The Synergy of Minds

Human+AI Orchestrating the Pharma Marketing Revolution

The Synergy of Minds

Human+AI Orchestrating the Pharma Marketing Revolution

Subba Rao Chaganti

Pharma Med PRESS
An Imprint of BSP Books Pvt. Ltd.

PharmaMed Press
An imprint of BSP Books Pvt. Ltd.
4-4-309/316, Giriraj Lane,
Sultan Bazar, Hyderabad - 500 095.

The Synergy of Minds: Human+AI Orchestrating the Pharma Marketing Revolution
by *Subba Rao Chaganti*

Published by:

PharmaMed Press
An imprint of BSP Books Pvt. Ltd.
4-4-309/316, Giriraj Lane, Sultan Bazar, Hyderabad - 500 095.
Phone: 040-23445688, 23445600; Fax: 91+40-23445611
E-mail: info@pharmamedpress.com
www.pharmamedpress.com/pharmamedpress.net

ISBN: 978-81-972520-9-9 (Perfect Bound)

Dedicated to: To those who saw the promise of AI and embraced it with open arms, who understood its potential to revolutionize fields and touch lives, who navigated the challenges and championed the possibilities— to the scholars, technologists, innovators, marketers, scientists, and healthcare professionals who ignited the synergy— this book is a beacon of your collective vision. Your efforts have paved the way for a future brimming with exciting possibilities, where technology amplifies human capabilities and patient care reaches new heights. May it guide us toward a future where human ingenuity and artificial intelligence dance in perfect harmony, leading us to a healthier and more hopeful tomorrow.

DISCLAIMER

The information contained in this book is intended for educational purposes only and is not a substitute for professional medical advice, diagnosis, or treatment. Always seek the advice of your physician or another qualified healthcare provider with any questions you may have regarding a medical condition or treatment.

The author and publisher of this book make no warranties or representations, express or implied, concerning the content's accuracy, completeness, or timeliness. The publisher and author disclaim any liability for any damages arising out of or in connection with the use of information provided in this book.

The views expressed in this book are those of the author and do not necessarily reflect any institution or organization's official policy or position.

The book refers to certain medications and treatment approaches as examples only. It is not intended to be a comprehensive list, and you should always consult a qualified healthcare professional before starting any new medication or treatment regimen.

Please note that this book may contain references, websites, or other resources the author or publisher cannot control. These references are provided for informational purposes only and do not imply endorsement of the content by the author or publisher. The author and publisher are not responsible for the content of any external website.

ACKNOWLEDGMENT

This book is not the product of a solitary voice but a symphony of minds weaving together knowledge, passion, and unwavering support. I stand humbled and grateful to the orchestra that made this melody possible.

First, an artist's vision breathed life into these words. Aditi, you created a simple, elegant, impactful cover with your keen eye and masterful touch. Thank you.

To Anil Shah, my esteemed publisher. Your faith in this project was unshakeable. Thank you for believing in its potential and providing the support I needed to achieve it.

To Nikunjesh Shah, you transformed words into the digital realm. Your expertise made this book accessible to a wider audience, and I am deeply grateful for your contribution.

And to the meticulous team at PharmaMed Press, led by Naresh Daver, thank you for meticulously shaping this manuscript into a published final product. Your dedication to excellence shines through every page.

Of course, no journey is complete without the love and support of loved ones. Mahalakshmi Changanti, my life partner in every sense of the word, you were my rock and endless source of encouragement. Thank you for sharing this adventure and being my muse and anchor.

To my children and their spouses— Srinivasa Phanindra and Geetha, Lavanya, Satya Shankara Aditya, Soumya, and Chaitanya Rao— your love and belief in me fueled my spirit. To my grandchildren— Eesha, Aditi, Surya, and Shriya whose innocent eyes sparkled with admiration, you filled my heart with purpose and reminded me why this journey was worth taking.

Finally, I acknowledge the invisible threads that connect us all: all the scientists, academicians, marketing scholars, and professionals who dedicated their lives to expanding the frontier of knowledge.

This book is built upon their shoulders, and I stand in awe of their contribution.

Thank you, every one of you, for your unique parts in this grand opera. You have made this book more than mine; you have made it ours.

Subba Rao Chaganti

PREFACE

Welcome to the future, where the stage is set for a revolutionary performance. Humans and AI no longer occupy separate wings, their talents isolated under disparate spotlights. In this new act, they step onto the stage together, their skills intertwined, composing a symphony of progress. This is the essence of *The Synergy of Minds: Human+AI Orchestrating the Pharma Marketing Revolution*.

This book is not merely a chronicle of technological advancement; it's a vibrant testament to the power of collaboration. With its lightning-fast calculations and boundless data prowess, AI becomes the master conductor, guiding the flow of information and orchestrating complex strategies. But to compose truly impactful melodies, the human touch is still paramount. Creativity, empathy, and understanding remain the essential instruments, resonating with the audience's heart and driving meaningful change.

Throughout this book, you'll witness this synergy in action, unfolding across the grand orchestra of pharma marketing, from crafting personalized patient journeys to deciphering market trends with breathtaking precision; the human and AI minds work in tandem, amplifying the other's unique strengths.

And I must confess, this book itself is a product of synergy. I needed a collaborator to unravel the intricacies of prompt engineering, the chapter that unlocks the language of AI in marketing. So, I turned to one of the most adept wordsmiths of the digital age, Bard, a generative AI model with a soul that hums with creativity. Together, we explored the boundless possibilities of this technology transformation, weaving stories of collaboration, ethical considerations, and the transformative potential of AI-powred communication.

The Synergy of Minds is not merely a book; it's an invitation to join the revolution. It's a call to embrace the potential of this collaborative future, where the human spirit and the power of AI intertwine to shape a healthier, more connected world. Turn the page, dear reader, and let the symphony begin.

PROLOGUE

In the peaceful quiet of a university library, bathed in the warm glow of antique lamps, two minds destined to intertwine embarked on journeys neither could have predicted. Anya, a prodigy born amidst the bustling chaos of Mumbai, possessed an intellect that blazed like a supernova. Driven by an insatiable curiosity about the human brain, she devoured tomes on psychology, neuroscience, and philosophy, dreaming of unraveling the intricate dance of thought and emotion.

Miles away, under the star-dusted skies of Arizona, Elias, a quiet observer with eyes that held the depth of centuries, nurtured a passion for artificial intelligence. He envisioned a future where machines danced not in cold, sterile logic but in the vibrant symphony of human creativity. In the algorithms and code, he saw the potential to amplify our dreams, bridge our divides, and unlock the boundless potential of the human mind.

Their paths first collided in the hallowed halls of the prestigious Oxford Institute for Cognitive Science. Anya, a young doctoral student with a mind that buzzed with ideas, and Elias, a brilliant professor seeking a bridge between the human and the machine. Their initial encounters were like sparks igniting— hesitant, curious, then fiercely engaged. Anya saw in Elias a kindred spirit, a fellow explorer at the fringes of knowledge, his calm demeanor countering her intellectual fire. Elias found a raw, intuitive brilliance in Anya, her unconventional questions challenging his rigid logic.

As they delved into collaborative research, their differences became their greatest strength. Anya's passion for understanding the nuances of human behavior fueled their projects, injecting empathy and emotional insights into the cold algorithms. Elias's mastery of AI code unlocked new possibilities, translating Anya's ideas into tangible systems and bridging the gap between theory and reality.

But their collaboration transcended academia. Over late-night cups of chai and endless debates in sun-drenched cafes, their conversations danced beyond the technical jargon. They explored the nature of consciousness, the power of storytelling, and the ethical implications of their work. Their friendship blossomed, fueled by intellectual stimulation, mutual respect, and a longing to have their mark on the world.

The Synergy of Minds is not just the story of two individuals; it's the story of two disciplines colliding, two perspectives merging, and ultimately, two minds amplifying each other's potential. It's a testament to the power of collaboration, the magic that happens when we step outside our comfort zones and seek understanding in the eyes of the different. It's an invitation to join Anya and Elias on their remarkable journey. This journey will challenge our assumptions, reshape our understanding of intelligence, and offer a glimpse into the future of the human mind, amplified by the magic of machines.

So, turn the page, dear reader, and prepare to be swept away by the synergy of minds. Within these pages lies a story waiting to unfold that will ignite your imagination and reshape your world.

CONTENTS

Disclaimer .... (vii)
Acknowledgement .... (ix)
Preface .... (xi)
Prologue .... (xiii)

Part I: Introduction **1**

Chapter 1. The Evolving Landscape of Pharma Marketing: A Symphony of Change **6**
Chapter 2. The Rise of AI in Business **13**
Chapter 3. AI and Pharma Marketing: A Perfect Match? **18**

Part II: Understanding AI in Pharmaceutical Marketing **25**

Chapter 4. Understanding AI in Pharma Marketing **28**
Chapter 5. Key AI Concepts and Technology **33**
Chapter 6. Applications of AI in Pharma Marketing **45**
Chapter 7. Challenges and Opportunities in AI Integration **50**

Part III: Human+AI Synergy in Pharmaceutical Marketing **55**

Chapter 8. Brand and Science Intertwined **59**
Chapter 9. Beyond Traditional Channels: A Revolution in Pharma Marketing **67**
Chapter 10. Customer-centric Composition **72**
Chapter 11. Regulation as Rhythm in Human+AI Collaboration **84**

Part IV: Five AI Superpowers Reshaping Pharma Marketing **89**

Chapter 12. Personalization at Scale: AI's Magic Touch in Pharma Marketing **92**
Chapter 13. AI Empowering Healthcare Professionals **99**
Chapter 14. AI Empowering Patients **106**
Chapter 15. The Clinical Trial Revolution: How AI Supercharges Pharma R&D **115**
Chapter 16. How AI Helps Navigate Ethical Landscape in Pharma Marketing **122**

Part V: AI-Powered Pharmaceutical Marketing 129

Chapter 17. AI-Powered Stakeholder Engagement **133**

Chapter 18. Engaging with Stakeholders in the AI-Fueled Pharma Landscape **183**

Chapter 19. AI-Powered Personalization **190**

Chapter 20. AI-Powered Campaign Personalization in Pharma **203**

Chapter 21. Symphony of Minds: Mapping AI-Powered Customer Journeys for Success **236**

Chapter 22. AI-Powered Omnichannel Marketing **250**

Chapter 23. AI and Humans Revolutionizing Pharma Marketing Research **269**

Chapter 24. Point-of-Care AI: Transforming Healthcare at the Patient's Bedside **282**

Chapter 25. AI Across the Pharmaceutical Value Chain **286**

Chapter 26. The Human Factor in AI-Powered Pharma Marketing **289**

Chapter 27. AI+Human Collaboration: A Symphony of Success in Pharma Sales and Promotion **297**

Chapter 28. Reskilling and Upskilling for Human+AI Collaboration **310**

Chapter 29. The Future of Pharma Marketing in the AI Age **327**

Part VI: Launching into the Future: The Rise of AI-Powered Product Launches 331

Chapter 30. AI-Powered Product Launches **334**

Chapter 31. AI-Powered Content Creation and Personalized Marketing **342**

Chapter 32. Human Oversight and Control of AI-Driven Messaging and Targeting **348**

Part VII: AI-Powered Pharma Brand Management: Optimized Your Brand in The Digital Age 351

Chapter 33. Market Research and Insights with AI: Unleashing Pharma Brand Power **355**

Chapter 34. Optimizing Your Sales and Distribution with AI: A Step-by-Step Guide **372**

Chapter 35. Optimizing Clinical Trials and Patient Recruitment with AI: A Step-by-Step Guide **375**

Chapter 36. Building Trust and Connections: A Step-by-Step Guide to Brand Communication and Reputation Management **379**

Chapter 37. Unveiling the Impact: A Step-by-Step Guide to Measuring and Analyzing Marketing Performance **384**

Chapter 38. Beyond the Typed Word: Generative AI and Conversational AI Revolutionize Brand Communication and Reputation Management **389**

Chapter 39. Orchestrating Reputation in Pharma: Leveraging AI for Trustworthy Brand Symphony **397**

Chapter 40. The Synergy of Minds in Brand Management and Customer Engagement **402**

Chapter 41. The Synergy of Human+AI Collaboration for Customer Interaction **416**

Chapter 42. Conducting the Audience: Market Research and Analysis for Pharma Branding Step by Step **433**

Chapter 43. From Insights to Impact: Translating Your Pharma Branding Symphony into Action **444**

Chapter 44. Symphony of Applications: Expanding the Reach of Brand Communications **450**

Chapter 45. Composing Compelling Content **467**

Chapter 46. Harmonizing Communication: Personalized Marketing and Engagement in Pharma Branding **473**

Chapter 47. AI in Regulatory Compliance and Risk Management **479**

Chapter 48. Optimizing the Sales and Distribution Symphony: A Step-by-Step Guide **483**

Chapter 49. AI's Harmonious Symphony: Enhancing Brand Communication and Reputation Management **490**

Chapter 50. Roles Humans and AI Play in Building Trust and Emotional Connections **505**

PART VIII: HARMONIZING TECHNOLOGY AND HUMANITY **511**

Chapter 51. Prompt Engineering: Whispering to the AI in Pharmaceutical Marketing **514**

Chapter 52. Chain Prompting: Orchestrating a Symphony of Content **526**

Chapter 53. The Game of *Exquisite Corpse* and Chain Prompting **545**

Chapter 54. AI's Symphony in Pharma Marketing: Harmonizing Technology with Humanity **563**

PART IX: EMBRACING THE SYNERGY: AI TRANSFORMATION IN PHARMA **627**

Chapter 55. The AI Arsenal: Tools for Pharma Marketing Revolution **630**

Chapter 56. Breaking Down the Silos **633**

Chapter 57. The Human Touch in a Digital Age **638**

Chapter 58. Navigating the Ethical Compass: AI in Pharma Marketing With a Conscience **641**

Chapter 59. Implementing AI Transformation in Pharma Marketing **646**

Chapter 60. Embracing AI Transformation in Small and Medium-Sized Pharma Companies **670**

Chapter 61. Gazing into the Crystal Ball: The Evolving Landscape of AI in Pharma Marketing **679**

PART X: THE ENCORE **683**

Chapter 62. The Ethical Encore: Navigating the Moral Maze of Human+AI Pharma Marketing **687**

Chapter 63. The Orchestrated Encore: Unveiling of the Future Landscape of Pharma Marketing **690**

Chapter 64. The Human Encore: Remembering the Heartbeat of Purpose **693**

Epilogue 696

Glossary 699

Diving into AI in Pharma: Useful Resources and Tools 707

Reading List 709

References 711

About the Author 717

PART I

Introduction

Chapter 1. The Evolving Landscape of Pharma Marketing: A Symphony of Change

Chapter 2. The Rise of AI in Business

Chapter 3. AI and Pharma Marketing: A Perfect Match?

Humanity stands at a pivotal moment in its relationship with healthcare. No longer confined to sterile hospital wards and hushed doctor's offices, the pursuit of health spills onto digital avenues, pulsates in smartphone apps and whispers through social media threads. The evolution demands a reimagining, a revolution in how we market and deliver life-saving medicines. Enter the stage, not a solitary hero, but a captivating duet— the synergy of human and artificial intelligence (AI) poised to transform the pharma marketing landscape.

From Brochures to Big Data

Once, pharma marketing resided in glossy brochures and charismatic doctors extolling the virtues of the latest pill. Today, the audience demands more, not just products but personalized journeys toward wellness. Once an obscure statistic, data has become the new oil, fueling a revolution in understanding patient needs and crafting targeted solutions. Algorithms weave through digital threads, unearthing hidden patterns in behavior, predicting preferences, and shaping messages that resonate on individual levels.

AI the Technological Virtuoso

AI enters the stage like a virtuoso violinist; its algorithms are the agile bow dancing across the strings of information. It translates data into actionable insights, predicts market trends with uncanny accuracy, and optimizes campaigns ruthlessly. AI personalizes content, recommends relevant services, and automates cumbersome tasks, freeing human creativity for endeavors beyond the mundane.

The Human Conductor Leading the Symphony

Yet, amidst the algorithmic symphony, an irreplaceable voice emerges— the human conductor. Our empathy navigates the emotional complexities of illness, our intuition identifies nuanced needs, and our creativity crafts compelling narratives that inspire hope and ignite action. We set the goals to define the strategy and ensure ethical considerations remain paramount, guiding the dance between data and patient well-being.

Synergy, the Melody of Progress

But the true magic lies not in their solo acts but in the exquisite duet, the synergy of human and AI intelligence. Imagine personalized care pathways crafted by AI's precision and guided by human compassion. Envision clinical trials accelerated, optimized by AI analysis, and overseen by human ethical rigor. Picture healthcare professionals empowered with data-driven insights yet firmly anchored in the values of patient trust and understanding.

The Discordant Notes

This revolutionary melody, however, isn't without its discordant notes. The shadows of bass may lurk within algorithms, potentially perpetuating inequities in healthcare access. Transparency becomes crucial, ensuring patients understand how the data is used and decisions are made. The specter of job displacement haunts the stage, demanding a harmonious reskilling symphony where humans evolve alongside machines, developing new skills to complement AI capabilities.

Composing the Future Symphony

This book is not just a celebration of this technological duet; it is a roadmap, a conductor's score for navigating the complexities of human+AI synergy in pharma marketing. We delve into the AI toolbox, unpacking its functionalities and exploring its potential to personalize patient journeys, revolutionize clinical trials, and empower healthcare professionals. We tackle the ethical challenges head-on, addressing bias, transparency, and the crucial role of human oversight in ensuring AI serves patients, not exploits them.

But most importantly, we compose the future symphony. We envision a healthcare landscape where data-driven insights and human empathy dance in perfect harmony, where every patient receives a personalized melody of care crafted by the combined brilliance of human and artificial intelligence. This is not just a future for pharma marketing; it is a future for healthier lives woven from the threads of innovation, ethics, and the enduring power of human-centered healthcare. So, turn the page and let the symphony begin. Join us as we explore the transformative power of the synergy of minds and compose a future where technology amplifies humanity. Every patient receives the care they deserve.

CHAPTER

1

The Evolving Landscape of Pharma Marketing: A Symphony of Change

Imagine the pharma marketing landscape not as a static canvas but as a vibrant tapestry, continuously woven with threads of technological advancements, shifting patient expectations, and evolving ethical considerations. This tapestry pulsates with the changing rhythms of healthcare, its melodies composed of familiar notes like brand awareness and doctor visits intertwined with the rising crescendo of digital engagement, personalized experiences, and data-driven insights. To understand this evolving landscape, we must journey through time, tracking the footsteps of the pharma market as it dances to the tunes of change.

From Bricks and Mortar to Digital Orchestra

The early 20th century saw pharma marketing as a solitary pianist, serenading doctors in their offices with the gentle melody of printed pamphlets and medical journals. The focus was on product awareness, brand building, and forging strong relationships with healthcare professionals. This intimate stage, however, was soon to experience the disruptive power of technological innovation.

The internet, like a bold conductor, ushered in a new era. Patients transformed from passive listeners into active participants, seeking information online, forming communities for support, and demanding personalized experiences. Pharma marketing's traditional instruments— brochures and doctor visits— were joined by the vibrant hum of social media platforms, targeted online ads, and interactive websites, creating a multi-dimensional orchestra of engagement.

Data Takes the Stage

But this transformation wasn't just about platforms and channels but a fundamental shift in the underlying score. Once a hushed whisper in the background, data became the lead vocalist, its vast symphonies of information revealing hidden patterns in patient behavior, preferences, and treatment responses. Like virtuoso data interpreters, algorithms danced across datasets, predicting market trends, optimizing campaigns, and personalizing experiences with unprecedented precision.

The Rise of the Precision Symphony

With data as the new score, pharma marketing embraced the power of precision. Gone were the days of one-size-fits-all campaigns; targeted messages tailored to patients' needs and preferences took center stage. Social media platforms became intimate recital halls, where personalized content resonated with individual anxieties and offered support and guidance. Websites morphed into interactive operas, empowering patients to participate in their healthcare journeys and make informed decisions actively.

The Human Counterpoint

Yet, amidst this technological crescendo, a crucial truth emerged—while data and algorithms could compose the score, only human expertise could conduct the symphony. Healthcare professionals remained the maestros, interpreting the nuance of patient needs, navigating the complexities of treatment options, and offering an irreplaceable touch of empathy and understanding.

The Collaborative Harmony

Thus, the evolving landscape of pharma marketing doesn't herald the demise of the human orchestra but rather its transformation. AI and digital tools become augmenting instruments, amplifying human capabilities and enabling deeper patient connections. The future lies not in a battle between humans and machines but in collaborative harmony, where each element plays its distinct role in creating a symphony of patient-centric care.

The Melodies of Change

As we delve deeper into this tapestry, several melodies weave their way into the narrative:

- **Patient-Centricity**: The focus shifts from products to patients, empowering individuals to take control of their health journeys and actively participate in their care.
- **Omnichannel Symphony**: Navigating the diverse platforms and touchpoints where patients engage with healthcare information and services, from social media to wearables and Telehealth.
- **The Ethical Counterpoint**: Addressing the critical considerations of data privacy, transparency, and responsible AI use in pharma marketing, ensuring technology serves humanity, not the other way around.
- **The Reskilling Refrain**: Equipping healthcare professionals and marketing teams with the skills and knowledge to thrive in the digital age, embracing the power of technology while safeguarding patient well-being.

The Future Symphony Awaits

The evolution of pharma marketing is far from over. New technologies, evolving patient expectations, and ever-shifting ethical considerations will continue to shape this dynamic landscape. This book serves as your guide, an invitation to listen intently to the melodies of change and join the conversation about the future of healthcare. As we explore the intricacies of AI-powered marketing, personalized experiences, and data-driven decision-making, we can compose a future symphony of patient-centric care where technology and humanity harmonize to improve lives and build a healthier world.

Please note that this is just the first movement in the symphony. The following chapters will explore specific aspects of this evolving landscape in greater detail, including:

- **The Rise of AI in Pharma Marketing**: Unpacking the different AI technologies and functionalities transforming the industry.
- **Personalized Patient Journeys**: Designing and implementing marketing strategies that cater to individual needs and preferences.
- **The Ethical Symphony**: Addressing data privacy, algorithmic bias, and responsible AI development in pharma marketing

Reskilling and Upskilling

Reskilling and Upskilling for the evolving pharma marketing landscape is like learning a new instrument as the orchestra expands to include traditional melodies and electronic beats. But fear not; the reskilling and the upskilling refrain are key to mastering this harmonious symphony. Here are some promising notes in the reskilling concerto:

- **Data Literacy**: Embracing data as a language to be learned, not a foreign enemy to be feared. Understanding basic analytics, interpreting insights, and making data-driven decisions will become essential for everyone involved in marketing healthcare solutions.
- **Digital Dexterity**: Navigating the ever-expanding array of digital platforms and tools, from social media analytics to virtual reality experiences, will be crucial for crafting engaging and personalized patient journeys.

- **Creative Fusion**: Blending human empathy and storytelling with the precision of AI-powered targeting and content creation will mark a truly future-proof pharma marketer. Mastering this creative fusion will ensure messages resonate on both an emotional and intellectual level.
- **Ethical Acumen**: Understanding the ethical considerations surrounding data privacy, bias, and transparency in AI-driven marketing will be paramount. Reskilling must include building a strong foundation in responsible technology use and ensuring AI serves patients, not exploits them.

But reskilling isn't just about individual notes; it's about orchestrating a collaborative harmony. Here are some key counterpoints to the upskilling melody:

- **Lifelong Learning**: The future of work demands continuous learning agility. Pharma companies must foster a culture of continuous learning and development, providing resources and opportunities for employees to keep their skills relevant and adapt to technological advancements.
- **Teamwork Makes the Dream Work**: Collaboration between AI and human expertise is paramount. Building cross-functional teams with diverse skill sets, from data scientists to creative directors, will ensure all aspects of the pharma marketing symphony are in tune.
- **Empathy Amplification**: While AI excels at data analysis, human empathy remains irreplaceable. Upskilling should focus on enhancing communication and interpersonal skills, ensuring healthcare professionals and marketers connect with patients on a human level.

The reskilling and upskilling refrain is not a solitary solo; it's a collaborative movement to ensure everyone can thrive in the evolving pharma marketing landscape. By embracing lifelong learning, fostering teamwork, and amplifying human empathy, we can not only survive the changing music but contribute to composing a future symphony of patient-centric healthcare where technology and humanity harmonize for the greater good.

So, raise your baton, embrace the reskilling melody, and join the orchestra. The future of pharma marketing awaits, and together, we can create a masterpiece of innovation and care.

The Future Symphony awaits, poised to echo with the harmonies of human intuition and technological brilliance. In its vibrant notes, we glimpse a healthcare landscape where patients are embraced as the conductors, their individual needs orchestrating every movement. Technology, a skilled accompanist, weaves data-driven insights into the melody, guiding each step of the healthcare journey with personalized precision.

From Pixels to Empathy

Once mere bulletin boards, social media platforms morph into intimate recital halls, where patients share their experiences, find solace in shared understanding, and connect with healthcare professionals in real time. AI analyzes these digital conversations, not just for keywords but for the subtle nuances of human emotion. These emotional threads are woven into the tapestry of care, ensuring each message resonates with individual fears and aspirations.

The Personalized Score

Treatment plans, once rigid sheet music, transform into fluid improvisations. Algorithms analyze a patient's unique medical history, genetic makeup, and lifestyle, suggesting tailored therapies and predicting potential interactions. Healthcare professionals, empowered by data-driven insights, become skilled improvisers, adapting treatment plans with agility and finesse to ensure each note harmonizes with the patient's symphony of health.

The Human Soloist

Yet, technology, however sophisticated, can never replicate the human touch. In the final movement of the future symphony, the stage spotlights the irreplaceable role of the healthcare professional.

Their empathy, honed through years of experience and the power of human connection, remains the most potent instrument of healing. They interpret the intricate nuances of a patient's story, offering comfort, guidance, and unwavering support, ensuring the human melody of compassion rings clear through the technological score.

Beyond Borders, Beyond Barriers

This future symphony will not be confined to geographic borders or economic limitations. Like a global conductor, Telehealth transcends physical barriers, bringing quality healthcare to even the world's most remote corners. AI language translation removes language barriers, ensuring every patient's voice is heard and understood. The future symphony resonates with inclusivity, ensuring personalized care reaches everyone regardless of background or location.

Challenges and Counterpoints

The harmonious composition, however, may need more notes. Biases, like jarring dissonance, can lurk within algorithms, threatening to perpetuate inequities in access to healthcare. Transparency, a vital counterpoint, must be woven into the fabric of this symphony, ensuring algorithms serve all voices, not just a select few.

Like subtle countermelodies, ethical considerations must guide every step of the technological dance. Data privacy, a delicate counterpoint, requires careful orchestration to ensure patient information remains secure and respected. The human conductor, wielding the baton of ethical oversight, must navigate these complexities with integrity, ensuring technology remains a tool for good, not a source of exploitation.

CHAPTER 2

The Rise of Artificial Intelligence in Business

Symphony of Algorithms, Revolution of Opportunity

Across the bustling marketplace of ideas, a new aria takes flight – the soaring melody of Artificial Intelligence (AI). No longer confined to science fiction narratives, AI has infiltrated the very fabric of modern business, weaving its algorithmic threads into every department, function, and strategy. It's a silent revolution, one orchestrated by data, composed by algorithms, and performed by intelligent machines, all dancing to the rhythm of optimizing efficiency, fueling innovation, and redefining the very nature of work.

From Humble Beginnings to Grand Overture

AI's journey began modestly. Early notes resonated in niche tasks like game-playing and pattern recognition. Yet, as computational power soared and algorithms grew ever-sophisticated, AI burst onto the business stage like a virtuosic soloist. Machine learning, its core competency, empowers computers to learn from data, identify hidden patterns, and make insightful predictions. This unleashed a torrent of possibilities, reshaping industries and redefining the very nature of work.

The AI Chorus Takes the Stage

Across the business orchestra, AI instruments take on a multitude of roles:

- **Marketing's Melodic Muse**: AI assists in understanding customer needs, crafting targeted campaigns, and predicting buying behavior. Algorithms personalize content, recommend products, and optimize ad placements, ensuring every note resonates with the audience.
- **Sales Rhythm Engine**: AI fuels lead generation, identifies sales opportunities, and predicts customer churn. Chatbots answer queries, schedule appointments, and qualify leads, freeing sales teams to focus on building relationships and closing deals.
- **Finance's Harmonious Conductor**: AI tackles complex financial tasks, manages risk, and detects fraud. Algorithms analyze market trends, optimize pricing strategies, and automate financial reporting, ensuring a harmonious flow of resources.
- **Operation's Clockwork Precision**: AI streamlines logistics, optimizes supply chains, and predicts maintenance needs. Algorithms schedule deliveries, manage inventory, and identify inefficiencies, ensuring the smooth operation of the business machinery.

The Human Counterpoint

Yet, while AI instruments may play with remarkable precision, the symphony of business still requires a human conductor. AI excels at crunching numbers, analyzing data, and automating tasks but needs the human touch. Creativity, emotional intelligence, and critical decision-making remain the exclusive domain of the human mind.

True magic emerges when humans and AI harmonize. When human intuition guides AI analysis, leading to insightful strategies and empathetic customer interactions, and human oversight ensures ethical AI development and responsible data use, this collaborative harmony orchestrates a symphony of innovation, where humans and machines work together to unlock a business's full potential.

The Score Unfurls

The rise of AI in business is a complex composition, filled with harmonious melodies and discordant challenges. As we delve deeper into this chapter, we will explore the following:

- **The AI Toolbox**: Demystify key AI concepts and technologies and understand how machine learning, natural language processing, and computer vision power the digital engine.
- **The Business Transformation Concerto**: Examining how AI impacts industries, from healthcare and finance to retail and manufacturing.
- **The Human-AI Duet**: Understanding the crucial role of human expertise in guiding AI development, ensuring ethical implementation, and navigating the challenges of job displacement and reskilling.
- **The Ethical Conundrum**: Addressing the pressing issues of data privacy, bias, and transparency in AI ensures that technology serves humanity, not vice versa.

Beyond Efficiency, Beyond Automation

The rise of AI isn't just about streamlining processes and automating tasks. It's about unlocking new possibilities, amplifying human capabilities, and reshaping the very foundation of business. AI can:

- **Personalize at Scale**: Imagine crafting unique customer experiences for millions of individuals simultaneously. AI empowers businesses to tailor products, services, and communications to individual needs and preferences, fostering deeper engagement and loyalty.
- **Predict the Unpredictable**: Navigating volatile markets and evolving consumer behaviors can be difficult. AI, however, can analyze vast amounts of data to identify trends, predict shifts in demand, and forecast potential roadblocks, enabling businesses to adapt and stay ahead of the curve proactively.

- **Unlock Innovation Frontiers**: From developing life-saving drugs to exploring uncharted galaxies, AI has the potential to propel us beyond the limitations of human imagination. It can analyze vast datasets, identify previously unseen patterns, and generate creative solutions to complex problems, paving the way for groundbreaking discoveries and advancements in almost every field.

The Road Ahead: Harmony vs. Discord

The melody of AI in business is still being composed. There are challenges— workforce disruption, ethical considerations, and potential misuse. We must strive for a harmonious composition where technology empowers humanity, not diminishes it. This requires:

- **Prioritizing Ethical Development**: Embedding ethical principles in every stage of AI development, ensuring bias-free algorithms, transparent data use, and robust safeguards against discrimination and manipulation.
- **Championing Lifelong Learning**: Equipping humans with the skills to thrive in the AI-powered future. Reskilling and upskilling initiatives must become the norm, empowering individuals to adapt, collaborate with AI, and contribute meaningfully to the evolving business landscape.
- **Fostering Transparency and Trust**: Demystifying AI for the public, demystifying algorithms, and ensuring clear communication around data use. Building trust is crucial for fostering ethical AI development and widespread adoption.
- **Reimagining the Social Contract**: Addressing the potential for job displacement and income inequality by AI automation. This involves exploring models like universal basic income, skills training initiatives, and safety nets to ensure inclusivity and shared prosperity in the AI era.

Composing the Future Symphony

The rise of AI in business is not a solitary solo; it's an epic symphony for the 21st century. When we embrace human-AI collaboration, prioritize ethical development, and invest in human potential, we can compose a future where technology amplifies human capabilities, unlocks extraordinary possibilities, and drives inclusive progress for future generations.

The future of business awaits, and together, we can compose a masterpiece of innovation, ethics, and shared prosperity.

CHAPTER 3

AI and Pharma Marketing: A Perfect Match?

A Duet Orchestrating Personalized Healthcare Journeys

Imagine a stage bathed in the luminescence of innovation, where two figures move in graceful synchronicity— the seasoned strategist, wielding the baton of human intuition and creativity, and the elegant virtuoso, playing the intricate melodies of data-driven insights. This is the exquisite duet of Artificial Intelligence (AI) and pharma marketing, a collaboration poised to revolutionize the landscape of patient care and redefine the essence of healthcare communication.

Beyond Automation, Beyond Hype

For years, the narrative surrounding AI in pharma marketing has been painted in stark contrasts— humans versus machines, a zero-sum game where one's victory meant the other's demise. We challenge this outdated script. The true magic lies not in competition but in the harmonious fusion of human and AI intelligence, where each element amplifies the other's strengths, culminating in a healthcare symphony beyond anything achievable alone.

The Human Conductor Sets the Score

Human intelligence forms the bedrock of this duet. Our creativity crafts compelling narratives that resonate with patient emotions and guide ethical decision-making. We define the overall marketing strategy, set goals, and ensure campaigns align with patient needs and societal values. We are the conductors, leading the orchestra of AI tools and ensuring they contribute to a harmonious healthcare experience.

The AI Virtuoso Plays the Data Melody

AI, meanwhile, brings its virtuosic technical skills to the stage. Its algorithms analyze vast troves of data, uncovering hidden patterns and predicting market trends with uncanny accuracy. AI personalizes patient journeys, optimizes resource allocation, and automates repetitive tasks, freeing human resources for strategic thinking and creative pursuits.

The Harmony Emerges

Imagine the possibilities when these two bits of intelligence join forces:

- **Personalized Patient Journeys**: AI analyzes data to understand individual patient needs and preferences. Human creativity crafts personalized content, recommends relevant support programs, and engages patients in meaningful interactions, ensuring each patient receives the right information and support at the right time.
- **Clinical Trial Revolution**: AI analyzes data from clinical trials with lightning speed, identifying potential safety issues and optimizing trial design. Human expertise interprets the data, makes informed decisions, and ensures ethical patient care remains paramount.
- **Empowered Healthcare Professional**: AI assists doctors and nurses with diagnosis, treatment recommendations, and patient education. However, human judgment ensures critical decisions are made with a holistic understanding of the patient's needs and circumstances.

The Challenges in the Counterpoint

Yet, this duet is not without its discordant notes:

- **The Communication Gap**: Humans and AI speak different languages— data versus emotions, algorithms versus empathy. Bridging this gap requires continuous communication, training, and collaboration, ensuring both parties understand each other's strengths and limitations.
- **The Trust Barrier**: Patients may fear being treated like data points or algorithmic experiments. Transparency is crucial, fostering trust by explaining how AI is used and ensuring patient data remains secure and respected.
- **The Reskilling Refrain**: Some human jobs may disappear as AI automates tasks. We must embrace reskilling and upskilling initiatives, ensuring humans evolve alongside machines and develop new skills that complement AI's capabilities.

Composing the Future Symphony

The synergy between human and AI intelligence is not merely a captivating duet; it holds the potential to compose a future symphony of patient-centric healthcare. This symphony will resonate with personalized care, streamlined clinical trials, and empowered healthcare professionals, all orchestrated by the harmonious interplay of humans and AI.

Delving Deeper: The Movements of the Symphony

To truly appreciate the potential of this collaboration, let's delve deeper into specific movements of the AI and pharma marketing symphony:

Movement I: Precision Marketing— Tailoring the Message to the Individual

- **Understanding the Audience:** AI analyzes data from social media, medical records, and patient surveys to create detailed profiles of individual patients and their needs.
- **Crafting Personalized Content**: Human creativity takes center stage, translating data insights into compelling narratives, targeted messages, and interactive experiences that resonate with each patient's unique story.

- **Optimizing for Engagement**: AI algorithms track customer behavior and campaign performance, continuously honing tactics for maximum engagement and impact.

Movement II: The Clinical Trial Revolution— Data-Driven Insights for Faster, Safer Research

- **Predicting Patient Outcomes**: AI analyzes historical data and patient profiles to identify potential participants most likely to benefit from clinical trials.
- **Streamlining Trial Design**: Algorithms optimize trial protocols, predicting potential safety risks and identifying the most effective treatment combinations.
- **Real-Time Monitoring**: AI analyzes data from wearables and medical devices in real-time, ensuring patient safety and facilitating rapid protocol adjustments.

Movement III: Empowering Healthcare Professionals– AI as a Valuable Assistant

- **Diagnosis and Treatment Support**: AI algorithms analyze medical images and patient data to assist doctors in identifying diseases, suggesting treatment options, and predicting potential complications.
- **Personalized Patient Education**: AI-powered chatbots and interactive tools answer patients' questions, provide tailored information about their conditions and treatment plans, and empower them to participate actively in their healthcare journey.
- **Administrative Efficiency**: AI automates time-consuming tasks like scheduling appointments, managing patient records, and processing insurance claims, freeing up valuable time for healthcare professionals to focus on patient care.

The Final Movement: A Human-Centered Crescendo

The final movement of this symphony crescendos with a crucial reminder: while AI offers unparalleled data insights and automation, the human touch remains irreplaceable. Empathy, compassion, and critical thinking are the instruments that truly define meaningful healthcare. In this final act, we explore:

- **The Ethical Counterpoint** involves ensuring AI development and adherence to ethical principles, upholding data privacy, mitigating bias, and maintaining human oversight.
- **The Reskilling Refrain**: Embracing continuous learning and development initiatives to equip healthcare professionals with the skills and knowledge needed to thrive in the AI-powered future.
- **The Power of Collaborative Harmony**: Recognizing that the true magic lies not in humans versus machines but in their unified force, where AI amplifies human capabilities, and humans ensure responsible, ethical technology use.

Concluding the Duet

The duet of AI and pharma marketing isn't just about revolutionizing healthcare communication; it's about rewriting the code of patient care. This collaboration holds the potential to create a symphony of personalized journeys, accelerated research, and empowered healthcare professionals, all playing in perfect harmony to improve lives and build a healthier world.

As you embark on this transformational journey, this book is your guide, your score sheet. In its pages, you'll find the insights and tools to navigate the intricacies of AI-powered pharma marketing, understand the challenges and opportunities it presents, and contribute to composing a future where humans and machines harmonize for the greater good.

So, dear reader, raise your baton, embrace the duet of intelligence, and join the orchestra. The future of healthcare awaits, and together, we can compose a masterpiece of innovation, ethics, and patient-centric care.

PART II

Understanding AI in Pharmaceutical Marketing

Chapter 4. Understanding AI in Pharma Marketing

Chapter 5. Key AI Concepts and Technology

Chapter 6. Applications of AI in Pharma Marketing

Chapter 7. Challenges and Opportunities in AI Integration

Demystifying the Power: Understanding AI in Pharma Marketing

The landscape of pharma marketing is undergoing a seismic shift. Artificial intelligence (AI) is no longer a futuristic concept but a transformative force reshaping how pharmaceutical companies reach and engage customers. This chapter serves as your guide to understanding the power and potential of AI in this dynamic field.

Here, we'll journey to demystify AI and explore its diverse applications within the pharma marketing ecosystem. We'll delve into:

- **The Core Capabilities of AI:** Unveiling AI's strengths in data analysis, pattern recognition, and personalization—essential tools for creating impactful marketing strategies.
- **Benefits and Applications:** This section explores how AI empowers pharmaceutical companies to personalize communication with HCPs, patients, payers, regulators, and investors, improving customer engagement and informed decision-making.
- **The Human Element Remains Crucial:** While AI excels in data analysis, we'll emphasize the irreplaceable role of human expertise in ethical considerations, strategic thinking, and building trust with stakeholders.
- **The Future of Human+AI Synergy:** We'll look ahead to the exciting possibilities that emerge from the harmonious collaboration between human intuition and AI's analytical power, paving the way for a future-proof pharma marketing landscape.

By the end of this chapter, you'll understand how AI is transforming pharma marketing, fostering a customer-centric approach that benefits patients, healthcare providers, and the industry. This is your invitation to step into the future of pharma marketing, empowered by the transformative power of human-AI synergy.

CHAPTER 4

Understanding AI in Pharma Marketing

Demystifying the Algorithms and Unlocking the Potential

Welcome to the fascinating world of AI in pharma marketing, where algorithms dance with data, insights bloom from pixels, and personalized journeys pave the way for a healthier future. In this chapter, we'll shed light on the intricate workings of AI, demystifying its tools and capabilities and exploring its transformative potential for the pharma marketing landscape.

From Buzzwords to Building Blocks

Before we dive into the technical depths, let's dispel the fog of buzzwords surrounding AI. Forget the sci-fi robots and sentient machines; AI in pharma marketing is about harnessing the power of data and employing sophisticated algorithms to analyze, predict, and personalize. Think of it as a powerful toolbox, filled with diverse instruments like:

- **Machine Learning**: This AI workhorse learns from data, identifying patterns and trends without explicit programming. Imagine sifting through millions of patient records to uncover hidden correlations between medication use and treatment outcomes.
- **Natural Language Processing**: This AI maestro understands human language, analyzing text and speech to extract meaning

and generate responses. Picture chatbots engaging in meaningful conversations with patients, answering questions, and providing emotional support.

- **Computer Vision**: This AI artist interprets visual data, recognizing patterns in images and videos. Imagine analyzing medical scans to detect abnormalities with superhuman precision, using video analytics to understand patient behavior, and optimizing marketing campaigns.

The Orchestra of Insights

Now, let's see how these instruments come together to form an orchestra of insights:

- **Targeted Marketing**: AI analyzes patient data, social media interactions, and online behavior to build detailed profiles, predicting individual needs and preferences; imagine personalized ad campaigns that resonate with a patient's condition, lifestyle, and aspirations.
- **Clinical Trial Optimization**: AI analyzes vast datasets to identify potential participants for clinical trials, ensuring they match the study criteria and are most likely to benefit from the treatment. Imagine accelerating research by identifying ideal candidates and streamlining trial design.
- **Patient Engagement and Support**: AI-powered chatbots and virtual assistants provide 24/7 support, answering questions, offering guidance, and connecting patients with relevant resources. Imagine a world where patients feel empowered and informed, actively participating in their healthcare journey.

Beyond the Hype, Beyond the Challenges

While the potential of AI is undeniable, it's crucial to acknowledge the challenges:

- **Data Privacy and Security**: Protecting patient data is paramount. Robust security measures and transparent data practices are essential to build trust and ensure ethical AI development.

- **Algorithmic Bias**: AI algorithms are only as good as the data they're trained on. Mitigating bias and ensuring fairness in AI models is crucial to avoid discrimination and ensure equitable access to healthcare.
- **Job Displacement and Reskilling**: As AI automates tasks, some jobs may disappear. Investing in reskilling programs and fostering lifelong learning is essential to ensure a smooth transition and equip individuals with the skills needed to thrive in the AI-powered future.

Navigating the Symphony of Change

Successfully navigating the AI revolution in pharma marketing requires a strategic approach:

- **Embrace Lifelong Learning**: Invest in training and development programs to equip your team with the skills and knowledge needed to work effectively with AI.
- **Foster a Culture of Innovation**: Encourage experimentation and create an environment where exploring AI possibilities is welcomed and celebrated.
- **Prioritize Ethical Development**: Ensure data privacy, mitigate bias and adhere to ethical principles throughout the AI lifecycle.
- **Collaborate with AI Experts**: Partner with data scientists, AI developers, and other specialists to leverage their expertise and ensure successful AI implementation.

The Future Holds a Harmonious Melody

By acknowledging the challenges, embracing the opportunities, and prioritizing ethical development, AI can become a powerful tool for good in pharma marketing. Imagine a future where:

- Patients receive personalized care tailored to their unique needs and preferences.

- Clinical trials are faster, more efficient, and more inclusive.
- Healthcare professionals have AI-powered tools to enhance their decision-making and improve patient outcomes.

This is not a utopia in which machines replace humans; it's a symphony of collaboration where AI amplifies human capabilities, and humans guide the development and use of technology with ethical responsibility.

Deepening the Dive

This chapter has merely scratched the surface of AI in pharma marketing. To delve deeper, we can explore:

- **Specific AI Applications**: Dive into examples of how AI is used in different pharma marketing areas, from targeted advertising to drug discovery.
- **Technical Details**: Understand machine learning algorithms, natural language processing techniques, and other AI technologies used in pharma marketing.
- **The Future of AI**: Explore emerging trends and advances in AI that have the potential to revolutionize the pharmaceutical marketing landscape further.

Remember, understanding AI is not about becoming a tech wizard but a translator. A translator between the language of data and human needs. In this pursuit, you will become fluent in the vocabulary of insights, adept at interpreting the nuanced melodies of patient journeys, and equipped to compose a truly personalized healthcare experience.

This understanding also empowers you to become a conductor of the AI orchestra. You'll set the strategic goals, guide the development of AI tools, and ensure they harmonize with healthcare's ethical values and human-centric ideals. Remember, AI is not a solo act; it thrives in collaboration, where human intuition steers the course and ethical considerations act as the guiding tempo.

Key Questions

As you delve deeper into the subject, consider these questions:

- How can AI be used to personalize the patient journey in your specific area of pharma marketing?
- What ethical considerations need to be prioritized when implementing AI solutions?
- What skills and knowledge would you acquire to collaborate with AI developers and data scientists confidently?
- How can you foster a culture of innovation within your organization that welcomes exploration and experimentation with AI?

By actively engaging with these questions and exploring the intricacies of AI in pharma marketing, you'll become not just a witness to the revolution but an active participant, composing a future where technology and humanity orchestrate a symphony of patient-centric care.

CHAPTER

5

Key AI Concepts and Technology

Unlocking the Mysteries of Machine Intelligence

Imagine a world where machines reason, learn, and adapt like humans. This isn't just science fiction; it's the exhilarating reality of Artificial Intelligence(AI), a field revolutionizing everything from healthcare and transportation to art and entertainment. But behind the buzzwords and headlines lies a complex landscape of concepts and technologies. So, dear reader, grab your intellectual compass and prepare to navigate the fascinating world of key AI concepts and technologies.

Beyond Buzzwords, Beyond Science Fiction

Before diving into specifics, let's dispel some common misconceptions. AI isn't about robots taking over, nor is it magic. It's a collection of sophisticated algorithms and techniques that enable machines to mimic human intelligence in various ways. From pattern recognition and problem-solving to decision-making and language comprehension, the possibilities are as vast as our imagination.

A Symphony of Concepts

To understand AI's power, we must grasp its foundational concepts:

- **Machine Learning**: At the heart of AI is learning from data without explicit programming. Imagine a machine analyzing millions of pictures to distinguish cats from dogs— that's machine learning in action.

- **Deep Learning**: Inspired by the human brain, deep learning utilizes complex neural networks to process information in layers, mimicking how we perceive and understand the world. Think of it as the engine driving sophisticated AI applications like facial recognition and self-driving cars.
- **Natural Language Processing:** (NLP) is a fascinating technology that bridges the gap between humans and machines by enabling computers to understand and generate human language. Imagine chatbots carrying on conversations or translating language in real time—that's NLP at work.
- **Computer Vision**: Have you ever wondered how machines "See"? Computer vision algorithms analyze images and videos, interpreting visual data to identify objects, track movements, and even understand emotions. This technology powers features like facial recognition in social media and autonomous vehicle navigation.
- **Robotics**: AI and robotics go hand-in-hand, with AI algorithms controlling and optimizing robot movements and actions. Imagine robots performing delicate surgery or exploring deep-sea environments—that's the incredible synergy of AI and robotics.

Technology— The Orchestra that Brings Concepts to Life

These concepts come alive through various AI Technologies:

- **Big Data and Data Analytics**: AI thrives on data, and big data platforms store and analyze massive amounts of information. Analytics tools extract insights and patterns from this data, fueling AI algorithms.
- **Cloud Computing**: The powerful processing required for AI isn't confined to individual computers. Cloud computing platforms provide vast computational resources to train and run complex AI models.

- **Internet of Things (IoT)**: With billions of sensors and devices constantly generating data, the IoT creates a rich tapestry of information for AI analysis. The IoT and AI are unlocking revolutionary possibilities from smart homes to connected cities.

Expanding the Orchestra: More Technologies within the AI Symphony

The melody of AI extends far beyond the initial instruments described above. Let's delve deeper into the orchestra pit and explore some additional technologies that add harmony and complexity to the symphony of machine intelligence.

1. **Reinforcement Learning**: Imagine an AI agent learning to play a video game like Go, mastering intricate strategies through trial and error and self-optimization. That's the power of reinforcement learning, where AI learns by interacting with its environment and receiving rewards for achieving goals. This technology revolutionizes robotics, game development, and even personalized healthcare plans.
2. **Generative AI**: From composing music indistinguishable from human-made scores to crafting hyperrealistic portraits, generative AI pushes the boundaries of creativity. This technology harnesses deep learning to generate new content, text, images, music, or code. Applications range from artistic expression and entertainment to product design and drug discovery.
3. **Explainable AI (XAI)**: The need for transparency and understanding grows as AI algorithms become increasingly complex. XAI focuses on making AI models interpretable, allowing us to understand how they reach their decisions. This is crucial for building trust, identifying potential biases, and ensuring responsible development. Techniques like attention mechanisms and feature importance analysis are helping to demystify the black box of AI.

4. **Multi-Agent Systems**: Imagine several AI agents collaborating to achieve a complex goal, like coordinating autonomous vehicles in a bustling city. Multi-agent systems allow multiple AI entities to learn, communicate, and act together, solving problems beyond the capabilities of individual agents. This technology holds promise for areas like traffic management, resource allocation, and even collaborative robotics.
5. **Cognitive Computing**: Inspired by the human brain, cognitive computing aims to simulate human thought processes within a machine. This technology integrates various AI techniques like natural language processing, reasoning, and machine learning to enable machines to perceive, understand, and respond to information in a human-like way. Applications include intelligent assistants, personalized learning systems, and even robots capable of basic emotional understanding.

The Evolving Soundscape

These additional technologies, alongside those previously discussed, constantly evolve and interact, creating a dynamic and ever-changing soundscape. New advancements like neuromorphic computing, natural language generation and understanding, and explainable AI tools continuously enrich the AI symphony.

Beyond Instruments

Remember, the true beauty of the AI orchestra lies not only in the individual techniques but also in their harmonious interplay. By combining expertise in software, hardware, neuroscience, and ethics, we can create a symphony of innovation, empowering AI to address our most pressing challenges and push the boundaries of what is possible.

A Call to Action

Whether you're a tech enthusiast, a policymaker, or simply someone curious about the future, take your seat in the audience and engage with the AI symphony. Learn about the different instruments, understand their potential and limitations, and join the conversation about shaping the future of AI for the benefit of all. By actively participating in the melody, AI resonates with harmony, progress, and a shared vision for a brighter tomorrow.

Further Exploration

This is just a taste of the diverse technologies within the AI orchestra. To delve deeper, consider exploring:

- **The Intersection of Specific AI Technologies**: Investigate how different AI techniques synergize and complement each other in areas like self-driving cars, personalized medicine, or climate change mitigation.
- **The Ethical Considerations of Emerging Technologies**: Discuss the potential risks and benefits of technologies like explainable AI, cognitive computing, and generative AI, ensuring responsible development and application.
- **The Future of Work in the AI Era**: Analyze how AI technologies will impact job markets, workforce dynamics, and the necessary skills for future success in the AI-powered world.

By venturing beyond the initial instruments and actively engaging with the AI symphony, we can write a future where technology elevates human capabilities, addresses global challenges, and enriches our lives in ways we can only begin to imagine.

Emerging Technologies

Venturing beyond the AI orchestra pit and into the bustling streets of emerging technology, let's explore the exciting realms of Augmented Reality (AR), Virtual Reality (VR), Extended Reality (XR), Mixed Reality (MR), and Blockchain. Each holds immense potential to transform how we live, work, and interact with the world.

1. **AR (Augmented Reality)**: AR overlays digital elements onto the real world, enriching our perception with virtual information.

Imagine seeing repair instructions superimposed on a broken machine, navigating a city with real-time directions overlaid on your view, or interacting with virtual characters within your living room. AR boasts applications in education, gaming, entertainment, healthcare, and countless other fields.

2. **VR (Virtual Reality)**: VR immerses you in a completely simulated environment, transporting you to new worlds and experiences. Explore the ocean's depths, climb Mount Everest, or attend a concert with friends across the globe—all from the comfort of your living room. VR holds promise in gaming, entertainment, education, training, and therapeutic applications like pain management.
3. **XR (Extended Reality)**: XR is an umbrella term encompassing both AR and VR, representing the entire spectrum of technologies that blur the lines between physical and digital. Think of it as a vast technological ocean in which AR and VR are like different islands. As technology advances, the boundaries between these islands will likely fade, creating increasingly immersive and blended experiences.
4. **MR (Mixed Reality)**: MR takes things further, seamlessly merging the real and virtual worlds. Imagine manipulating virtual objects in your physical environment, collaborating with remote colleagues in a shared virtual space, or receiving training instructions on real-world equipment. MR offers unique possibilities in design, collaboration, education, and industrial applications.
5. **Blockchain**: This revolutionary technology decentralizes trust by creating a secure and transparent digital ledger. Imagine a system where transactions are recorded on a shared network, eliminating the need for intermediaries and guaranteeing the authenticity of data. Blockchain has immense potential in finance, supply chain management, healthcare, and voting systems.

Understanding the Symphony

While these technologies may seem distinct, they share a common theme: pushing the boundaries of our interaction with the digital world. They offer unique strengths and limitations, creating a symphony of possibilities. Imagine AR enhancing VR experiences with real-world context or blockchain-securing data transactions within immersive XR environments. The potential for collaboration and synergy is immense.

Challenges and Considerations

Despite their exciting potential, each technology faces challenges:

- **Accessibility and Affordability**: Ensuring equitable access to these technologies requires addressing issues like cost, device availability, and accessibility for individuals with disabilities.
- **Ethical Considerations**: Concerns about privacy, data security, and potential misuse of these immersive experiences need careful consideration and robust ethical frameworks.
- **User Experience and Interface**: Creating intuitive and user-friendly interfaces for interacting with these technologies is crucial for widespread adoption and positive user experiences.

Composing the Future

By addressing these challenges and harnessing the potential of these technologies responsibly, we can write a future where:

- **Education Transcends Geographic Boundaries**: Students can explore historical events in immersive VR environments or dissect virtual frogs in AR anatomy labs.
- **Collaboration Defies Physical Limitations**: Teams can work together on projects in shared virtual spaces, regardless of location.
- **Healthcare Becomes Proactive and Personalized**: AI-powered AR/VR tools can guide medical professionals during

surgery, and patients can participate in therapeutic VR experiences to manage pain or anxiety.

The Invitation to Explore

This is a brief glimpse into the exciting world of AR, VR, XR, MR, and Blockchain. To delve deeper, consider exploring:

- **Specific Applications and Case Studies**: Investigate how these technologies are used in various industries, gaining inspiration from real-world examples.
- **The Ethical Landscape of Each Technology**: Discuss potential risks and benefits, analyzing ways to develop and implement these technologies responsibly.
- **The Future of Work and Education**: Imagine how these technologies will reshape how we work and learn, preparing ourselves for the skills and opportunities they present.

Remember, the future of technology is not a solo performance. It's a collaborative symphony where instruments like AI, AR, VR, and Blockchain create a harmonious and transformative experience for all. So, please pick up your instrument, join the orchestra, and help compose a future where technology empowers us to connect, learn, and create in exciting and unimaginable ways.

The Symphony's Melodies: Benefits and Applications

This intricate collaboration of concepts and technologies unlocks a world of benefits:

- **Enhanced Healthcare**: AI diagnoses diseases with unprecedented accuracy, predicts patient outcomes, and develops personalized treatment plans. Its impact on drug discovery and healthcare delivery is revolutionizing the medical landscape.

- **Personalized Experiences**: Whether recommending products you love or tailoring news feeds to your interests, AI personalizes digital experiences, making them more relevant and engaging.
- **Increased Efficiency and Productivity**: From automating tasks in manufacturing to optimizing logistics and supply chains, AI is streamlining workflows and boosting efficiency across industries.
- **Scientific Breakthroughs**: From analyzing astronomical datasets to predicting climate change patterns, AI is accelerating scientific discovery and helping us better understand the world around us.

The Counterpoint: Challenges and Considerations

Despite its promise, AI isn't without challenges:

- **Bias and Discrimination**: AI algorithms trained on biased data can perpetuate inequities. Mitigating bias and ensuring fair and ethical AI development is crucial to preventing discrimination and building trust.
- **Job Displacement**: Automation through AI raises concerns about job losses. Reskilling initiatives and adapting our workforce to a changing landscape are essential to navigate this transition smoothly.
- **Safety and Security**: Cybersecurity threats and potential misuse of AI pose serious risks. Developing robust security measures and responsible AI frameworks are necessary to safeguard privacy and prevent misuse.
- **Transparency and Explainability**: Complex AI algorithms can be opaque. Ensuring transparency and explainability in AI decision-making is crucial to building trust and addressing concerns about black box algorithms.

Composing the Future: Towards Responsible and Ethical AI

To address these challenges and ensure AI benefits all, we must:

- **Prioritize Ethical Development**: Implement robust ethical frameworks, mitigate bias, and ensure transparency throughout the AI lifecycle.
- **Invest in Research and Education**: Fund AI research and development and equip our workforce with the skills and knowledge needed to thrive in the AI-powered world. To harness the full potential of AI while mitigating its risks, we must prioritize ongoing research and education.
- **Funding Research Initiatives**: Investing in fundamental AI research is crucial to pushing the field's boundaries and discovering new applications. This includes supporting academic institutions, public-private partnerships, and independent research labs dedicated to advancing AI development responsibly and ethically.
- **Enhancing AI Literacy**: It is vital to equip everyone—from policymakers and business leaders to citizens and students—with a basic understanding of AI concepts, potential benefits and limitations, and ethical implications. Educational programs and public awareness can bridge the knowledge gap and foster informed dialogue about AI's societal role.
- **Reskilling and Upskilling the Workforce**: Automation through AI will undoubtedly change the job landscape. Proactive reskilling and upskilling initiatives are essential to prepare our workforce for the evolving needs of the AI-powered economy. This includes training in complementary skills like critical thinking, creativity, and collaboration, which will remain irreplaceable in the face of AI advancements.

Building a Bridge: Collaboration and Open Dialogue

Effective navigation of the AI landscape requires open dialogue and collaboration among diverse stakeholders:

- **Academia-Industry Partnerships**: Collaboration between academic researchers and industry leaders can bridge the gap between theoretical advancements and practical applications. By working together, they can ensure responsible AI development, address practical challenges, and accelerate the transfer of research into real-world solutions.
- **International Cooperation**: The challenges and opportunities presented by AI are global. International collaboration on ethical frameworks, data governance standards, and AI safety measures is crucial to ensure responsible development and equitable access to its benefits.
- **Public Engagement and Inclusion**: Open dialogue with the public about AI's potential impact on society, concerns about data privacy and bias, and ethical considerations is essential to build trust and ensure AI advancements serve the needs of all people. This includes diverse community engagement, transparent communication, and opportunities for public input in AI policy and development.

Beyond the Horizon: A Symphony of Human and Machine Intelligence

By prioritizing ethical development, investing in research and education, and fostering collaboration, we can ensure that AI becomes a force for good in our world. Imagine:

- AI-powered tools assist doctors in making accurate diagnoses and personalized treatment plans, leading to improved health outcomes for all.
- Educational platforms powered by AI tailoring learning experiences to individual needs, fostering inclusive and effective education for every child.
- Sustainable energy solutions and environmental monitoring systems developed through AI help combat climate change and build a greener future.

This is not a dystopian future where machines control us; it's a hopeful vision where human intelligence and AI synergize, complementing each other to create a more equitable, prosperous, and sustainable world. It's a symphony where technology amplifies our capabilities, addresses our challenges, and empowers us to create a brighter future for future generations. So, dear reader, pick up your instrument, join the orchestra of voices shaping AI's future, and let responsible, ethical AI music play on.

Further Exploration

This chapter offers a glimpse into the vast world of key AI concepts and technologies. To delve deeper, consider exploring:

- **Specific AI Applications in Various Fields**: Explore the diverse applications of AI in healthcare, education, environmental protection, and other sectors, understanding the unique challenges and opportunities in each domain.
- **Emerging AI Advancements**: Stay up-to-date on the latest developments in AI research, like quantum computing, neuromorphic computing, and advancements in natural language processing, understanding their potential impact in the future of AI.
- **The Ethical Landscape of Specific AI Technologies**: This section delves into the concerns surrounding autonomous weapons, facial recognition systems, and social media algorithms, exploring potential solutions and mitigation strategies to ensure responsible development and use.

By continuously learning, adapting, and engaging in open dialogue, we can ensure that the symphony of AI and human intelligence continues to evolve, composing a future filled with harmony, progress, and shared prosperity for all.

CHAPTER 6

Applications of AI in Pharma Marketing

Harnessing the Power of AI in Specific Marketing Activities

Let's delve deeper into how AI can transform specific pharma marketing activities:

1. **Targeting and Segmentation**
    - **Predictive Patient Targeting**: AI can identify high-value patient segments with specific medication needs by analyzing patient data and social media trends. Imagine targeting doctors treating patients with rare diseases based on AI-powered analysis of online forums and medical literature.
    - **Dynamic Customer Segmentation**: AI algorithms can continuously update and refine customer segments based on real-time data feeds. This agility ensures marketing campaigns stay relevant and impactful, adapting to evolving patient needs and market dynamics.
2. **Content Creation and Optimization**
    - **AI-powered Medical Writing**: Imagine generating accurate and insightful reports for healthcare professionals or personalized medication summaries for patients, all powered by AI. This frees medical writers to focus on complex content while ensuring information accuracy and relevance.

- **Chatbots and Virtual Assistants**: Personalized chatbots powered by NLP can answer patient questions, provide medication reminders, and offer self-care tips. This 24/7 patient support builds trust and improves medication adherence.
- **Data-Driven Video and Audio Content**: AI can analyze audience preferences and trends to generate customized video and audio content, ensuring maximum engagement and effectiveness in online campaigns.

3. **Customer Engagement and Relationship Management**
    - **Hyper-Personalized Email Marketing**: Imagine crafting and sending emails with individual patient names, relevant medication information, and tailored offers, all powered by AI's understanding of each recipient. This personalization increases engagement and conversion rates.
    - **Social Media Listening and Engagement**: AI tools can monitor social media conversations about specific medications and diseases, allowing pharma companies to engage with patients, address concerns, and build brand loyalty.
    - **Sentiment Analysis and Reputation Management**: By analyzing online reviews and feedback, AI can identify potential reputational risks and inform proactive public relations strategies, maintaining a positive brand image.
4. **Clinical Trial Recruitment and Management**
    - **Predictive Patient Matching:** AI can identify potential trial participants with specific characteristics based on medical data and lifestyle factors, streamlining the recruitment process and improving trial success rates.
    - **Virtual Trial Assistants**: AI-powered chatbots can answer patient questions about clinical trials, address concerns, and guide them through the participation process, leading to higher enrollment and participant satisfaction.

- **Real-time Data Monitoring and Analysis**: AI can analyze clinical trial data in real-time, identifying safety concerns or efficacy trends, enabling proactive adjustments, and optimizing outcomes.

5. **Regulatory Compliance and Reporting**
   - **Automated Content Compliance Checks**: AI tools can flag potentially non-compliant marketing materials before publication, ensuring regulatory adherence and minimizing compliance risks.
   - **Streamlined Reporting and Documentation**: AI can automate reporting processes, analyze safety data, and generate regulatory reports, saving time and resources while guaranteeing accuracy and completeness.
   - **Predictive Regulatory Compliance**: AI can analyze historical data and regulatory trends to predict potential compliance challenges and inform proactive risk mitigation strategies.

Challenges and Considerations

Implementing AI in pharma marketing requires careful planning and consideration of potential challenges.

- **Data Governance and Security**: Robust data governance frameworks and data security measures are crucial to protect sensitive patient information.
- **Model Validation and Explainability**: Ensuring the accuracy and validity of AI models and making their decision-making processes transparent is essential for building trust with stakeholders.
- **Human in the Loop Approach**: AI should complement, not replace, human expertise and empathy in patient interactions and healthcare communication.
- **Cost and Infrastructure**: Implementing AI technology requires investments in infrastructure, training, and skilled personnel.

Beyond the Hype, a Symphony of Innovation

The integration of AI in pharma marketing is not just a technological trend; it's a symphony of innovation promising a future where:

- Patients receive personalized care and support empowered by AI-driven communication and engagement tools.
- Healthcare professionals experience streamlined workflows and data-driven insights, enabling them to make informed decisions and provide better patient care.
- Pharma companies achieve integrated marketing campaigns, optimize resource allocation, and contribute to improved health outcomes for all.

The future will not be built solely on technology; it requires a collaborative effort from pharmaceutical companies, regulatory bodies, healthcare professionals, and patients. By prioritizing ethical development, responsible implementation, and continuous learning, we can ensure that AI becomes a force for good in pharmaceutical marketing, transforming how we communicate and engage and ultimately improving health outcomes for everyone.

Further Exploration

We can delve even deeper into AI in pharma marketing, exploring specific examples, ethical considerations, and the future landscape of this exciting field. Consider the following:

1. **Deeper Dive into Specific Applications**
   - **AI in Pharma Sales**: Imagine AI-powered sales assistants guiding reps through personalized interactions with healthcare professionals, providing real-time data on patient needs and treatment options.
   - **AI for Drug Pricing and Market Access**: AI algorithms can analyze complex market data and predict pricing strategies, optimizing market access for new drugs and ensuring patient affordability.

- **AI-Driven Pharmacovigilance**: By monitoring social media conversations, online forums, and healthcare databases, AI can detect potential adverse drug reactions in real time, improving pharmacovigilance and patient safety.

2. **Ethics and Responsible AI in Pharma Marketing**
    - **Mitigating Bias in AI Algorithms**: Exploring strategies to ensure AI algorithms used in pharma marketing are trained on unbiased data and do not perpetuate inequalities in healthcare access.
    - **Transparency and Explainability in AI Decision-Making**: Discussing frameworks for making AI-driven decisions in pharma marketing transparent and understandable for patients, healthcare professionals, and regulators.
    - **AI and the Future of Medical Privacy**: Addressing patient data privacy and security concerns in AI-powered Healthcare Communication and Marketing.
3. **The Future Landscape of AI in Pharma Marketing**
    - **The Rise of Explainable AI (XAI)**: Explores how XAI tools can provide insights into the reasoning behind AI algorithms used in pharma marketing, building trust, and addressing concerns about black box algorithms.
    - **The Integration of Blockchain**: Discuss the potential for combining AI and blockchain technology to create secure, transparent data platforms for pharmaceutical marketing research.
    - **The Human-AI Partnership**: This initiative addresses how AI can empower and collaborate with healthcare professionals and marketing teams, leading to a more human-centric approach to pharmaceutical marketing.

CHAPTER 7

Challenges and Opportunities of AI Integration

A Symphony of Challenges and Opportunities

The fusion of Artificial Intelligence (AI) and pharma marketing paints a vibrant canvas of possibilities. Imagine hyper-personalized patient engagement, data-driven campaign optimization, and market insights gleaned from a vast ocean of information. However, beneath this dazzling surface lies a complex world brimming with challenges and opportunities, demanding an orchestra of careful consideration and ethical implementation.

Challenges: Navigating the Crossroads of Innovation and Responsibility

1. **Ethical Maze of Data Privacy and Security**: Protecting the sensitive tapestry of patient data is paramount. Concerns lie in potential breaches, algorithmic bias, and the opaque nature of some AI models. Robust data governance frameworks, transparency measures, and continuous vigilance are crucial to prevent misuse and build trust.
2. **Explainability and Algorithmic Bias**: It is vital to unpack the black box of AI decision-making. Algorithms trained on skewed data can perpetuate inequalities, marginalizing specific demographics. Demystifying algorithms, ensuring diversity in training data, and human oversight are key to combating potential bias and fostering fairness.

3. **Skillset Symphony, Re-orchestrating the Workforce**: AI's automation potential can disrupt traditional landscapes. While it may augment capabilities, reskilling and upskilling initiatives are crucial for healthcare professionals and marketing teams to adapt and thrive in this evolving ecosystem.
4. **Regulatory Rhythms: Harmonizing Innovation and Compliance**: Regulatory frameworks must embrace innovation while safeguarding patient well-being. Clear guidelines and collaborative dialogues between pharma companies, regulators, and ethical experts are essential to navigating the regulatory landscape of AI in healthcare.
5. **Cost and Infrastructure, and The Overture of Investment**: Embracing AI necessitates investment in infrastructure, skilled personnel, and ongoing research. Careful planning, resource allocation, and strategic partnerships can orchestrate a cost-effective integration that maximizes return on investment.

Opportunities: Amplifying the Potential of AI in Pharma Marketing

1. **Hyper-Personalized Engagement:** AI can weave a tapestry of personalized patient experiences. Imagine chatbots offering 24/7 support, tailored medication reminders, and content curated to individual needs. This would foster trust, improve medication adherence, and empower patients to actively participate in their healthcare journey.
2. **Data-Driven Insights Symphony**: AI can analyze vast troves of data, unveiling hidden patterns and predicting market trends with uncanny accuracy. Imagine anticipating patient needs, optimizing clinical trial recruitment, and tailoring campaigns to resonate with specific audiences. This data-driven approach leads to targeted campaigns, efficient resource allocation, and improved health outcomes.
3. **Augmenting Human Expertise**: AI isn't here to replace but to amplify the unique capabilities of healthcare professionals

and marketing teams. Imagine AI-powered assistants providing real-time data and insights, streamlining workflows, and enabling healthcare professionals to dedicate more time to personalized patient care. Similarly, AI can analyze customer sentiment, optimize campaign content, and guide marketing teams toward data-driven strategies, maximizing outreach and impact.

4. **Innovation through Collaboration**: This symphony of AI in pharma marketing requires a harmonious ensemble of stakeholders. Collaboration between pharma companies, universities, tech giants, and regulatory bodies fosters innovation, ethical development, and responsible implementation. Joint research initiatives, knowledge-sharing platforms, and open dialogues can pave the way for a future where AI benefits members of the healthcare ecosystem.
5. **Revolutionizing Clinical Research**: AI can accelerate clinical research, bringing life-saving drugs to patients faster. Imagine AI-powered virtual assistants screening potential participants, identifying promising drug targets, and analyzing clinical trial data in real-time. This would increase efficiency, enhance patient safety, and accelerate the path to new treatments.

Composing a Future Where AI Harmonizes with Humanity

Integrating AI in pharma marketing demands a holistic approach. We must acknowledge and address the challenges while remaining enthralled by the vast potential to improve patient care, enhance healthcare experiences, and ultimately contribute to a healthier future for all. Here are some key insights to guide our composition:

- **Ethical Harmony**: Prioritize ethical considerations and responsible AI development, ensuring data privacy, mitigating bias, and fostering transparency.
- **Human+AI Collaboration**: Embrace AI to empower, not replace, human expertise and empathy in healthcare communication and patient engagement.

- **Continuous Learning and Innovation**: Foster a culture of continuous learning and adaptation, staying abreast of evolving AI technologies and their ethical implications.
- **Open Dialogue and Collaboration**: Encourage open dialogue among stakeholders to address concerns, share best practices, and navigate the ethical landscape of AI healthcare.
- **Investing in the Future**: Invest in research, education, and infrastructure to ensure equitable access to AI's benefits in healthcare and bridge the digital divide.

By playing our instruments in harmony, we can ensure that AI becomes a force for good in pharma marketing, composing a future where technology empowers healthcare professionals and personalized patient experiences and ultimately contributes to a healthier world for everyone.

PART III

Human+AI Synergy in Pharmaceutical Marketing

Chapter 8. Brand and Science Intertwined

Chapter 9. Beyond Traditional Channels: A Revolution in Pharma Marketing

Chapter 10. Customer-centric Composition

Chapter 11. Regulation as Rhythm in Human+AI Collaboration

Introduction: Harmony Amidst Complexity

The pharmaceutical industry stands at a pivotal crossroads. Innovation explodes from laboratories, birthing a dizzying array of treatments, while the healthcare landscape undergoes seismic shifts in regulation, reimbursement, and patient expectations. In the maelstrom, success no longer dances to the side tunes of individual marketing channels. Instead, a new maestro leads the orchestra—Synergy. Synergy in pharma marketing transcends mere collaboration. It's a strategic alchemy where diverse elements—scientific data, brand storytelling, digital outreach, and customer insights— fuse into a potent concoction. This potent concoction transcends limitations, amplifies impact, and unlocks transformative growth. Yet, harnessing this synergistic power demands a nuanced understanding of its multifaceted application.

Part III embarks on a deep dive into the symphony of synergy in pharma marketing. We dissect its various instruments, each resonating with distinct strengths and challenges. We explore the intricate arrangements— cross-channel integration, data-driven insights, and the rise of digital platforms— that weave a captivating melody of brand engagement and market influence.

A Chorus of Catalysts

- **Brand and Science Intertwined:** Scientific advancements deserve compelling narratives. We delve into the art of translating complex data into stories that resonate with healthcare professionals and patients, forging powerful emotional connections that amplify brand value.
- **Beyond Traditional Channels**: We move past the familiar beats of print ads and sales reps, examining the dynamic rise of digital ecosystems, social media engagement, and personalized experiences. From virtual reality consultations to AI-powered analytics, we unveil the transformative potential of these platforms in nurturing long-term brand loyalty.

- **Data Drives Melody:** Information is not just power; it's the conductor orchestrating the entire performance. We explore the intricate dance between data analytics and marketing strategy, demonstrating how data-driven insights can inform targeted campaigns, optimize resource allocation, and personalize patient journeys.
- **Customer-Centric Composition:** The audience dictates the tune. We spotlight the crucial role of understanding and catering to diverse customer segments— healthcare professionals, patients, and payers— building trust and forging collaborative partnerships for sustainable success.
- **Regulations as Rhythm:** Legal and ethical frameworks set the parameters of the performance. We navigate the complex regulatory landscape of pharma marketing, ensuring compliance while utilizing its constraints as springboards for creative and impactful messaging.

Harmonious Convergence

Part III culminates in a grand finale, showcasing how these individual instruments continue to create a unified masterpiece. We examine real-world success stories where synergistic marketing orchestrated remarkable brand transformations, improved patient outcomes, and redefined industry standards. The concluding segment also offers a glimpse into the future of pharma marketing, where synergy takes center stage, fueled by emerging technologies like artificial intelligence, blockchain, and immersive experiences.

This journey through the application of synergy in pharma marketing is not merely an intellectual exercise; it's a clarion call. It's a call to embrace the complexity, to break down silos, and to unlock the transformative power of collaboration. For in the harmonious convergence of diverse elements lies the melody of success, waiting to be played out on the vast stage of the pharmaceutical industry.

Ready to join the orchestra? Turn the page, and let the symphony of synergy begin.

CHAPTER 8

Brand and Science Intertwined

The Challenge: Translating Complexity into Connection

The pharmaceutical industry thrives on scientific innovation, constantly unlocking groundbreaking discoveries. However, these advancements often exist as complex data, statistics, and clinical trial results— a language inaccessible to most patients and even many healthcare professionals (HCPs). This is where the art of translation comes in.

The Art of Storytelling: Bridging the Gap

The power of storytelling bridges the intricate world of science and the human desire for connection. By weaving narratives around scientific advancements, you can:

- **Make Complex Data Relatable:** Translate dry statistics into engaging stories that resonate with audiences. Use metaphors, analogies, and visuals to break complex concepts into easily digestible pieces.
- **Evoke Emotions:** Connect with audiences on an emotional level. Highlight the human impact of scientific breakthroughs, showcasing how they improve lives, alleviate suffering, and offer hope.
- **Spark Engagement:** Ignite curiosity and interest in the science behind the brand. Encourage audiences to learn more, ask questions, and participate in the healthcare journey.

Examples of Synergy in Action:

- **Patient Testimonials:** Share the stories of real patients whose lives have been transformed by a new treatment. Their struggles, triumphs, and emotions resonate deeply and make the science tangible.
- **Animated Explainer Videos:** Use animation to visually represent complex biological processes or drug mechanisms clearly and engagingly.
- **Interactive Data Visualization:** This allows audiences to explore data themselves, fostering a sense of discovery and deeper understanding.
- **Doctor Interviews:** Feature HCPs explaining the science behind a new drug in clear, concise language, building trust and credibility with their peers.

Amplifying Brand Value:

You achieve more than education by effectively intertwining brand and science through storytelling. You:

- **Build Trust and Credibility:** Showcase your commitment to scientific rigor and transparency.
- **Differentiate Your Brand:** Stand out in a crowded market by connecting with audiences on a deeper level.
- **Foster Emotional Connections:** Create a lasting impression beyond just product features.
- **Drive Engagement and Action:** Motivate patients to seek treatment and HCPs to prescribe your medication.

Remember:

- **Authenticity is Key:** Ensure your stories are genuine, ethical, and patient-centric.
- **Tailor Your Message:** Adapt your storytelling approach to resonate with different audience segments (patients, HCPs, and investors).

- **Embrace New Formats:** Explore innovative storytelling methods like podcasts, virtual reality experiences, and interactive games.

By mastering the art of intertwining brand and science, you can unlock the true potential of pharma marketing, fostering deeper connections, building trust, and improving patient outcomes. This synergy embodies the spirit of "The Synergy of Minds," where human creativity and scientific advancements join forces to revolutionize healthcare.

The Power of Storytelling in Pharma Marketing: Weaving Compelling Narratives

Storytelling isn't just a literary device; it's a powerful tool in pharma marketing, forging emotional connections and amplifying brand value. Here's how to craft a compelling story about a new diabetic drug:

Understanding the Audience:

- **Who are You Targeting:** Patients, healthcare professionals (HCPs), or both? Tailor your story accordingly.
- **What Are Their Needs and Aspirations?** Patients yearn for hope and control, while HCPs seek efficacy and patient well-being.

Crafting Your Narrative:

1. **Define the Hero:** Is it the patient struggling with diabetes, the dedicated HCP, or the innovative drug itself?
2. **Establish the Challenge:** What are the daily struggles and anxieties associated with managing diabetes?
3. **Introduce the Solution:** How does your new drug address these challenges— with better sugar control, minimal side effects, and convenient dosing?
4. **Showcasing the Transformation:** Highlight the positive impact on the hero's life— improved health, greater freedom, or stronger relationships.

5. **End with a Call to Action:** Encourage patients to talk to their doctors and HCPs to learn more about the drug.

Hypothetical Story

Scene: Sarah, a vibrant 42-year-old with Type 2 diabetes, juggles multiple medications, finger pricks, and constant worry about her blood sugar. She feels limited, missing out on spontaneity and fearing complications.

Challenge: Sarah's current regimen is complex, with side effects affecting her energy and social life. The constant monitoring casts a shadow over her day.

Solution: Enter "GlucoEase," a new once-daily pill offering better sugar control with minimal side effects. Sarah starts experiencing:

- **Stable Blood Sugar:** Freedom from constant worry and finger pricks.
- **Reduced Side Effects:** More energy and confidence to participate in life.
- **Improved Well-being:** Enjoying activities and spending quality time with loved ones.

Transformation: Sarah embraces a more active lifestyle, travels with less anxiety, and feels empowered to manage her diabetes. She even shares her story with friends facing similar challenges.

Call to Action: Patients are encouraged to ask their doctors about GlucoEase, and HCPs are invited to attend webinars or download clinical trial data.

Remember:

- **Authenticity:** Avoid exaggerated claims; focus on genuine patient experiences and benefits.
- **Emotional Connection:** Tap into the core desires and anxieties of your audience.

- **Credibility:** Balance emotional appeal with factual information and scientific backing.
- **Clarity and Conscience:** Deliver your message effectively within time constraints.
- **Multi-channel Storytelling:** Utilize various formats like videos, social media posts, and patient testimonials.

By weaving a compelling story, you can transform a new drug from a product into a life-changing solution, resonating deeply with your audience and driving successful pharma marketing.

Storytelling in Pharma: An Example

A Slice of Life: Sarah's Sweet Success with GlucoEase!

Concept: This campaign leverages AI+human collaboration to tell the story of Sarah, a young woman with type 2 diabetes, and her positive experience with GlucoEase (a hypothetical diabetes medication brand with superior blood sugar control with minium side effects). AI personalizes the narrative based on viewer demographics and interests, while human expertise ensures emotional resonance and ethical messaging.

Human Touch:

- **Story Development:** A team of writers crafts Sarah's narrative, capturing her challenges, anxieties, and eventual joys after starting GlucoEase.
- **Emotional Storytelling:** Humor, relatable anecdotes, and genuine portrayal of Sarah's journey evoke empathy and connection with viewers.
- **Ethical Considerations:** Transparent communication about drug benefits and limitations, respecting patient privacy, and avoiding unrealistic expectations.

AI Power:

- **Interactive Website:** AI tailors Sarah's story based on viewer demographics (age, gender, location) and diabetes type (1 or 2).
- **Personalized Video Thumbnails:** AI highlights story segments relevant to the viewer's interests (e.g., managing weight, enjoying social events, or traveling with diabetes).
- **Dynamic Infographics:** AI visualizes Sarah's Improved blood sugar control and overall well-being.
- **Multilingual Support:** AI translates the story and website contents into various languages, expanding reach and inclusivity.

Synergy in Action

- Viewers aged 25-35 with an active lifestyle see Sarah thriving at a music festival, managing her blood sugar seamlessly with GlucoEase.
- Viewers over 55 with type 2 diabetes see Sarah enjoying a delicious family dinner, confidently discussing her dietary choices with GlucoEase support.
- Interactive elements allow viewers to explore Sarah's daily routine, exercise choices, and emotional responses to managing diabetes.
- Real-time analytics reveal which story segments and emotional cues resonate most with different audiences, informing future content optimization.

Expected Outcomes

- Increased brand awareness and positive perception of GlucoEase.
- Deeper engagement with personalized storytelling that fosters trust and connection.

- Empowerment for diabetes patients to see themselves reflected in a relatable and successful story.
- Improved patient education and understanding of managing diabetes effectively.

Ethical Considerations:

- **Data Privacy:** Ensure informed consent for data collection and transparent communication about its use for personalization.
- **Avoiding Bias:** Train AI models with diverse datasets and monitor for potential biases in personalization to ensure fair representation.
- **Balanced Portrayal:** Present GlucoEase as a helpful tool, not a miracle cure, emphasizing responsible diabetes management alongside its benefits.

Driven by AI + human collaboration, Sarah's story is just one example of how storytelling can revolutionize pharmaceutical marketing. By harnessing both strengths, we can create narratives that resonate, educate, and empower patients while upholding ethical responsibility and building brand trust. Remember, in the ever-evolving healthcare landscape, it's not just about selling drugs but connecting with human experiences and sparking positive change.

A Satisfied Diabetic Patient: Example of a Story

From Rollercoaster to Rhythm: Clara's Journey with GlucoEase!

Sarah used to live in a world of "maybes" and "what-ifs." As a Type 2 diabetic, her blood sugar levels resembled a wild rollercoaster, spiking after meals, plummeting unexpectedly, and leaving her constantly on edge. Every bite of food, every activity, became a calculated risk. "Can I have this? Will it send me soaring? Should I rest now? Might I crash it later?" The joy of spontaneity, the freedom of a carefree day, vanished, replaced by a constant drumbeat of worry.

GlucoEase wasn't just a drug; it was a lifeline. When Sarah started taking it, the rollercoaster ride began to smooth out. The unpredictable peaks and valleys morphed into gentle ripples, then gentle slopes, until finally, her blood sugar found its steady rhythm. It wasn't a miracle cure, mind you. Sarah still monitored her diet, exercised regularly, and took her medication meticulously. But now, she did it with confidence, not fear.

The change wasn't just physical; it was emotional. The "maybes" and "what-ifs" began to fade, replaced by "yeses" and "I can." Sarah could finally indulge in a slice of birthday cake without guilt, knowing GlucoEase had her back. She could join her friends for spontaneous hikes, the crisp mountain air no longer a potential trigger for a crash. The little things mattered most— the freedom to savor a sweet treat, the unplanned dance party in the kitchen, the simple act of walking without wondering if her body would rebel.

But Sarah's story wasn't just about self-indulgence. GlucoEase empowered her to take control of her health. She embraced cooking healthy meals, discovering a hidden passion for creating vibrant vegetable stir-fries and experimenting with gluten-free desserts. Exercise became a source of joy, not drudgery, as she discovered the exhilaration of a morning run and the quiet mindfulness of a yoga session. She even joined a local support group, sharing her experiences and learning from others, becoming a source of strength and encouragement.

Life, for Sarah, became a symphony. The once discordant notes of her disease blended into a harmonious melody. The steady thrum of her GlucoEase, the rhythm of her healthy habits, and the joyful notes of life rediscovered— all played perfectly. She wasn't cured, but she was free. Free from fear, free from limitations, free to live her life to the fullest, one sweet, spontaneous, worry-free moment at a time.

And that, as Sarah would tell you with a smile brighter than any sunrise, was truly something to sing about.

CHAPTER

9

Beyond Traditional Channels: A Revolution in Pharma Marketing

The pharma marketing landscape is evolving rapidly, and more than traditional channels like print ads and rep visits are needed to reach and engage diverse audiences. A new wave of digital ecosystems, social media engagement, and personalized experiences is shaping the industry, demanding a bold exploration of 'Beyond Traditional Channels."

Beyond Traditional Channels

Digital Ecosystems Take Center Stage

- **Virtual World, Real Connections:** Virtual consultations and immersive experiences powered by VR and AR transform patient interactions. Imagine healthcare professionals showcasing treatment solutions through 3D models of the human body or patients experiencing virtual simulations of potential treatment outcomes. This personalized approach builds engagement and understanding like never before.
- **AI-Powered Insights and Automation:** Artificial intelligence is no longer science fiction. AI-powered platforms assist in analyzing vast data, identifying market trends, and driving targeted campaigns. By optimizing campaign performance and personalizing outreach, AI opens doors to reaching the right audience at the right time with the right message.

- **Mobile-First Mindset:** Smartphones are ubiquitous, making mobile engagement essential. Pharma brands must develop user-friendly apps, interactive tools, and educational content tailored for mobile consumption. This ensures accessibility, fosters ongoing communication with patients and healthcare professionals, and builds loyalty through immediate access to information and support.

Social Media: Amplifying Brand Resonance

- **Patient Communities and Advocacy:** Social media platforms facilitate powerful patient communities. By fostering online support groups, encouraging patient testimonials, and engaging with influencers, pharma brands can cultivate trust, generate authentic content, and gain valuable insights into patient needs and experiences.
- **Targeted Outreach and Education:** Social media advertising tools enable highly targeted campaigns, reaching specific demographics and healthcare professionals with educational content about treatment options, disease awareness, and medication adherence. This fosters engagement, drives website traffic, and improves patient outcomes.
- **Real-Time Conversation and Crisis Management:** Social media opens a two-way dialogue with audiences. Brands can proactively address concerns, manage crises, and respond to inquiries in real time, building trust and transparency with stakeholders.

Personalization: The Key to Resonant Engagement

- **Tailored Content and Experience:** Gone are the days of one-size-fits-all messaging. Big data analytics allows personalized content delivery, tailoring communications based on individual preferences, medical history, and treatment needs. This ensures relevance, enhances engagement, and drives better patient outcomes.

- **Interactive Tools and Assessments:** Personalized quizzes, symptom trackers, and medication reminders on mobile apps empower patients to actively participate in their healthcare journey. This fosters a sense of control, improves medication adherence, and strengthens the relationship between patients and their healthcare providers.
- **Gamification and Reward Systems:** Gamification elements like points, badges, and leaderboards can be integrated into patient education platforms and apps. This incentivizes engagement, increases knowledge retention, and promotes healthy behaviors, ultimately improving patient outcomes.

Moving Forward: Navigating the Digital Frontier

While the potential beyond traditional channels is immense, pharma brands must navigate the landscape with ethical considerations and regulatory compliance in mind. Data privacy, transparency, and responsible engagement with online communities are paramount. The future of pharma marketing lies in embracing this digital revolution, utilizing its power to reach and engage audiences meaningfully while prioritizing patient well-being and ethical conduct.

How Data Drives the Melody

There are several ways data can drive the melody in the context of pharma marketing:

1. **Identifying Trends and Patterns**
   - **Market Research:** Analyzing data on demographics, disease prevalence, and treatment preferences can inform the development of targeted marketing campaigns, ensuring messages resonate with the right audiences.
   - **Predictive Analytics:** Data on past marketing performance and market factors can predict future trends and customer behavior, allowing brands to allocate resources and effectively tailor strategies.

- **Competitive Insights:** Analyzing competitor data can reveal their strengths and weaknesses, enabling brands to differentiate themselves and position their products strategically.

2. **Optimizing Message and Content**
   - **A/B Testing:** Data can be used to test different versions of ad copy, email marketing, and website content to identify the most effective messaging and visuals.
   - **Personalization:** Data on individual preferences and behavior can be used to personalize content and communication, making it more relevant and engaging to each audience member.
   - **Sentiment Analysis:** Analyzing social media and customer feedback data can help understand audience sentiment towards a brand or treatment, allowing real-time adjustments to messaging and communication strategies.
3. **Measuring and Improving Performance**
   - **Campaign Tracking:** Data on website traffic, social media engagement, and lead generation can track the effectiveness of marketing campaigns and inform future iterations.
   - **Marketing Attribution:** Advanced analytics tools can identify the specific touchpoints within a marketing campaign that drive conversions, allowing for focused optimization and ROI maximization.
   - **Customer Journey Mapping:** Data can be used to map the customer journey from awareness to purchase, highlighting pain points and opportunities for improvement in the overall marketing experience.

Data Drives Melody: Some Examples:

- Imagine a pharma brand using data to identify regions with a high prevalence of a specific disease and then developing targeted ad campaigns tailored to the local population with educational content.

- Another brand might use A/B testing to discover that videos featuring real patient testimonials perform better than animated illustrations, prompting them to shift their video content strategy accordingly.
- Finally, data analysis might reveal that patient engagement drops at a specific point in their treatment journey, prompting the brand to develop targeted interventions like reminder messages or educational resources to address this challenge.

In essence, data plays the role of the conductor in an orchestra, guiding the melody of your marketing strategy. By analyzing and leveraging data insights, pharma brands can make informed decisions, refine their approach, and ultimately achieve greater success in reaching and engaging their target audiences.

CHAPTER 10

Customer-Centric Composition

The "Customer-centric Composition" in Human+AI collaboration in pharma marketing is a fascinating yet somewhat ambiguous phrase. To better understand its meaning, let's break it down:

Customer-centric: This emphasizes putting the customer (healthcare professionals, patients, or payers) at the heart of every marketing decision. It means understanding their needs and preferences and tailoring messaging and strategies accordingly.

Composition: This term could have various interpretations here. It might refer to:

- **Content Creation:** Crafting marketing materials (ads, website content, videos) that resonate with customers and address their specific needs.
- **Campaign Structuring:** Designing marketing campaigns involving AI and human elements, each contributing their strengths to achieve optimal results.
- **Decision-making:** Combining AI-driven insights with human expertise and judgment to make informed marketing decisions that benefit the customers.

The Human+AI collaboration highlights the power of combining artificial intelligence's efficiency and analytical capabilities with human creativity, empathy, and ethical considerations. It represents a synergistic approach where AI and humans contribute to delivering superior customer-centric marketing.

So, putting it together, "Customer-centric Composition" in Human+AI collaboration in pharma marketing could suggest:

- Developing marketing materials like stories, videos, or educational resources tailored to specific customer segments using AI data analysis crafted by human creative minds, ensuring relevance and emotional resonance.
- Designing marketing campaigns that leverage AI for tasks like audience targeting and personalized engagement while humans guide the overall strategy, ensuring ethical considerations and brand alignment.
- Making data-driven marketing decisions informed by AI insights but ultimately filtered through human judgment and understanding of the customer landscape.

The Synergy between Humans and AI

The synergy between humans and AI holds immense potential for creating customer-centric, impactful campaigns in pharma marketing. Here's how they can collaborate effectively:

Human Strengths

- **Creativity and Storytelling:** Humans excel at creating compelling narratives that resonate emotionally with audiences. AI can analyze data and suggest target segments, but human empathy and insight translate data points into relatable stories that connect with customers.
- **Strategic Direction and Oversight:** Humans possess the strategic vision and ethical sensibilities to define campaign goals, align them with brand values, and ensure messaging remains compliant and responsible. AI can provide invaluable data-driven insights, but ultimately, humans guide the campaign's ethical compass.

- **Understanding Nuance and Content:** Humans are adept at interpreting emotional cues, anticipating unspoken needs, and navigating the complexities of human behavior. AI can track broad trends and patterns, but humans decipher the subtle nuances that make campaigns resonate with specific audiences.

AI Strengths

- **Data Analysis and Insights:** AI algorithms can process vast amounts of data far faster than humans, identifying hidden patterns, customer segments, and predictive trends. This provides invaluable insights for tailoring campaigns and targeting the right audiences.
- **Personalization and Optimization:** AI can personalize campaign elements like content, timing, and delivery channels based on individual customer data. This ensures highly relevant messaging and maximizes campaign effectiveness.
- **Automation and Efficiency:** AI can automate routine tasks like data analysis, reporting, and ad placement, freeing up human time and resources for higher-level strategic thinking and creative endeavors.

Creating Synergy

- **Collaborative Brainstorming:** Combine AI-generated data insights with human brainstorming sessions to spark creative ideas for campaign themes, content, and storytelling approaches.
- **Data-Driven Storytelling:** Use AI data to inform the factual foundation of your narratives, but let human creativity weave it into stories that resonate emotionally with customers.
- **Human-in-the-Loop Optimization:** Use AI tools for A/B testing and campaign optimization, but consider human judgment and ethical considerations in making final decisions.

- **Transparent Collaboration:** Clearly define roles and responsibilities for both humans and AI within the campaign. This fosters trust and ensures optimal utilization of each party's strengths.

Examples of Customer-Centric Compositions

- Interactive video campaign based on AI-identified patient trends, featuring real patient testimonials and human-crafted storytelling to drive empathy and understanding.
- Personalized email content with treatment adherence tips generated by AI algorithms based on individual patient data but reviewed and nuanced by human healthcare professionals.
- Targeted social media ad campaign utilizing AI data to identify specific audience segments but employing human copywriters to craft emotionally evocative messaging that resonates with each segment.

By leveraging the unique strengths of both humans and AI, pharma marketing campaigns can achieve a powerful synergy, leading to more customer-centric, impactful, and successful campaigns. Remember, it's not about replacing humans with AI but harnessing their combined strengths to create something remarkable.

Creating an Interactive Video Campaign

Here's an example of an interactive video campaign that combines AI and human expertise to drive empathy and understanding:

Campaign Title: A Day in the Life of Clara

Target Audience: Healthcare Professionals (HCPs) specializing in chronic pain management

Concept:

- The video follows Clara, a young woman with chronic pain, through her daily routine.

- AI analysis of patient data (survey responses, medical records) identifies common challenges and emotional experiences shared by individuals with chronic pain.
- These insights inform the storyline, ensuring it authentically reflects the daily realities of living with chronic pain.
- However, experienced human storytellers craft and voice the narrative, injecting empathy, humor, and vulnerability into Clara's experience.

Interactive Elements:

- **Choice Points:** At key moments in the video, viewers (HCPs) can choose how Clara responds to a situation, offering a personalized experience and fostering engagement.
- **Emotion Tracker:** An overlay on the screen shows Clara's changing emotional state (frustration, fatigue, hope) throughout the video based on their chosen actions.
- **Pop-up-Facts:** Clicking on specific objects or actions triggers pop-up windows with relevant medical information related to chronic pain management.
- **Reflection Questions:** After watching the video, viewers are prompted with questions to reflect on Clara's experiences and consider their interactions with patients with chronic pain.

Impact:

- By experiencing Clara's story firsthand, HCPs gain a deeper understanding of the emotional and practical challenges faced by patients with chronic pain.
- The interactive elements promote active engagement and reflection, solidifying learning and encouraging empathy towards patients.
- The data gathered from viewer choices and reflections can be used further to refine future initiatives and personalized patient care strategies.

Human-AI Synergy

- **AI:** Identifies key patient trends and provides data-driven insights to inform the storyline's authenticity.
- **Humans:** Craft a compelling narrative, inject emotion and nuance, and ensure ethical storytelling to prevent AI-generated coldness.

This is just an example, and the possibilities are endless. You can adapt to different diseases, patient personas, and storytelling formats. The key is to leverage AI's analytical power alongside human creativity and empathy to create truly impactful experiences that drive understanding and change.

This should inspire you to develop innovative ways to utilize AI and human collaboration in pharma marketing.

Creating a Personalized Email Campaign

Here's an example of a personalized email campaign featuring treatment adherence tips, co-designed by an AI algorithm and human healthcare professionals.

Campaign Title: **"Stay on Track: Personalized Tips for (Your Medication Name) Success"**

Target Audience: Patients currently taking (Your Medication Name) for (Disease Name)

Content Creation:

- **AI Algorithm:** Analyzes patient data, including medication refill history, appointment attendance, and clinical markers.
  - Identifies challenges and potential reasons for non-adherence based on previously successful adherence interventions and common pitfalls.
  - Generates personalized tips and reminders tailored to each patient's needs.

- **Human Healthcare Professionals:**
  - Review and refine the AI-generated tips, ensuring medical accuracy, ethical messaging, and appropriate language for the target audience.
  - Inject empathy and understanding into the tone and messaging.
  - Add human-created content like success stories or inspirational quotes for patient encouragement.

Email Content:

- **Personalized Subject Line:** "Sarah, don't forget your next (Your Medication Name) dose."
- **Opening:** Greeting the patient by name and acknowledge their medication and disease
- **AI-Generated Tips:** Based on individual data, the email might suggest:

  Setting convenient reminders on their phone/smartwatch.

  Linking medication intake to daily routines.

  Packing medication for travel or work.

  Addressing side effects through lifestyle changes or additional medication.
- **Human-Reviewed Content:** Doctors offer encouraging words, share a relatable anecdote, or provide links to educational resources.
- **Closing:** A friendly reminder to contact their healthcare team if they need support or have questions.

Benefits:

- **Increased Adherence:** Personalized tips address specific patient needs, leading to improved adherence and potentially better treatment outcomes.

- **Enhanced Patient Engagement:** Receiving personalized messaging fosters a sense of care and connection with the healthcare team.
- **Scalability and Efficiency:** AI handles data analysis and personalized content generation, allowing HCPs to focus on higher-level interventions and patient interaction.

Human+AI Synergy:

- **AI:** Analyzes individual data, identifies specific challenges, and generates targeted tips.
- **Humans:** Ensure medical accuracy and ethical messaging, inject empathy, and add human-curated elements for patient connection.

This is just a basic example, and the content can be further customized based on the specific disease, medication, and patient segment. The key is to find the right balance between AI's data-driven insights and human expertise to create truly personalized and impactful communication that improves patient well-being.

1. **Example of Sample Email to a Patient with Type 2 Diabetes:**

   Subject: Let's Conquer Your Metformin Misadventures! (No bloating required!)

   Hi, (Patient's Name),

   Managing type 2 diabetes can sometimes feel like a superhero quest, and it's okay if there are days when your trusty sidekick—Metformin—gets left behind in the Fortress of Forgetfulness.

   - We've all been there, battling bloating, gas, and maybe the occasional "Oops, did I take that already?" Moment.

   But let's face it: Metformin is your secret weapon in this fight. It helps keep your blood sugar in check, and that's a major victory for your health.

   So, how do we ensure those little blue pills become your reliable allies instead of temporary hostages?

Here are some battle tactics to help you conquer your Metformin misadventures:

- **Team up with Technology:** Set reminders on your phone, pair your pillbox with an app, or even invest in a fancy "smart cap" that tells you if you missed a dose. Teach your friend in this fight.
- **Befriend Routine:** Take your Metformin at the same time every day, like when you brush your teeth or make your morning coffee. Routine is the kryptonite to forgetfulness!
- **Embrace the Snack Attack:** Feeling bloated or gassy after taking your Metformin? Try splitting your dose into smaller ones spread throughout the day. Sometimes, a little snack attack can be the solution!
- **Rally Your Support System:** Talk to your doctor or pharmacist about managing side effects. And let your family or friends know about your goals— accountability is a powerful weapon!
- **Celebrate the Wins:** Every dose you take is a victory! Track your progress with a fun chart or reward yourself for consistent Metformin-ing.

Remember, you're not alone in this quest. Millions of people with type 2 diabetes face similar challenges every day. But with a little planning, support, and even some laughter at the occasional gas monster, you can make Metformin your best friend in the fight for healthier blood sugar. Let's keep those little blue superheroes doing their magic!

If you have any questions or need extra help taming your Metformin mishaps, don't hesitate to contact your doctor or pharmacist. They're your super team allies!

Onward to victory,

The (Your Clinic/Brand Name) Team

P.S. Check out our blog for fun tips and tricks for managing type 2 diabetes!

This email aims to be motivational and action-oriented, combining a lighthearted tone with practical advice. Remember to personalize it further by referencing your specific clinic/brand name and including links to your blog or other resources.

2. **Example of Sample Email to an HCP:**

   Here is a sample email from an email campaign reiterating Metformin's (an oral diabetic medication) importance and prominent place in diabetes management. This is necessary as many later drugs to treat diabetes have eroded Metformin's market share.

   Subject: Rethinking Metformin: A Powerful Ally in the Type 2 Diabetes Toolbox

   Dear (HCP Name),

   In the ever-evolving landscape of type 2 diabetes management, the merits of Metformin sometimes get overshadowed by newer medication options. However, it's important to revisit this established agent and recognize its enduring value, especially in light of recent research and clinical experience. Metformin boasts a unique combination of benefits:

   Proven Efficacy: Its effectiveness in controlling glucose and reducing HbA1c is well-documented. For a good reason, it remains a cornerstone of treatment.

   Favorable Tolerability Profile: Contrary to common perception, research suggests Metformin's side effects, particularly bloating and gastrointestinal issues, are often transient and can be mediated with proper dosing and patient education. Compared to newer medications, overall discontinuation rates due to side effects are lower with Metformin.

   Cost-Effectiveness: Metformin significantly reduces the financial burden on patients and the healthcare system as a generic medication, making it an accessible and responsible choice.

   Predictable Glucose Control: Metformin works with the body's natural mechanisms, leading to steady and predictable reductions in blood sugar levels. This minimizes the risk of hypoglycemia, a major concern for many patients.

Recent Studies Further Showcase Metformin's potential:

- **The New England Journal of Medicine study** demonstrated similar cardiovascular benefits with Metformin compared to newer DPP-4 inhibitors, highlighting its role in comprehensive diabetes management.
- **Research on Long-Term Safety and Side Effects** indicates that with proper patient selection and management, Metformin can be tolerated by most patients, often exceeding initial concerns.

Therefore, I encourage you to:

- **Reassess Metformin as a First-Line or Early-Line Option** for appropriate patients, especially those cost-conscious, concerned about side effects, or seeking predictable glucose control.
- **Utilize Patient Education and Tailored Dosing Strategies** to optimize tolerability and maximize adherence.
- **Consider Metformin's Holistic Benefits** beyond HbA1c reduction, including its potential cardiovascular and metabolic advantages.

Metformin remains a powerful tool in our armamentarium against type 2 diabetes. By acknowledging its strengths and addressing common misconceptions, we can ensure more patients reap the benefits of this safe, effective, and accessible medication.

Please don't hesitate to reach out if you have questions or require additional resources on Metformin.

Sincerely,

(Your Name/Affiliation)

For Non-Prescribing HCPs

You May Consider the Following for HCPs Who are Not Prescribing Metformin:

While prescribing medication falls outside your immediate scope, please consider advocating for Metformin's value in patient interactions and discussions with colleagues. Understanding its benefits can further promote informed discussions and ensure wider utilization of this valuable therapeutic option.

Remember, every voice advocating for evidence-based, accessible management of type 2 diabetes makes a difference.

This email aims to inform, reassure, and encourage HCPs to consider Metformin more readily. You can personalize it by adding specific clinical scenarios or local data relevant to your practice or region. Adjust the content and tone to suit your audience and professional goals.

CHAPTER

11

Regulation as Rhythm in Human+AI Collaboration

The phrase "Regulation as Rhythm in Human+AI collaboration in Pharma Marketing" is an interesting metaphor, and its interpretation can vary depending on your perspective. Here are some ways to understand it:

1. **Regulations as the Metronome:**
   - Regulations (FDA, EMA, etc.) are the steady beat in the orchestra of Human+AI collaboration, ensuring both parties play their roles in compliance and ethical marketing practices.
   - Like a metronome keeps the tempo, regulations provide a framework for responsible data use, accurate information, and patient safety.
   - AI and humans must adapt to the rhythm of regulations, constantly adjusting their strategies and approaches to adhere to established guidelines.
2. **Regulations as a Balancing Act:**
   - Integrating AI and humans in pharma marketing requires a delicate balance between innovation and compliance.
   - Regulations guide this balance, ensuring AI advancements don't overstep ethical boundaries while encouraging creativity and effective marketing strategies.

- AI and humans must be mindful of the regulatory constraints, utilizing their strengths within the permitted space to achieve optimal results.

3. **Regulations as a Dance of Dialogue**
   - The interpretation and application of regulations are often open to discussion and adaptation. This opens up avenues for continuous dialogue between AI and humans.
   - AI can analyze data and identify potential regulatory inconsistencies or areas for improvement, prompting collaborative discussions with humans to refine marketing strategies within the regulations' spirit.
   - This ongoing dialogue ensures regulations remain relevant and adaptable, fostering a harmonious partnership between technology and human experience.
4. **Regulations as a Symphony of Trust**
   - Ultimately, effective Pharma marketing relies on building trust with healthcare professionals and patients.
   - Adherence to regulations plays a crucial role in establishing this trust, demonstrating a commitment to ethical practices, transparency, and patient safety.
   - AI and humans must conduct themselves within the regulatory rhythm, contributing to a harmonious symphony of trust that strengthens the pharma marketing landscape.

Remember, the meaning of "Regulation as Rhythm" is open to interpretation, and these are just possible perspectives. Regardless of how you understand it, the essence lies in recognizing the critical role of regulations in shaping and guiding the AI+human collaboration in pharma marketing while creating a responsible and trustworthy landscape for healthcare communication.

Harmonious Convergence

Achieving harmonious convergence between AI and humans in pharma marketing requires a nuanced approach that leverages the strengths while bridging the potential gaps. Here are some key strategies to consider:

1. **Define Roles and Responsibilities:**
   - **Humans:** Strategic direction, ethical oversight, creative storytelling, emotional intelligence, and stakeholder relationship-building.
   - **AI**: Data analysis, insights generation, campaign optimization, personalization, and automation of routine tasks.

   Clearly defining roles ensures synergy and avoids overlap or underutilization of resources.

2. **Foster Collaboration and Communication**
   - Establish open communication channels to regularly exchange ideas, concerns, and feedback between AI specialists and marketing teams.
   - Encourage joint brainstorming sessions and workshops to leverage human creativity and AI's data-driven strengths.

   Collaboration fosters trust and understanding, creating a unified team working towards shared goals.

3. **Prioritize Transparency and Explainability**
   - Use human expertise to interpret and explain AI-generated insights, ensuring transparency and building trust with healthcare professionals and patients.
   - Avoid "black box" algorithms and encourage explainable AI models that provide the rationale behind results.

   Transparency ensures the ethical application of AI and enhances stakeholder confidence.

4. **Invest in Training and Education**
   - Train marketing teams on AI capabilities and limitations, enabling them to guide and utilize AI tools effectively.
   - Educate AI specialists on healthcare regulations, ethical considerations, and the nuances of pharma marketing.

Shared knowledge creates a common ground for collaboration and mutual respect.

5. Focus on Ongoing Improvement

- Track and measure the impact of AI+human collaboration in pharma marketing campaigns, continually learning and refining approaches.
- Encourage experimentation and iterative development, adapting strategies based on real-world results and feedback.

Continuous improvement ensures that collaboration evolves and remains relevant in a dynamic environment.

Additional Tips

- Emphasize human oversight and control over AI decision-making, especially in sensitive areas like targeting and messaging.
- Prioritize data privacy and security, ensuring patient information is handled ethically and responsibly.
- Advocate for responsible AI development and adoption within pharma marketing.

Remember, harmonious convergence is not a one-time achievement but an ongoing process. By continuously fostering collaboration, communication, and ethical practices, humans and AI can create a powerful synergy that revolutionizes pharma marketing while upholding patient safety and trust.

PART IV

Five AI Superpowers Reshaping Pharma Marketing

Chapter 12. Personalization at Scale: AI's Magic Touch in Pharma Marketing

Chapter 13. AI Empowering Healthcare Professionals

Chapter 14. AI Empowering Patients

Chapter 15. The Clinical Trial Revolution: How AI Supercharges Pharma R&D

Chapter 16. How AI Helps Navigate Ethical Landscape in Pharma Marketing

The pharmaceutical landscape is undergoing a metamorphosis fueled by a potent elixir: artificial intelligence. No longer relegated to science fiction, AI has become a powerful tool, ready to unlock five fundamental pharmaceutical superpowers: personalization at scale, the clinical trial revolution, empowering HCPs and patients, and navigation of the ethical pharma marketing landscape.

Imagine crafting bespoke campaigns that resonate with individual healthcare professionals and patients— not through guesswork but through laser-sharp targeting of AI. Envision streamlining clinical trials, optimizing patient selection, and predicting outcomes with a once unthinkable precision. Picture a future where AI empowers HCPs, freeing them from administrative burdens and equipping them with insights to deliver personalized care. Visualize empowered patients playing a more active role in their healthcare journeys like never before. However, this transformative journey demands a compass— a clear understanding of the ethical considerations that guide the responsible application of AI in healthcare.

This Section delves into these five AI superpowers, demystifying their potential and illuminating their path to navigate their ethical complexity. We'll explore how AI, wielded with purpose and responsibility, can transform pharma marketing from a broad brush to a pointillist masterpiece, where every touchpoint is meticulously tailored to individual needs and aspirations. Prepare to embark on a pharma marketing journey powered by five superpowers of AI— a journey that promises to redefine the future of healthcare engagement.

So, fasten your seatbelts, fellow pioneers. We're about to witness the rise of AI superpowers, ready to propel pharma marketing into a new era of personalized, efficient, and ultimately more human healthcare.

CHAPTER 12

Personalization at Scale

AI's Magic Touch in Pharma Marketing

Imagine a world where medicine isn't a one-size-fits-all proposition, where treatment plans dance to the rhythm of individual needs, and patients receive precisely the information and support they crave, not a generic broadcast lost in the static mass communication. This dear reader, is the exquisite symphony of personalization at scale orchestrated by the virtuosic power of AI pharma marketing.

Beyond Targeting, Beyond Segmentation

For decades, the marketing playbook relied on broad demographics and psychographics, casting a wide net to capture fragmented audiences. Personalization at scale shatters this outdated model. It delves into the depths of individual data, understanding a patient's unique medical history, lifestyle, and preferences. It's about crafting bespoke melodies rather than playing the same predictable tune for everyone.

The AI Maestro Conducts the Data Orchestra

AI is the maestro in this personalized symphony, wielding powerful algorithms to analyze vast data. Here is how it plays out:

- **Understanding the Individual Score**: AI analyzes medical records, social media transactions, and online behavior to create detailed patient profiles. Imagine understanding a patient's struggles with a chronic condition, their preferred communication style, and even their fear of needles before administering an injection.

- **Composing Customized Messages**: With these insights, AI tailors content and messaging to resonate with each individual. From targeted ad campaigns featuring relatable testimonials to personalized educational materials addressing specific concerns, every note rings true in the patient's unique story.
- **Optimizing the Patient Journey**: AI goes beyond static content. It dynamically adjusts the patient journey based on real-time interactions. Imagine adjusting the frequency of reminders for medication adherence based on a patient's forgetfulness or recommending alternative treatment options based on their genetic makeup.

The Harmony Emerges, Personalized Symphonies of Care

This personalized approach unlocks a multitude of benefits:

- **Enhanced Patient Engagement**: When patients feel truly understood and supported, they become more proactive participants in their healthcare journey. Engagement increases, leading to better adherence to treatment plans and improved health outcomes.
- **Increased Marketing ROI**: Targeted messaging resonates more effectively, leading to higher conversion rates and a better return on investment for marketing campaigns.
- **Building Trust and Brand Loyalty**: Personalization fosters a sense of connection and care, building trust between patients and pharma companies. This translates into long-term brand loyalty and a positive reputation.

The Counterpoint: Challenges in the Composition

However, this personalized symphony isn't without its discordant notes:

- **Data Privacy Concerns:** Collecting and analyzing patient data necessitates robust security measures and transparent data practices. Addressing privacy concerns and building trust are crucial for ethical implementation.
- **Algorithmic Bias:** AI algorithms are only as good as the data they're trained on. Mitigating bias and ensuring fair representation in patient profiles is essential to avoid discrimination and provide equitable access to personalized healthcare.
- **Technology and Human Harmony:** While AI excels at data analysis and personalization, the human touch remains irreplaceable. Ensuring healthcare professionals guide AI development and use, emphasizing empathy and critical thinking, is key to maintaining a patient-centric focus.

Composing the Future of Personalized Healthcare

To navigate these challenges and unlock the full potential of personalized care, we must:

- **Prioritize Ethical Development**: Implement robust data governance, mitigate bias, and ensure transparency throughout the AI lifecycle.
- **Invest in Data Security**: Employ state-of-the-art cybersecurity measures and empower patients with control over their data.
- **Foster Collaboration**: Bridge the gap between AI developers and healthcare professionals, fostering joint initiatives and promoting ongoing learning and knowledge sharing.
- **Humanize the Technology**: Personalization is not about automation but understanding and responding to the human experience.

Beyond Algorithms, Beyond Data

By acknowledging the challenges, prioritizing ethics, and fostering collaboration, we can ensure that personalization at scale doesn't become a cold symphony of algorithms but a warm and empathetic chorus of care. Imagine:

- Patients receive timely reminders and encouragement tailored to their needs, boosting medication adherence and improving health outcomes.
- Clinicians empowered with AI-driven insights to personalize treatment plans and predict potential complications, ensuring proactive and effective care.
- Pharma companies craft marketing campaigns that resonate deeply with individual patients, forging trust and building long-lasting relationships.

This is not a dystopian future of robotic healthcare; it's a hopeful vision where technology augments human capabilities, amplifying compassion and understanding to personalize the patient journey. It's a symphony where data dances with empathy, algorithms harmonize with intuition, and human-centered care takes center stage.

Delving Deeper into the Score

This chapter offers a glimpse into the world of personalization at scale. To explore this intricate melody further, we can explore case studies.

Case Studies: Personalization at Scale in Action

To truly appreciate the transformative power of personalization at scale, let's dive into the captivating melodies of real-world case studies, showcasing how AI is changing the game in pharma marketing:

1. **Tailoring Treatment Support for Diabetes Patients**

   Imagine a world where patients with diabetes receive daily personalized messages of encouragement, tailored reminders for medication adherence, and even grocery recommendations based on their dietary needs. Thanks to a pharmaceutical company's AI-powered platform, this is the reality for hundreds of people with diabetes. Leveraging patient data from connected devices and medical records, the platform creates detailed profiles, predicting individual challenges and proactively offering personalized support. The result? A significant increase in medication adherence, improved blood sugar control, and a positive shift in patient morale.

2. **Building Trust and Engagement with HIV Patients**

   In another powerful case study, a pharmaceutical company tackled the challenge of reaching and engaging HIV patients who often face stigma and social isolation. Their AI solution analyzed social media platforms to identify online communities frequented by HIV patients. Leveraging natural language processing, the AI developed culturally relevant and empathetic posts, offering educational resources, connecting patients with support groups, and addressing their specific concerns. This personalized approach dramatically increased online engagement, a strengthened sense of community, and a greater willingness to engage with healthcare professionals.

3. **Optimizing Clinical Trial Recruitment**

   Traditional methods of recruiting participants for clinical trials often need to be faster and more efficient. AI, however, is changing the game. In a recent clinical trial for a novel cancer treatment, researchers employed AI to analyze patient data from electronic health records across numerous hospitals. The AI identified potential participants who closely matched the trial criteria, significantly reducing the recruitment time and increasing the diversity of participating patients. This accelerated the research process and ensured the trial results were more representative of the broader population.

4. **Empowering Pharmacists with Personalized Medication Alerts**

   Pharmacists play a crucial role in patient care but often lack real-time data about patient's medications and potential interactions. A leading pharmacy chain implemented an AI system that analyzes individual patient medication profiles, identifying potential drug interactions and notifying pharmacists before dispensing medications. This proactive approach has prevented countless medication errors, improving patient safety and fostering trust between pharmacists and patients.

5. **Crafting Compelling and Relevant Ad Experiences**

   Traditional pharmaceutical advertising often bombards patients with generic messages that fail to resonate. A biotech company, however, took a different approach. Utilizing AI-powered audience segmentation and dynamic content creation, they crafted personalized ad experiences tailored to individual patients' medical conditions, interests, and online behavior. The result? A drastic increase in ad click-through rates, higher engagement with educational content, and a shift in patient's perception of the biotech company, recognizing them as a provider of relevant and valuable information.

The Chorus Concludes

These case studies demonstrate the extraordinary potential of personalization at scale in pharma marketing. From revolutionizing patient support to optimizing clinical trials and empowering healthcare professionals, AI is composing a beautiful symphony of patient-centric care. As we embrace ethical development, foster collaboration, and prioritize human insight, this symphony will continue to grow, its harmonious melodies reaching every corner of the healthcare landscape.

Beyond the Case Studies

This chapter scratches the surface of personalization at scale's capabilities. To further explore this dynamic realm, consider:

- **Investigating Emerging Technologies**: Learn about advancements in natural language processing, computer vision, and other AI techniques that are pushing the boundaries of personalization.
- **Focusing on Specific Therapeutic Areas**: Learn how personalization impacts specific illnesses or disease states, understanding each domain's unique challenges and opportunities.
- **Exploring Future Horizons**: Imagine the possibilities of AI-powered personalized medicine, where treatment plans are customized to individual genetic profiles and real-time health data.

By continuously learning and adapting, we can ensure that personalization at scale remains a symphony of ethical innovation, human-centered care, and improved health outcomes for all. So, dear reader, raise your baton, embrace the intricate personalization score, and join the orchestra. Together, we can compose a future where technology amplifies empathy, data enriches understanding, and patients receive the unique melody of care they deserve.

CHAPTER
13

AI Empowering Healthcare Professionals

AI as a Symphony of Support, Not Replacement

Imagine a world where repetitive tasks don't burden doctors, nurses have readily available insights to personalize care, and healthcare professionals thrive with AI as their capable teammate, not a looming replacement. This is the symphony of empowered healthcare professionals orchestrated by the transformative power of Artificial Intelligence (AI).

Beyond Administrative Hurdles, Beyond Information Overload

Healthcare professionals battle administrative burdens, mountains of paperwork, and a constant influx of medical information daily. AI steps in as a tireless assistant, automating mundane tasks, extracting meaningful insights from data, and empowering professionals to focus on what truly matters: patient care.

The AI Maestro Conducts the Data Orchestra

In this empowering symphony, AI plays the role of a brilliant maestro, wielding diverse instruments to support healthcare professionals:

- **Clinical Decision Support**: AI analyzes patient data, medical literature, and real-time vitals to provide evidence-based recommendations for diagnosis, treatment planning, and medication selection. Imagine doctors having instant access to the latest research and personalized insights, leading to more informed and effective decisions.

- **Streamlined Administration Tasks**: AI automates time-consuming tasks like appointment scheduling, insurance claim processing, and medical record transcription. Freed from these burdens, nurses can dedicate more time to patient interaction, education, and emotional support.
- **Personalized Patient Care**: AI analyzes patient data and preferences to tailor care plans, predict potential complications, and proactively address individual needs. Imagine nurses receiving early alerts about a patient's risk of falls or a doctor customizing a treatment plan based on a patient's genetic makeup.

The Harmony Emerges: Enhanced Efficiency, Improved Outcomes

This AI-powered support leads to a multitude of benefits:

- **Improved Clinical Decision-Making**: Evidence-based insights and real-time data analysis lead to more accurate diagnoses, effective treatment plans, and reduced medical errors.
- **Enhanced Patient Care and Experience**: Healthcare professionals have more time for patient interaction, personalized care, and emotional support, which increases patient satisfaction and improves health outcomes.
- **Increased Efficiency and Productivity**: Automating administrative tasks frees up valuable time for healthcare professionals to focus on patient care, streamline workflows, maximizing resource utilization.

The Counterpoint: Challenges in Composition

However, this harmonious symphony isn't without its discordant notes:

- **Job Displacement Concerns**: Automation through AI raises concerns about job losses in healthcare. Addressing these concerns through reskilling initiatives and ensuring human oversight remains crucial.
- **Algorithmic Bias**: AI algorithms are only as good as the data they are trained on. Mitigating bias and ensuring fair representation in healthcare data is essential to avoid discrimination and provide equitable access to AI-powered tools.
- **Human Expertise Remains Irreplaceable**: AI excels at data analysis and automation, but human intuition, critical thinking, and empathy are irreplaceable in healthcare. Ensuring AI complements, not replaces, human decision-making is paramount.

Composing the Future of Empowered Professionals

To navigate these challenges and unlock the full potential of AI in empowering healthcare professionals, we must:

- **Prioritize Ethical Development**: Implement robust data governance, mitigate bias, and ensure transparency throughout the AI lifecycle.
- **Invest in Reskilling and Training**: Equip healthcare professionals with the skills and knowledge needed to work effectively with AI and adapt to changing workflows.
- **Foster Collaboration**: Bridge the gap between AI developers and healthcare professionals, promoting joint initiatives, ongoing learning, and knowledge sharing.

- **Humanize the Technology**: Remember that AI is a tool to enhance, not replace, human capabilities. Ensure a human-centered approach to AI implementation, prioritizing patient care and professional well-being.

Beyond Algorithms, Beyond Data

By acknowledging the challenges, prioritizing ethics, and fostering collaboration, we can ensure that empowering healthcare professionals with AI isn't just about efficiency and data; it's about human-centered care and improved patient outcomes. Imagine:

- Doctors use AI-powered tools to diagnose rare diseases with newfound accuracy, giving hope to patients who previously went undiagnosed.
- Nurses receive real-time alerts about a patient's deteriorating condition, allowing for swift intervention and preventing complications.
- Healthcare professionals have more time for meaningful conversations with patients, building trust, and providing emotional support.

This is not a dystopian future where robots replace doctors; it's a hopeful vision where technology augments human expertise, amplifies care, and empowers healthcare professionals to be the heroes they truly are. It's a symphony where data dances with empathy, algorithms amplify human intuition, and patient-centered care takes center stage.

Delving Deeper into the Score

This chapter offers a glimpse into the world of empowered healthcare professionals. To further explore this intricate melody, we can delve deeper into case studies to analyze real-world examples of how AI empowers professionals in specific areas.

Case Studies: AI Empowering Healthcare Professionals in Action

1. **Diagnosing Rare Diseases with Accuracy**: Dr. Tracy Garcia, a rural physician, often faced the frustration of undiagnosed patients exhibiting unusual symptoms. She analyzed their genetic data and medical history using an AI-powered diagnostic tool. Within minutes, the AI identified a rare metabolic disorder, prompting Dr. Garcia to refer the patient to a specialist for confirmatory tests and treatment. This timely diagnosis saved the patient from potentially life-threatening complications and empowered Dr. Garcia to tackle future cases more confidently.
2. **Predicting and Preventing Hospital Readmissions**: Nurse manager Emily Jones grappled with the challenge of readmissions among cardiac patients. Utilizing an AI-driven prediction model, she identified patients at high risk of readmission based on their medical history and social determinants of health. Proactive interventions, including home visits, medication reminders, and dietary counseling, significantly reduced readmission rates, freeing up hospital beds and improving patient outcomes.
3. **Enhancing Surgical Precision and Efficiency**: Dr. David Chen, a surgeon specializing in complex procedures, embraced AI-powered surgical robots. The robot, guided by Dr. Chen's expertise, assisted in delicate maneuvers, minimizing tremors and ensuring greater precision. This collaboration shortened surgery times, reduced complications, and improved patient recovery.
4. **Personalized Care Plans for Cancer Patients**: Oncology nurse practitioner Alice Kim found conventional treatment plans for cancer patients often lacked individualization. Implementing an AI-powered tool, she analyzed each patient's tumor genomic profile and treatment response data. This enabled her to recommend personalized treatment regimens, leading to improved remission rates and reduced side effects.

5. **Mental Health Support Through AI-Powered Chatbots**: Dr. Maria Lopez, a psychiatrist, recognized the limitations of in-person consultations in addressing mental health needs. Integrating an AI-powered chatbot into her practice, she provided patients with 24/7 access to emotional support, self-management tools, and crisis intervention resources. This readily available support system empowered patients to manage their mental health and improved their overall well-being.

The Chorus Concludes

These case studies demonstrate the diverse applications of AI in empowering healthcare professionals across various domains. From enhancing diagnostic accuracy to personalizing care plans and providing accessible mental health support, AI is composing a symphony of improved healthcare outcomes and strengthened patient-professional relationships.

As we embrace ethical development, foster collaboration, and prioritize human oversight, this symphony will continue to evolve, its powerful melodies reaching every corner of the healthcare landscape.

Beyond the Case Studies

This chapter scratches the surface of AI's potential in empowering healthcare professionals. To further explore this dynamic realm, consider:

- **Investigating Emerging AI Technologies**: Dive into advancements in natural language processing, computer vision, and other AI techniques that are pushing the boundaries of professional support and patient engagement.
- **Focusing on Specific Healthcare Specialties**: Learn how AI impacts specific areas like mental health, surgery, or chronic disease management, understanding the unique challenges and opportunities in each domain.

- **Exploring Ethical Considerations**: Discuss the impact of AI on healthcare workforce dynamics, data privacy, and potential biases, ensuring ethical implementation and addressing professional concerns.

By continuously learning and adapting, we can ensure that AI-empowered healthcare professionals remain in a symphony of innovation, ethical practice, and improved patient care for all. So, dear reader, raise your baton, embrace the intricate score of empowered professionals, and join the orchestra. Together, we can compose a future where technology strengthens the human touch, amplifies expertise, and empowers healthcare professionals to be the heroes they truly are.

CHAPTER

14

AI Empowering Patients

AI as the Conductor of Patient Empowerment: A Look at the Power of Technology

Patient empowerment is no longer a utopian dream; it's a real-time symphony orchestrated by the powerful baton of AI. This technology, once confined to science fiction, is now transforming healthcare, giving patients the tools and knowledge to participate actively in their well-being. Let's dive deep into how AI empowers patients, vividly portraying this transformative revolution.

1. **Personalized Healthcare Journeys**: Imagine a future where your treatment plan is as unique as your fingerprint. AI analyzes your medical history, genetic makeup, and lifestyle to craft personalized medication dosages, predict individual responses to therapies, and even tailor preventive measures. This level of precision minimizes side effects, optimizes efficacy, and puts you in the driver's seat of your health journey.

   Example: John, managing a chronic heart condition, utilizes an AI-powered platform that recommends his ideal medication dosage based on his genetic markers and daily routines. This personalization avoids unnecessary side effects and optimizes his treatment, empowering him to live a healthier, more active life.

2. **Knowledge is Power: Demystifying Medical Jargon**: No more drowning in a sea of technical terms! AI is your translator, simplifying complex medical information into understandable language. Accessing reliable disease explanations, treatment options, and research findings becomes a breeze, empowering you to make informed decisions about your care.

   Example: Asha, recently diagnosed with diabetes, uses an AI-powered app that explains her condition clearly, in layperson's terms. It provides personalized insights into managing her diet, medication, and lifestyle, ensuring she understands her diagnosis and actively participates in her treatment plan.

3. **Proactive Monitoring and 24/7 Support**: Gone are the days of waiting for doctor appointments to address health concerns. AI-powered wearables and telehealth platforms continuously monitor your vital signs, medication adherence, and overall health. This constant feedback loop empowers you to proactively manage your health, identify potential issues early, and stay connected with your healthcare team 24/7.

   Example: Maria, recovering from surgery, wears an AI-powered wristband that tracks her pain, sleep patterns, and activity levels. The AI detects a sudden rise in temperature and alerts both Maria and her doctor, enabling prompt intervention and preventing a potential infection.

4. **Shared Decision-Making From Passive Patient to Active Collaborator**: Medical advice no longer comes shrouded in a mystique. AI empowers you with access to data, research, and evidence-based options personalized to your situation. You can participate in shared decision-making with your doctor, feeling confident and informed about your choice.

   Example: Daniel, facing a cancer diagnosis, utilizes an AI-powered platform that compiles relevant research papers, treatment options, and potential side effects based on his specific case. This empowers him to ask informed questions, discuss options with his doctor, and actively participate in decision-making.

5. **Beyond the Pill: Mental Health Support at Your Fingertips**: AI-powered chatbots and virtual assistants become your non-judgmental companions, providing mental health resources, personalized coping mechanisms, and emotional support for anxiety, depression, and other mental health challenges. This readily available, confidential support empowers individuals to manage their mental well-being and seek help when needed.

   Example: Emily, struggling with anxiety, utilizes an AI-powered chatbot that provides mindfulness exercises, breathing techniques, and personalized coping strategies based on her mood and symptoms. This readily available support helps her manage her anxiety, reducing the need for frequent doctor visits and fostering self-reliance.

Remember, AI is a powerful tool, but its effectiveness relies on human expertise and compassion. Patient empowerment thrives in an environment where AI complements, not replaces, human interaction. Building trust, ensuring data privacy, and mitigating algorithmic bias is crucial to creating a symphony of empowered patients where technology harmonizes with humanity.

This is just the beginning of the story. As AI evolves, its potential to improve patients will continue to unfold. Imagine AI-powered virtual coaches guiding patients through personalized exercise routines, AI-driven rehabilitation programs accelerating recovery, and AI-facilitated language translation breaking down communication barriers between patients and healthcare providers. The future of healthcare is a harmonious collaboration between humans and AI, where patients hold the conductor's baton, empowered to compose their health journeys.

These case studies showcase how AI empowers patients. Remember, you can further personalize this narrative by adding real-life case studies, addressing ethical considerations, and exploring emerging AI applications in patient empowerment. By weaving your unique story into this transformative landscape, you can inspire and empower patients to take control of their health and participate actively in their well-being.

Empowered Patients: The Harmony Emerges

In the grand symphony of healthcare, a new melody rises— the empowered patient. Driven by AI-powered tools, information access, and a growing sense of agency, patients are stepping onto the stage, their voices resonating with newfound confidence. This is the essence of "Empowered Patients—The Harmony Emerges," celebrating the transformative potential of patient empowerment and its harmonious convergence with technological advancements. Empowerment, however, is not a solo act. It's a delicate orchestration where challenges and opportunities intertwine, forming the counterpoint to this harmonious movement.

The Counterpoint: Challenges in the Composition of Patient Empowerment

Just as any beautiful melody requires contrast to shine, the path to patient empowerment is fraught with challenges. Here, we delve into the counterpoint of this transformative movement.

- **Digital Divide**: Only some have access to the technology and internet connectivity needed to harness the power of AI-powered healthcare tools. Bridging this digital divide is crucial to ensuring equitable access to empowerment.
- **Information Overload**: The abundance of information online can be overwhelming and confusing for patients, potentially leading to misinterpretations and anxieties. Cultivating digital literacy and providing reliable, curated information sources are essential.
- **Data Privacy Concerns**: Sharing personal health data with digital platforms raises concerns about privacy and security. Building trust through robust data governance and transparency is vital.

- **Algorithmic Bias**: AI algorithms can perpetuate societal inequalities, leading to biased recommendations and unequal access to care. Mitigating bias and ensuring the ethical development of healthcare AI is crucial.
- **Human Connection Gap**: Technology should complement, not replace, human interaction in healthcare. Maintaining the role of empathy, compassion, and human connection while embracing AI is essential.

These challenges are manageable, but they require careful attention and innovative solutions. By addressing them effectively, we can develop a symphony of patient empowerment that resonates with inclusivity, trust, and ethical harmony.

Composing the Future of Empowered Patients

The future of patient empowerment is a breathtaking score waiting to be written. In this section, we explore potential ways to harness the power of technology and human understanding to compose harmonious movement to healthcare.

- **Personalized Healthcare Journeys**: Leveraging AI to tailor treatment plans, medication management, and educational materials to individual needs and preferences.
- **Patient-Centered Research**: Actively involving patients in research design, data collection, and decision-making, ensuring their voices guide the future of healthcare.
- **AI-powered Decision Support**: Providing patients with accessible tools and algorithms to analyze their health data, understand diagnostic results, and make informed choices about their care.
- **Telehealth and Remote Monitoring**: Expanding access to healthcare through virtual consultations, remote monitoring technologies, and AI-powered chatbots to support and guidance.

- **Strengthening Patient-Provider Communication**: Using AI to bridge the communication gap, translate medical jargon, and facilitate informed conversations between patients and healthcare providers.

By embracing these opportunities, we can compose a future where patients are not just passive recipients of care but active participants in their health journeys, harmoniously collaborating with technology and healthcare professionals to achieve optimal well-being.

Beyond Algorithms, Beyond Data

Empowerment transcends algorithms and data. It's about fostering a culture of patient agency, where individuals feel confident in their ability to advocate for their health, ask questions, and make informed decisions. This section explores the human elements that shape a truly empowered patient.

- **Health Literacy**: Educating patients about their health conditions, treatment options, and healthcare systems empowers them to participate actively in their care.
- **Critical Thinking Skills**: Equipping patients with the ability to analyze information, challenge assumptions, and ask probing questions ensures they make informed choices based on evidence and individual needs.
- **Community Support**: Building networks of peer support groups, patient advocates, and community health programs can empower patients by providing resources, sharing experiences, and fostering a sense of belonging.
- **Mental and Emotional Well-being**: Prioritizing mental and emotional well-being alongside physical health is crucial for empowering patients to navigate their healthcare journeys with resilience and confidence.
- **Cultural Sensitivity**: Recognizing and respecting cultural differences in healthcare beliefs and practices ensures inclusive patient empowerment and avoids reinforcing existing disparities.

These human elements form the soul of patient empowerment. By nurturing them alongside technological advancements, we can create a symphony of healthcare where individuals are empowered by data and knowledge, critical thinking, community, and a holistic approach to well-being.

Delving Deeper into the Score: Case Studies of Empowered Patients

To truly understand the impact of patient empowerment, we need to hear the stories of individuals who have transformed their healthcare journeys through agency and knowledge. In this section, we delve into real-life case studies of empowered patients, each playing a unique instrument in the harmony of health:

Case Study 1: The Tech-Savvy Patient: Sarah, diagnosed with diabetes, uses an AI-powered app to track her blood sugar, analyze trends, and adjust her medication and diet based on personalized insights. This proactive approach helps her manage her condition effectively and prevents complications.

Case Study 2: **The Community Advocate**: David, living with a rare chronic illness, joins an online patient forum where he shares his experiences, connects with others facing similar challenges, and actively participates in research studies. This collective empowerment leads to an improved understanding of the condition and advocacy for better treatment options.

Case Study 3: **The Culturally Informed Patient**: Maria, a recent immigrant navigating the healthcare system, utilizes translated patient education materials and culturally sensitive community health programs to understand her diagnosis and make informed decisions about her care. This empowers her to bridge cultural gaps and access appropriate healthcare services.

Case Study 4: The Peer Support Champion: John, overcoming addiction, volunteers as a peer mentor, using his experience and knowledge to empower others on their recovery journeys. This act of shared agency creates a ripple effect of hope and support within the community.

Case Study 5: The Mental Health Advocate: Emily, diagnosed with anxiety and depression, leverages a chatbot app for mindfulness exercises and personalized coping strategies. This readily available support empowers her to manage her mental health and connect with resources outside of traditional therapy sessions.

Like individual notes on a musical score, these case studies form a powerful melody of empowerment. They showcase the diverse ways patients harness technology, knowledge, and community to take control of their health and contribute to a more inclusive healthcare landscape.

Beyond Case Studies: A Continuous Symphony

By studying these empowering narratives, we learn that the potential for patient agency is vast and ever-evolving. Just as a musical composition requires constant practice and revision, the symphony of patient empowerment demands ongoing collaboration and innovation. Here are some areas for future exploration:

- Developing accessible patient-driven research frameworks to ensure diverse voices inform healthcare advancements.
- Integrating AI ethics and data privacy considerations into designing and implementing patient empowerment tools.
- Investing in digital literacy programs to bridge the digital divide and ensure equitable access to empowering technologies.
- Cultivating an environment of patient-centered care where informed consent, shared decision-making, and open communication are the cornerstones of every interaction.
- Recognizing and celebrating the diverse ways patients empower themselves and each other, including traditional knowledge and community support.

Algorithms and data do not solely define the future of patient empowerment; it's an ongoing composition shaped by human experiences, technological advancements, and a shared commitment to creating a healthcare system where every individual can actively participate in their well-being. By listening to the diverse voices within this symphony, we can continue to refine the score, ensuring that the melody of empowerment resonates for all.

CHAPTER

15

The Clinical Trial Revolution

AI Orchestrates A Symphony of Faster, More Efficient Research

Imagine a world where clinical trials, the cornerstone of medical discovery, move with a ballerina's skill rather than a bear's lumbering gait. Groundbreaking cures aren't delayed by years of cumbersome processes but emerge with the grace of a perfectly timed leap. This is a symphony of the clinical trial revolution orchestrated by the virtuosic power of Artificial Intelligence (AI).

Beyond Paperwork, Beyond Delays

For decades, clinical trials have been plagued by inefficiencies. Mountains of paperwork, slow recruitment process, and outdated data analysis methods often resulted in costly delays and missed opportunities. Enter AI, its algorithms armed with the power to streamline workflows, predict outcomes, and unlock the hidden potential of patient data.

The AI Maestro Conducts the Data Orchestra

In this clinical trial revolution, AI plays the role of a brilliant maestro, directing and amplifying the efforts of researchers through various instruments:

- **Patient Identification and Matching**: AI analyzes vast datasets of electronic health records, identifying potential participants who fit the study criteria with uncanny accuracy. Imagine finding the ideal candidate for a rare disease trial in minutes, not months, accelerating recruitment and ensuring diverse and representative patient populations.

- **Predictive Analytics**: AI analyzes historical data from past trials and real-time patient data to predict potential risks and adverse events. This proactive approach allows researchers to adjust protocols, ensuring patient safety and preventing unnecessary trial disruptions.
- **Streamlining Trail Design and Operations**: AI optimizes trial protocols, suggesting effective dosage ranges, optimizing visit schedules, and predicting participant dropouts. Imagine eliminating unnecessary procedures and reducing the overall patient burden, improving trial efficiency and participant retention.

The Harmony Emerges— Faster Cures, Improved Outcomes:

This AI-powered revolution leads to a multitude of benefits:

- **Accelerated Drug Development**: Faster recruitment, optimized protocols, and real-time monitoring lead to shorter trial durations, bringing life-saving medications to patients quicker.
- **Increased Trial Success Rates**: With improved patient matching and predictive analytics, the chances of trial success increase, maximizing investments and bringing more effective treatments to market.
- **Enhanced Patient Safety**: Proactive risk prediction and real-time data monitoring ensure participant safety remains paramount, minimizing potential adverse events and building trust in the research process.

The Counterpoint: Challenges in the Composition

However, this harmonious symphony isn't without its discordant notes:

- **Data Privacy Concerns**: Collecting and analyzing patient data necessitates robust security measures and transparent data practices. Addressing privacy concerns and building trust are crucial for ethical AI implementation in clinical trials.
- **Algorithmic Bias**: AI algorithms are only as good as the data they're trained on. Mitigating bias and ensuring fair representation in patient datasets is essential to avoid discrimination and ensure equitable access to clinical trials.
- **Human Expertise Remains Irreplaceable**: While AI excels at data analysis and automation, human intuition and critical thinking are essential for interpreting results, making ethical decisions, and ensuring patient well-being throughout the trial.

Composing the Future of Clinical Trials

To navigate these challenges and unlock the full potential of AI in clinical trials, we must:

- **Prioritize Ethical Development**: Implement robust data governance, mitigate bias, and ensure transparency throughout the AI lifecycle.
- **Invest in Data Security**: Employ state-of-the-art cybersecurity measures and empower patients with control over their data.
- **Foster Collaboration**: Bridge the gap between AI developers and medical researchers, promoting ongoing learning and knowledge sharing.
- **Balance Automation with Human Oversight**: Remember that AI is a tool, not a replacement. Human expertise remains crucial for ethical decision-making, patient care, and ensuring the research serves the greater good.

Beyond Algorithms, Beyond Data

By acknowledging the challenges, prioritizing ethics, and fostering collaboration, we can ensure that the clinical trial revolution isn't just about faster results, ethical research, and improved patient care. Imagine:

- Thanks to AI-powered patient identification, patients with rare diseases participate in trials tailored to their needs.
- Clinical trials proactively adapt to real-time data insights, minimize risks, and ensure participant safety.
- Thanks to AI-driven efficiency and optimized research processes, new, life-saving medications reach patients years sooner.

This is not a dystopian future of cold, machine-driven research; it's a hopeful vision where technology empowers clinicians, accelerates discovery, and improves patient outcomes. It's a symphony where data dances with empathy, algorithms amplify human expertise, and the pursuit of cures takes center stage.

Delving Deeper into the Score

This chapter offers a glimpse into the world of the clinical trial revolution. To further explore this intricate melody, we can delve deeper into case studies and analyze real-world examples of how AI transforms clinical trials across different therapeutic areas.

Case Studies: AI Orchestrating Faster, More Efficient Clinical Trials

1. **Accelerating Cancer Treatment Research**: In the fight against cancer, time is of the essence. A leading oncology research center employed AI to analyze patient data from across its network of hospitals. The AI identified potential participants for a novel immunotherapy trial with remarkable accuracy, significantly reducing recruitment time and allowing researchers to begin the trial months sooner. This swift action

benefitted the initial participants and paved the way for faster development of this potentially life-saving treatment.

2. **Improving Patient Safety in Cardiovascular Trials**: Cardiovascular trials involve complex protocols and delicate procedures. A pharmaceutical company implemented AI to monitor real-time data from wearable devices worn by participants continuously. The AI identified subtle changes in patient vitals and predicted potential adverse events before they could occur. This proactive approach allowed researchers to intervene early, preventing serious complications and ensuring the safety of every participant.
3. **Democratizing Clinical Trial Access for Rare Diseases**: Patients with rare diseases often face insurmountable hurdles when accessing clinical trials. A non-profit organization partnered with an AI startup to develop a platform that analyzes medical records from across the globe. This platform identified potential participants for rare disease trials with unprecedented accuracy, even in geographically isolated regions. This revolutionized access to research for countless patients who would otherwise have been excluded, offering them a glimmer of hope and accelerating research for these often-overlooked conditions.
4. **Bringing Precision Medicine to Alzheimer's Research**: Alzheimer's disease research has long been plagued by broad patient populations and one-size-fits-all approaches. A research consortium employed AI to analyze genetic and imaging data from thousands of patients. The AI identified distinct patient subgroups with unique disease mechanisms, leading to the development of personalized treatment strategies and more targeted clinical trials. This personalized approach promises to unlock new avenues for Alzheimer's treatment and bring hope to millions of patients and their families.

5. **Enhancing Patient Engagement and Retention**: Clinical trial dropouts can significantly hamper research progress. A pharmaceutical company leveraged AI to develop an interactive mobile app for trial participants. The app provided educational resources, answered real-time questions, and addressed individual concerns. This personalized approach led to a dramatic increase in patient engagement and retention, improving the quality and reliability of the research data.

The Chorus Concludes

These case studies demonstrate AI's diverse applications in transforming clinical trials. From accelerating research to enhancing patient safety and engagement, AI is composing a symphony of scientific advancement and improved healthcare outcomes. As we embrace ethical development, foster collaboration, and prioritize human oversight, this symphony will continue to evolve, its powerful melodies reaching every corner of the medical research landscape.

Beyond the Case Studies

This chapter scratches the surface of AI's potential in clinical trials. To further explore this dynamic realm, consider:

- **Investigating Emerging AI Technologies**: Dive into advancements in machine learning, natural language processing, and other AI techniques pushing the boundaries of clinical trial efficiency and patient safety.
- **Focusing on Specific Therapeutic Areas**: Learn how AI impacts specific disease states or research challenges, understanding each domain's unique opportunities and complexities.
- **Exploring Legal and Regulatory Considerations**: As AI transforms clinical trial research, understanding the evolving legal and regulatory landscape is crucial for ethical and responsible implementation.

By continuously learning and adapting, we can ensure that AI-powered clinical trials remain a symphony of scientific progress, ethical practice, and improved patient care for all. So, dear reader, raise your baton, embrace the intricate score of the clinical trial revolution, and join the orchestra. Together, we can compose a future where technology accelerates discovery, strengthens safety nets, and brings hope to patients waiting for breakthroughs.

CHAPTER

16

How AI Helps Navigate the Ethical Landscape

Charting A Moral Course in the AI-Powered Pharma Seas

Imagine a boundless ocean of data churned by the powerful currents of Artificial Intelligence (AI). Aboard this vessel, the pharma industry charts its course towards innovative breakthroughs, promising life-saving medicines and better health outcomes. Yet, beneath the glistening surface lurk hidden reefs of ethical dilemmas, threatening to shipwreck progress and erode public trust. This, dear reader, is the treacherous yet exhilarating journey of navigating the ethical landscape in Pharma's AI waters.

Beyond Algorithms, Beyond Profits

Traditional approaches in pharma often prioritized scientific advancements and financial returns, sometimes overlooking the ethical implications of data collection, algorithm bias, and potential discrimination. AI amplifies these concerns with its powerful capabilities, demanding a new and robust ethical compass to guide the industry's voyage.

The Ethical Currents: Charting the Course

To sail these uncharted waters safely, we must be navigating by the guiding principles:

- **Transparency and Explainability**: Algorithms must be demystified, often cloaked in mathematical obscurity. Pharma companies must explain how AI tools work, how decisions are made, and how data is used, fostering trust and accountability.

- **Data Privacy and Security**: Patient data is fueling AI engines but must be handled carefully. Robust security measures and stringent data governance are essential to prevent breaches, misuse, and discrimination.
- **Fairness and Non-Discrimination**: AI algorithms trained on biased data can perpetuate inequalities. Pharma companies must actively mitigate bias and ensure AI serves all populations equitably, avoiding discrimination based on demographics, socioeconomic status, or health conditions.
- **Human Oversight and Accountability**: AI may be a powerful tool, but it shouldn't be the ship's captain. Human oversight and accountability remain paramount. Pharma companies must ensure ethical frameworks guide AI development and use, holding themselves accountable for responsible implementation.

The Rough Seas – Tackling Ethical Challenges

Navigating these ethical currents isn't without its fierce challenges:

- **Balancing Innovation and Public Trust**: Advancing medical progress often intersects with ethical concerns. Striking a balance between innovation and public trust requires open dialogue, public awareness campaigns, and actively incorporating ethical considerations into decision-making processes.
- **Mitigating Algorithmic Bias**: Unfortunately, data mirrors our world's biases. Addressing algorithmic bias in healthcare AI necessitates diverse datasets, rigorous testing for fairness, and ongoing monitoring to prevent discriminatory outcomes.
- **Addressing Job Displacement**: Automation through AI raises concerns about job losses in pharma. Proactive reskilling

initiatives, adapting workflows, and prioritizing human-AI collaboration are crucial to navigating this transition without leaving people behind.

- **Protecting Vulnerable Populations**: Children, pregnant women, and individuals with rare diseases often face unique vulnerabilities in healthcare AI implementations. Robust safeguards, ethical frameworks, and community engagement are necessary to protect these vulnerable groups and ensure equitable access to AI-powered healthcare.

Anchoring in Responsibility— Building a More Ethical Future

To successfully navigate these ethical complexities, we must:

- **Invest in Ethical AI Development**: Allocate resources to develop AI tools that are transparent, fair, and accountable, prioritizing ethical considerations from the outset.
- **Foster Industry-Wide Collaboration**: Share best practices, collaborate on ethical frameworks, and engage in open dialogue across the pharma industry, academia, and regulatory bodies to tackle shared challenges.
- **Prioritize Public Engagement and Empowerment**: Educate the public about AI in healthcare, address concerns transparently, and empower patients with control over their data and participation in developing and using AI tools.
- **Continuously Adapt and Evolve**: The ethical landscape is constantly shifting. Continuous learning, adaptability, and openness to feedback ensure ethical considerations remain at the forefront of AI development and deployment in pharma.

Beyond Compliance, Beyond Regulations

Navigating the ethical landscape isn't just about ticking boxes and complying with regulations. It's about building a future where AI in pharma serves humanity with integrity, inclusivity, and a deep respect for individual rights. Imagine:

- AI tools optimize clinical trials, ensuring diverse patient representation and ethical research practices.
- Personalized drug recommendations powered by AI, improving treatment efficacy and minimizing side effects while respecting patient autonomy.
- Accessible mental health support powered by AI chatbots, reaching underserved communities and providing readily available resources.

This is not an Orwellian future where AI dictates healthcare decisions; it's a hopeful vision where technology is a responsible partner, amplifying human expertise and driving progress with ethical principles firmly anchored at its core. It's a journey where pharma companies, researchers, and the public sail together, navigating the ethical currents and leaving a wake of positive change in the vast ocean of AI-powered healthcare.

Diving Deeper into the Charts: Exploring the Ethical Seas of AI in Pharma

1. **Case Studies in Ethical Navigation**
    - **Mitigating Bias in AI-Powered Drug Dosing:** Imagine a pharmaceutical company developing an AI algorithm to personalize drug dosages. To prevent bias against racial or ethnic minorities, they actively collect diverse data, employ fairness testing throughout development, and involve community stakeholders in validation processes. This proactive approach ensures the AI tool's recommendations are equitable and effective for all populations.
    - **Transparency in Clinical Trial AI Tools**: A research organization leverages AI to identify potential participants for a rare disease trial. They develop a user-friendly dashboard that explains the AI's selection criteria, allows researchers to review individual patient profiles, and

provides clear opt-out options for data inclusion. This transparent approach fosters trust and empowers participants to make informed decisions about their involvement in the trial.

- **Addressing Job Displacement Concern in AI Automation**: A pharma company implements AI-powered robots to automate repetitive tasks in manufacturing. Instead of mass layoffs, they invest in reskilling programs, training displaced workers to operate and maintain robots, and creating new roles that leverage human expertise alongside the efficiency of AI. The proactive approach mitigates job losses and fosters a collaborative human-AI work environment.

2. **Navigating Specific Ethical Currents**
   - **Balancing Innovation with Public Trust in Genetic Testing**: Explore the ethical complexities of using AI to analyze genetic data for disease prediction and treatment recommendations. Consider balancing the potential for personalized healthcare with concerns about genetic discrimination and data privacy.
   - **Protecting Vulnerable Populations in AI-Powered Mental Health Tools**: Discuss the ethical considerations of deploying AI chatbots for mental health support. Analyze how to protect children and vulnerable individuals from potential risks like misinformation or lack of human connection while ensuring equitable access to these resources.
   - **Addressing the Environmental Impacts of AI in Pharma**: Consider the environmental footprint of AI research and development, including energy consumption and data storage. Explore strategies for minimizing environmental impact and promoting sustainable practice within the pharma industry's AI initiatives.

3. **Anchoring in Collaboration and Continuous Learning**:
   - **International Collaboration on Ethical AI Frameworks**: Analyze the development of international guidelines and frameworks for ethical AI in healthcare. Discuss the challenges and opportunities of harmonizing ethical standards across countries and legal systems.
   - **Public-Private Partnerships for Responsible AI Development**: Explore the potential of partnerships between government agencies, pharma companies, and academic institutions to drive responsible AI development in healthcare. Consider how such collaborations can foster shared resources, expertise, and ethical perspectives.
   - **Continuous Learning and Adaptation in the Ethical Landscape**: Discuss the importance of ongoing research, dialogue, and adaptation in navigating the evolving ethical challenges of AI in pharma. Emphasize the need for agile frameworks and a commitment to learning from past mistakes and emerging issues.

By venturing into these specific currents and embracing collaborative learning, we can ensure that AI's voyage in pharma remains innovative, ethically sound, and inclusive. It's a journey where technology acts as a compass, guiding us toward a future where healthcare is personalized, accessible, and driven by the unwavering principles of respect and responsibility. So, dear reader, set your sail, engage in open dialogue, and chart a more ethical future where AI empowers a healthier world for all.

PART V

AI-Powered Pharmaceutical Marketing

Chapter 17. AI-Powered Stakeholder Engagement

Chapter 18. Engaging with Stakeholders in the AI-Fueled Pharma Landscape

Chapter 19. AI-Powered Personalization

Chapter 20. AI-Powered Campaign Personalization in Pharma

Chapter 21. Symphony of Minds: Mapping AI-Powered Customer Journeys for Success

Chapter 22. AI-Powered Omnichannel Marketing

Chapter 23. AI and Humans Revolutionizing Pharma Marketing Research

Chapter 24. Point-of-Care AI: Transforming Healthcare at the Patient's Bedside

Chapter 25. AI Across the Pharmaceutical Value Chain

Chapter 26. The Human Factor in AI-Powered Pharma Marketing

Chapter 27. AI+Human Collaboration: A Symphony of Success in Pharma Sales and Promotion

Chapter 28. Reskilling and Upskilling for Human+AI Collaboration

Chapter 29. The Future of Pharma Marketing in the AI Age

AI-Powered Pharma Marketing – Orchestrating the Revolution with Human+AI Synergy

The pharmaceutical marketing landscape is undergoing a seismic shift. Artificial intelligence (AI) is no longer a futuristic vision; it's a potent force actively shaping the industry. This transformative technology offers unprecedented opportunities to unlock deeper patient insights, personalize communication with precision, and ultimately elevate the patient experience.

However, within pharma marketing, AI is not a solitary player. It thrives in a dynamic partnership with human expertise – a **synergy of minds** that orchestrates the true revolution. This book, "The Synergy of Minds: Human+AI Orchestrating the Pharma Marketing Revolution," delves into this powerful collaboration, exploring how the combined strengths of human empathy and AI's analytical prowess reshape how we connect with patients and healthcare professionals.

This specific section, "AI-powered Pharma Marketing," serves as your roadmap to understanding the diverse applications of AI within this evolving landscape. We'll delve into specific chapters exploring:

- **AI-powered Stakeholder Engagement:** Fostering deeper, more meaningful connections with patients, healthcare professionals, and policymakers.
- **AI-Powered Customer Journey Mapping:** Crafting personalized patient journeys that cater to individual needs and preferences.
- **AI-Powered Market Research:** Utilizing AI to gain deeper insights and predict market trends, informing data-driven marketing strategies.
- **AI-powered Point-of-care:** Transforming how healthcare professionals interact with patients, optimizing treatment plans, and empowering patient self-management.

- **AI across the Pharmaceutical Value Chain:** Exploring the broader impact of AI beyond marketing, from drug discovery to personalized medicine development.

Remember, AI's true power lies not in itself but in its synergy with human ingenuity. As you journey through these chapters, you'll gain the knowledge and inspiration to harness this transformative force, crafting a future of patient-centric pharma marketing and, ultimately, a healthier world for all. Prepare to be a part of the revolution. Welcome to the age of Human+AI in pharma marketing!

CHAPTER

17

AI-Powered Stakeholder Engagement

The symphony of brand communication extends beyond its audience, resonating with a diverse choir of stakeholders whose engagement and trust are crucial for success. In this ever-evolving landscape, artificial intelligence (AI) is reshaping the conductor's baton, offering the potential to compose a richer, more impactful melody of stakeholder engagement and relationship building.

This chapter delves into the burgeoning world of AI-powered stakeholder engagement, exploring how intelligent technologies transform the way we interact and build relationships with those who impact our brands. We'll explore the various instruments within this AI orchestra, from identifying diverse stakeholders and tailoring communication to predicting sentiment and fostering long-term relationships.

However, like any grand symphony, a harmonious performance requires more than powerful instruments. Ethical considerations, responsible data handling, and the ever-present human touch remain crucial for a sustainable and successful approach. Join us as we examine AI's benefits and potential pitfalls in stakeholder engagement, ultimately providing a roadmap for composing a symphony of trust, collaboration, and mutual success.

Are you ready to explore AI's potential in your stakeholder engagement strategy? Turn the page, and let the music begin!

Orchestrating Harmony: AI-Powered Stakeholder Engagement and Relationship Building

Picture a bustling marketplace, not of goods but of ideas and collaborations. Stakeholders of all walks— investors, employees, communities, regulators— gather around your brand, their voices forming a diverse chorus that shapes your success. How can you ensure each voice is heard, understood, and engaged meaningfully in this dynamic ecosystem?

Enter the transformative melody of Artificial Intelligence (AI). Just as a conductor wields their baton to harmonize a complex orchestra, AI offers new tools to orchestrate a symphony of stakeholder engagement and relationship building. From identifying diverse stakeholders and tailoring communication to predicting sentiment and fostering long-term connections, AI promises a richer, more impactful way to navigate this intricate landscape.

Imagine:

- **Identifying Stakeholder Ecosystems**: AI algorithms can analyze vast datasets to map out complex relationships, uncovering previously unseen connections and influencers within your ecosystem.
- **Personalizing Communication**: Tailored messages delivered through the most relevant channels resonate with individual stakeholders, fostering deeper understanding and trust.
- **Predicting Sentiment**: Anticipate potential concerns or opportunities by analyzing social media mentions, news articles, and other data sources. This allows for proactive engagement and conflict resolution.
- **Building Lasting Relationships**: Chatbots and virtual assistants provide 24/7 support and answer basic inquiries, while AI-powered platforms facilitate meaningful dialogues and collaboration.

- **Measuring and Optimizing**: Gain real-time insights into stakeholder engagement metrics, enabling data-driven adjustments to your strategy for continuous improvement.

However, a harmonious performance requires more than just powerful instruments. Just as an orchestra needs a skilled conductor, so does AI-powered stakeholder engagement, which requires careful consideration of ethical implications, responsible data handling, and the irreplaceable human touch. Transparency, fairness, and a commitment to human-centered values are critical to building trust and ensuring AI serves as a tool for good, not a source of alienation.

Identifying Stakeholder Ecosystems

Mapping your stakeholder ecosystem is the first step in harnessing the power of AI for meaningful engagement. Here's a step-by-step guide:

1. **Define Your Scope**:
    - **Start with Your Industry**: Identify key stakeholders in your value chain (suppliers, distributors, customers, regulators).
    - **Consider Your Specific Brand**: Who directly or indirectly impacts your brand's success (e.g., investors, community groups, media)?
    - **Think of Future Stakeholders**: Include emerging groups potentially relevant to your long-term goals (e.g., sustainability influencers, future workforce demographics).

    Example: A pharmaceutical company might consider patients, doctors, pharmacists, research institutions, regulators, advocacy groups, community leaders, and environmental organizations for sustainability initiatives.
2. **Gather Data**:
    - **Internal Sources**: Utilize existing customer databases, employee directories, and partner information.

- **External Sources**: Leverage industry reports, news articles, social media mentions, and government records.
- **Stakeholder Engagement**: Conduct surveys, interviews, and focus groups to gather direct insights and identify hidden stakeholders.

Example: The pharmaceutical company can analyze CRM (Customer Relationship Management) data, partner contracts, and social media mentions to identify key doctors, advocacy groups, and potential community partners.

3. **Leverage AI Tools**:
   - **Text Analysis**: Analyze textual data to identify relevant stakeholder types, interests, and relationships.
   - **Social Network Analysis**: Map connections between stakeholders based on mentions and engagements online.
   - **Clustering Algorithms**: Group stakeholders with similar characteristics for targeted engagement strategies.

   Example: AI algorithms can analyze the company's social media mentions to identify influential patient groups, doctors discussing their products, and potential new partners for clinical trials.

4. **Refine and Iterate**:
   - **Validate Your Findings**: Cross-check with human experts and stakeholder feedback to ensure accuracy and avoid biases.
   - **Update Regularly**: Track changes in the ecosystem and update your map as stakeholder relationships evolve.
   - **Use Findings for Action**: Design targeted communication, engagement activities, and relationship-building strategies for each stakeholder group.

   Example: The company might organize educational webinars for specific doctor groups identified through AI analysis, partnering with influential patient groups for awareness campaigns, and engaging community leaders in sustainability initiatives.

Remember:

- **AI is a Tool, not a Replacement**: Human judgment and understanding of the context remain crucial.
- **Focus on Ethical Data Collection and Use**: Respect privacy and transparency.
- **Continuous Improvement is Key**: Regularly review and adapt your stakeholder ecosystem map as your brand and landscape evolve.

By following these steps and responsibly leveraging AI, you can identify and understand your stakeholder ecosystem, paving the way for more effective and impactful engagement strategies.

System for Identifying Different Stakeholder Types: A Step-by-Step Guide

Identifying and understanding your diverse stakeholders is crucial for successful communication and relationship building. Here's a step-by-step guide to categorize key stakeholders like HCPs, patients, payers, regulators, and investors:

Step 1: Define Your Brand and Industry:

- **Industry Analysis**: Identify key stakeholder groups relevant to your industry. For example, pharmaceutical companies might consider research institutions, distributors, and regulatory bodies.
- **Brand-Specific Stakeholders**: Pinpoint groups directly or indirectly impacting your brand (e.g., specific patient segments, media outlets relevant to your niche).
- **Future Considerations**: Include emerging stakeholder groups relevant to your long-term goals (e.g., sustainability influencers, future workforce demographics).

Example: A medical device manufacturer might consider HCPs (surgeons, nurses), patients with specific conditions, insurance companies, regulatory bodies (FDA), and investors focused on healthcare technology.

Step 2: Gather Data:

- **Internal Sources**: Utilize CRM data, customer databases, employee directories, and partner information.
- **External Sources**: Leverage industry reports, news articles, social media mentions, government records, and market research.
- **Stakeholder Engagement**: Conduct surveys, interviews, and focus groups to gain direct insights and identify hidden stakeholders.

Example: The medical device manufacturer can analyze sales data to identify key HCPs using their products, social media mentions to understand patient concerns, and industry reports to track insurance reimbursement policies.

Step 3: Apply Differentiation Criteria for Each Stakeholder Group:

- **Interests**: What are their primary concerns and motivations? (e.g., HCPs: Patient outcomes, cost-efficiency, cost-effectiveness; Patients: health improvement, affordability, access).
- **Influence**: How much power do they have to shape your brand's success? (For example, regulators have significant influence through approvals, while community groups might influence public perception.)
- **Information Needs**: What information do they require from you? (For example, HCPs need scientific data, patients need clear product information, and investors need financial performance updates.)

- **Communication Channels**: How do they prefer to receive information? (e.g., HCPs through medical conferences, patients through social media, and investors through financial reports).

  Example: The manufacturer can categorize HCPs by specialty (surgeon vs. cardiologist) and patients by condition (chronic vs. acute) and differentiate investors based on their risk appetite and investment focus.

Step 4: Leverage AI Tools:

- **Text Analysis**: Analyze textual data to identify keywords, interests, and relevant keywords, interests, and relationships between stakeholders.
- **Social Network Analysis**: Map stakeholder connections based on online interactions and mentions.
- **Clustering Algorithms**: Group stakeholders with similar characteristics for targeted communication strategies.

Example: AI can analyze social media mentions to identify influential patient groups, HCPs discussing specific needs, and potential partners for clinical trials.

Step 5: Refine and Iterate:

- **Validate Findings**: Cross-check with human experts and stakeholder feedback to ensure accuracy and address potential biases.
- **Update Regularly**: Monitor changes in the stakeholder landscape and update categorization as needed.
- **Actionable Insights**: Use your findings to develop targeted communication, engagement activities, and relationship-building strategies for each stakeholder group.

Example: The manufacturer can organize webinars for specific HCP groups, partner with patient advocacy groups for awareness campaigns, and tailor their communication to address investor concerns about regulatory approvals.

Remember:

- **AI is a Tool**: Utilize it alongside human expertise and qualitative understanding of stakeholder needs.
- **Ethical Considerations**: Ensure responsible data collection, transparency, and respect for individual privacy.
- **Continuous Improvement**: Regularly review and adapt your stakeholder categorization as your brand and industry evolve.

By implementing this system and responsibly leveraging AI, you can better understand your diverse stakeholders, paving the way for more effective and impactful communication, collaboration, and brand success.

Tailored Communication for Diverse Stakeholders: A Step-by-Step Guide

Crafting effective communication requires understanding your audience. Here's a step-by-step approach to tailoring messages for key stakeholders like HCPs, patients, payers, regulators, and investors.

Step 1: Define Your Messaging Goals:

- **Identify Objectives**: What do you aim to achieve with each stakeholder group? (e.g., educate HCPs, inform patients, influence regulators, attract investors).
- **Align with Stakeholder Interests**: Ensure your message resonates with their priorities and addresses their needs.

Example: A pharma company aims to launch a new diabetes medication. Their goals are:

- **HCPs**: Educate them on the medication's efficacy and safety profile, highlighting clinical trial data and benefits for patients.
- **Patients**: Improve awareness and understanding of the disease and treatment options, emphasizing the medication's potential impact on their quality of life.

- **Payers**: Demonstrate the drug's cost-effectiveness and value proposition compared to existing options.
- **Regulators**: Provide comprehensive safety and efficacy data to secure regulatory approval.
- **Investors**: Highlight the market potential and financial viability of the new medication.

Step 2: Research and Segmentation:

- **Gather Insights**: Conduct research (surveys, focus groups) to understand each stakeholder group's information needs, preferred communication channels, and potential concerns.
- **Segment Audiences**: Divide each group into sub-segments based on specific characteristics (e.g., HCPs by specialty, patients by disease stage).

Example: The company can segment HCPs by diabetes specialization (endocrinologists, primary care physicians), segment patients by age and disease severity, and categorize investors by risk tolerance and investment focus.

Step 3: Craft Tailored Messages:

- **Content and Tone**: Adapt your message content and tone to resonate with each segment's specific interests and concerns (e.g., use technical language for HCPs, plain language for patients, and focus on financial metrics for investors).
- **Channels and Formats**: Utilize different communication channels each group prefers (e.g., medical conferences for HCPs, social media for patients, and investor relations platforms for financial updates).
- **Personalization**: To increase engagement, consider personalization strategies (e.g., targeted email campaigns, addressing HCPs by name).

Example: For HCPs, the company can create detailed clinical presentations with data and case studies. And for patients the company can develop educational video content and infographics. Also, the company can prepare cost-effectiveness analyses and budget impact models for payers. Comprehensive dossiers with thorough safety and efficacy data can be submitted to regulators. Investors can be presented with financial projections and market research reports.

Step 4: Utilize AI Tools:

- **Segmentation and Targeting**: Leverage AI algorithms to analyze vast data sets and identify specific audience segments within each stakeholder group.
- **Content Creation**: Explore AI-powered tools for personalized content generation, tailoring messages to individual interests and preferences.
- **Performance Measurement**: Utilize AI dashboards to track engagement metrics across different channels and assess the effectiveness of your communication strategies.

Example: AI can help analyze social media data to identify patient communities concerned about specific diabetes symptoms, allowing for targeted awareness campaigns. Additionally, AI can personalize patient email content based on their medical history and medication use, providing relevant information and recommendations.

Step 5: Continuous Improvement:

- **Monitor Feedback**: Track stakeholder response and gather feedback through surveys, social media monitoring, and direct interactions.
- **Refine Your Approach**: Based on feedback and performance data, adjust your messaging, channels, and personalization strategies for each stakeholder group.
- **Embrace Iterative Optimization**: Continuous monitoring and adaptation ensure your communication remains relevant and effective in a dynamic environment.

Remember:

- **Ethical Considerations**: Maintain data privacy and transparency throughout the communication process.
- **Human Oversight**: AI is a tool; human judgment and ethical decision-making remain crucial.
- **Authenticity and Empathy**: Tailor your communication to resonate with human emotions and values, not just data points.

By following these steps and utilizing AI responsibly, you can create a symphony of tailored communications that resonate with each stakeholder group, building trust, fostering engagement, and ultimately achieving your goals.

Personalizing Communication for Different Stakeholder Groups

Personalizing Communications for HCPs: Step by Step

Healthcare professionals (HCPs) are a diverse group with specific needs and preferences. Tailoring communication to individual HCPs can significantly increase engagement and message effectiveness. Here's step-by-step guide:

Step 1: Gather Data and Insights:

- **Internal Data**: Utilize CRM (Customer Relationship Management) systems, sales reports, and conference attendance records to identify relevant HCPs.
- **External Data**: Use medical databases, publications, and social media profiles to learn about specialties, research interests, and areas of expertise.
- **Engagement Activities**: Conduct surveys, polls, and in-person interactions to gather direct feedback and preferences.

Example: A medical device company can analyze sales and prescription data to identify HCPs using their products, track social media activity to understand areas of discussion, and conduct surveys at conferences to learn about specific challenges and needs.

Step 2: Segment Your Audience:

- **Specialty And Interest**: Categorize HCPs by specialty (e.g., cardiologists, oncologists), subspecialty (e.g., electrophysiologists, medical oncologists), or specific interests (e.g., minimally invasive surgery, pediatric care).
- **Practice Setting**: Differentiate HCPs based on their practice setting (e.g., hospitals, clinics, private practice) to consider workflow and patient population differences.
- **Experience and Adoption Level**: Segment your product or solution based on your customers' experience level or adoption (e.g., early adopters, established users).

Example: The medical device company might segment cardiologists by subspecialty (electrophysiologists vs. interventional cardiologists), private practice vs. hospital settings, and early adopters of their new technology vs. established users of competitor devices.

Step 3: Craft Personalized Messages:

- **Content Relevance**: Tailor content to each segment's specific needs and challenges. Present clinical data relevant to their specialty, address common questions in their practice setting, and highlight benefits based on their adoption level.
- **Communication Channels**: Use preferred communication channels, such as medical conferences, online portals, targeted email campaigns, or personalized video messages.
- **Formatting and Language**: Adapt the message format (e.g., white papers, case studies, infographics) and language (technical vs. plain language) to their preferences and level of expertise.

Example: The company can share detailed white papers on their new device's technical features and clinical trial data for early adopter electrophysiologists. For established users in private practice, they can create video testimonials showcasing improved patient outcomes with the device.

Step 4: Utilize AI Tools:

- **Personalization Engine**: Leverage AI to personalize email content based on HCP's specialties, previous interactions, and interests.
- **Dynamic Content Generation**: Explore AI-powered tools to adapt presentations or case studies with specific data relevant to each HCP's practice and patient population.
- **Social Media Monitoring**: Utilize AI to identify HCPs discussing relevant topics and engage them with personalized responses or targeted content.

Example: AI can analyze an HCP's social media activity to identify their research interests and tailor targeted email campaigns highlighting relevant clinical studies or white papers. Additionally, AI can personalize presentation slides with patient demographics and practice-specific data for each HCP during sales meetings.

Step 5: Measure and Improve:

- **Track Engagement Metrics**: Monitor open rates, click-through rates, and video completion rates for personalized communication.
- **Gather Feedback**: Conduct surveys or solicit direct feedback from HCPs to assess the effectiveness of your personalization efforts.
- **Refine Your Approach**: Based on data and feedback, continuously improve your segmentation, content tailoring, and personalization strategies.

Remember:

- **Privacy and Ethics**: Ensure responsible data collection, use, and transparency in all personalization efforts.
- **Human Touch Remains Essential**: AI is a tool to enhance personalization, but human insights and judgment are crucial for effective communication.

- **Build Trust and Relationships**: Personalized communication is a tool to foster trust and engagement, not just sell products.

By following these steps and leveraging AI responsibly, you can create a symphony of personalized communications that resonate with individual HCPs, driving deeper engagement and better healthcare outcomes.

Personalizing Communication for Patients Step-by-Step

Patients are no longer a homogenous group. They have diverse needs, preferences, and health literacy levels. Tailoring communication to individual patients can foster trust, improve understanding, and ultimately improve health outcomes. Here is a step-by-step guide:

Step 1: Gather Data and Insights:

- **Medical Records**: Leverage anonymized data to understand patients' diagnoses, treatment history, and potential communication needs.
- **Surveys and Questionnaires**: Gather insights into patients' preferred communication channels, information needs, and concerns about their health condition.
- **Social Media Monitoring**: Analyze online discussions to understand patient sentiment and identify common questions or anxieties.

Example: A diabetes management app can collect data on patients' glucose levels, medication adherence, and preferred communication channels. They can also conduct surveys to understand patients' challenges and fears about managing their diabetes.

Step 2: Segment Your Audience:

- **Condition and Severity**: Segment patients based on their specific diagnosis, stage of disease, and treatment needs (e.g., newly diagnosed vs. long-term management).

- **Demographics and Cultural Background**: Consider age, language, and cultural preferences to communicate clearly and respectfully.
- **Digital Literacy and Information Needs**: Segment based on comfort level with technology and preferred level of detail in the information provided.

Example: The diabetes app can segment patients by type of diabetes (type 1 vs. type 2), consider language preferences based on user demographics, and differentiate between patients who want daily glucose level updates or those who prefer weekly summaries.

Step 3: Craft Personalized Messages:

- **Content Relevance**: Tailor information to each segment's specific condition, concerns, and treatment plan. Provide actionable steps and resources relevant to their stage of disease.
- **Visual and Language Clarity**: Use simple language, understandable visuals, and accessible formats (e.g., short videos and infographics) to cater to varying digital literacy levels.
- **Empathy and Emotional Tone**: Acknowledge patients' anxieties and challenges, offering support and personalized encouragement.

Example: For newly diagnosed type 1 diabetic teenagers, the app can provide educational content on managing diet, exercise, and insulin injections presented in a visually engaging way. For long-term type 2 diabetic patients, the app can offer reminders for medication adherence and personalized goal-setting based on health data.

Step 4: Utilize AI Tools:

- **Chatbots and Virtual Assistants**: Implement AI-powered tools to answer patients' common questions, provide basic support, and offer personalized health information based on their medical history.

- **Content Personalization Engines**: Leverage AI to adapt educational materials and messages to individual patients' reading levels, cultural backgrounds, and specific condition details.
- **Sentiment Analysis**: Utilize AI to monitor patient feedback and social media mentions, identifying concerns and opportunities for personalized outreach or support.

Example: The app can integrate a chatbot to answer FAQs about managing diabetes, suggest healthy recipes based on the patient's dietary restrictions, and personalize medication reminders with encouraging messages. Additionally, AI can analyze patient feedback to identify common concerns and proactively address them through targeted educational content or support messages.

Step 5: Measure and Improve:

- **Track Engagement Metrics**: Monitor app usage, click-through rates on educational materials, and response rates to personalized messages.
- **Gather Patient Feedback**: Conduct surveys or solicit direct feedback to understand if patients feel the communication is relevant and helpful.
- **Refine Your Approach**: Continuously adapt your segmentation, content, and personalization strategies based on data and feedback to ensure ongoing effectiveness.

Remember:

- **Privacy and Security**: Ensure adherence to data privacy regulations and transparent communication about data usage.
- **Human Oversight is Crucial**: AI remains a tool, and empathy and understanding are essential for genuine patient connection.

- **Focus on Empowerment**: Personalized communication should empower patients to manage their health, not replace human interaction with healthcare professionals.

By following these steps and leveraging AI responsibly, you can create a symphony of personalized communication that resonates with individual patients, leading to improved health outcomes, increased engagement, and stronger patient-provider relationships.

Personalizing Communication with Payers, Step-by-Step

Navigating the complex world of healthcare payers requires targeted and insightful communication. Personalizing your approach to each payer can build trust, demonstrate value, and ultimately secure favorable coverage decisions for your product or service. Here is a step-by-step guide:

Step 1: Gather Data and Insights:

- **Payer Landscape**: Analyze the competitive landscape, identifying key payers in your target market and their coverage policies.
- **Payer-Specific Data**: Research each payer's formulary guidelines, reimbursement criteria, and past coverage decisions for similar products.
- **Industry Trends**: Keep up with healthcare policy changes, cost-containment measures, and emerging technologies influencing payer decisions.

Example: A pharmaceutical company launching a new drug for a specific disease must identify the major national and regional payers covering that patient population. They should research each payer's preferred medications for that condition, past coverage decisions for similar drugs, and any specific cost-effectiveness requirements.

Step 2: Segment Your Audience:

- **Payer Type**: Differentiate between commercial payers, government programs (Medicare, Medicaid), and self-insured employers, each with distinct priorities and decision-making processes.
- **Patient Population**: Consider the specific patient groups each payer covers, as their needs and cost pressures vary.
- **Financial Considerations**: Segment payments based on their financial outlook, risk tolerance, and willingness to adopt innovative treatments.

Example: The drug company might segment commercial payers by size (national vs. regional) and patient population focus (general health vs. specialty care). They could also differentiate Medicare plans based on geographic location and patient demographics.

Step 3: Craft Tailored Messages:

- **Value Proposition**: Highlight the unique value your product brings to each payer segment, focusing on cost-effectiveness, improved patient outcomes, and alignment with their coverage priorities.
- **Data and Evidence**: Provide robust clinical data, cost-effectiveness analyses, and real-world evidence tailored to each payer's requirements and evaluation criteria.
- **Communication Channels**: Utilize preferred communication channels, such as formal proposals, targeted presentations, or one-on-one meetings adapted to each payer's decision-making process.

Example: When presenting to a cost-conscious commercial payer, the company can emphasize the medication's potential to decrease hospital admissions and long-term care costs for its specific patient population. A Medicare plan concerned with patient outcomes can present data demonstrating improved quality of life and reduced complications for its beneficiaries.

Step 4: Leverage AI Tools:

- **Market Analysis Tools**: Utilize AI-powered platforms to track evolving payer market trends, competitor activity, and emerging reimbursement policies.
- **Data Analysis and Insights**: Analyze large datasets to identify payer-specific cost drivers, patient characteristics, and potential areas for value proposition customization.
- **Personalized Communication Platforms**: Explore AI-powered tools to generate targeted proposals, presentations, and reports adapted to each payer's unique needs and language.

Example: AI can analyze hospital admission data to identify specific cost reductions achievable with the new drug for each payer's patient population. Additionally, AI can generate personalized reports highlighting relevant clinical data and cost-effectiveness metrics tailored to each payer's evaluation criteria.

Step 5: Measure and Improve:

- **Track Engagement Metrics**: Monitor proposal response rates, meeting scheduling requests, and overall dialogue with each payer.
- **Gather Feedback**: Conduct surveys or debriefing sessions with payer representatives to understand their perspectives on your communication effectiveness.
- **Refine Your Approach**: Continuously adapt your segmentation, messaging, and personalization strategies based on data, feedback, and evolving payer landscapes.

Remember:

- **Transparency and Ethics**: Ensure data accuracy, communication transparency, and industry regulation adherence when using AI.

- **Human Expertise Remains Crucial**: AI can enhance your understanding of payers, but human judgment and relationship building are essential for success.
- **Long-Term Engagement**: Build trust and understanding with payers through ongoing dialogue and value demonstration.

By following these steps and leveraging AI responsibly, you can create a symphony of personalized communication that resonates with individual payers, securing optimal coverage decisions and improving patient access to your healthcare solutions.

Personalizing Communication with Regulators, Step-by-Step

Navigating the complex world of regulatory agencies requires targeted and compliant communication. Personalizing your approach to each regulator can ensure alignment with their expectations, expedite the approval process, and build trust for future interactions. Here is a step-by-step guide:

Step 1: Gather Data and Insights:

- **Regulatory Landscape**: Analyze the specific agency you're interacting with, their area of jurisdiction, and recent regulatory guidelines related to your product or service.
- **Past Interactions**: Research the agency's history with similar submissions, identifying potential concerns or areas of particular focus.
- **Industry Trends**: Keep up with regulatory reforms, emerging technologies, and potential shifts in regulatory interpretations that might impact your submission.

Example: A medical device company seeking FDA approval for a novel diagnostic tool must research the agency's recent guidance on AI-powered medical devices, identify past approvals for similar tools, and stay updated on ongoing discussions about cybersecurity for connected healthcare devices.

Step 2: Segment Your Audience:

- **Agency Divisions and Reviewers**: Differentiate between scientific reviewers, legal experts, and policy analysts within the agency, each with distinct roles and evaluation criteria.
- **Regional Regulatory Bodies**: When working with international markets, consider each relevant regulatory agency's specific requirements and cultural nuances.
- **Level of Experience and Expertise**: Adapt your communication to the reviewer's background and familiarity with your specific technology or field.

Example: The medical device company might tailor its submission materials differently for scientific reviewers focused on technical specifications and clinical data versus the legal experts reviewing compliance with safety regulations. Additionally, if seeking approval in the EU, it would need to consider the specific requirements of the European Medicines Agency.

Step 3: Craft Tailored Messages:

- **Clarity and Compliance**: Ensure your communication is concise and strictly adheres to the agency's submission format and content requirements.
- **Data-Driven Approach**: Present comprehensive data, evidence, and scientific rationale tailored to the agency's concerns and evaluation criteria.
- **Addressing Potential Concerns**: Based on past interactions and industry trends, anticipate questions or objections and proactively address them in your submissions.

Example: When presenting pre-clinical data, the company can highlight studies specifically designed to address concerns raised by the FDA in previous approvals of similar devices. Additionally, they can offer alternative testing methods if standard protocols might not apply to their unique technology.

Step 4: Leverage AI Tools:

- **Regulatory Intelligence Platforms**: Utilize AI-powered tools to track evolving regulatory landscapes, identify relevant guidance documents, and predict potential approval hurdles.
- **Data Analysis and Mining**: Explore AI to analyze your existing data and identify potential gaps or areas requiring further evidence to address regulatory concerns.
- **Personalized Communication Generation**: Consider AI-powered tools to generate compliant cover letters, summaries, and responses to reviewers' questions tailored to the specific agency and reviewer's level of expertise.

Example: AI can analyze FDA approval pathways for similar technologies to predict potential review timelines and identify areas where more data might be needed. Additionally, AI can analyze large datasets of clinical data to identify subgroups of patients potentially benefiting most from the new device, addressing specific reviewer concerns about patient selection and generalizability.

Step 5: Measure and Improve:

- **Track Feedback and Review Cycles**: Monitor reviewers' feedback and adapt your communication based on their comments and questions.
- **Gather Regulatory Feedback**: Participate in agency workshops, public forums, and meetings to understand ongoing regulatory priorities and adapt your communication accordingly.
- **Refine Your Approach**: Continuously refine your segmentation, messaging, and data presentation strategies based on feedback and evolving regulatory landscapes.

Remember:

- **Transparency and Ethics**: Ensure responsible data use, transparency in communications, and strict adherence to regulatory guidelines when utilizing AI.
- **Human Expertise Remains Crucial**: AI can enhance your understanding of regulators, but human judgment, scientific expertise, and relationship building are essential for success.
- **Long-Term Engagement**: Foster ongoing dialogue and transparency with regulators, building trust and facilitating a smoother approval process for future submissions.

By following these steps and leveraging AI responsibly, you can create a symphony of personalized communication that resonates with individual regulators, expedite approval processes, build trust, and ensure your innovations have a safe and effective introduction to the market.

Personalizing Communication with Investors, Step-by-Step

Building and maintaining strong relationships with investors requires targeted communication that resonates with their unique interests and investment goals. Personalizing your approach can foster trust, attract and retain investors, and drive long-term financial success. Here is a step-by-step guide:

Step 1: Gather Data and Insights:

- **Investor Profiles**: Analyze current and potential investor backgrounds, investment styles, and risk tolerance.
- **Market Trends**: Stay informed about market sentiment, industry trends, and potential risks relevant to your company and sector.
- **Investor Relations History**: Review past interactions, feedback, and areas of interest expressed by different investor groups.

Examples: A publicly traded technology company might categorize investors by size (individuals vs. institutional), investment focus (growth vs. value), and previous interactions with the company. They would also track current economic trends and potential disruptions impacting their industry.

Step 2: Segment Your Audience:

- **Investment Objectives:** Differentiate between investors seeking short-term returns, long-term capital appreciation, or dividend income.
- **Geographic Location and Cultural Nuances**: Adapt communication to align with different investor groups' cultural expectations and preferred communication styles.
- **Information Needs**: Segment based on their familiarity with your company and industry, tailoring the depth and detail of information provided.

Example: The technology company might tailor presentations for growth investors focusing on future market potential and disruptive innovation while presenting financial stability and dividend consistency to income-focused investors. Additionally, they would adapt their communication style and materials when presenting to international investors from different cultural backgrounds.

Step 3: Craft Tailored Messages:

- **Value Proposition**: Highlight your company's unique value proposition, focusing on key metrics and achievements relevant to each investor segment's goals.
- **Future Outlook**: Provide clear and compelling insights into your company's growth prospects, market opportunities, and strategic paths.
- **Transparency and Trust**: Communicate openly and honestly, addressing potential risks and challenges while demonstrating a commitment to ethical business practices.

Example: For growth investors, the company might emphasize its innovative product pipeline, market share expansion, and potential for disruptive impact. For income-focused investors, the company would showcase consistent revenue growth, profitability, and commitment to maintaining a sustainable dividend payout.

Step 4: Leverage AI Tools:

- **Investment Sentiment Analysis**: Utilize AI to analyze news articles, social media mentions, and financial reports to understand investor sentiment toward your company and industry.
- **Personalized Communication Platforms**: Explore AI-powered tools to generate targeted investor reports, presentations, and Q&A responses tailored to each segment's information needs and concerns.
- **Investment Risk Prediction Models**: Consider AI-powered models to assess potential risks and opportunities, informing your communication and strategic decision-making.

Example: AI can analyze social media sentiment to identify concerns among specific investor groups, allowing for proactive communication addressing those concerns. Additionally, AI can generate personalized investor reports highlighting relevant financial metrics and future projections tailored to each segment's investment objectives.

Step 5: Measure and Improve:

- **Track Engagement Metrics**: Monitor investor relations event attendance, website traffic, and interactions with communication materials.
- **Gather Feedback**: Conduct surveys or individual investor meetings to understand their perception of your communication and areas for improvement.

- **Refine Your Approach**: Continuously adapt your segmentation, messaging, and AI tools based on data and evolving market conditions.

Remember:

- **Transparency and Ethics**: Uphold the highest ethical standards in data collection, use, and communication, building trust with investors.
- **Human Touch is Irreplaceable**: AI offers valuable insights, but genuine relationship building and investor engagement require human interaction and empathy.
- **Long-Term Focus**: Cultivate long-term relationships with investors through consistent, transparent communication and alignment with their interests.

By following these steps and leveraging AI responsibly, you can create a symphony of personalized communication that resonates with individual investors, fostering trust, attracting capital, and ultimately achieving your financial goals.

Optimizing Pharma Stakeholder Engagement with Predictive Analytics, Step-by-Step

The pharmaceutical industry thrives on relationships. Understanding and engaging stakeholders effectively is crucial for success, from patients and healthcare providers (HCPs) to payers and regulators. Predictive analytics can be a powerful tool in this endeavor, unlocking valuable insights to personalize communication and strengthen relationships. Here's step-by-step guide:

Step 1: Define Goals and Stakeholders:

- **Identify Key Stakeholder Groups:** Patients, HCPs, regulators, investors, and community organizations.
- **Set Specific Goals**: Define what you want to achieve (e.g., increased patient adherence, improved physician adoption of new drugs, positive media coverage).

Example: A pharma company launching a new diabetes medication might aim to optimize patient adherence, identify high-prescribing HCPs, and predict potential regulatory hurdles.

Step 2: Data Collection and Integration:

- **Gather Diverse Data**: Collect patient data (e.g., demographics, medical records, prescription history), HCP engagement data (e.g., conference attendance, online interactions), and external data (e.g., social media sentiment, market trends).
- **Combine Internal and External Data**: Integrate clinical trial data, sales data, and competitor analysis with external sources to paint a holistic picture).

Example: The company can collect patient data from electronic health records, analyze social media discussions about diabetes management, and integrate HCP prescription data with their expertise and conference attendance information.

Step 3: Building Prediction Models:

- **Choose Relevant Algorithms**: Identify suitable algorithms based on your goals and data types (e.g., patient churn prediction models and network analysis for HCP relationships).
- **Train and Refine Models**: Train models on historical data to predict future behavior (e.g., medication adherence, HCP prescribing patterns, potential safety concerns).

Example: The company can build a model predicting which patients are more likely to be non-adherent based on past behavior and socio-economic factors. They can also create a network analysis model to identify influential HCPs within specific disease specialties.

Step 4: Actionable Insights and Personalization:

- **Extract Actionable Insights**: Use your models to predict individual stakeholder needs, preferences, and potential risks.

- **Personalize Communication and Engagement**: Based on these insights, tailor patient education materials, HCP outreach strategies, and regulatory submissions.

Example: For patients at risk of non-adherence, the company can develop personalized reminders, educational content, and support programs. To HCPs, they can create targeted webinars and educational materials relevant to their practice and patient population. Regulatory submissions can be tailored to address specific concerns identified through data analysis.

Step 5: Continuous Improvement and Feedback:

- **Monitor Performance and Feedback**: Track the impact of your personalized engagement strategies on key metrics (e.g., patient adherence, HCP adoption, regulatory approval timelines).
- **Adapt and Refine Your Approach**: Learn from data and feedback to refine your models and personalization strategies.

Example: The company can track how adherence rates change with personalized interventions and adapt their approach based on feedback from patients and HCPs. They can also monitor regulatory feedback and use it to refine future submissions.

Additional Considerations:

- **Data Privacy and Ethics**: Ensure responsible data collection, use, and transparency according to regulations and ethical standards.
- **Explainability and Interpretability**: Choose models that allow explanation of predictions, fostering trust and stakeholder understanding.
- **Human-in-the-Loop Approach**: Leverage AI insights to inform, not replace, human decision-making and relationship-building.

Examples Across Pharma Stakeholders:

- **For Patients**: Predict and address medication adherence challenges and personalize communication based on health literacy and preferences.
- **For HCPs**: Identify key opinion leaders, tailor educational content to their specialty and interests, and predict drug adoption potential.
- **For Payers**: Predict the cost-effectiveness of treatments, develop personalized reimbursement strategies, and anticipate potential payer concerns.
- **For Regulators**: Predict potential safety risks based on real-world data and personalize communication based on agency priorities.

By following these steps and responsibly using predictive analytics, pharma companies can gain a deeper understanding of their stakeholders, personalize their engagement strategies, and build stronger, more sustainable relationships, ultimately leading to better patient outcomes and business success.

Building Lasting Stakeholder Relationships

Building Lasting Relationships with HCPs: A Step-by-Step Guide

Healthcare professionals (HCPs) are crucial partners in ensuring patient well-being. Building and nurturing lasting relationships with them requires trust, value-driven interactions, and personalized engagement. Here's a step-by-step guide exploring how AI can enhance each step:

Step 1: Understand Their Needs and Challenges:

- **Conduct Surveys and Focus Groups**: Gather feedback from HCPs on their needs, preferred communication channels, and pain points.

- **Analyze Social Media Discussions**: Utilize AI-powered sentiment analysis to understand broader HCP concerns and industry trends.
- **Leverage Market Research**: Stay informed about evolving healthcare landscapes and challenges different HCP specialties face.

Example: A medical device company can conduct surveys with cardiologists to understand their preferences for learning about new technologies and their biggest challenges in treating heart failure patients. Additionally, AI can analyze online forums and social media discussions to identify broader concerns about patient care and emerging treatment options.

Step 2: Segment and Personalize Outreach:

- **Segment by Specialty, Practice Setting, and Interests**: Cater to the specific needs of cardiologists, oncologists, or primary care physicians. Consider hospital vs. private practice settings and individual research interests.
- **Utilize Content Personalization**: Leverage AI to tailor educational materials, case studies, and product information to each HCP's specialty, practice setting, and areas of interest.
- **Personalized Communication Channels**: Utilize preferred communication channels like email, online portals, or targeted social media advertising based on individual preferences.

Examples: The company can create different educational webinars for cardiologists in hospitals vs. private practice, focusing on relevant clinical data and addressing specific challenges based on their setting. AI can personalize email content with relevant product information tailored to each HCP's research interests and patient population.

Step 3: Offer Value Beyond Products:

- **Provide Ongoing Service Beyond Products**: Offer CME-accredited webinars, case studies, and clinical decision support tools relevant to their practice.

- **Facilitate Peer-to-Peer Learning**: Utilize AI-powered platforms to connect HCPs with similar interests for knowledge sharing and collaboration.
- **Partner in Research and Innovation**: Engage HCPs in co-creating educational content for product development or conducting clinical trials.

Example: The company can develop an AI-powered platform where cardiologists can share best practices, discuss complex cases, and learn from each other's experiences. Additionally, they can partner with HCPs on research projects to validate the effectiveness of their new devices in real-world clinical settings.

Step 4: Build Trust and Transparency:

- **Be Transparent about Data Practices and AI Usage**: Communicate how you collect, use, and protect HCP data to ensure responsible AI implementation.
- **Address their Concerns Proactively**: Monitor feedback and address potential concerns about data privacy, algorithmic bias, or conflicts of interest.
- **Foster Open and Honest Communication**: Encourage two-way dialogue, actively listen to HCPs' perspectives, and respond promptly to their inquiries.

Example: The company can publish detailed data privacy policies, explain how AI personalizes its outreach, and actively seek feedback on AI-powered tools. They can also establish advisory boards with HCPs to ensure transparency and ethical use of AI in their interactions.

Step 5: Continuously Measure and Improve:

- **Track Engagement Metrics**: Monitor website traffic, webinar attendance, and interactions with educational materials to assess HCP engagement.

- **Gather Feedback Through Surveys and Interviews**: Regularly solicit feedback from HCPs to understand their perceptions of your communication and value proposition.
- **Refine Your Approach Based on Data and Feedback**: Continuously adapt your segmentation, content personalization, and AI-powered tools based on insights and evolving HCP needs.

Remember:

- **AI is a tool, Not a Replacement**: Human relationships and genuine interactions remain crucial for building trust and lasting partnerships with HCPs.
- **Focus on Value, Not Just Promotion**: Offer valuable resources, support, and educational opportunities that genuinely benefit HCPs in their practice.
- **Ethical Considerations are Paramount**: When using AI, ensure responsible data collection, transparency, and alignment with HCPs' best interests.

By following these steps and leveraging AI responsibly, you can build strong, lasting relationships with HCPs, fostering trust, collaboration, and, ultimately, better patient outcomes.

Building Lasting Relationships with Patients, Step-by-Step with AI

The foundation of healthcare lies in the patient-provider relationship. Building trust, fostering engagement, and ensuring patients feel seen and heard are crucial for long-term health outcomes and positive experiences. Here's a step-by-step guide on how AI can enhance your efforts:

Step 1: Understand Their Needs and Preferences:

- **Conduct Surveys and Focus Groups**: Gather direct patient feedback about their concerns, communication preferences, and desired level of involvement in their care.

- **Analyze Social Media Discussions**: Utilize AI-powered sentiment analysis to understand broader patient concerns and identify topics of high interest.
- **Leverage Patient Data and Insights**: Analyze medical records and past interactions to understand individual patient needs, motivations, and potential communication gaps.

Example: A hospital can conduct surveys to see if patients prefer email, text message, or phone call reminders for appointments. Additionally, AI can analyze social media discussions to identify concerns about specific conditions or treatment options. Combining this with insights from medical records can reveal which patients might benefit from additional educational resources or emotional support.

Step 2: Personalize Communication and Care:

- **Segment Patients Based on Condition, Demographics, and Preferences**: Tailor communication and resources to their needs and comfort levels.
- **Utilize AI for Content Personalization**: Generate educational materials, appointment reminders, and discharge instructions in language and formats (e.g., easy-to-read text, infographics) suitable for each patient's literacy level and cultural background.
- **Offer Personalized Care Plans and Interventions**: Leverage AI to analyze patient data and suggest personalized lifestyle modifications, medication adherence support, or mental health resources.

Example: A diabetes clinic can segment patients based on diabetes type, age, and preferred language. AI can then personalize education materials on managing blood sugar levels and medication reminders with visuals and language specific to their needs. Additionally, AI can analyze data to identify patients at risk for complications and suggest personalized interventions like nutrition coaching or mental health support.

Step 3: Foster Engagement and Two-Way Communication:

- **Utilize AI-Powered Chatbots in Basic Questions and Support**: This allows patients to easily access information, schedule appointments, or ask basic questions through chatbots, freeing up healthcare professionals for more complex concerns.
- **Create Online Communities and Forums**: Facilitate peer-to-peer support and information sharing through AI-moderated online communities where patients can connect and learn from each other's experiences.
- **Enable Feedback and Co-Creation Opportunities**: Utilize AI-powered surveys and feedback mechanisms to continuously gather patient input and involve them in shaping care delivery or educational resources.

Example: A cancer treatment center can develop an AI-powered chatbot to answer frequently asked questions about side effects, manage appointment scheduling, and offer basic emotional support. They can also create an online forum where patients can share their experiences, connect with others facing similar challenges, and provide feedback on their care journey.

Step 4: Build Trust and Transparency:

- **Be Transparent About Data Practices and AI Usage**: Communicate how patient data is collected, used, and protected, ensuring responsible AI implementation.
- **Address Privacy Concerns Proactively**: Actively address potential concerns about data privacy and algorithmic bias, demonstrating a commitment to the ethical use of AI.
- **Emphasize Human Touch and Empathy**: Ensure AI-powered interactions complement, not replace, human interaction and compassionate care from healthcare professionals.

Example: The hospital can publish detailed privacy policies, explain how AI personalizes communication, and actively address patient concerns about AI use in healthcare. Additionally, they can train healthcare professionals to effectively interact with patients who have used AI-powered tools or resources.

Step 5: Continuously Measure and Improve:

- **Track Engagement Metrics**: Monitor patient portal usage, chatbot interactions, and participation in online communities to assess engagement with AI-powered tools.
- **Gather Feedback through Surveys and Interviews**: Regularly solicit patient feedback on their experience with communication, personalization, and overall level of engagement.
- **Refine Your Approach Based on Data and Feedback**: Continuously adapt your segmentation, content personalization, and AI-powered tools based on insights and evolving patient needs and preferences.

Remember:

- **AI Should Empower, not Replace**: The human connection between patients and healthcare professionals remains essential. AI should enhance communication, support, and empower patients to actively participate in their healthcare journey.
- **Focus on Building Trust and Empathy**: Transparency, ethical data practices, and prioritizing patient well-being are crucial for building lasting relationships.
- **Data Privacy and Security are Paramount**: Ensure responsible data collection, use, and protection to preserve patient trust and privacy.

By following these steps and leveraging AI responsibly, you can build stronger, more personalized relationships with patients, improving health outcomes, increased patient satisfaction, and a more collaborative approach to healthcare.

Pharma and AI Building Lasting Relationships with Patients – A Step-by-Step Guide

While pharma companies may not have direct relationships with individual patients, fostering trust and positive perceptions among patients is crucial for brand reputation, product adoption, and successful patient outcomes. Here's how AI can help build these lasting relationships:

Step 1: Understand Patient Needs and Concerns:

- **Analyze Social Media Discussions and Online Forums**: Utilize AI-powered sentiment analysis to understand patient concerns, hopes, and experiences related to specific conditions and treatments.
- **Partner with Patient Advocacy Groups**: Collaborate with relevant organizations to gain deeper insights into specific patient populations' needs and challenges.
- **Analyze Real-World Data**: Leverage anonymized patient data sources (e.g., electronic health records) to understand medication adherence rates, side effects, and treatment outcomes.

Example: A pharmaceutical company developing a new diabetes medication can analyze online forums to understand patient frustrations with current options, their desired features in a new drug, and potential concerns about side effects. Collaborating with diabetic patient advocacy groups can provide deeper insights into the population's needs and challenges.

Step 2: Offer Personalized Patient Support and Resources:

- **Develop AI-powered Chatbots**: Design chatbots to answer frequently asked questions, provide basic education about conditions and medications, and connect patients with relevant resources.
- **Personalize Patient Education Materials**: Leverage AI to tailor educational content (e.g., videos, infographics) based

on individual patient demographics, medical history, and learning preferences.

- **Facilitate Peer-to-Peer Support**: Utilize AI-moderated online communities where patients can connect, share experiences, and encourage each other.

Example: The diabetes medication company can develop a chatbot to answer questions about their new medication, its side effects, and how to manage diabetes effectively. AI can then personalize education materials about blood sugar control or healthy eating habits based on patient needs and preferences. Additionally, they can create an online community for patients taking the medication to connect, share tips, and support each other.

Step 3: Foster Transparency and Trust:

- **Be Transparent About Data Practices and AI Usage**: Communicate how patient data is collected, used, and protected, ensuring compliance with regulations and ethical considerations.
- **Address Patient Concerns About AI and Data Privacy**: Proactively address potential concerns about data security, algorithmic bias, and how AI is used in patient interactions.
- **Partner with Patients in Research and Development**: Engage patients in clinical trials, advisory boards, or co-creation initiatives to build trust and incorporate their perspectives.

Example: The company can publish detailed data privacy policies, explain how AI is used to personalize patient support, and actively address concerns about data security. They can also involve patients in advisory boards to inform the development of future patient support tools and educational materials.

Step 4: Measure and Refine Your Approach:

- **Track Patient Engagement Metrics**: Monitor chatbot interactions, usage of educational materials, and participation in online communities to assess patient engagement with AI-powered tools.

- **Gather Feedback Through Surveys and Interviews**: Regularly solicit patient feedback on their experience with patient support resources, educational materials, and overall satisfaction with the pharma company.
- **Refine Your AI Tools and Communication Based on Data and Feedback**: Continuously adapt your communication strategies based on patient needs, preferences, and technological advancements.

Remember:

- **Focus on Patient Empowerment, Not Marketing**: Use AI to empower patients with knowledge, support, and resources, not solely promote your products.
- **Empathy and Human Connection are Crucial**: AI should complement, not replace, human interaction and empathy in patient support initiatives.
- **Ethical Considerations are Paramount**: Ensure responsible data collection, transparency, and alignment with patient well-being in all AI-driven initiatives.

By following these steps and leveraging AI responsibly, pharma companies can build trust, empathy, and lasting relationships with patients, ultimately contributing to better health outcomes and a more patient-centric approach to healthcare.

Building Lasting Relationships with Payers with AI: A Step-by-Step Guide

Developing strong, collaborative relationships with payers is crucial for pharmaceutical companies to ensure market access, optimize reimbursement, and navigate an increasingly complex healthcare landscape. Here's a step-by-step guide exploring how AI can enhance each step:

Step 1: Understand Their Needs and Priorities:

- **Analyze Payer Reports and Public Filings**: Gain insights into payers' strategic objectives, cost-containment measures, and preferred therapeutic areas.
- **Engage in Dialogue with Key Stakeholders:** Build relationships with payer decision-makers by understanding their needs, evaluation criteria, and preferred communication channels.
- **Leverage Market Research and Industry Trends**: Stay informed about evolving payer landscapes, reimbursement policies, and emerging technologies impacting access and pricing.

Example: A medical device company seeking reimbursement for a new heart failure treatment can analyze public reports to understand payers' focus on cost-effectiveness and quality of care. Engaging with payer representatives can reveal their specific evaluation criteria for new technology and preferred submission data formats. Additionally, monitoring industry trends can uncover the impact of digital health integration on reimbursement policies.

Step 2: Segment and Personalize Value Proposition:

- **Segment Payers Based on Size, Region, and Therapeutic Focus**: Tailor communication and evidence packages to align with each payer's specific priorities and patient population.
- **Utilize AI for Data-Driven Insights**: Leverage AI to analyze claims data, patient demographics, and competitor analysis to identify high-value segments and predict potential payer responses.
- **Develop Personalized Pricing and Contracting Strategies**: Tailor pricing models and contracting terms based on each payer's needs and willingness to pay.

Examples: The device company can segment payers by size (national vs. regional) and focus on those specializing in cardiovascular care. AI analysis can reveal which payer segments value cost savings the most and predict potential challenges based on past reimbursement decisions for similar technologies. Based on these insights, the company can personalize cost-effectiveness models and propose innovative contracting options aligned with specific payer needs.

Step 3: Offer Value Beyond Products:

- **Provide Real-World Data and Patient Outcomes**: Utilize AI to analyze real-world data and generate insights demonstrating the value and cost-effectiveness of your product compared to alternatives.
- **Develop Collaborative Research Initiatives**: Partner with payers on research projects to co-create solutions addressing their specific concerns, like reducing readmissions or improving patient adherence.
- **Offer Digital Health Integration and Value-Based Care Solutions**: Leverage AI to develop digital tools that seamlessly integrate with payer platforms and support value-based care initiatives.

Example: The company can leverage AI to analyze real-world data showing how their device reduces long-term hospital stays for heart failure patients, presenting this data to specific payers interested in cost savings. Additionally, they can partner with payers on research projects studying the impact of the device on patient readmissions, demonstrating its value for both parties. Furthermore, they can develop AI-powered tools that integrate with payer platforms to track patient adherence and generate predictive models for potential complications, contributing to value-based care initiatives.

Step 4: Build Trust and Transparency:

- **Be Transparent About Data Practices and AI Usage**: Communicate how you collect, use, and protect payer data to ensure responsible AI implementation.

- **Address Payer Concerns About Data Privacy and Algorithmic Bias**: Proactively address potential concerns about data security, algorithmic fairness, and how AI is used in payer interactions.
- **Maintain Open and Honest Communication**: Foster ongoing dialogue with payers, actively listen to their feedback, and respond promptly to inquiries.

Example: The company can publish detailed data privacy policies, explain how AI is used to analyze data and generate insights, and actively address payer concerns about potential bias in algorithms. They can also establish advisory boards with payer representatives to ensure transparency and ethical use of AI in their interactions.

Step 5: Continuously Measure and Improve:

- **Track Key Performance Indicators (KPIs)**: Monitor metrics like market access rates, reimbursement levels, and payer satisfaction to assess the effectiveness of your relationship-building strategies.
- **Gather Feedback Through Surveys and Interviews**: Regularly solicit feedback from payers on their experience with your communication, data insights, and overall collaboration.
- **Refine Your Approach Based on Data and Feedback**: Continuously adapt your segmentation, value proposition, and AI-powered tools based on insights and evolving payer needs and preferences.

Remember:

- **AI is a Tool, Not a Replacement**: Genuine relationships and transparent communication with payers remain essential for building trust and collaboration.
- **Focus on Mutual Benefit**: Your approach should demonstrate how your products and solutions contribute to payers' goals of cost-effectiveness, improved patient outcomes, and better population health management.

- **Long-Term Commitment is Key**: Building lasting relationships with payers requires consistent engagement, continuous value creation, and adaptability to a dynamic healthcare landscape.

Additional Considerations:

- **Compliance with Regulations and Ethical Standards**: Ensure all data collection, analysis, and communication with payers comply with relevant regulations and adhere to ethical principles.
- **Explainability and Interpretability of AI Insights**: Choose AI models that clearly explain their outputs, fostering trust and understanding with payers.
- **Human-in-the-Loop Approach**: Leverage AI insights to inform, not replace, human decision-making and relationship-building with payers.

Examples Across Payer Types:

- **For Commercial Payers**: Tailor value propositions to fit their cost-containment priorities, leverage real-world data to demonstrate cost-effectiveness, and explore innovative contracting models.
- **For Government Payers**: Collaborate on research projects aligned with public health goals, provide data insights supporting population health management initiatives, and demonstrate adherence to specific regulatory requirements.
- **For Managed Care Organizations (MCOs)**: Develop integrated care solutions that fit within their care delivery models, personalize communication-based on patient populations, and offer data-driven insights to support value-based care initiatives.

By following these guidelines and leveraging AI ethically and responsibly, pharmaceutical companies can build strong, collaborative relationships with payers, ultimately leading to improved market access, optimized reimbursement, and a more sustainable healthcare ecosystem for all.

Building Lasting Relationships with Regulators with AI: A Step-by-Step Guide

Navigating the regulatory landscape is crucial for any industry, and building positive, collaborative relationships with regulators is key to ensuring smooth product approvals, market access, and long-term success. Here's a step-by-step guide on how AI can enhance your efforts:

Step1: Understand Their Priorities and Processes:

- **Analyze Regulatory Guidance Documents and Public Statements** to gain insights into regulators' current priorities, concerns, and preferred approaches to data analysis and scientific evidence.
- **Engage with Regulatory Representatives**: Build relationships with key decision-makers within regulatory agencies to understand their internal processes, communication preferences, and evaluation criteria.
- **Monitor Regulatory Trends and Emerging Technologies**: Stay informed about evolving regulatory landscapes, potential policy changes, and AI's impact on regulatory processes.

Example: A medical device company developing a novel diagnostic tool can analyze recent FDA guidance documents on AI-powered medical devices to understand their evaluation criteria and preferred data formats. Engaging with FDA representatives can offer insights into their internal review processes and potential concerns about algorithmic bias. Additionally, monitoring industry trends can reveal the impact of AI on regulatory frameworks for diagnostic tools.

Step 2: Proactive and Transparent Communication:

- **Maintain Open Communication Channels**: Regularly engage with regulators throughout the development and submission process, proactively addressing potential concerns and providing timely updates.

- **Utilize AI for Data-Driven Submissions**: Leverage AI to organize, analyze, and visualize massive datasets effectively, providing regulators with clear, well-structured evidence.
- **Develop Explainable AI Models**: Choose AI models that clearly explain their outputs, fostering trust and understanding with regulators regarding AI-driven insights.

Example: The company can establish regular meetings with FDA officials to discuss the development process, anticipated submissions, and potential changes. They can utilize AI to analyze clinical trial data and generate comprehensive reports highlighting the device's safety and efficacy in a clear, digestible format for regulators. Additionally, they can use explainable AI models to demonstrate how the diagnostic tool arrives at its results, addressing potential concerns about algorithmic bias.

Step 3: Demonstrate Rigorous Science and Ethical AI Practices:

- **Adhere to Regulatory Guidelines and Best Practices**: Ensure all data collection, analysis, and development processes comply with relevant regulatory and ethical standards.
- **Be Transparent About Data Privacy and Security Practices**: Communicate how you collect, use, and protect patient data, demonstrating responsible use of AI throughout the development process.
- **Address Potential Ethical Concerns About AI**: Proactively address concerns about algorithmic fairness, bias, and interpretability in your AI-powered tools and data analysis methodologies.

Example: The company can publish detailed data privacy policies, explain how AI is used in development, and actively address regulatory concerns about potential bias in its algorithms. They can also participate in industry efforts to establish ethical guidelines for AI use in medical devices, demonstrating their commitment to responsible development and regulatory compliance.

Step 4: Build Long-Term Collaboration and Trust:

- **Partner with Regulators on Research Initiatives**: Collaborate on research projects exploring the potential of AI in healthcare, contributing to regulatory knowledge and demonstrating your commitment to innovation.
- **Provide Ongoing Education and Support**: Offer training sessions or workshops to educate regulators on how your AI-powered tools work and address their potential concerns.
- **Be Receptive to Feedback and Adapt Your Approach**: Continuously seek and actively listen to feedback from regulators, adapting your communication, data analysis methods, and AI tools based on their insights.

Example: The company can partner with the FDA on research projects exploring the use of AI in medical diagnostics, contributing to developing regulatory frameworks for such technologies. They can also offer training sessions for FDA officials on their specific AI-powered tools and actively solicit feedback on their data analysis methods and regulatory submissions.

Remember:

- **AI is a Tool, Not a Replacement**: Building genuine relationships and trust with regulators requires human interaction, transparency, and open communication.
- **Focus on Data Quality and Scientific Rigor**: Ensure your data analysis and AI-powered tools are based on high-quality data and adhere to sound scientific principles.
- **Ethical Considerations are Paramount**: Responsible data collection, transparency, and alignment with regulatory and ethical standards are crucial for building lasting relationships with regulators.

By following these steps and leveraging AI responsibly, companies can foster positive, collaborative relationships with regulators, achieving smoother approvals, market access, and a more efficient and innovative healthcare ecosystem.

Additional Considerations:

- **Adapt Your Approach Based on Scientific Regulatory Agencies**: Tailor your communication strategies and AI-powered tools to align with the requirements and priorities of each relevant regulatory agency.
- **Stay Informed About Evolving Regulatory Landscapes**: Continuously monitor changes in regulations and policies relevant to AI use in your industry to ensure compliance and adapt your approach accordingly.
- **Build a Culture of Compliance and Ethical AI Practices**: Embed responsible AI use in your company culture.

Building Lasting Relationships with Investors with AI: A Step-by-Step Guide

Securing and fostering strong investor relationships is crucial for any company seeking growth and long-term success. But how can AI help build lasting relationships beyond just attracting initial investment? Here's a step-by-step guide:

Step 1: Understand Their Needs and Priorities:

- **Analyze Investor Reports and Public Statements**: Gain insights into their investment theses, preferred industries, and risk tolerance levels.
- **Engage Directly with Potential and Existing Investors**: Build relationships by understanding their specific objectives, concerns, and preferred communication channels.
- **Monitor Market Trends and Investor Sentiment**: Stay informed about evolving market conditions, emerging technologies, and their impact on investor decisions.

Example: A biotech startup developing a new cancer treatment can analyze recent investment reports from health-care-focused venture capitalists to understand their priorities in cancer therapeutics. Engaging with these investors can reveal their specific investment criteria, risk tolerance for early-stage ventures, and preferred communication formats (e.g., detailed data packages and concise investor decks). Additionally, monitoring industry trends can highlight how AI and personalized medicine influence investment decisions in the biotech sector.

Step 2: Foster Transparency and Trust:

- **Provide Regular and Accurate Updates on Company Performance**: Utilize AI for data-driven reports and visualizations to communicate progress, milestones achieved, and plans.
- **Be Transparent About Risks and Challenges**: Proactively address potential hurdles, mitigation strategies, and your approach to navigating uncertainties.
- **Maintain Open Communication Channels**: Encourage questions, feedback, and investor dialogue, demonstrating your commitment to accountability and partnership.

Example: The startup can leverage AI to analyze clinical trial data and generate insightful reports showcasing the therapeutic potential of their treatment. They can also utilize AI-powered visualization tools to present complex data on market size, competitor landscape, and projected financials in a clear, digestible format for investors. Additionally, they can host regular webinars or Q&A sessions to address investor concerns and foster open communication.

Step 3: Offer Personalized Value and Insights:

- **Segment Investors Based on Their Interests and Risk Profiles**: Tailor communication, financial projections, and data-driven insights resonate with each investor's needs.
- **Utilize AI for Sentiment Analysis and Predictive Modeling**: Gain deeper insights into investor concerns and anticipate

potential questions, proactively providing relevant information and addressing potential objections.

- **Develop Investor-Specific Materials and Presentations**: Leverage AI to personalize financial models, market analysis reports, and investment proposals based on each investor's interests and risk appetite.

Example: The biotech company can segment its investor base by focusing on those interested in early-stage oncology ventures with high-growth potential. AI can then analyze investor communication to identify potential concerns about market competition or regulatory approval timelines. With these insights, the company can create personalized presentations highlighting its competitive advantages and mitigation strategies for potential risks.

Step 4: Demonstrate Long-Term Value Creation:

- **Focus on Metrics that Align with Investor Objectives**: Highlight key performance indicators (KPIs) that matter most to your targeted investors, such as patient enrollment rates, technology advancements, or strategic partnerships.
- **Utilize AI for Scenario Planning and Risk Management**: Leverage AI to model different market scenarios and demonstrate your preparedness for future challenges, enhancing investor confidence.
- **Showcase Your Commitment to Sustainable Growth**: Highlight your long-term vision, ethical practices, and environment/social impact, aligning with values increasingly important to investors.

Example: The Company can showcase its commitment to patient well-being by highlighting ongoing clinical trials and real-world data analysis conducted with ethically sourced patient data. Additionally, they can use AI to model different market adoption scenarios and present mitigation strategies for potential risks, demonstrating their resilience and preparedness for various market conditions.

Step 5: Build Ongoing Relationships and Trust:

- **Participate in Relevant Industry Events and Conferences**: Engage with potential and existing investors through networking opportunities and presentations.
- **Provide Ongoing Support and Education**: Offer exclusive webinars, data access, or early insights to foster deeper connections and demonstrate value beyond financial returns.
- **Actively Seek Feedback and Adapt Your Approach**: Regularly solicit feedback from investors and utilize it to refine your communication, data analysis methods, and overall investor engagement strategy.

Example: The company can participate in industry conferences focused on oncology and personalized medicine, presenting their advancements and engaging with potential investors. They can also offer exclusive access to anonymized clinical trial data or AI-powered insights into market trends for their existing investor base, demonstrating transparency and commitment to value creation. Additionally, they can actively seek feedback through surveys or meetings, utilizing these insights to refine their investor communication and engagement strategies.

Remember:

- **AI is a Tool, Not a Replacement**: Genuine relationships and trust with investors require human interaction, transparency, and open communication.
- **Focus on Long-Term Value Creation**: Building lasting relationships goes beyond short-term financial gains. Demonstrate your commitment to innovation, social responsibility, and sustainable growth to align with evolving investor priorities.
- **Ethical Considerations are Paramount**: To maintain investor trust and confidence, ensure responsible data collection, transparent AI practice, and alignment with industry best practices.

- **Adapt Your Approach Based on Investor Types**: Tailor your communication, data analysis, and AI-powered tools to resonate with different investor segments, such as venture capitalists, angel investors, or institutional investors.

Additional Considerations:

- **Leverage Social Media and Online Communities:** Utilize platforms like LinkedIn to connect with investors, share relevant content, and engage in meaningful discussions.
- **Partner with Investor Relationship Firms:** Consider collaborating with experienced professionals to enhance your investor communication strategies and relationship management efforts.
- **Continuously Evaluate and Improve AI-powered Tools:** Ensure your AI models are updated with the latest data and provide accurate, unbiased insights to maintain investor trust and avoid potential biases.

By following these steps and leveraging AI responsibly, companies can build strong, lasting relationships with investors, secure valuable partnerships, foster long-term support, and achieve sustainable growth in a competitive market.

CHAPTER 18

Engaging with Stakeholders in the AI-Fueled Pharma Landscape

AI is transforming the internal workings of pharma companies and reshaping their relationships with external stakeholders. Let's delve into how AI can impact engagement with:

1. **HCPs:**

   Healthcare professional (HCP) engagement is a crucial piece of the puzzle in the future of pharma with AI. Here's how AI can revolutionize the way pharma companies interact with HCPs:

   Personalized Learning and Education:

   - **AI-Powered Adaptive Learning Platforms**: Tailored to individual HCPs' knowledge level and preferred learning styles, these platforms will offer targeted educational modules on new drugs, treatment protocols, and emerging medical advancements. Imagine HCPs accessing bite-sized, personalized learning experiences that fit their busy schedules and educational needs.
   - **Virtual Simulations and Immersive Training**: AI-powered VR simulations will put HCPs in realistic clinical scenarios, allowing them to practice diagnosis and treatment decisions and hone their skills in a safe and controlled environment. Imagine surgeons rehearsing complex procedures virtually before entering the operating room or physicians navigating rare disease cases through interactive simulations.

Enhanced Communication and Collaboration:

- **AI-Powered Medical Chatbots**: HCPs can access real-time drug information, answer patient inquiries, and even receive clinical decision support through chatbots that are available 24/7. Imagine busy physicians getting quick and accurate drug information at their fingertips or receiving AI-powered suggestions for potential diagnoses based on patient symptoms.
- **Personalized Medical Intelligence Platforms**: AI can analyze vast amounts of clinical data, patient registries, and real-world evidence to generate insights and personalized reports for HCPs on specific disease areas, treatment outcomes, and emerging trends. Imagine physicians accessing a personalized "knowledge vault" tailored to their practice areas, empowering them to make better-informed decisions.

Empowered Patient Care:

- **AI-Powered Shared Decision-Making Tools**: HCPs can use AI-powered visualization tools and decision aids to engage patients in interactive discussions about treatment options, potential risks and benefits, and personalized care plans. Imagine patients leaving consultations feeling empowered, with a clear understanding of their treatment options and a sense of shared decision-making with their healthcare provider.
- **Digital Therapeutics and AI-Powered Behavioral Interventions**: AI-powered apps and programs will offer patients personalized support for managing chronic conditions, adhering to medication regimens, and improving health outcomes. Imagine patients with diabetes receiving personalized exercise recommendations based on their blood sugar levels or individuals with depression participating in AI-guided cognitive behavioral therapy programs.

Of course, addressing ethical considerations like patient privacy, data security, and potential bias in algorithms is crucial. Transparency and collaboration between pharma companies, HCPs, and Patients will be paramount.

By harnessing the power of AI responsibly and collaboratively, we can build a future where HCPs have access to the latest knowledge and tools, allowing them to provide patients with personalized, evidence-based care. This, in turn, will lead to improved health outcomes and a more robust healthcare ecosystem for all.

2. **Patients:**

AI is transforming healthcare in many ways, and patient engagement is a key area where it's showing promise. Here are some ways AI helps optimize patient engagement:

Personalization and Targeting:

- **Identifying High-Risk Patients**: AI analyzes data to identify patients at risk of poor outcomes or non-adherence to treatment plans. This allows healthcare providers to prioritize outreach and interventions for those in need.
- **Tailored Communication**: AI-powered chatbots and educational tools can deliver personalized messages and resources based on individual needs and preferences, making information more relevant and engaging for patients.
- **Predictive Analytics**: AI can predict future health risks and behaviors, allowing for proactive interventions and preventive care. For example, AI can predict which patients are most likely to miss appointments and send them reminders beforehand.

Improved Communication and Convenience:

- **Chatbots and Virtual Assistants**: AI chatbots can answer basic questions, schedule appointments, and complete administrative tasks, freeing up healthcare providers' time for more complex interactions with patients.

- **Remote Monitoring**: AI-powered devices can track vital signs and health data remotely, allowing for early detection of problems and improved communication between patients and providers.
- **24/7 Support**: AI-powered tools can provide patients access to information and support 24/7, even outside regular clinic hours.

Enhanced Care Experience:

- **Automated Follow-up**: AI can automate reminders and follow-up messages after appointments, ensuring patients stay on track with their care plans.
- **Self-Management Tools**: AI-powered tools can help patients manage their chronic conditions more effectively, leading to better health outcomes.
- **Translation and Accessibility Features**: AI can translate information into different languages and adapt it for different reading levels, making it accessible to a wider range of patients.

It's important to remember that AI is a tool, and its effectiveness depends on how it's used. Here are some key considerations:

- **Data Privacy and Security**: Patient data must be protected and used ethically.
- **Transparency and Explainability**: Patients should understand how AI is being used and what data is being collected.
- **Human Connection**: AI should not replace the human touch in healthcare. It should be used to enhance communication and collaboration between patients and providers.

Overall, AI has the potential to significantly improve patient engagement by making healthcare more personalized, convenient, and effective. However, it is important to use it responsibly and ethically to ensure it benefits all patients.

3. **Payers:**
   - **Value-Based Pricing and Outcomes-Driven Models**: AI can analyze real-world data to predict treatment costs and effectiveness, enabling personalized pricing models based on patient outcomes. Imagine pharma companies negotiating reimbursement for new drugs based on actual health improvements in specific patient populations.
   - **AI-Powered Disease Forecasting and Resource Allocation**: Payers can utilize AI to predict potential disease outbreaks and optimize resource allocation, ensuring efficient healthcare spending. Imagine predicting flu seasons weeks in advance, allowing for targeted vaccination campaigns and reducing the overall burden on healthcare systems.
4. **Regulators:**
   - **AI-Powered Risk Assessment and Safety Monitoring**: AI algorithms can analyze vast amounts of safety data from clinical trials and real-world use, enabling proactive identification and mitigation of potential adverse events. Imagine regulators having access to real-time safety signals, allowing for swift interventions and improved patient safety.
   - **Streamlined Approvals and Regulatory Processes**: AI can automate parts of the regulatory review processes, like data analysis and document verification, speeding up drug approvals without compromising safety standards. Imagine faster access to innovative treatments for patients in dire need.
5. **Investors:**
   - **AI-Powered Drug Discovery and Development Platforms**: Investors can analyze AI-driven prediction models to assess the potential success of new drug candidates and make informed investment decisions.

Imagine identifying highly promising drug candidates early on, attracting investors, and accelerating their development.

- **Predictive Market Analytics and Demand Forecasting**: AI can analyze market trends and patient data to predict future demand for specific drugs, helping investors identify potentially lucrative opportunities. Imagine investors having access to a crystal ball predicting which therapies will be the next big breakthroughs.

AI holds immense potential to reshape Pharma's relationships with external stakeholders, promoting value-based healthcare, efficient resource allocation, faster drug development, and informed investment decisions. However, navigating ethical considerations, ensuring transparency, and fostering collaboration will be crucial to ensuring AI benefits all stakeholders and contributes to a healthier future for all.

Cultivating Lasting Connections with AI

The potential of AI to transform stakeholder engagement and relationship building is undeniable. By leveraging its data analysis, personalization, and automation capabilities, organizations can navigate the complexities of stakeholder interactions more effectively. However, genuine and lasting relationships require more than just technological prowess.

Building trust and respect with stakeholders remains paramount. This necessitates responsible AI practices, transparency in data usage, and a human-centered approach that values genuine communication and empathy. As you embark on your AI-powered stakeholder engagement journey, remember:

- **Focus on Value Creation**: Every interaction with a stakeholder should offer value, be it through insightful data-driven insights, personalized engagement, or simply demonstrating a genuine understanding of their needs.

- **Build Human Connections**: AI should complement, not replace, human interaction. Foster meaningful conversations, actively listen to feedback, and build trust through transparency and honesty.
- **Continuously Adapt and Evolve**: The stakeholder landscape is dynamic. Regularly measure your efforts, gather feedback, and be willing to adapt your AI-powered tools and strategies based on evolving needs and emerging technologies.

By embracing AI thoughtfully and ethically, organizations can cultivate deeper, more meaningful relationships with their stakeholders, creating a foundation for sustainable success in an increasingly complex and interconnected world. Remember, AI is a powerful tool, but the human touch builds lasting connections.

CHAPTER 19

AI-Powered Personalization

Let's dive into the fascinating world of AI-powered personalization in pharma marketing, where human empathy meets technological precision to craft unique experiences for patients, HCPs, and payers. This chapter will guide you in navigating the entire spectrum of personalized marketing, from audience segmentation and persona creation to delivering targeted, impactful campaigns.

1. **Unveiling the Layers: Personalized Segmentation and Personas**
   - **Beyond Demographics**: AI analyzes vast data sets, encompassing medical records, social media interactions, and online behavior, to segment patients, HCPs, and payers based on deeper insights and psychographics.
   - **Patient Personas**: AI helps create rich patient personas, understanding their medical conditions, anxieties, motivations, and preferred communication channels. Think Sarah, the tech-savvy diabetes patient seeking discreet support tools, or John, the anxious cancer survivor needing empathetic guidance.
   - **HCP Profiles**: AI builds nuanced profiles of HCPs, factoring in their area of expertise, treatment preferences, and learning styles. Imagine Dr. Lee, the data-driven cardiologist, and

Dr Garcia, the relationship-oriented oncologist, each requiring tailored educational content.

- **Payer Insights**: AI uncovers different payer segments' priorities and decision-making processes, including cost-conscious PBMs (Pharmacy Benefit Managers) and value-driven health insurers.

2. **Orchestrating the Content: The AI-Powered Personalization Process:**
   - **Dynamic Content Generation**: AI generates personalized content, crafting articles, infographics, and videos aligned with specific patient personas, HCP profiles, and payer needs. Imagine targeted blog posts for anxious cancer survivors or interactive learning modules for data-driven cardiologists.
   - **Real-Time Relevance:** AI analyzes real-time data, like medication adherence or treatment response, to dynamically adjust content and recommendations, ensuring ongoing relevance and impact.
   - **Multi-Channel Delivery**: AI optimizes content delivery across preferred channels, from email and social media to mobile apps and in-clinic experiences for seamless engagement.

3. **Symphony of Action: Targeted and Personalized Campaigns:**
   - **Patient Engagement Campaigns**: AI personalizes patient outreach, delivering targeted educational materials, medication reminders, and support resources based on individual needs and preferences. Imagine Sarah receiving discreet text message reminders or John accessing a personalized online support group.
   - **HCP-Focused Initiatives**: AI tailors educational webinars, clinical trial opportunities, and product information to specific

HCP profiles, fostering deeper engagement and knowledge sharing. Think Dr. Lee receiving AI-powered data summaries or Dr. Garcia connecting with relevant patient testimonials.

- **Payer Partnerships**: AI facilitates data-driven collaborations with payers, developing personalized disease management programs and value-based payment models that benefit patients and healthcare systems.

4. **The Human Touch: Ethical Considerations and Collaborative Harmony:**
   - **Transparency and Trust**: Maintaining transparency about data usage and ensuring patient privacy are paramount to building trust.
   - **Human Oversight and Accountability**: AI is a powerful tool, but human expertise and ethical principles guide its application and decision-making.
   - **Collaborative Synergy**: Combining humans' creativity and empathy with AI's analytical power leads to the most effective and ethical personalization strategies.

By embracing AI-powered personalization, pharma companies can forge genuine connections with patients, HCPs, and payers, transforming marketing from one-size-fits-all messaging to a symphony of tailored experiences that empower individuals, improve healthcare outcomes, and ultimately contribute to a healthier future.

This chapter is just the beginning of the personalized pharmaceutical marketing revolution. Feel free to ask further questions about specific aspects, such as AI platforms used for segmentation, ethical considerations for patient data, or practical examples of personalized campaigns for each audience segment. This chapter aims to inspire readers to embrace the transformative power of human+AI synergy in pharmaceutical marketing.

Remember, the future of pharma marketing is not about technology alone but about leveraging it to build meaningful connections and empower individuals to take charge of their health. Let's create a future where healthcare is truly personalized, patient-centric, and driven by the harmonious symphony of human empathy and AI intelligence.

Personalization Powerhouse: Deep Dives into Each Facet

We have laid the groundwork for a comprehensive chapter on AI-powered personalization in pharma marketing. Now. Let's delve deeper into each facet, unveiling the intricate workings and potential of this game-changing approach:

1. **Unveiling the Layers:**
   - **Beyond Demographics**: Move past age and location. AI analyzes medical records databases, social media interactions, online behavior, and treatment profiles to identify subtle patterns and hidden connections. Imagine uncovering clusters of patients based on medication adherence patterns, preferred information sources, or emotional responses to treatments.
   - **Patient Personas**: AI helps craft rich, multidimensional patient personas. It helps understand medical conditions, anxieties, motivations, and preferred communication channels. Think Sarah, the tech-savvy diabetes patient struggling with discreetly managing her condition, or John, the anxious cancer survivor seeking emotional support and community.
   - **HCP Profiles**: Go beyond specialties. AI builds nuanced profiles of HCPs, factoring in their areas of expertise, treatment preferences, learning styles, and technological adoption. Imagine Dr. Lee, the data-driven cardiologist who thrives on interactive case studies, and Dr. Garcia, the relationship-oriented oncologist who connects best through patient testimonials and shared stories.
   - **Payer Insights**: Unmask the complexities of payer landscapes. AI analyzes claims data, cost models, and

regulatory frameworks to understand different payer segments' priorities and decision-making processes. Imagine identifying cost-conscious PBMs seeking medication adherence solutions and value-driven health insurers focused on preventative care initiatives.

2. **Orchestrating the Content: The AI-Powered Personalization Process**
   - **Dynamic Content Generation**: AI isn't just repurposing generic content. It crafts articles, infographics, videos, and educational materials tailored to specific personas and needs. Imagine personalized blog posts outlining coping strategies for anxious cancer survivors or interactive learning modules for data-driven cardiologists delving into specific clinical trial data.
   - **Real-Time Relevance**: AI analyzes real-time data, like medication adherence or treatment response, to dynamically adjust content and recommendations. Imagine Sarah receiving customized tips on improving adherence based on her recent challenges or Dr. Lee's personalized dashboard updating with relevant clinical trial results as new data emerges.
   - **Multichannel Delivery**: AI optimizes content delivery across preferred channels. Mobile apps, social media, email, and in-clinic experiences are seamlessly integrated to ensure the right message reaches the right person at the right time. Imagine John searching for a personalized support group forum on his phone while Sarah receives discreet medication reminders via text message.

3. **Symphony in Action: Targeted and Personalized Campaigns:**
   - **Patient Engagement Campaigns:** AI personalizes patient outreach, delivering targeted educational materials, medication reminders, and support resources based on

individual needs and preferences. Imagine Sarah receiving discreet text message reminders or John accessing a personalized online support group tailored to his concerns.

- **HCP-Focused Initiatives**: AI tailors educational webinars, clinical trial opportunities, and product information to specific HCP profiles, fostering deeper engagement and knowledge sharing. Think Dr. Lee receiving AI-powered data summaries of relevant clinical trials or Dr. Garcia connecting with patient testimonials that align with her empathetic approach.
- **Payer Partnerships**: AI facilitates data-driven collaborations with payers, developing personalized disease management programs and value-based payment models that benefit patients and healthcare systems. Imagine co-creating medication adherence programs with PBMs based on AI-driven patient segmentation or developing cost-effective preventative care initiatives with health insurers using predictive modeling.

4. **The Human Touch: Ethical Considerations and Collaborative Harmony**
   - **Transparency and Trust**: Maintaining transparency about data usage and ensuring patient privacy are crucial to building trust. Communicate how data is used to personalize experiences and always offer opt-out options.
   - **Human Oversight and Accountability**: AI is a powerful tool, but human expertise and ethical principles guide its application and decision-making. Regularly assess algorithms for bias, ensure fairness in content generation, and prioritize human understanding over blind automation.
   - **Collaborative Synergy**: The magic lies in combining humans' creativity and empathy with AI's analytical power. Let human insights steer persona development, content creation, and campaign goals while AI fuels data-driven targeting and real-time optimization.

Remember, personalization is not just about technology; it's about building empathy, trust, and genuine connections. Each facet of this approach offers a treasure trove of examples, specific AI applications, and ethical considerations to explore. Personalization is not just a buzzword but a true symphony of individual engagement and empowered healthcare.

Personalized Personas: Unveiling the Minds and Motivations

Personalization thrives on understanding your audience. Let's delve into detailed profiles of patients, oncologists, and payers, exploring their hopes, needs, and preferred interactions with pharma companies:

1. **Patient Profile: Sarah, the Tech-Savvy Diabetic**
    - **Demographics:** 32-year-old female, working professional, living in an urban area.
    - **Medical Condition:** Type 1 diabetes diagnosed at age 10.
    - **Challenges:** Managing insulin injections discreetly at work, finding reliable support resources, and staying motivated with long-term treatment.
    - **Tech-Savvy:** Uses smartphones, health apps, and social media extensively.
    - **Communication Preferences:** Personalized content delivered through mobile app notifications, text messages, and interactive online platforms.
    - **Engagement Style:** Appreciates practical tips, discreet support options, and data-driven insights into her health.
    - **Pharma Value:** Sarah seeks discreet support tools, personalized medication reminders, and access to online communities for sharing experiences and learning from others.
2. **Oncologist Profile: Dr. Lee, the Data-Driven Cardiologist**
    - **Specialty:** Cardiology.
    - **Years of Experience:** 15 years.

- **Practice Focus:** Precision medicine and data-driven decision-making.
- **Information Sources:** Clinical research journals, industry conferences, and peer-to-peer networks.
- **Learning Style:** Prefers interactive learning modules, detailed analysis of clinical trial data, and real-time case studies.
- **Communication Preferences:** Secure online platforms for accessing personalized educational materials and data updates.
- **Engagement Style:** Seeks evidence-based insights, personalized treatment recommendations, and opportunities to contribute to research and knowledge sharing.
- **Pharma Value:** Dr. Lee values AI-powered data summaries, cutting-edge clinical trial data access, and collaborative research opportunities with pharma companies.

3. **Payer Profile: Ms. Garcia, the Value-Driven Health Insurance Executive**
    - **Role:** Director of Population Health Management at a large health insurance company.
    - **Focus:** Cost-effectiveness, preventative care, and improving patient outcomes.
    - **Priorities:** Managing healthcare costs, optimizing medication utilization, and promoting healthy lifestyles.
    - **Data Utilization:** Analyzes claims data, population trends, and cost models to inform decision-making
    - **Communication Preferences:** Secure data-sharing platforms, collaborative workshops, and presentations showcasing evidence-based solutions.
    - **Engagement Style:** Prefers data-driven insights, cost-effectiveness analyses, and personalized proposals for joint initiatives with pharma companies.

- **Pharma Value:** Ms. Garcia seeks partnerships to develop value-based payment models, co-create medication adherence programs, and implement preventative care initiatives with measurable outcomes.

These are just a few examples, and the possibilities are endless. Remember, personalizing goes beyond basic demographics. By understanding each segment's deeper motivations, preferred communication styles, and specific needs, pharma companies can craft truly valuable and impactful interactions.

Crafting a Symphony of Personalization: Step-by-Step Guide to Targeted Campaigns

Identifying patient, HCP, and payer personas is the foundation, but the magic happens when you translate these insights into targeted, personalized campaigns. Here's a step-by-step guide to guide your process:

Step 1: Define Campaign Goals and Objectives:

- **Patient Focus:** Are you aiming to improve medication adherence, promote healthy lifestyle choices, or raise awareness about a new treatment option?
- **HCP Focus:** Do you want to educate about a new drug, encourage the adoption of clinical guidelines, or facilitate participation in clinical trials?
- **Payer Focus:** Are you looking to implement a value-based payment model, improve medication utilization, or promote preventative care initiatives?

Step 2: Leverage Persona Insights for Targeting:

- **Patient Segment:** Use AI to identify specific patient subgroups based on their traits, like Sarah's tech-savviness or John's need for emotional support.

- **HCP Specialization and Learning Style:** Target Dr. Lee with data-driven presentations and Dr. Tracy Garcia with patient testimonials based on their preferences.
- **Payer Priorities and Data Utilization:** Align your campaign with Ms. Garcia's focus on cost-effectiveness and data-driven solutions.

Step 3: Craft Personalized Content and Messaging:

- **Content Tailor-Made:** Create content that resonates with each persona's interests, challenges, and preferred communication channels.
- **Personalized Tone and Language:** Adapt your tone to match each segment's emotional state and communication style.
- **Data-Driven Insights:** Integrate personalized data points like medication adherence or risk factors into content for relevant patients.

Step 4: Choose the Right Delivery Channels:

- **Multichannel Approach:** Utilize a combination of channels Sarah frequents, like mobile apps and text messages, and Dr. Lee's preferred platforms, like secure online platforms.
- **Consideration of Privacy:** Ensure data privacy and opt-out options are communicated, particularly for patient outreach.
- **Seamless Integration:** Create a cohesive experience across channels with consistent messaging and personalized content tailored to each touchpoint.

Step 5: Real-Time Optimization and A/B Testing:

- **Track Engagement and Response:** Monitor metrics like click-through rates, app downloads, or HCP interactions to gauge campaign effectiveness.
- **Continuously Optimize:** Use AI to analyze data and refine your content, targeting, and delivery based on real-time insights.

- **A/B Testing:** Test different content variations, delivery channels, and personalization elements to identify the most effective approach for each segment.

Step 5: Building Trust and Transparency:

- **Data Privacy and Security:** Be transparent about data usage, implement robust security measures, and prioritize ethical considerations.
- **Human-Centered Approach:** Always remember that AI is a tool to empower human connection, not replace it.
- **Open Communication:** Clearly explain goals and personalize information, fostering trust and understanding with your audience.

Remember, there is no one-size-fits-all approach. Continuously iterate, optimize, and learn from your audience to refine your targeting, personalize content, and deliver impactful campaigns that resonate with each persona. By embracing AI-powered personalization as a symphony of human empathy and technological precision, you can build stronger relationships, improve health outcomes, and revolutionize pharma marketing.

AI and Humans: A Symphony of Roles and Responsibilities

In personalized pharma marketing campaigns, AI and humans play distinct yet complementary roles, forming a powerful synergy that drives success. Let's delve deeper into their specific responsibilities:

AI's Strengths:

- **Data Analysis and Segmentation:** AI excels at crunching vast amounts of data from medical records, social media, and other sources, identifying hidden patterns, and segmenting patients, HCPs, and payers based on their unique characteristics and needs.
- **Content Personalization and Delivery:** AI can tailor content to each persona, crafting compelling messages, infographics,

and videos in the preferred format and language and delivering them through the most effective channels.

- **Real-Time Optimization and A/B Testing:** AI continuously monitors campaign performance, analyzing engagement metrics and optimizing content, targeting, and delivery strategies in real time for maximum impact.
- **Predictive Modeling and Insights:** AI can identify trends and predict patient behavior, allowing for proactive intervention and personalized support based on anticipated needs.

Human Strengths:

- **Strategic Direction and Ethical Guidance:** Humans set the overall campaign goals, ensuring they align with ethical considerations and patient well-being.
- **Creative Storytelling and Empathy:** Humans craft the campaign's emotional tone, inject empathy into content, and personalize messages to resonate with each audience segment.
- **Data Interpretation and Insights:** Humans interpret AI-generated data, providing context and drawing actionable insights to guide campaign decisions.
- **Human Oversight and Accountability:** Humans ensure data privacy and ethical use of AI, taking ultimate responsibility for campaign outcomes and ensuring alignment with regulatory guidelines.
- **Building Trust and Human Connection:** Humans foster trust by providing clear communication, explanations, and opportunities for feedback, enabling the campaign to be human-centered and supportive.

The Synergy of Collaboration:

The magic happens when AI and humans work together, leveraging their unique strengths to create personalized campaigns that are both effective and ethical.

Imagine:

- AI identifies Sarah's struggle with medication adherence and generates a personalized mobile app reminder with motivational messages tailored to her tech-savviness.
- Dr. Lee receives AI-powered data summaries of relevant clinical trials, while humans provide personalized interpretations and insights to inform his treatment recommendations.
- Ms. Garcia collaborates with AI to develop a cost-effective medication adherence program while human expertise guides the implementation and patient communication strategies.

By embracing this symphony of AI and human collaboration, pharmaceutical companies can unlock the full potential of personalized marketing. AI empowers data-driven insights and real-time optimization while humans ensure ethical guidance, empathy, and trust-building connections. Together, they can craft campaigns that resonate with individual needs, improve health outcomes, and revolutionize pharmaceutical marketing for a healthier future.

CHAPTER 20

AI-Powered Campaign Personalization in Pharma

AI-powered campaign personalization in pharma marketing revolves around using artificial intelligence to tailor marketing messages and content to specific audiences of healthcare professionals (HCPs) and patients. This level of personalization goes beyond traditional segmentation and aims to deliver highly relevant and impactful messaging at an individual level.

The campaign personalization in pharma marketing involves several factors, such as:

1. Data-Driven Audience Segmentation
2. Personalized Content Creation
3. Dynamic Content Optimization
4. Website Personalization
5. Targeted Email Marketing
6. Social Media Engagement
7. Programmatic Advertising
8. Mobile Marketing

Now, let's dive into each of these aspects:

1. **Data-Driven Audience Segmentation**

   Audience segmentation divides a broad customer base into smaller, more specific groups with similar needs, characteristics, and behaviors. Traditionally, segmentation might be based on demographics like age or gender. In pharmaceutical marketing, data-driven segmentation goes beyond basic demographics. Here is what sets it apart:

- **Rich Data Sources**: Pharma companies leverage a vast array of data sources, including:
  - Patient demographics and medical history.
  - HCP prescribing behavior and areas of specialization.
  - Online behavior on the company website and social media platforms.
  - Real-world data on medication usage and patient outcomes (once privacy considerations are addressed.
- **Advanced Analytics**: AI and machine learning algorithms analyze this data to identify hidden patterns and create highly granular audience segments.

Benefits of Data-Driven Segmentation in Pharma:

- **Targeted Communication**: Pharma companies can tailor their communication to resonate more deeply by understanding each segment's specific needs and preferences.
- **Personalized Content Creation**: Segmentation allows for targeted content (e.g., educational videos, blog posts) that address each group's concerns and information needs.
- **Improved Campaign Performance**: Targeted communication campaigns directed at specific segments tend to have higher engagement rates, leading to better conversions (e.g., medication adherence and HCP adoption of new treatments).
- **Resource Optimization**: By allocating marketing resources to the most relevant segments, pharma companies can maximize their return on investment (ROI).

Pharmaceutical Segmentation Examples:

Example 1: Targeting Patients with a New Asthma Medication:

- **Data Analysis might reveal patient segments with asthma based on the following**:
    - **The severity of the condition:** Mild, moderate, or severe.
    - **Trigger type:** Allergic asthma, exercise-induced asthma, etc.
- **Previous medication usage**:
    - New patients are not currently on any medication.
    - Patients using a different medication class.
- **The pharmaceutical company can then create targeted communication for each segment**:
    - **For newly diagnosed patients:** Educational content explaining asthma basics and treatment options.
    - **For Patients with severe asthma:** Information about how the new medication can manage their condition.
    - **For patients using a different medication class:** Content highlighting the advantages and potential benefits of switching to the new medication.

Example 2: Engaging Healthcare Professionals with a New Oncology Treatment:

- **Segmentation might consider factors like**:
    - **HCP specialty**: Oncologists, hematologists, etc.
    - **Geographic location**: Targeting HCPs in regions with a high prevalence of the specific cancer the new treatment addresses.
    - **Previous prescribing behavior**: Focusing on HCPs with a history of prescribing similar medications.
- **The company can then tailor outreach**:
    - **Webinars for oncologists**: Detailed presentations on the new treatment's clinical trials data and efficacy.

- **Targeted email campaigns for HCPs in high-prevalence regions**: Information about upcoming educational events and patient support services.
- **Detailed ad campaigns** showcasing the medication's benefits to HCPs with relevant prescribing history.

Conclusion:

Data-driven audience segmentation is a powerful tool for pharma marketing. By leveraging rich data and advanced analytics, pharmaceutical companies can create highly targeted communication strategies that resonate with specific patient and healthcare provider groups. This leads to a more effective and efficient marketing approach, ultimately contributing to improved patient care and medication adherence.

2. Personalized Content Creation

Personalized content creation is a cornerstone of effective pharma marketing in the age of Artificial Intelligence (AI). It allows companies to move beyond generic messages and craft content that truly resonates with individual patients and healthcare professionals (HCPs). Here is a deeper look at this concept:

Understanding Personalized Content Creation:

Personalized content creation goes beyond simply using a name in a salutation. Here is what sets it apart:

- **Leveraging Data**: AI and machine algorithms analyze various data sources, such as demographics, online behavior, and past interactions, to understand user preferences and needs.
- **Content Tailoring**: Based on this data, content can be tailored in various ways:
- **Topic selection**: Focus on topics most relevant to a user's specific condition, stage of treatment, or area of expertise.
- **Language and Tone**: Adjust the content's language complexity and tone to match the user's level of

understanding (e.g., using simpler language for newly diagnosed patients compared to HCPs).

- **Formatting and Delivery**: Personalize the content format (e.g., video tutorials for visual learners, text articles for those who prefer reading) and delivery channels (e.g., email, social media, mobile app notifications).

Benefits of Personalized Content Creation in Pharma:

- **Increased Engagement**: Content directly addressing a user's specific needs and interests is more likely to capture their attention and lead to higher engagement.
- **Improved Information Retention**: People are more likely to remember information that is relevant to them personally.
- **Enhanced Brand Trust**: Personalized content demonstrates that a pharmaceutical company understands its audience and cares about their needs, fostering trust and loyalty.
- **Measurable Results**: By tracking user interaction with personalized content, companies can gauge its effectiveness and optimize their content creation strategies.

Personalized Content in Pharma: Examples

Example 1: Supporting Patients with a Chronic Illness:

- A patient with a chronic illness might receive personalized content based on their condition and disease stage:
  - **For a newly diagnosed patient**: Educational videos explaining the basics of the illness, treatment options, and managing side effects.
  - **For a patient in long-term treatment**: Content focused on healthy living tips, managing stress, and potential medication adherence strategies.
- The content could be delivered through:
  - **Targeted email campaigns** with personalized greetings and relevant content suggestions.

- **Push notifications** on a mobile app reminding patients about medication adherence or upcoming appointments.
- **Social media content feeds** showcasing patient success stories and inspirational content tailored to their specific condition.

Example 2: Educating HCPs on a New Medication:

- Personalized content for HCPs might consider factors like:
  - **Area of specialization**: Tailored presentations focusing on how the new medication benefits their specific patient population.
  - **Previous prescribing behavior**: Highlighting case studies relevant to medications they frequently prescribe.
  - **Geographical location**: Sharing data on the prevalence of the condition the new medication treats in their region.
- The personalized content could be delivered through:
  - **Targeted email campaigns** with clinical trial data summaries and upcoming webinars relevant to their expertise.
  - **Interactive online tools** allow HCPs to explore the medication's efficacy based on specific patient demographics and medical history.
  - **Social media advertising** showcases the medication's benefits to HCPs interested in similar treatment options.

Conclusion:

Personalized content creation powered by AI and data analysis is a game-changer in pharma marketing. By moving beyond a "one-size-fits-all" approach, pharmaceutical companies can create content that resonates with individual patients and HCPs, leading to a more effective and patient-centric strategy.

3. **Dynamic Content Optimization in Pharma Marketing Campaigns**

   Running marketing campaigns can be slow and cumbersome in the pharmaceutical industry, where regulations and approvals are strict. This is especially true for traditional methods that involve creating many static ads, each requiring individual review.

Dynamic campaign optimization offers a solution to this problem. Here's the breakdown:

- **Dynamic Creative**: Instead of creating individual ads, a template is used. This template can automatically populate information like location or specific details about the medication.
- **Real-time Targeting**: The right ad variation is shown to the right audience based on demographics, browsing history, or weather (for certain medications).
- **Faster Approval Process**: Because the core message and safety information remain consistent, these variations can gain approval quicker than entirely new ads.

Dynamic campaign optimization allows pharma companies to deliver targeted messaging to patients more efficiently while adhering to regulatory requirements.

Dynamic campaign optimization in pharma leverages technology to personalize patient ad experiences while following strict regulations. Here's a closer look at the process:

1. **Template Creation**: Marketers design a master template for the campaign. This template includes the core message, branding elements, and disclaimers about the medication, all compliant with regulations.
2. **Data Integration**: The campaign platform integrates patient data from various sources, such as demographics, medical history (when possible), and online behavior.
3. **Real-time Personalization**: When a patient encounters the ad, the platform uses the template and their specific data to personalize elements like:
   - **Location**: Inserting the nearest clinic or pharmacy.

    - **Condition details**: Highlight specific symptoms the medication addresses.
    - **Creative elements**: Tailoring visuals or headlines to resonate with the patient's age group.
4. **Approval Workflows**: Since the core message remains consistent, these personalized variations might require a streamlined approval process compared to entirely new ads. However, regulations still need to be followed.
5. **Performance Monitoring**: The campaign platform tracks how different ad variations perform. Marketers can then analyze this data to optimize the campaign further, such as adjusting the targeting or creative elements.

Benefits for Pharma Companies:

- **Increased Efficiency**: Dynamic campaigns streamline ad creation and approval processes.
- **Improved Targeting**: Patients see messages most relevant to their needs.
- **Enhanced Engagement**: Personalized ads can lead to better patient engagement.
- **Measurable Results**: Data allows for ongoing optimization and improved campaign performance.

Challenges to Consider:

- **Regulatory Compliance**: Navigating regulations around personalized medical messaging remains crucial.
- **Data Privacy**: Ensuring patient data is collected and used ethically is essential.
- **Technical Expertise**: Implementing dynamic campaigns might require specialized marketing technology skills.

Overall, dynamic campaign optimization offers pharma companies a powerful tool for reaching patients with targeted and compliant messaging in a data-driven way.

Here are some concrete examples of how dynamic campaign optimization plays out in the pharmaceutical industry:

Scenario 1: Allergy Medication Campaign

- **Template**: The campaign promotes a new allergy medication. The template includes a consistent message about the drug's benefits and safety information and the brand logo.
- **Data Integration**: Patient data like location and browsing history is integrated.
- **Real-time Personalization**:
  - **Location**: For someone searching for "allergy relief" in a specific city, the ad might display the nearest pharmacy that carries the medication.
  - **Trigger**: If the patient recently looked at articles about pollen allergies, the ad might highlight the medication's effectiveness against that specific allergy type.
- **Approval Workflow**: Since the core message remains the same, approval for these variations might be faster.
- **Performance Monitoring**: The campaign tracks which variations (location focus, allergy type focus) resonate more with patients. This data helps refine the campaign further.

Scenario 2: Awareness Campaign for a New Diabetes Drug

- **Template**: The campaign focuses on raising awareness about a new diabetes medication. The template showcases the drug's benefits and includes disclaimers about consulting a doctor.
- **Data Integration**: Data on demographics and online behavior is used.
- **Real-time Personalization**:
  - **Demographics**: The ad might display visuals or headlines targeted toward specific age groups most commonly affected by diabetes.
  - **Online Behavior**: If a user has been browsing diabetic recipes, the ad might emphasize the medication's ability to help manage blood sugar levels.

- **Approval Workflow**: Similar to the allergy example, a streamlined approval process might be possible due to the consistent core message.
- **Performance Monitoring**: The campaign tracks which variations (age group focus, recipe browsing trigger) generate the most interest. This data helps optimize ad spending and target the right audience.

Benefits in Action:

These scenarios showcase how dynamic campaigns can:

- **Reach the right patients**: By personalizing messages based on location, demographics, and online behavior, the campaign reaches patients with a higher potential to benefit from the medication.
- **Increase engagement**: Personalized ads are more likely to grab attention and lead patients to learn more about the medication.
- **Optimize spending**: Data-driven insights help allocate budget towards ad variations that perform best, maximizing campaign effectiveness.

While regulations and data privacy remain important considerations, dynamic campaign optimization offers pharma companies a valuable approach to navigating the complex world of patient outreach.

A dynamic campaign optimization is a powerful tool that empowers pharma companies to create adaptive and data-driven marketing campaigns. By leveraging real-time data and AI's analytical capabilities, they can ensure their messages resonate with the right audience at the right time, ultimately leading to better patient outcomes and a successful marketing strategy. Here's how it works:

- **Real-Time Data Analysis**: AI algorithms analyze data from various sources, including website traffic, social media engagement, email open rates, and ad click-through rates (CTRs).

- **Predictive Analytics**: AI can identify emerging trends, allowing for proactive campaign adjustments.
- **Automated A/B Testing**: The system can automatically test different versions of ad copy, landing pages, or email subject lines to determine what resonates best with the target audience.
- **Multi-Channel Optimization**: Optimization happens across all channels simultaneously, ensuring a consistent and personalized brand experience.

Benefits of Dynamic Campaign Optimization:

- **Improved Campaign Performance**: By constantly optimizing content and targeting based on real-time data, campaigns become more effective at reaching the desired audience and achieving marketing goals.
- **Increased Engagement**: Dynamically adjusting content and messaging based on user behavior ensures it's relevant and engaging, leading to higher click-through rates, conversions, and overall campaign performance.
- **Optimized Resource Allocation**: Data-driven insights help allocate the marketing budget more effectively toward channels and messages, yielding the best results.
- **Faster Campaign Learning**: AI allows for continuous learning and improvement, enabling campaigns to adapt quickly to changing audience behavior and market trends.

Pharmaceutical Campaign Optimization Examples:

Example 1: Optimizing a Social Media Campaign for a New Migraine Medication:

A pharmaceutical company launches a social media campaign promoting a new migraine medication:

- **Dynamic optimization might reveal:**
  - **Target audience segments**: Younger women are likelier to engage with video content, while older demographics prefer text-based posts.

    - **High-performing ad copy**: Headlines mentioning "fast relief" generate more clicks than those focusing on long-term prevention.
- **Based on this data, the AI can automatically**:
    - **Adjust ad targeting**: Focus on showing video ads to younger women and text-based ads to older demographics.
    - **Optimize ad copy**: Prioritize headlines with "fast-relief" for higher engagement.

Example 2: Tailoring Email Marketing for Medication Adherence:

- A pharmaceutical company launches an email campaign to remind patients about taking their new high-blood pressure medication.
- **Dynamic optimization might reveal**:
    - **Patient behavior**: Some patients open emails early in the morning, while others check them in the evening.
    - **Engagement with previous emails**: Patients who haven't opened reminders might need a different approach.
- Based on this data, the AI can automatically:
    - **Schedule emails for optimal delivery**: Remind patients of the time of day they are most likely to check their email.
    - **Personalize email content**: For patients who have not opened previous reminders, use stronger calls to action or offer additional educational resources.

4. Website Personalization in Pharma

Website personalization in pharma marketing involves tailoring a company website's content and user experience to individual visitors. This goes beyond simply addressing someone by name. Here's a deeper look at website personalization:

Understanding Website Personalization:

Website personalization leverages data and AI to create a dynamic, user-centric website experience. Here is how it works:

- **Data Collection**: The website collects data about visitors through various means:
    - **Website behavior**: Pages viewed, time spent on specific sessions, links clicked.
    - **Demographics**: Location, device used, language preference (if available).
    - **Previous interactions**: Past visits, content downloads, forms submitted.
    - **Integration with other data sources**: CRM data for logged-in HCPs or patient portals.
- **Content Personalization**: The website dynamically displays content relevant to visitors based on the collected data. This could include:
    - **Targeted landing pages**: Highlight specific medications, treatment options, or clinical trial information relevant to the visitor's condition or area of interest.
    - **Personalized product recommendations**: Recommending medications or educational resources based on the visitor's browsing behavior.
    - **Dynamic calls to action**: Tailoring CTAs (calls to action) based on the visitor's stage in the patient journey. For example, "Learn More" for new patients or "Start Your Free Trail" for repeat visitors.

Benefits of Website Personalization in Pharma:

- **Enhanced User Experience**: Personalized content creates a more encouraging and relevant experience for visitors, leading to higher satisfaction and longer website engagement.
- **Improved Conversion Rates**: By tailoring calls to action and information to user needs, website personalization can increase

the likelihood of visitors taking desired actions, such as signing up for a medication assistance program or downloading educational materials.

- **Better Lead Generation**: Personalization allows for collecting more qualified leads by capturing visitor information relevant to their specific needs.
- **Stronger Brand Perception**: A personalized website experience demonstrates that a pharmaceutical company understands its audience and cares about its needs, fostering trust and brand loyalty.

Pharmaceutical Website Personalization Examples:

Example 1: A Patient Researching High Cholesterol:

- A patient visits a pharmaceutical company website searching for information about high cholesterol.
- **Website personalization might**:
    - Display a landing page focused on high cholesterol, including causes, risk factors, and treatment options.
    - Recommend blog posts or articles discussing healthy lifestyle changes for managing cholesterol.
    - Feature a prominent call to action to download an e-book on cholesterol medication and its side effects.

Example 2: An HCP Looking for Information on a New Medication:

- A healthcare professional visits the website to learn more about a new medication for Type 2 Diabetes.
- **Website personalization might**:
    - Direct the HCP to a dedicated section with detailed clinical trial data, dosage recommendations, and potential drug interactions.
    - Offer access to exclusive webinars or downloadable presentations on the new medication.

- Provide a secure login option for HCPs to access additional resources and connect with the company's medical affairs team.

5. Targeted Email Marketing

Targeted email marketing is a cornerstone of any successful marketing strategy. It allows you to reach specific audiences with personalized messages that resonate with their needs and interests. Here's a deeper dive into this concept:

Targeted email marketing goes beyond sending mass emails to a generic list of subscribers. Here is what sets it apart:

- **Audience segmentation**: The subscriber list is divided into smaller groups (segments) based on various criteria, such as:
  - **Demographics**: Age, gender, location.
  - **Health conditions**: Specific diseases or treatments.
  - **Online Behavior**: Past interactions with emails, website visits, and downloaded content.
  - **HCP specialty**: For healthcare professionals (HCPs), targeting based on area of expertise.
- **Personalized Content**: Emails are tailored to each segment with content that addresses their specific needs and interests. This can include:
  - **Subject lines**: Using relevant keywords and addressing pain points to encourage opens.
  - **Email body**: Highlighting information and benefits relevant to the specific condition or area of interest.
  - **Calls to action**: Tailoring CTAs (calls to action) based on the audience segment. For example, "Learn More" for awareness, "Download Guide" for education, or "Schedule an Appointment" for action-oriented campaigns.

Benefits of Targeted Email Marketing in Pharma:

- **Increased Engagement**: Personalized emails that resonate with recipients' needs will likely be opened, read, and acted upon.

- **Improved Conversation Rates**: Targeted CTAs tailored to specific segments are more likely to lead to desired actions, such as visiting a website, downloading resources, or signing up for a program.
- **Enhanced Brand Trust**: Personalized communication demonstrates that a company understands its audiences, fostering trust and brand loyalty.
- **Measurable Results**: Email marekting platforms provide detailed analytics on open rates, click-through rates, and conversions, allowing for campaign optimization and measurement of ROI.

Targeted Email Marketing in Pharma: Examples:

Example 1: Educating Patients About a New Medication:

- A pharmaceutical company launches a new medication for migraine. They segment their email list based on demographics and past interactions:
  - **Segment 1**: Patients who previously signed up for migraine information.
  - **Segment 2**: Women aged 25 - 45 who haven't interacted with the company before.
- They send targeted email campaigns:
  - **Segment 1**: Email highlighting the new medication's benefits, efficacy data, and potential side effects.
  - **Segment 2**: An introductory email introducing the company and explaining how its new medication can help manage migraines. The company might offer a downloading guide on "Living with Migraines."

Example 2: Engaging HCPs with Upcoming Webinars:

- A pharmaceutical company segments its HCP email list based on specialty:
  - **Segment 1**: Cardiologists
  - **Segment 2**: General Practitioners

They send targeted emails promoting an upcoming webinar on a new heart medication:

- **Segment 1**: In-depth email with detailed information on the webinar agenda, focusing on clinical trial data and how the medication benefits cardiologists' specific patient populations.
- **Segment 2**: General overview email highlighting the webinar's relevance to managing heart health, focusing on key benefits and patient outcomes.

Email Marketing

AI is revolutionizing email marketing in the pharmaceutical industry, allowing companies to deliver more personalized, relevant, and effective messages to healthcare professionals (HCPs) and patients. Here is how AI is optimizing pharma email marketing:

1. **Hyper-Segmentation and Targeting**:
    - AI can analyze vast amounts of data such as demographics, medical specialty, past interactions, and email engagement history.
    - This allows for highly specific segmentation of HCP and patient email lists. Pharma companies can target emails based on a doctor's area of practice or a patient's specific condition.

Example: A company launches a new medication for a specific type of cancer.

- AI segments its HCP email list by oncology subspecialties. Medical oncologists specializing in the relevant cancer type receive emails highlighting clinical trial data and treatment benefits.

2. **Personalized Email Content and Design:**
    - AI can personalize email content based on recipient data. Emails for HCPs might contain technical information and clinical trial results, while patient emails could focus on disease management tips and medication adherence strategies.

- AI can personalize email design elements like subject lines and visuals to cater to different audience preferences.

Example: A patient with diabetes receives an email from a company offering a new blood sugar monitoring device.

- The email leverages the patient's medical history (with consent) to showcase how the device can help manage their specific type of diabetes.
- The email might include personalized recommendations for healthy living habits based on the patient's age and lifestyle.

3. AI-Powered Send Time Optimization:

- AI can analyze historical data to identify the optimal time to send emails to maximize open and click-through rates. This takes into account factors like recipient location and typical email usage patterns.

Example: An HCP in a busy practice might be more likely to open emails during evenings or weekends.

- AI schedules email delivery for this HCP when they are more likely to check their inbox, leading to higher engagement.

4. Real-Time Performance Analysis and Improvement:

- AI can track and analyze real-time email campaign performance, including open, click-through, and unsubscribe rates.
- AI can automatically adjust future email campaigns based on this data to continuously improve and optimize email marketing strategies.

Example: An email campaign promoting a new drug webinar has a low click-through rate for the registration link.

- AI identifies that the link placement within the email might be hindering clicks.
- The AI system automatically A/B tests different link placement options in future emails to improve user experience and click-through rates.

Benefits of AI-Powered Email Marketing in Pharma:

- **Increased Engagement and Conversions**: Personalized emails with relevant content lead to higher open rates, click-through rates, and conversions.
- **Improved Patient Education and Care**: Targeted emails can educate patients about treatment options, medication adherence, and disease management strategies.
- **Enhanced Brand Reputation**: Personalized communication fosters trust and strengthens relationships with HCPs and patients.

Challenges and Considerations:

- **Data Privacy and Security**: Patient data privacy is paramount. Strict adherence to data protection regulations and transparent communication are essential.
- **Spam Filters and Deliverability**: AI can help craft engaging content, but ensuring emails avoid spam filters and reach inboxes requires a focus on clean email lists and permission-based marketing.
- **Human Touch and Relationship Building**: While AI personalizes content, building trust with HCPs requires genuine human interaction.

By leveraging AI responsibly, pharmaceutical companies can create effective email marketing campaigns that deliver valuable information to HCPs and empower patients to manage their health more effectively.

Conclusion:

Targeted email marketing powered by data and audience segmentation is a game-changer in pharma marketing. By crafting email campaigns that resonate with specific audiences, pharmaceutical companies can increase engagement, drive conversions, and build stronger relationships with patients and healthcare professionals. This ultimately leads to a more efficient and effective marketing strategy that benefits patients and the company.

6. **Social Media Engagement**

Social media engagement is a crucial aspect of pharmaceutical marketing in today's digital age. It allows companies to connect with patients, healthcare professionals (HCPs), and other stakeholders more personally, fostering brand awareness, education, and community building. Here's a deeper look at social media engagement in pharma:

Social media engagement goes beyond simply posting content. It's about fostering two-way communication and building relationships with your audience. Here are key aspects:

- **Content Strategy**: Creating valuable and informative content tailored to your target audience's needs. This could include:
  - **Educational posts**: Sharing infographics, videos, and articles about diseases, treatment options, and healthy living tips.
  - **Patient stories**: Featuring testimonials and success stories from patients using your medications.
  - **Live Q&A Sessions**: Hosting interactive sessions with medical experts to answer audience questions.
- **Community Management**: Monitor and respond to comments, messages, and mentions. This demonstrates that the company values its feedback and builds trust.
- **Social Listening**: Using social media listening tools to understand online conversations about your brand, industry trends, and patient concerns.

Benefits of Social Media Engagement in Pharma:

- **Increased Brand Awareness**: Social media presence helps build brand recognition and reach a wider audience.
- **Improved Patient Education**: Sharing educational content empowers patients to make informed decisions about their health.

- **Enhanced Brand Reputation**: Positive social media interactions foster trust and loyalty towards the company.
- **Valuable Patient Insights**: Social listening helps companies understand real-time patient needs, concerns, and emerging trends.

Social Media Engagement in Pharma: Examples:

Example 1: Building a Community for Patients with Diabetes

- A pharmaceutical company creates a Facebook group specifically for patients with Type 2 Diabetes.
- **Engagement Strategies**:
  - **Live Q&A sessions**: Host monthly sessions with diabetes educators or registered dieticians to answer patients' questions about managing their conditions.
  - **Recipe sharing**: Encourage patients to share healthy and delicious recipes for diabetic diets.
  - **Support Groups**: Foster a safe space for patients to connect, share experiences, and offer peer-to-peer support.

Example 2: Launching a New Asthma Medication on Twitter (X, now):

- A pharmaceutical company has launched a new medication for asthma and wants to raise awareness among patients and HCPs.
- **Engagement Strategies**:
  - **Patient education campaign**: Use the #MyAsthma Journey hashtag to encourage patients to share their experiences and challenges.
  - **Patients with asthma influencers**: Collaborate with relevant patient advocates or healthcare professionals to promote the medication and answer questions from their audience.
  - **Twitter (X, now) polls**: Conduct polls to understand patient concerns and preferences regarding asthma treatment.

Social Media Engagement in Pharma

Social media offers a powerful platform for pharmaceutical companies to connect with healthcare professionals (HCPs), patients, and advocacy groups. However, navigating the dynamic world of social media can be challenging. Here is how AI can optimize social media engagement in pharma:

1. **Audience Targeting and Content Personalization**:
    - AI can analyze vast social media data such as demographics, interests, and online behavior. This allows for the creation of targeted audience segments for specific campaigns.
    - AI-powered content creation Tools can generate personalized content based on audience preferences. For example, AI can tailor social media posts for cardiologists to focus on specific drug benefits for heart disease. In contrast, posts for patient groups might emphasize treatment options and support resources.

Example: **A pharma company launches a new diabetes medication.**

- AI identifies HCPs specializing in diabetes care and patients with Type 2 diabetes on social media.
- The company creates separate campaigns:
    - **For HCPs**: Social media posts highlight clinical trial results and treatment benefits for patients.
    - **For Patients**: Content focuses on managing diabetes, medication information, and links to support groups.

2. **Community Management and Brand Monitoring:**
    - AI-powered chatbots can answer basic inquiries on social media platforms, freeing up time for human interaction on more complex topics.
    - AI can monitor brand mentions and sentiment analysis to identify trends, address concerns, and participate in relevant

conversations. This allows for proactive engagement with the audience and building trust.

Example: A patient tweets about experiencing side effects with a company's medication.

- AI identifies the tweet and flags it for a social media manager.
- The manager can empathize with the patient, offer resources, and direct them to appropriate channels for reporting side effects.

3. Content Optimization and Performance Analysis:

- AI can analyze social media engagement metrics such as likes, shares, and comments to understand what content resonates best with the audience.
- AI can recommend adjustments to a content strategy based on performance data, allowing for continuous improvement and optimization of social media campaigns.

Example: A pharmaceutical company posts two educational videos on a new drug— one with a formal presentation style and another with an animated explainer format.

- AI analyzes engagement metrics and discovers that the explainer video receives significantly higher views, shares, and positive comments.
- Based on this data, the company can prioritize creating more explainer videos for future social media campaigns.

Benefits of AI-Powered Social Media Engagement:

- **Increased Reach and Engagement**: AI helps target the right audience and deliver personalized content, leading to better engagement and brand awareness.
- **Improved Community Management**: AI empowers faster response times and proactive communication with the audience.
- **Data-Driven Content Strategy**: AI provides insights to optimize content based on what resonates with the audience, maximizing the impact of social media campaigns.

Challenges and Considerations:

- **Transparency and Trust**: Building trust with the audience is crucial. Be transparent about how AI is used and prioritize human interaction for sensitive topics.
- **Regulatory Compliance**: Ensure all social media content adheres to pharmaceutical industry regulations.
- **Ethical Considerations**: Avoid using AI for manipulative marketing tactics. Focus on providing valuable information and fostering genuine connections.

By leveraging AI responsibly, pharma companies can unlock the full potential of social media to connect with their audience, educate patients and HCPs, and ultimately improve patient care.

Conclusion

Social media engagement is a powerful tool for pharmaceutical companies to connect with their audience, build brand loyalty, and improve patient care. By creating valuable content, actively engaging with users, and leveraging social listening tools, pharma companies can establish a strong social media presence that positively impacts the healthcare landscape.

7. Programmatic Advertising in Pharma

Programmatic advertising has become a linchpin of digital marketing strategies across all industries, and pharma is no exception. It allows pharmaceutical companies to automate buying and selling ad space across a vast network of websites, apps, and other digital platforms, leading to more targeted and efficient campaigns. Here's a deeper dive into programmatic advertising in pharma.

Understanding Programmatic Advertising:

Traditionally, media buying involved manual negotiations with individual publishers to secure ad placements. Programmatic advertising streamlines this process by:

- **Ad Exchanges**: These act as marketplaces where advertisers (pharmaceutical companies) bid on ad space publishers offer (websites, apps) through real-time auctions.

- **Demand-Side Platforms (DSPs)**: These platforms allow advertisers to manage their programmatic campaigns, set budgets, target specific audiences, and choose the ad formats they want to display.
- **Data Management Platforms (DMPs)**: These platforms aggregate and analyze data from various sources (demographics, online behavior, past interactions) to create audience profiles for targeting.

Benefits of Programmatic Advertising in Pharma:

- **Increased Targeting Precision**: Programmatic advertising leverages audience data to create highly targeted campaigns targeting specific patient segments or HCP specialties.
- **Improved Efficiency**: Automating the bidding process saves time and resources compared to manual media buying.
- **Real-Time Optimization**: DSPs allow real-time campaign monitoring and adjustments based on performance metrics, ensuring optimal budget allocation.
- **Reduced Ad Fraud**: Reputable ad exchanges have robust measures to prevent fraudulent ad placements.

Pharmaceutical Programmatic Advertising Examples:

Example 1: Targeting Patients with High Cholesterol:

- A pharmaceutical company is launching a new medication for high cholesterol. It wants to reach the patients most likely to benefit from it.
- **Programmatic Advertising Strategy**:
  - **Target audience**: People aged 45+ who have shown interest in health topics or searched for information about cholesterol online.
  - **Ad placements**: Health and wellness websites, fitness apps, and social media platforms frequented by the target audience.
  - **Ad formats**: Display ads featuring the medication's benefits, video testimonials from patients who manage their

cholesterol, or interactive quizzes to assess heart health risks.

Example 2: Raising Awareness Among HCPs for a New Cancer Treatment:

- A pharmaceutical company develops a new, targeted therapy for a specific type of cancer. They want to raise awareness among oncologists specializing in that area.
- **Programmatic Advertising Strategy**:
  - **Target audience**: Oncologists who frequently visit medical journals or online resources about the specific cancer type.
  - **Ad placements**: Professional medical websites, online publications for oncologists, and social media groups frequented by HCPs.
  - **Ad formats**: Rich media ads showcasing the medication's mechanism of action and clinical trial data or targeted email marketing campaigns with detailed information for download.

Programmatic Advertising in Pharma

Programmatic advertising allows pharmaceutical companies to automate ad-buying, reaching targeted audiences across various online platforms. AI is transforming this approach in pharma by injecting intelligence and data-driven insights into every stage.

1. **Audience Targeting and Segmentation**:
   - AI can analyze vast datasets, including demographics, health interests, online behavior, and disease associations. This allows for highly specific audience segmentation beyond basic demographics.
   - AI can go beyond simple keyword targeting and identify users actively researching specific conditions, browsing relevant medical websites, or participating in online patient communities.

Example: A company launches a new medication for migraines.

- AI goes beyond targeting users searching for "migraine medication." It identifies users on health forums discussing migraine symptoms, browsing articles on specific migraine triggers, or following patient advocacy groups focused on. Migraines.

2. **Dynamic Ad Creative and Personalization:**
   - AI can generate ad creatives that adapt to different audience segments. For HCPs, ads might showcase clinical trial data and treatment benefits. For patients, ads could focus on improved quality of life or disease management tips.

Example: An ad campaign for a new allergy medication encounters users with different allergy types (pollen, dust mites, etc.).

- AI tailors the ad content to display the medication's effectiveness against the specific allergy type the user is likely experiencing based on their online behavior.

3. **Real-Time Bidding Optimization and Budget Allocation:**
   - AI algorithms can analyze real-time campaign performance data, including impressions, clicks, and conversions.
   - AI can automatically adjust bids for ad placements on various platforms, optimizing budget allocation towards placements yielding the best results.

Example: An ad campaign runs across various health websites and social media platforms.

- AI identifies that ad placements on a specific medical news website generate many qualified leads from patients interested in the medication.
- The AI system automatically increases the bid for ad placements on this website, maximizing reach and conversions within the allocated budget.

4. **Fraud Detection and Brand Safety:**
   - AI can identify and prevent fraudulent activity, such as click bots that inflate ad costs without generating genuine leads.

- AI can ensure brand safety by filtering out websites with inappropriate content or not aligning with the company's brand image.

Benefits of AI-Powered Programmatic Advertising in Pharma:

- **Increased Efficiency and Cost-Effectiveness**: AI automates processes and optimizes spending, maximizing reach and conversions within budget constraints.
- **Improved Targeting and Relevance**: AI delivers ads to the right audience at the right time with relevant messaging, leading to higher engagement.
- **Enhanced Brand Reputation**: Reaching targeted audiences and avoiding irrelevant placements protects the brand image and builds trust with patients and HCPs.

Challenges and considerations:

- **Data Privacy Regulations**: Data collection and targeting practices must comply with evolving privacy regulations like HIPAA and GDPR.
- **Transparency and Explainability**: Understanding how AI algorithms make targeting and ad delivery decisions is crucial for ensuring fairness and avoiding bias.
- **Integration with Existing Systems**: AI solutions should integrate seamlessly with existing marketing automation and data management platforms.

By harnessing AI responsibly and ethically, pharmaceutical companies can leverage programmatic advertising to reach the right audience with impactful messages, ultimately improving brand awareness and patient education.

Conclusion:

Programmatic advertising offers pharmaceutical companies a powerful data-driven approach to reaching their target audiences across the digital landscape. By leveraging automation, precise targeting capabilities, and real-time optimization, programmatic advertising allows pharmaceutical companies to deliver impactful campaigns that raise awareness, educate patients and HCPs, and ultimately contribute to better health outcomes.

8. Mobile Marketing in Pharma

Mobile marketing has become an essential aspect of any pharmaceutical marketing strategy. With the ever-increasing use of smartphones and tablets, it is crucial to reach patients and healthcare providers (HCPs) on their mobile devices. Here's a deeper dive into mobile marketing for pharma, along with examples to illustrate its effectiveness.

Mobile marketing encompasses various strategies to reach target audiences through smartphones and tablets. Here are some key aspects:

- **Mobile Responsive Websites**: Ensure your company website is optimized for mobile viewing, with easy navigation and clear calls to action (CTAs).
- **Mobile Apps**: Developing patient-centric apps for medication adherence reminders, educational content, or managing treatment side effects. Companies might also develop HCP-specific apps for prescribing information or drug interaction tools.
- **SMS Marketing** involves sending targeted text messages for appointment reminders, medication refill alerts, or educational campaigns (with explicit consent).
- **Mobile Advertising**: Utilizing programmatic advertising platforms to target specific patient groups or HCPs with relevant mobile website and app ads.

Benefits of Mobile Marketing in Pharma:

- **Enhanced Patient Engagement**: Mobile marketing allows reaching patients directly on their most used devices, fostering better engagement and medication adherence.
- **Improved HCP Outreach**: Reaching HCPs on their mobile devices provides timely access to medication information and educational resources at the point of care.

- **Personalized Communication**: Mobile marketing allows targeted messaging and content based on user data and behavior.
- **Measurable Results**: Mobile marketing analytics provide valuable insights into campaign performance, user engagement, and app usage, allowing for continuous optimization.

Pharmaceutical Mobile Marketing Examples:

- AI presents a game-changer for mobile marketing in the pharmaceutical industry. Here is how AI can be harnessed to create targeted, effective mobile campaigns that reach the right patients and healthcare professionals (HCPs).
- AI can analyze vast datasets, including demographics, location data, app usage, and online behavior. This allows for highly specific audience segmentation on mobile platforms.
- Pharmaceutical companies can target mobile campaigns to HCPs specializing in specific areas based on their app usage (e.g., medical journals) or conference attendance data. Patients with particular conditions can be reached through apps related to their health concerns.

Example 1: Medication Adherence App for Patients:

- A pharmaceutical company develops a mobile app for patients taking their new medication for hypertension.
- **App features**:
    - **Daily medication reminders**: Customizable alerts to remind patients to take their medication on time.
    - **Educational content**: Information about hypertension, healthy lifestyle tips, and potential side effects of the medication.
    - **Progress tracking**: Charts and graphs to visualize medication adherence and blood pressure readings (with proper privacy measures).

Example 2: SMS Appointment Reminders for HCPs:

- A pharmaceutical company launches a new pain medication and wants to remind HCPs about upcoming educational webinars about its benefits.
- **Mobile Marketing Strategy**:
  - The company sent targeted SMS messages to HCPs who previously expressed interest in pain management solutions, reminding them about the webinar date and registration link.
  - Short and informative message: Briefly mention the webinar topic, date, and a clear CTA to register.

Example 3: **A company launches a new medication for a rare lung disease.**

- AI identifies pulmonologists who frequently use medical reference apps and attend relevant conferences.
- The company creates a targeted mobile ad campaign showcasing the drug's benefits, delivered through these medical apps.

Personalized Mobile Ad Experiences:

- AI can personalize mobile ad content based on user data and in-app behavior. For HCPs, ads might highlight clinical trial results and drug efficacy. Patients might see ads on improved quality of life or disease management tips.
- Interactive elements like quizzes or surveys within mobile ads can further personalize the experience and gather valuable user insights.

Example 4: **A patient with high blood pressure sees a mobile ad for a new blood pressure medication.**

- The ad leverages the patient's health data (if available with consent) to showcase the medication's effectiveness in specific blood pressure ranges.

- The ad might include a short, interactive quiz to assess the patient's understanding of the condition and connect them with resources for managing their blood pressure.

3. **Real-Time Optimization and Budget Allocation:**
   - AI can analyze real-time campaign performance data, including click-through rates, app downloads, and conversions.
   - AI can automatically adjust mobile ad campaigns based on performance, optimizing budget allocation towards strategies yielding the best results.

Example 5: A pharma company runs a mobile ad campaign across various health and wellness apps.

- AI analyzes data and identifies that ads in a specific fitness app generate many qualified leads from patients interested in the medication.
- The AI system automatically increases the budget allocated to this app, maximizing reach and conversions.

4. **Location-Based Mobile Marketing:**
   - AI can leverage location data (with user content) to deliver geographically relevant mobile ads. For example, patients searching for nearby pharmacies can be shown ads for specific medicatons available at those locations.
   - Geo-fencing technology allows targeted ads to be displayed when users enter specific areas, such as hospitals or clinics specializing in the relevant condition.

Example 6: A patient with symptoms of a migraine searches for a nearby pharmacy on a mobile app.

- Based on the user's location and search query, AI delivers an ad for a migraine medication available at a nearby pharmacy.

Benefits of AI-Powered Mobile Marketing in Pharma:

- **Increased Engagement and Conversions**: Personalized, relevant mobile ads increase engagement and conversions, driving patients towards desired actions.

- **Improved ROI**: AI optimizes campaigns for maximum impact, ensuring efficient budget allocation and strong return on investment.
- **Enhanced Patient Education and Care**: Mobile marketing can raise awareness of treatment options and empower patients to take charge of their health.

Challenges and Considerations:

- **Privacy Concerns**: Transparency and user consent are crucial when collecting and utilizing location data.
- **Data Security**: Robust data security measures are essential to protect patient privacy.
- **Integration with Existing Systems**: AI solutions must integrate seamlessly with existing marketing and data management platforms.

By harnessing AI responsibly and ethically, pharmaceutical companies can create impactful mobile marketing campaigns that reach the right audience with the right message, ultimately improving patient care and brand awareness.

Conclusion:

Mobile marketing offers a unique opportunity for pharmaceutical companies to connect with patients and HCPs in a personalized and convenient way. By leveraging the power of mobile devices and tailoring strategies to specific audiences, pharma companies can improve patient care, medication adherence, and brand awareness in the ever-evolving mobile landscape.

CHAPTER 21

Symphony of Minds: Mapping AI-Powered Customer Journeys for Success

In the intricate pharma world, understanding customer journeys is no longer a luxury but a necessity. This chapter delves into the powerful art of customer journey mapping, where human empathy harmonizes with AI analysis to craft a multi-faceted symphony of experiences by patients, healthcare professionals (HCPs), and payers.

1. **The Conductor: Orchestrating Patient Journeys**:
   - **Understanding the Patient Perspective**: AI analyzes medical records, social media conversations, and online forums to uncover patient needs, anxieties, and expectations at every stage of their illness journey.
   - **Mapping the Touchpoints**: From diagnosis to treatment and beyond, humans meticulously chart the touchpoints patients encounter with healthcare providers, pharmaceutical companies, and support services.
   - **Identifying Friction Points**: AI pinpoints moments of frustration, confusion, or unmet needs within the patient journey, guiding human intervention to create a smoother and more supportive experience.

Example: A pharma company developing a new cancer medication uses AI to discover that patients find the post-treatment follow-up process fragmented and overwhelming. They then work with patient advocacy groups to map a cohesive follow-up journey with streamlined communication and personalized support resources.

2. **Engaging the Ensemble: HCP Treatment Journey Mapping**:
   - **Emphasizing the HCP Role**: AI analyzes clinical trial data, prescribing patterns, and industry publications to understand the challenges and priorities HCPs face in treating specific conditions.
   - **Deconstructing the Decision-Making Process**: Humans map the touchpoints HCPs encounter when evaluating treatment options, factoring in scientific evidence, a patient's needs, and regulatory considerations.
   - **Removing Roadblocks**: AI pinpoints areas where information gaps or logistical hurdles impede optional treatment decisions, allowing humans to develop targeted educational resources and streamlined communication channels.

Example: A pharma company developing a new diabetes medication uses AI to discover that HCPs lack resources to educate patients about proper insulin injection techniques. They then map a journey for HCPs, including access to instructional videos, downloadable patient materials, and support hotlines.

3. **Harmonizing the Finance: Payer Journey Mapping**:
   - **Decoding Reimbursement Decisions**: AI analyzes payer data, cost-effectiveness studies, and regulatory frameworks to understand the factors influencing medication coverage decisions.
   - **Navigating the Approval Process**: Humans map the payers' interactions with pharma companies, regulatory agencies, and patient advocacy groups throughout the medication approval and reimbursement.
   - **Building Value Propositions**: AI identifies key data points that demonstrate the economic benefits of a new

medication, enabling humans to craft compelling evidence-based arguments for payer acceptance.

Example: A pharma company developing a new orphan drug uses AI to analyze potential cost savings associated with reduced hospitalizations due to medication effectiveness. They then map a journey for payers, highlighting this data alongside patient testimonials and clinical evidence to advocate for broader coverage.

The Final Harmony

This synergistic blend of human empathy and AI analysis transforms customer journey mapping into a powerful tool for pharma success. By understanding the individual journeys of patients, HCPs, and payers, pharma companies can:

- Develop patient-centric medications and support services.
- Enhance HCP understanding and adoption of new treatments.
- Secure payer acceptance and optimize market access.
- Ultimately, it contributes to improved patient outcomes and a more efficient healthcare ecosystem.

AI Optimizing Customer Journeys

Here's how AI can optimize each of the customer journeys in the pharma landscape:

1. **Patient Journey Optimization:**
    - **Diagnosis and Prognosis:** AI can analyze medical scans and genomic data to provide faster, more accurate diagnoses and personalized risk assessments.
    - **Treatment Selection and Management:** AI-powered recommendation systems can suggest optimal treatment options based on individual patient characteristics and predict potential side effects, allowing personalized treatment plans.

- **Patient Support and Education:** AI chatbots and virtual assistants can provide on-demand support, answer questions, and deliver educational resources tailored to each patient's needs and stage of treatment.
- **Remote Monitoring and Support:** Wearable devices and smartphone apps integrated with AI can monitor vital signs, medication adherence, and treatment response, enabling proactive intervention and personalized care follow-up.

Example: A cancer patient uses an AI-powered app to track their medication schedule, side effects, and emotional well-being. The app analyzes the data and recommends adjustments to the treatment plan or suggests additional support services, leading to improved treatment outcomes and quality of life.

2. HCP Journey Optimization:

- **Clinical Decision Support:** AI algorithms can analyze vast medical literature and clinical trial data to provide HCPs with real-time evidence-based insights for improved treatment decisions.
- **Personalized Patient Management:** AI can analyze patient data and suggest personalized treatment plans, medication dosage, and follow-up schedules, streamlining HCP workflows and optimizing patient care.
- **Administrative Efficiency:** AI tools can automate tasks like prescription generation, prior authorization requests, and insurance verification, freeing up HCPs' time to focus on patient care.
- **Continuous Learning and Education:** AI-powered platforms can personalize educational content and deliver targeted updates on new medications, clinical studies, and treatment guidelines, empowering HCPs to stay current with the latest advancements.

Example: A cardiologist uses an AI platform to assess a patient's risk of heart failure based on their medical history and genetic profile. The platform suggests a personalized treatment plan with tailored medication dosages and follow-up schedules, improving patient outcomes.

3. **Payer Journey Optimization:**
   - **Medication Cost-Effectiveness Analysis:** AI can analyze data on medication efficacy, side effects, and long-term outcomes to predict cost savings associated with specific treatments, supporting payers in making informed coverage decisions.
   - **Fraud and Abuse Detection:** AI can analyze claims data and identify patterns suggestive of fraudulent activity, helping payers manage healthcare costs and ensure efficient resource allocation.
   - **Predictive Modeling and Budgeting:** AI can forecast future medication needs and healthcare costs based on population trends and disease patterns, enabling payers to optimize their budgets and resource allocation.
   - **Value-Based Payment Design:** AI can support the development of value-based payment models that reward providers for achieving improved patient outcomes and cost-effectiveness, aligning payer and provider goals.

Example: A health insurance company uses the cost-effectiveness of a new medication for their insured population. The analysis reveals significant potential cost savings due to reduced hospitalizations, leading the payer to approve coverage for the medication.

Remember, AI is not a silver bullet; responsible implementation is crucial. Ethical considerations, data privacy, and human oversight are paramount to ensure trust and prevent unintended consequences.

Integrating AI into these customer journeys allows pharma companies to create a more patient-centric, efficient, and value-driven healthcare ecosystem. This collaboration between humans and AI holds immense potential to transform the pharma landscape and ultimately improve the lives of patients around the world.

Optimizing Customer Journeys with AI: A Glimpse into the Future

Now, let's glimpse into the future and understand how AI can help optimize our customer journeys (a hypertensive patient, an oncologist, and a pharmacy benefit manager):

1. **The Hypertensive Patient's Journey**

   Touchpoints:

   - **Diagnosis:** Initial GP visit, blood pressure monitoring, genetic testing.
   - **Treatment Initiation:** Consultation with a cardiologist, prescription for medication, appointment scheduling.
   - **Medication Management:** Adherence to a medication schedule, monitoring of side effects, refills, and adjustments.
   - **Long-term Management:** Regular check-ups with a doctor, lifestyle adjustments, and managing other health conditions.

   AI Optimization:

   - **Diagnosis and Prognosis:** AI analyzes genetic data and lifestyle factors to predict individual risk of hypertension and potential complications.
   - **Personalized Treatment Plans:** AI algorithms suggest optimal medication combinations, dosages, and lifestyle adjustments based on the patient's unique profile.
   - **Smart Medication Dosing:** AI-powered apps remind patients to take medications, track adherence, and suggest adjustments based on real-time data from wearable devices.
   - **Proactive Intervention:** AI models predict potential complications and alert doctors to schedule preventive interventions or adjust treatment plans.

Pharma Intervention:

- **Educational Chatbots:** AI-powered chatbots provide patients with 24/7 access to personalized information on hypertension, medication side effects, and healthy lifestyle tips.
- **Remote Monitoring and Support:** Pharma companies offer wearable devices and smartphone apps that track vitals, medication adherence, and mood, offering personalized feedback and support.
- **Targeted Loyalty Programs:** Reward patients for adherence and healthy habits, incentivizing long-term engagement and improved outcomes.

2. **The Oncologist's Journey:**

   Touchpoints:

   - **Patient Diagnosis and Evaluation:** Reviewing medical history, scans, and genetic tests.
   - **Treatment Planning:** Selecting optimal treatment options, considering risks and benefits for each patient.
   - **Treatment Delivery:** Coordinating care with other specialists, managing side effects, and monitoring response.
   - **Long-term Care Management:** Monitoring for recurrence, adapting treatment plans as needed, and providing supportive care.

AI Optimization:

- **Advanced Imaging Analysis:** AI algorithms analyze scans and biopsies to provide second opinions, identify subtle abnormalities, and predict treatment response.
- **Personalized Patient Monitoring:** AI simulates different treatment options based on the patient's unique tumor characteristics and predicts efficacy and potential side effects.
- **Real-time Patient Monitoring:** AI tools analyze wearable and implantable device data to detect early signs of complications or treatment inefficacy, enabling proactive intervention.

- **Clinical Trial Recruitment and Matching:** AI identifies eligible patients for clinical trials and matches them to the most promising therapy options based on their personalized profiles.

Pharma Intervention:

- **AI-powred Decision Support Systems:** Pharma companies provide oncologists access to AI platforms that offer real-time clinical evidence, treatment guidelines, and personalized therapy recommendations.
- **Virtual Tumor Boards:** AI facilitates remote collaboration between oncologists and specialists, enabling collective decision-making and sharing of expertise.
- **Educational Webinars and Resources:** Pharma companies offer AI-powered tools to personalize educational content for oncologists, keeping them up-to-date on the latest research and treatment advancements.

3. **The PBM's Journey:**

   Touchpoints:

   - Negotiating Drug Prices with Pharma Companies.
   - Developing Formularies: Selecting a list of covered medications based on cost, efficacy, and safety.
   - Managing patient claims and utilization.
   - Analyzing data to identify cost-saving opportunities and improve medication adherence.

AI Optimization:

- **Predictive Drug Pricing:** AI models forecast future drug costs and market trends, informing negotiation strategies with pharma companies.
- **Value-Based Formulary Design:** AI analyzes data on medication efficacy, cost-effectiveness, and patient outcomes to optimize formularies and deliver the best value for the covered population.

- **Fraud Detection and Claims Management:** AI algorithms identify fraudulent claims and potential medication misuse, streamlining administration and reducing costs.
- **Predictive Modeling for Resource Allocation:** AI anticipates future medication needs and healthcare costs, helping PBMs allocate resources efficiently and manage budgets effectively.

Pharma Intervention:

- **Real-world Data Sharing:** Pharma companies partner with PBMs to provide anonymized patient data on medication use and outcomes, supporting evidence-based formulary decisions and value-based agreements.
- **Cost-Effectiveness Modeling Tools:** Pharma companies develop AI-powered tools that demonstrate the economic value of their medications, facilitating negotiations and coverage decisions with PBMs.
- **Joint Patient Adherence Programs:** Pharma companies and PBMs work together to design AI-powered interventions that improve medication adherence and reduce healthcare costs.

These are just a few hypothetical examples, and the possibilities for AI optimization are constantly evolving. By embracing human-AI synergy, pharma companies can forge deeper and more meaningful connections with patients, HCPs, and payers, contributing to a healthier and more sustainable healthcare ecosystem.

Deep Dive into Optimized Journeys: AI Revolutionizing Pharma Customer Relationships

Let's now explore and understand how AI-powered customer journey revolutionizes pharma's customer relationship-building process :

1. **Deeper Engagements with AI (Touchpoints and Examples):**

   A. Hypertensive Patient:

   - **Touchpoint— Pharmacy Refill:**

- **AI:** Smart pill bottle alerts patients about potential medication interactions with over-the-counter drugs they purchase.
- **Touchpoint— Doctor's Appointment:**
- **AI:** Personalized virtual assistant analyzes blood pressure data and suggests lifestyle adjustments before the appointment, leading to a more focused consultation.
- **Touchpoint— Social Media:**
- **AI:** A pharmaceutical company utilizes AI-powered chatbots to address patient concerns about hypertension and healthy living in real time, building trust and fostering engagement.

B. Oncologist:

- **Touchpoint— Clinical Trial Recruitment**
- **AI:** The AI platform matches patients with compatible clinical trials based on their tumor profile and personal preferences, streamlining enrollment rates.
- **Touchpoint— Treatment Decision-Making:**
- **AI:** An AI-powered decision-support system integrates real-world data with tumor models, providing the oncologist with personalized treatment recommendations and potential outcomes for each option.
- **Touchpoint— Patient Follow-up:**
- **AI:** Wearable device data analyzed by AI detects early signs of treatment side effects or tumor progression, enabling proactive intervention and personalized adjustments.

C. PBM (Pharmacy Benefit Manager):

- **Touchpoint— Drug Price Negotiation**
- **AI:** Predictive pricing models forecast future drug prices and market trends, informing negotiation strategies and ensuring optimal value for the PBM.
- **Touchpoint— Formulary Review**
- **AI:** AI analyzes claims data and identifies medication

underutilization or potential alternatives with better cost-effectiveness and patient outcomes, optimizing the formulary.

- **Touchpoint— Patient Education and Adherence**
- **AI:** PBM collaborates with pharmaceutical companies to develop personalized medication adherence programs that use AI-powered reminders, targeted educational resources, and gamification elements.

2. **Navigating the Ethical Maze:**
   - **Bias and Fairness:** Ensure AI algorithms are trained on diverse datasets and regularly audited to avoid biased recommendations or discriminatory outcomes.
   - **Data Privacy and Security:** Implement robust data protection measures and transparent communication practices to build trust with patients and other stakeholders.
   - **Human Oversight and Accountability:** Maintain human oversight at all stages of AI implementation and clearly define ethical principles for responsible development and use.
3. **AI's Future Promise:**
   - **Personalized Medicine:** AI will enable the development of truly personalized treatments and prevention strategies tailored to individual genetic profiles and environmental factors.
   - **Real-time Healthcare:** Continuous data monitoring through AI-powered wearables and devices will facilitate proactive interventions and preventative measures, transforming healthcare into a real-time predictive system.
   - **Collaborative Ecosystems:** AI will foster deeper collaboration between pharma companies, HCPs, and patients, breaking down silos and creating a patient-centric, data-driven healthcare ecosystem.

Beyond the Basics: Uncovering Deeper Optimization with AI

Building on the previous examples, let's dive into even more touchpoints within each journey, highlighting the diverse ways AI can enhance customer relationships in pharma:

A. Hypertensive Patient:

- **Pre-diagnosis:**
  - **AI-powered Health Assessment Tools:** Analyze family history, lifestyle factors, and genetic marketers to identify individuals at risk of developing hypertension, enabling early intervention and prevention strategies.
  - **Virtual Health Assistants:** Guide individuals through self-monitoring blood pressure and provide personalized lifestyle recommendations based on real-time data.
- **Treatment Adherence:**
  - **Smart Pill Packaging:** Integrate medication reminders and adherence tracking into pill dispensers, motivating patients and providing valuable data for personalized interventions.
  - **Gamified Medication Adherence Programs:** Leverage AI to design engaging games and reward systems encouraging patients to adhere to their medication schedules.
- **Mental Well-being and Stress Management:**
  - **AI-Powered Stress Recognition and Coping Tools:** Analyze physiological data and user interactions to identify stress triggers and offer personalized relaxation techniques and emotional support resources.
  - **Peer Support Groups and Communities:** Utilize AI to match patients with similar experiences and build online communities for shared learning and encouragement.

B. Oncologist:

- **Tumor Diagnosis and Staging:**
  - **AI-Powered Image Analysis for Early Detection:** This technology analyzes scans and biopsies more accurately,

identifying even subtle abnormalities and enabling earlier cancer diagnosis.

- **Predictive Models for Personalized Risk Assessment:** Utilize AI for tumor progression and recurrent risk, informing treatment decisions and tailoring follow-up care.

- **Treatment Side Effect Management:**
  - **AI-powered Symptom Prediction and Mitigation:** Analyze patient data and treatment plans to predict potential side effects and suggest proactive interventions or adjustments to minimize their impact.
  - **Real-time Symptom Monitoring and Reporting:** Wearable devices and AI-powered apps enable patients to track and report side effects in real-time, allowing immediate response and treatment plan adjustment.
- **Survivorship and Post-treatment Support:**
  - **AI-Driven Survivorship Care Plans:** Generate personalized plans for long-term monitoring, rehabilitation, and managing potential late-stage effects, optimizing survivorship outcomes.
  - **Virtual Support Groups and Peer Mentoring:** Connect cancer survivors with AI-powered platforms to find mentors and relevant emotional and practical support resources.

C. PBM (Pharmacy Benefit Manager):

- **Patient Education and Medication Literacy:**
  - **AI-Powered Chatbots and Virtual Assistants:** Provide patients with accurate, personalized information about their medications, side effects, and potential interactions, improving medication literacy and promoting safe usage.
  - **Interactive Video Explainers and Educational Materials:** Utilizing AI to personalize educational content based on patient needs and preferences, increasing comprehension and engagement.

- **Cost-Efficiency and Resource Allocation:**
  - **AI-driven Claim Fraud Detection:** Identify and prevent fraudulent activity in real-time, minimizing financial losses and ensuring efficient resource allocation.
  - **Predictive Models for Medication Utilization:** Optimize inventory management and ensure patient medication availability for each future medication needs and potential drug shortages.
- **Collaboration and Data Sharing:**
  - **AI-Powered Data Marketplaces:** Securely share aggregated and anonymized patient data with pharma companies to facilitate research and development of new, personalized treatments.
  - **Joint Initiatives for Medication Adherence:** Partner with pharma companies to develop AI-powered adherence programs that improve patient outcomes and reduce long-term healthcare costs.

These are just a few additional touchpoints where AI can significantly impact customer journeys in pharma. Remember, the possibilities are constantly evolving, and the key is to embrace a collaborative approach where human expertise and ethical considerations guide the development and application of AI solutions for optimal patient care and enhanced customer relationships.

CHAPTER

22

AI-Powered Omnichannel Marketing in Pharma

What is omnichannel Marketing?

Omnichannel marketing is a customer-centric approach that integrates all online and offline channels to provide customers with a cohesive and consistent brand experience regardless of how they interact with the company.

Here's a deeper look at the rise of omnichannel marketing:

The Fragmented Customer Journey of the Past:

Traditionally, marketing focused on linear customer journeys. For example, a patient might see a television commercial for a new medication and then visit a doctor who prescribes it. This approach relied heavily on mass media and limited touchpoints.

The Challenge of Siloed Channels:

However, the rise of the internet and digital technologies fragmented the customer journey. Patients can now research medications online, read reviews on social media, and connect with healthcare providers through various platforms. This creates a complex web of touchpoints where customers gather information and make decisions.

The Power of Omnichannel Marketing:

Omnichannel marketing addresses this fragmentation by ensuring a unified brand experience across all channels. Here's how it works:

- **Consistent Messaging**: The core message about medication, its benefits, and brand values remains consistent across all touchpoints, from website content to social media posts and printed brochures.
- **Seamless Transitions**: Customers can easily transition between channels without experiencing a disconnect. For instance, a patient might see a social media ad for a medication, visit the company website for more detailed information, and consult a doctor who can prescribe it.
- **Personalized Communication**: Omnichannel marketing leverages data and AI to personalize communication-based on a customer's demographics, online behavior, and past interactions. This allows for targeted messaging that resonates more deeply with each individual.

Why Omnichannel Marketing is on the Rise:

Several factors have contributed to the rise of omnichannel marketing:

- **Customer Expectations**: Today's customers expect a seamless and consistent brand experience across all channels. They want information readily available, regardless of the device they use.
- **The Growth of Digital Channels**: The explosion of digital channels like social media, mobile apps, and online review platforms has created more touchpoints for customer interaction.
- **Data and Analytics**: The availability of rich customer data and advanced analytics allows companies to understand customer behavior and tailor their marketing strategies across channels.

- **Marketing Technology (MarTech)**: The rise of marketing automation tools and customer relationship management (CRM) platforms has made it easier for companies to manage and orchestrate omnichannel campaigns.

The Benefits of Omnichannel Marketing:

By implementing an omnichannel marketing strategy, pharmaceutical companies can reap several benefits:

- **Increased Customer Engagement**: A seamless and personalized experience across channels keeps customers engaged with the brand.
- **Improved Conversion Rates**: Targeted communication and a clear path to conversion across channels can lead to more patients starting and adhering to medication regimens.
- **Enhanced Brand Reputation**: A consistent and positive brand experience across all touchpoints fosters trust and loyalty among patients, HCPs, and other stakeholders.
- **Data-Driven Decision Making**: Omnichannel marketing allows for real-time data collection and analysis, enabling companies to optimize their campaigns and marketing spend based on what resonates with customers.

Overall, omnichannel marketing is no longer a luxury but a necessity for pharmaceutical companies to thrive in today's dynamic and customer-centric healthcare landscape.

This fragmented customer journey refers to the complex, non-linear path patients, healthcare providers (HCPs), and other stakeholders take when encountering information or making medication decisions. This contrasts with the traditional view of a linear customer journey with set touchpoints. Here's a deeper dive into why the customer journey has become fragmented:

The Explosion of Information Channels:

- **The Internet**: The Internet has become a primary source of information for patients and HCPs alike. Patients can research medications online, read reviews on platforms like WebMD or patient forums, and connect with support groups on social media. HCPs can access clinical trial data, research publications, and online educational resources.
- **The Rise of Mobile**: Smartphones and tablets have become ubiquitous, allowing patients and HCPs to access information online. This creates additional touchpoints where they might encounter marketing messages, medication information, or doctor reviews.
- **Social Media**: Social media platforms have become powerful information-sharing and community-building tools. Patients can connect, share experiences with medications, and even participate in online discussions with healthcare professionals.
- **Wearable Devices and the Internet of Things**: The rise of wearable health devices and the IoT adds another layer of complexity. These devices can collect health data (e.g., heart rate, blood pressure) that can be used to monitor medication effectiveness or inform treatment decisions.

Shifting Power Dynamics:

- **Empowered Patients**: The Internet has empowered patients to take a more active role in healthcare decisions. They are no longer passive recipients of information from doctors but actively seek information and participate in online communities to learn about medications and treatment options.
- **Evolving HCP Landscape**: HCPs are increasingly time-constrained and bombarded with marketing messages from pharmaceutical companies. They rely on various sources, including online resources, peer-to-peer networks, and patient feedback, to make informed prescribing decisions.

The Impact of Fragmentation:

This fragmentation of the customer journey presents several challenges for pharmaceutical companies:

- **Reaching the Right Audience**: With so many channels vying for attention, it's difficult for companies to ensure their message reaches the right audience at the right time.
- **Delivering a Consistent Message**: Maintaining a consistent brand message across all channels can be challenging, especially with such a wide variety of touchpoints.
- **Understanding Customer Needs**: The fragmented journey makes it difficult for companies to get a holistic view of customer needs and preferences.
- **Optimizing Marketing Efforts:** Measuring the effectiveness of marketing campaigns across multiple channels can be complex.

Conclusion:

The fragmented customer journey is a reality of the modern pharma marketing landscape. However, by understanding this complexity and leveraging AI-powered omnichannel marketing strategies, pharmaceutical companies can create a more cohesive and personalized experience for patients, HCPs, and other stakeholders, ultimately leading to better healthcare outcomes.

Omnichannel Marketing and Targeting

In the complex landscape of omnichannel marketing, where brands strive to deliver cohesive experiences across multiple touchpoints, the duet of AI and human expertise plays a crucial role in achieving effective targeting and engagement. Imagine an orchestra where AI provides the instruments of data and analysis while humans lead the melodies of creativity and strategy. Here is how this collaboration works:

The AI Conductor:

- **Data Collection and Unification:** AI gathers, cleans, and integrates data from various channels, including websites, social media, email, customer relationship management(CRM) systems, and point-of-sale (POS) data. This creates a holistic view of each customer.
- **Segmentation and Targeting:** AI analyzes customer data to identify distinct segments based on demographics, behavior, preferences, and intent. It then personalizes content and messaging for each segment across different channels.
- **Real-Time Insights and Optimization:** AI monitors real-time customer interactions, allowing for dynamic campaign adjustments and personalized recommendations based on individual behavior.

The Human Virtuoso:

- **Strategic Direction and Story Telling:** Humans define the omnichannel marketing strategy, setting goals and crafting compelling narratives that resonate with target audiences across all touchpoints.
- **Creative Content and Messaging:** Humans inject creativity into campaign assets, tailoring content formats, tones, and design elements to specific channels and audience preferences.
- **Ethical Considerations and Brand Consistency:** Humans ensure that personalization remains ethical and responsible, avoiding biases and manipulation while maintaining brand voice and messaging across all channels.

Harmonious Duet:

To achieve true omnichannel success, collaboration requires a harmonious blend of strengths.

- **Symbiotic Integration:** AI empowers humans, not replaces them. Imagine AI suggesting optimal ad placements based on data, but a human creates the targeted ad content.
- **Human Oversight and Guidance:** Humans evaluate and interpret AI insights, ensuring ethical practices and aligning campaigns with strategic goals.
- **Continuous Learning and Adaptation:** AI models and human understanding must evolve. AI requires regular updates with new data, while humans must effectively reskill technology and data analysis tools.

Examples of Omnichannel Targeting:

Imagine these scenarios:

- Customers receive a personalized email based on their recent website browsing, followed by a retargeting ad on social media with a special offer relevant to the product they viewed.
- A company sends birthday greetings through different channels— an email with a discount code, a social media post mentioning their favorite product, and even a personalized notification within their app.
- Potential customers receive targeted content throughout their purchase journey, from helpful blog posts on their browsing topic to a live chat offer when they hesitate at checkout.

Orchestrated Symphony: AI-Powered Omnichannel Marketing in Pharma

In today's dynamic pharma marketing landscape, effectively reaching and engaging customers requires a multifaceted approach. This chapter explores the transformative power of AI in orchestrating omnichannel marketing strategies, ensuring seamless communication across all touch points.

The Rise of Omnichannel Marketing:

- **The Fragmented Customer Journey**: Gone are the days of a linear customer journey. Patients, HCPs, and other stakeholders navigate a complex web of online and offline channels to gather information and make decisions.
- **The Power of Omnichannel**: Omnichannel marketing strives to create a unified and consistent brand experience across all touchpoints, from a company website to social media platforms, email marketing, and in-person interactions with sales representatives.

AI: The Conductor of the Omnichannel Orchestra:

- **Data-Driven Audience Segmentation**: AI analyzes vast datasets to segment customers into distinct groups based on demographics, online behavior, and past interactions. This allows for targeted communication tailored to each segment's specific needs.
- **Personalized Content Creation**: AI can generate or personalize content (e.g., blog posts, social media messages, educational videos) based on audience segment and their stage in the customer journey.
- **Dynamic Campaign Optimization**: AI tracks customer engagement metrics across various channels, allowing for real-time optimization of campaigns and content delivery strategies.

AI Applications Across Channels:

- **Website Personalization**: AI tailors website content and recommendations based on visitors' previous interactions and search queries.
- **Targeted Email Marketing**: AI personalizes email content, subject lines, and sending schedules based on recipient demographics and interests.

- **Social Media Engagement**: AI can analyze social media conversations to identify trending topics and engage with relevant audiences. It can also personalize social media ads for targeted reach.
- **Programmatic Advertising**: AI automates the buying and selling of ad space across various online platforms, ensuring targeted ad delivery to relevant customer segments.
- **Mobile Marketing**: AI can personalize push notifications, in-app messaging, and mobile ad experiences based on user behavior and location data (with appropriate privacy considerations).

The Human Touch in AI-Powered Omnichannel Marketing:

- **Content Curation and Creativity:** While AI can personalize content, human expertise remains crucial in crafting compelling and emotionally resonant messages.
- **Building Relationships and Trust**: Human representatives are irreplaceable in building rapport, addressing complex questions, and fostering customer trust.
- **Ethical Considerations**: Humans ensure that AI-powered omnichannel marketing adheres to ethical principles and data privacy regulations and avoids potential communication biases.

Omnichannel Marketing: Some Examples

The power of omnichannel marketing in pharma lies in its ability to create a seamless and personalized experience for patients, HCPs, and other stakeholders throughout their journey with a specific medication or pharmaceutical company. Here are some examples showcasing this power:

Example 1: Supporting a Patient with Migraines:

- **Imagine a patient experiencing frequent migraines**. They might start their journey by **searching online** for "migraine relief options."

- An omnichannel approach would ensure they encounter the pharmaceutical company's migraine medication across various touchpoints:
  - **Targeted online ads** featuring the medication and its benefits.
  - **Educational blog posts** on the company website explaining different types of migraines and treatment options.
  - **Social media content** from patient advocacy groups discussing the medication and sharing success stories.
- Once the patient decides to talk to their doctor, the company could ensure **HCPs** have access to:
  - **Detailed online resources** about the medication's efficacy and safety data.
  - **Webinars** hosted by medical experts discussing the latest migraine treatment options.
  - **Targeted email marketing** with clinical trial data and prescribing information.
- Finally, after the doctor prescribes the medication, the patient might receive:
  - **Personalized mobile app reminders** to take their medication on time.
  - **Educational content** within the app about managing migraines and potential side effects.
  - **A dedicated patient support hotline** staffed by nurses or pharmacists to answer any questions.

Example 2: Launching a New Diabetes Medication:

- A pharmaceutical company launches a new medication for Type 2 diabetes.
- An omnichannel approach can help them reach various stakeholders:
  - **Patients**: Educational videos on social media platforms explaining how the new medication works and its advantages.

- **HCPs**: Targeted email campaigns with detailed information about clinical trials, dosage recommendations, and potential interactions with other medications.
- **Payers**: Data-driven insights from AI analysis demonstrating the medication's cost-effectiveness compared to existing treatments.

The Benefits of Omnichannel in Pharma:

- **Increased Patient Engagement**: By providing patients with relevant information and support across channels, they are more likely to adhere to their medication regimen and experience better health outcomes.
- **Improved HCP Education**: Targeted omnichannel communication ensures HCPs stay up-to-date on the latest treatment options and can make informed prescribing decisions.
- **Enhanced Brand Reputation**: A consistent and positive brand experience across all touchpoints fosters trust and loyalty among patients, HCPs, and other stakeholders.
- **Measurable Results**: Omnichannel marketing allows for data-driven measurement of campaign effectiveness across various channels, enabling companies to optimize their marketing spend and strategies.

Conclusion:

In today's dynamic pharma marketing landscape, omnichannel marketing is no longer a luxury but a necessity. By creating a seamless and personalized experience across all touchpoints, pharmaceutical companies can build stronger relationships with stakeholders, improve patient care, and contribute to a healthier future.

Omnichannel Marketing: Role of AI and Humans

In omnichannel marketing, AI is crucial in data analysis, personalization, and automation. However, the human touch remains essential to ensure effective communication and build trust with patients and healthcare professionals (HCPs). Here is a breakdown of the human touch in AI-powered omnichannel marketing:

The Role of the Human Touch:

While AI excels at data analysis and automation, human qualities are irreplaceable in marketing, especially in pharma:

- **Creativity and Storytelling:** Humans can craft compelling narratives that resonate with emotions and inspire action. AI can assist with content generation, but human expertise is needed to curate and refine it for a targeted audience.
- **Empathy and Understanding:** Humans can understand the emotional nuances of patient experience and tailor communication accordingly. AI can personalize content based on data, but human intervention ensures messages are empathetic and address patient concerns.
- **Ethical Considerations:** AI algorithms need human oversight to ensure responsible marketing practices and adherence to industry regulations, particularly regarding patient privacy and data security.
- **Strategic Decision-Making:** Humans must interpret data insights from AI and translate them into actionable marketing strategies that align with overall business goals.

Examples of Human Touch in AI-Powered Omnichannel Marketing:

Example 1: Personalizing Email Marketing for Medication Adherence:

- **AI's Role:** AI analyzes patient data to identify those struggling with medication adherence

- **Human Touch:** A healthcare professional or marketing team member crafts personalized emails with a supportive tone. The emails might acknowledge potential challenges with medication adherence, offer practical tips, or connect patients with relevant resources.

Example 2: Building Trustworthy Chatbots:

- **AI's Role:** It powers a chatbot on the company website that answers basic patient questions about a new medication.
- **Human Touch:** The chatbot script is designed with a friendly and informative tone, avoiding overly technical language. It includes clear instructions for reaching a live customer service representative for complex inquiries.

Example 3: Enhancing Social Media Engagement:

- **AI's Role:** Monitors social media mentions and identifies potential customer service issues.
- **Human Touch:** A social media manager responds to comments and messages with a human voice, addressing concerns, offering support, and directing patients to appropriate resources when needed.

Conclusion:

AI and the human touch are not opposing forces but complementary elements in a successful omnichannel marketing strategy for pharma. By leveraging AI for data analysis and automation while maintaining a human-centric approach to communication, pharmaceutical relationships with patients and HCPs lead to better health outcomes.

The following case study about the launch of a new medication shows how omnichannel marketing plays out in pharmaceutical marketing:

Omnichannel Marketing Strategy for GlucoBalance, A Hypothetical Brand of a New Diabetes Medication:

Brand USP:

- Superior blood sugar control with minimal side effects compared to competitors.

Target Audience:

- Patients with Type 2 Diabetes
- Healthcare Professionals (HCPs) include endocrinologists, diabetologists, and primary care physicians.

Marketing Objectives:

- Increase brand awareness for GlucoBalance among patients and HCPs.
- Educate patients about the benefits of GlucoBalance and how it can improve their blood sugar control.
- Drive prescription of GlucoBalance by HCPs.

Omnichannel Strategy:

1. **Pre-Launch Phase (Generate Buzz and Educate):**
    - **Website:** Develop a user-friendly website with clear information about GlucoBalance, its mechanism of action, and clinical trial data highlighting superior blood sugar control and minimal side effects compared to competitors. Include patient testimonials and FAQs.
    - **Social Media Marketing:** Create engaging social media content (Facebook, Instagram, Twitter, now known as "X") to build brand awareness.
        - Partner with diabetes influencers to share their experiences with managing blood sugar.
        - Host live Q&A sessions with diabetes educators or medical professionals to address patient concerns.

    - Utilize relevant hashtags (#diabetes #bloodsugarcontrol #GlucoBalance) to increase search.

- **Content Marketing:**
    - Develop blog articles and infographics on diabetes management, healthy living tips, and the importance of blood sugar control.
    - Partner with patient advocacy groups to publish educational content about GlucoBalance on their platforms.
- **Public Relations:** Issue press releases announcing the upcoming launch of GlucoBalance, highlighting its unique selling points (USPs).

2. **Launch Phase (Drive Awareness and Trial):**
    - **Digital Advertising:** Utilize targeted display advertising across relevant websites and social media platforms to reach patients with diabetes.
    - **Search Engine Marketing (SEM):** Implement a strategic pay-per-click (PPC) campaign targeting relevant keywords related to diabetes, blood sugar control, and medication options.
    - **Video Marketing:** Create short, informative videos explaining GlucoBalance's benefits and how it works. Promote on platforms like YouTube and social media.
    - **Physician Outreach:** Develop educational materials for HCPs detailing GlucoBalance clinical trial data, efficacy, and minimal side effect profile compared to competitors.
    - **Organize Webinars** or in-person workshops for HCPs to learn more about GlucoBalance.
    - **Partner** with medical professional associations for wider reach.

3. **Post-Launch Phase (Sustain Engagement and Sales):**
    - **Patient Support Programs:** Develop a comprehensive patient support program offering personalized guidance, medication adherence reminders, and access to educational resources.
    - **Mobile Marketing:** Develop a mobile app for patients to track their blood sugar levels and medication intake and connect with healthcare providers.
    - **Email Marketing:** Create targeted email campaigns for patients, offering educational content, special offers, and reminders for prescription refills.
    - **Social Media Engagement:** Continue to engage with patients on social media, address their questions and concerns, and foster a supportive online community.
    - **Track and Analyze Results:** Continuously monitor the performance of marketing campaigns across all channels. Analyze data to identify what works best and optimize strategies for better results.

Metrics to Track:

- Website traffic and engagement
- Social media reach and engagement
- Lead generation (patient sign-ups, HCP inquiries)
- Conversion rates (prescription requests, product sales)

Overall Tone and Messaging:

- Maintain a professional, trustworthy, and informative tone across all channels.
- Focus on educating patients about diabetes management and how GlucoBalance can help them achieve better blood sugar control.
- Emphasize the safety profile of GlucoBalance with minimal side effects compared to competitors.

- Highlight patient success stories and testimonials to build trust and credibility.

GlucoBalance can effectively reach its target audience and generate brand awareness by implementing a well-coordinated omnichannel marketing strategy. Educate patients and HCPs, drive product adoption, and improve patient outcomes.

By harnessing the power of AI in omnichannel marketing, pharmaceutical companies can create a truly patient-centric experience. AI orchestrates seamless communication across channels, while human expertise ensures ethical considerations and fosters stakeholder trust. This synergy between human and machine intelligence will continue to evolve, paving the way for a future of pharma marketing that is both effective and ethical.

The Future of AI-Powered Omnichannel Marketing

The future of AI-powered omnichannel marketing is brimming with exciting possibilities that promise a more personalized, immersive, and data-driven experience for patients and healthcare providers (HCPs) in the pharmaceutical space. Here's a glimpse into what the future might hold:

Advanced Personalization:

- **AI-powered Micro-Segmentation**: AI will go beyond basic demographics and delve into psychographics and behavioral patterns to create ultra-specific audience segments. This allows for hyper-personalized content that resonates deeply with individual needs and preferences.
- **Predictive Content Delivery**: AI will anticipate user needs and proactively deliver relevant content across channels before they even express a search query. Imagine a patient receiving an educational video about potential side effects after picking up a new medication.

Seamless Omnichannel Experience:

- **Omnichannel Orchestration**: AI will act as the conductor, seamlessly integrating marketing efforts across all channels. For example, a patient's online product research might trigger a targeted ad on their mobile device with a special discount offer at a nearby pharmacy.
- **Omnichannel Attribution**: AI will accurately track customer journeys across touchpoints, showing how each channel contributes to conversions. This allows for data-driven decisions on budget allocation and campaign optimization.

AI-Powered Content Creation:

- **Automated Content Generation Tailored to Channels**: AI will create high-quality content like blog posts, social media captions, and video scripts specifically optimized for each channel's format and audience preferences.
- **Personalized Creative Assets**: Imagine AI generating visuals and personalized marketing materials that dynamically adapt based on user data. For example, a medication advertisement might showcase a model with a similar skin tone or age group to the target audience.

Evolving Customer Service:

- **AI-Powered Chatbots with Emotional Intelligence**: Chatbots will become more sophisticated, understanding and responding to the emotional undertones of user queries. This fosters a more natural and empathetic customer service experience.
- **Virtual Healthcare Assistants**: AI-powered virtual assistants might become commonplace, offering patients basic health information, medication reminders, and even preliminary symptom analysis to guide them toward seeking appropriate medical attention.

Ethical Considerations:

As AI becomes more integrated into marketing, ethical considerations will remain paramount. Transparency and user privacy will be crucial. Here are some aspects to consider:

- **Explainable AI**: Companies must explain how AI algorithms make decisions and personalize content to e**nsure fairness and avoid bias.**
- **User Control Over Data**: Patients and HCPs should control how pharmaceutical companies collect, use, and store their data.

Conclusion:

AI-powered omnichannel marketing in pharma is a future of deep personalization, seamless customer experiences, and intelligent content creation. However, human oversight and ethical considerations will remain essential to ensure the responsible use of AI and build trust with patients and healthcare professionals. As AI technology develops, the possibilities for omnichannel marketing in pharma are limitless.

CHAPTER 23

AI and Humans Revolutionize Pharma Marketing Research

The world of pharma marketing research, once reliant on traditional methods and siloed data, is undergoing a revolutionary transformation. At the forefront of this change stands the powerful synergy of human expertise and artificial intelligence (AI). This chapter delves into the transformative potential of collaboration, exploring how AI empowers humans to conduct market research, analyze competitors, gather competitive intelligence, and ultimately craft winning marketing strategies.

1. **Redefining Market Research**:
   - Traditional methods like surveys and focus groups are enriched by AI-powered sentiment analysis, social media mining, and real-time data acquisition.
   - AI-driven insights identify hidden trends, predict patient needs, and uncover previously inaccessible segments within the target markets.
   - Human-AI collaboration ensures ethical data collection, unbiased analysis, and a nuanced understanding of patient behaviors and motivations.

   Case Study: A Pharma company developing a new diabetes medication leverages AI to analyze online forums and social media conversations. They discover a previously unidentified segment of young, tech-savvy patients eager for convenient and discreet diabetes management solutions. This insight informs campaign development and product positioning, leading to a successful market launch.

2. **Supercharging Competitive Analysis**:
   - AI algorithms process vast amounts of data, including competitor marketing materials, clinical trial results, and financial reports, providing a comprehensive picture of the landscape.
   - Humans leverage AI-generated insights to identify competitor strengths and weaknesses, predict future moves, and develop differentiated marketing strategies.
   - By analyzing competitor websites, social media engagement, and advertising campaigns, AI reveals its target audiences, preferred messaging, and potential vulnerabilities.

   Case Study: A pharma company analyzing its competitors in the pain management market uses AI to identify a popular marketing campaign targeting athletes. Humans then develop a counter-campaign highlighting their own medication's effectiveness and safety for active individuals, successfully capturing market share.

3. **Unlock Competitive Intelligence**:
   - AI tools mine news articles, patent databases, and industry publications, delivering real-time updates on competitor developments, regulatory changes, and emerging trends.
   - Humans interpret AI-generated intelligence, assess its implications for their marketing strategies, and proactively adapt to market shifts and competitor actions.
   - By analyzing clinical trial data and patent filings, AI predicts upcoming competitor product launches and identifies potential areas for disruptive innovation.

   Case Study: A pharma company developing a new cancer treatment uses AI to monitor competitor clinical trials and regulatory filings. They anticipate potential delays in competitor approval and adjust their launch timeline and marketing messaging to capitalize on the first-mover advantage

4. **The Ethical Imperative**:
   - Transparency and data privacy are paramount throughout the AI-powered research process. Humans ensure ethical data collection and usage, avoiding bias and discrimination in analysis and interpretation.
   - Collaboration between AI and humans fosters critical thinking and ethical decision-making, preventing AI misuse and ensuring responsible marketing practices.
   - Monitoring and evaluating AI algorithms and research methods are crucial to maintaining ethical standards and building stakeholder trust.
5. **The Future of Pharma Marketing Research**:
   - The human-AI collaboration will continue to evolve with increasingly sophisticated AI tools and deeper integration into every aspect of research.
   - As AI capabilities expand, humans will focus on creative strategy development, communication, and ethical oversight, guiding the AI and ensuring its responsible application.
   - This synergistic approach holds immense potential to revolutionize pharma marketing research, paving the way for more targeted, impactful, and ethically sound marketing strategies that ultimately benefit patients and healthcare professionals.

AI-Powered Market and Marketing Research Processes: A Step-by-Step Guide:

Market Research:

- Market research in pharma is all about understanding the pharmaceutical market and the people in it. It helps drug companies make better decisions by gathering information on:

- **Market size and trends:** How big is the market for a particular drug or therapy? Is it growing or shrinking?
- **Customer needs:** What do doctors, patients, and caregivers need? What are they looking for in a new drug?
- **Competition:** Who are the competitors? What are their strengths and weaknesses?

This information is crucial for developing new drugs, marketing them effectively, and pricing them competitively.

Here are some of the ways that pharmaceutical companies conduct market research:

- **Surveys and interviews:** To get their insights, talk to doctors, patients, and caregivers.
- **Focus groups:** Bringing together a small group to discuss a particular topic.
- **Secondary research:** Analyzing data that other organizations have already collected.

Using market research, pharmaceutical companies can improve their chances of success in a competitive and ever-changing industry.

Here is a step-by-step guide to conducting market research in the pharmaceutical industry:

1. **Define Research Objectives:**
    - **Human**: Identify key questions about your target market, competitors, and industry trends.
    - **AI**: Analyze historical data, industry reports, and news to refine objectives and suggest additional areas of inquiry.
2. **Select Research Methods**:
    - **Human**: Choose appropriate methods like surveys, focus groups, or social media listening based on objectives.
    - **AI**: For faster and more cost-effective data gathering, automated data collection tools, online surveys, and social media analytics platforms.

3. **Collect Data:**
   - **Human**: Conduct surveys, interviews, or online research as chosen.
   - **AI**: Automate data collection through online surveys, social media scraping, and website analytics, reducing manual effort and increasing data volume.
4. **Analyze Data**:
   - **Human**: Employ traditional statistical analysis or qualitative coding techniques.
   - **AI**: Use advanced data analysis tools, such as machine learning and natural language processing, to identify hidden patterns, trends, and sentiments in large datasets.
5. **Generate Insights and Recommendations**:
   - **Human**: Interpret data, draw conclusions, and formulate actionable recommendations based on analysis.
   - **AI**: Provide visualizations, summaries, and predictive models to help interpret data and recommend specific insights-based strategies.

Marketing Research:

In the world of pharmaceuticals, marketing research goes beyond just understanding the market size. It's a strategic tool to develop and launch drugs that meet patient needs and succeed commercially. Here's a breakdown of its role:

Understanding Stakeholders: Pharmaceutical marketing research focuses on multiple stakeholders, not just patients. This includes:

- **Healthcare Providers (HCPs)** are doctors, nurses, and specialists who prescribe medications. Research helps understand their prescribing habits, preferences, and knowledge gaps related to new drugs.
- **Patients:** Understanding patient needs, concerns, and preferred treatment options is crucial. Research can involve disease burden, treatment adherence, and information needs.

- **Payers:** Insurance companies and government bodies that reimburse for medications. Research helps determine how a new drug might be priced and positioned for coverage.

Informing Key Decisions: Market research provides valuable data to guide various aspects of a drug's journey:

- **Product Development:** Research can influence dosage forms, delivery methods, and even naming based on patient preferences and HCP needs.
- **Marketing & Sales Strategies:** Market research is crucial for understanding competitor tactics, patient communication channels, and effective messaging for new drugs.
- **Pricing & Reimbursement:** Research helps determine a drug's value proposition and build a case for appropriate pricing and coverage by payers.

Types of Research Methods Used:

Pharmaceutical market research employs various methods to gather data:

- **Primary Research:** This involves collecting first-hand information through surveys, interviews, and focus groups with patients, HCPs, and payers.
- **Secondary Research:** Existing data from medical journals, government reports, and healthcare databases is analyzed to understand market trends and competitor landscapes.

The Evolving Landscape:

The pharmaceutical industry is constantly evolving. Market research adapts to this by using advanced analytics and market intelligence platforms. These allow for faster data processing, identification of emerging trends, and data-driven decisions throughout the drug development and marketing process.

By utilizing market research, pharmaceutical companies can ensure they're creating drugs that address unmet medical needs, are communicated effectively to the right audience, and have a higher chance of commercial success.

Here is a step-by-step guide for conducting marketing research in the pharmaceutical industry:

1. **Define Target Audience**:
   - **Human**: Analyze market research findings and develop detailed profiles of target customers.
   - **AI**: Utilize segmentation tools to cluster customers based on demographics, online behavior, and psychographics, creating more precise target segments.
2. **Analyze Competitor Marketing**:
   - **Human**: Monitor competitor campaigns, messaging, and product offerings.
   - **AI**: Track competitor activity across channels, analyze website content and copy, and identify their strengths and weaknesses.
3. **Evaluate Existing Marketing Materials**:
   - **Human**: Assess the effectiveness of current campaigns through website analytics, surveys, and social media monitoring.
   - **AI**: Analyze website traffic, customer engagement, and brand sentiment to identify areas for improvement in messaging and content.
4. **Optimize Marketing Strategy**:
   - **Human**: Develop new campaigns, refine messaging, and select channels based on research insights.
   - **AI**: Recommend personalized content, predict campaign performance, and suggest optimal channel mixes and content formats for target segments.

5. **Measure and Adapt**:
   - **Human**: Track campaign performance through analytics and refine strategies based on results.
   - **AI**: Provide real-time performance updates, identify emerging trends, and suggest adjustments to optimize campaigns continuously.

AI Optimization Benefits:

- **Speed and Efficiency**: Automate data collection, analysis, and reporting, saving time and resources.
- **Deeper Insights**: Uncover hidden patterns and trends in large datasets that need to be noticed by human analysis.
- **Personalization**: Tailor marketing strategies and content to specific customer segments for higher engagement and conversion rates.
- **Predictive Intelligence**: Forecast future trends in customer behavior to adapt campaigns proactively.
- **Data-Driven Decision-Making**: Base decisions on objective data and insights, minimizing guesswork and maximizing ROI.

Remember, AI is a valuable tool, not replacing human expertise. The best market and marketing research results from a synergistic blend of human creativity, critical thinking, and ethical considerations with the power and efficiency of AI-driven insights. By incorporating these steps and leveraging AI effectively, you can conduct comprehensive and optimized market and marketing research, leading to well-informed strategies and, ultimately, marketing success.

Dissecting the Competition: A Deep Dive into Pharma Competitor Analysis and Competitive Intelligence with AI

Staying ahead of the curve in high-stakes pharma relies heavily on understanding your competitors' strategies. Enter the crucial domains of competitor analysis and competitive intelligence, where human expertise and AI join forces to unveil important insights that inform every facet of your pharma marketing game plan:

Competitor Analysis:

1. **Identifying Competitors:**
    - **Humans:** Define the competitive landscape based on market share, therapeutic areas, and product pipelines.
    - **AI:** Analyze industry databases, financial reports, and news articles to identify emerging players and potential future competitors.

    Example: A pharma company developing a new diabetes medication analyzes market share data to identify its top three competitors. They further utilize AI to discover smaller startups focused on innovative insulin delivery systems, which could pose a future threat.

2. **Assessing Strengths and Weaknesses:**
    - **Humans:** Evaluate competitor marketing materials, clinical trial results, and financial performance.
    - **AI:** Analyze competitor websites, social media engagement, and patent filings to identify key strengths and potential vulnerabilities.

    Example: The diabetes medication company uses AI to analyze competitor websites, revealing one competitor has a strong patient support program while another struggles with negative brand sentiment on social media.

3. **Analyzing Product Portfolio:**
    - **Humans:** Compare competitor product offerings regarding efficacy, side effects, price, and target indications.
    - **AI:** To identify potential differentiation opportunities, use data mining tools to compare product features, clinical trial data, and regulatory filings.

    Example: The AI analysis reveals that a competitor's diabetes medication has higher side effects, while another is significantly more expensive. This information lets the company position its medication as a safe, affordable alternative.

Competitive Intelligence:

1. **Tracking Industry Trends:**
    - **Human:** Monitor industry publications, conferences, and regulatory agencies for emerging trends and potential disruptions.
    - **AI:** Set up real-time alerts for relevant keywords and news articles, informing the team about early signs of new technologies, regulatory changes, or competitor developments.

Example: The AI system identifies news about regulatory approval for a competitor's new glucose monitoring device. This prompts the company to investigate potential partnerships or develop competing technology.

2. **Monitoring Competitor Activity:**
    - **Humans:** Track competitor marketing campaigns, salesforce presentations, and social media activities.
    - **AI:** Utilize web scraping tools and social media listening platforms to gather competitor data automatically, providing a comprehensive picture of their marketing strategies and messaging.

Example: The AI monitoring reveals a competitor's upcoming launch campaign targeting similar patient segments. This allows the company to adjust its launch timing and messaging to avoid direct competition.

3. **Predicting Future Actions:**

- **Humans:** Analyze historical data and competitor behavior to anticipate their next moves and strategic focus.
- **AI:** Utilize predictive analytics models based on competitor data and industry trends to forecast potential product launches, clinical trial outcomes, and future market shifts.

Example: The AI model predicts a high probability of competitor approval for a new drug in the same therapeutic area. This prompts the company to accelerate its development efforts to prepare for a competitive market landscape.

The Synergistic Power of AI & Humans:

- **Human:** Provide strategic direction, interpret AI insights, and ensure ethical data collection and analysis.
- **AI:** It automates data collection, identifies hidden patterns, and delivers real-time updates, enabling faster and more informed decision-making.

Remember, competitive intelligence is not just about outsmarting the competition; it's about gaining a deeper understanding of the market and your strengths and weaknesses. By leveraging AI effectively and ensuring ethical practices, you can develop winning strategies that benefit your patients, your company, and the healthcare ecosystem as a whole.

AI Revolutionizing Pharma Marketing Research

Artificial intelligence is revolutionizing pharmaceutical marketing research— enabling companies to gather insights from patent analysis.

AI-Powered Insights: Decoding the Secrets of Pharma Patents

In the competitive world of pharmaceuticals, gaining insights from patient analysis is crucial for staying ahead of the curve. Traditionally, this involved laborious manual reviews by experts. However, artificial intelligence (AI) is transforming this landscape, offering faster, deeper, and more data-driven insights from patent analysis.

How AI Can Help in Patent Analysis:

Here's how AI can help draw insights from patent analysis in pharma:

1. **Unlocking Hidden Connections:**
   - AI excels at identifying relationships between seemingly disparate concepts within and across patents. This allows

researchers to discover emerging technological trends that might disrupt the market.

- Potential infringement risks from competitors.
- Unforeseen opportunities for combining existing technologies for breakthrough innovations.

Example: AI might analyze a new drug delivery system patent and identify connections to patents for specific materials or manufacturing processes, suggesting alternative production methods or potential patent infringement issues.

2. Predicting Future Directions:

- AI can analyze historical patent data and industry trends to predict the future direction of specific technologies or therapeutic areas. This enables companies to make informed R&D investments by allocating resources to promising areas with high potential.
- Position themselves strategically in the market by anticipating competitors' moves and potential disruptions.

Example: By analyzing patents related to gene editing technologies, AI could predict which diseases and treatment approaches will likely see future breakthroughs, guiding a pharma company's research priorities.

3. Benchmarking and Competitive Intelligence:

- AI can analyze competitors' patent portfolios, identifying their focus areas, strengths, and weaknesses. This empowers companies to develop differentiated strategies by avoiding areas where competitors are strong and focusing on emerging opportunities.
- Identify potential partners or acquisition targets with complementary technologies or expertise.

Example: AI could analyze patents filed by a rival company known for developing cancer therapies, revealing their focus on specific drug targets and potential blind spots. This would allow another pharmaceutical company to prioritize different targets and gain a competitive edge.

4. **Personalized Patent Search and Alerting:**
   - AI can learn individual researchers' preferences and interests, automatically identifying and delivering relevant patents and updates tailored to their needs. This saves time and ensures they stay informed about critical developments in their field.

Example: A researcher focused on developing new antibiotics could receive automatic alerts whenever new patents related to specific drug resistance mechanisms or delivery systems are published, keeping them at the forefront of their field.

5. **Extracting Actionable Insights:**
   - AI goes beyond raw data, interpreting the context and meaning of patent information. This helps researchers prioritize the most relevant patents, understand the technical details, and draw actionable insights.

Example: Instead of just providing a list of patents mentioning a specific protein target, AI could identify the specific claims related to therapeutic applications, highlighting potential drug development opportunities and potential roadblocks.

Benefits of Using AI in Pharma Patent Analysis:

- Uncovers hidden connections and trends.
- Predicts future technological directions.
- Provides competitive intelligence and benchmarking.
- Personalizes the patent search experience.
- Extracts actionable insights from raw data.

AI is becoming an indispensable tool for gaining insights from pharmaceutical patent analysis. By unlocking hidden connections, predicting future trends, and providing personalized information, AI empowers pharmaceutical companies to make informed decisions, stay ahead of the competition, and develop differentiated products that improve patient outcomes.

Remember, responsible use of AI and adherence to ethical principles like data privacy and transparency are crucial for building trust and maximizing the benefits of this powerful technology.

CHAPTER 24

Point-of-Care AI: Transforming Healthcare at the Patient's Bedside

Point-of-care AI is the application of artificial intelligence directly at the patient's bedside, in clinics, pharmacies, or even in their homes. Unlike traditional AI used in research or analytics, point-of-care AI operates in real-time, delivering insights and aiding healthcare professionals in making immediate decisions. This has the potential to improve patient outcomes significantly by:

1. **Faster and More Accurate Diagnosis**:
    - AI algorithms can analyze medical images, vital signs, and other data to more accurately and quickly identify diseases or risk factors, leading to earlier diagnoses and quicker treatment initiation.
2. **Personalized Treatment and Care**:
    - AI can analyze patient data (medical history, genetics, lifestyle) to recommend personalized treatment plans and interventions tailored to their needs and risks.

Example: Point-of-care AI can analyze a patient's blood sugar levels and suggest adjustments to their insulin dosage based on their response patterns, optimizing their diabetes management.

3. **Improved Treatment Monitoring and Adherence**:
    - AI-powered wearable devices can continuously monitor vital signs and medication adherence, allowing real-time adjustments and personalized feedback to improve treatment outcomes.

Example: Smart inhalers with AI-powered sensors can track medication usage and alert patients or healthcare providers if they miss a dose, potentially preventing asthma flare-ups.

4. **Enhanced Decision-Making and Support**:
   - AI can analyze vast amounts of medical data and provide real-time insights to healthcare professionals, aiding them in making informed decisions about diagnosis, treatment, and resource allocation.

Example: Point-of-care AI can analyze a patient's medical history and current symptoms to suggest potential diagnoses and treatment options, supporting doctors in their decision-making process.

5. **Remote Patient Monitoring and Support:**
   - AI-powered telehealth platforms can remotely connect patients with healthcare providers, allowing continuous monitoring and support, especially in rural or underserved areas.

Example: Patients with chronic conditions can use AI-powered chatbots to answer questions, track symptoms, and receive personalized health guidance, improving their overall well-being.

How Point-of-Care AI Works

1. **Data Collection**: Vital signs, medical images, patient history, and other relevant data are collected through various sensors, devices, and medical records.
2. **Data Processing**: The data is pre-processed and fed into AI algorithms specifically designed for point-of-care applications.
3. **AI Analysis**: The algorithms analyze the data and identify patterns, correlations, or potential risks.
4. **Insights Generation**: AI generates insights, recommendations, or alerts based on the analysis presented to healthcare professionals in an understandable format.

5. **Decision-Making and Action**: Healthcare professionals leverage AI insights to make informed decisions about diagnosis, treatment, or further investigation.

Challenges and Considerations:

- **Data Privacy and Security**: Ensuring patient data privacy and security is paramount when using AI at the point of care.
- **Algorithmic Bias**: Training and monitoring AI algorithms to avoid biases that could lead to unfair or discriminatory outcomes is crucial.
- **Integration and Workflow**: Seamless integration of point-of-care AI into existing healthcare workflows and training healthcare professionals is essential.
- **Accessibility and Affordability**: Ensuring equitable access to point-of-care AI across diverse populations and healthcare settings requires careful planning and resource allocation.

Point-of-care AI holds immense potential to revolutionize healthcare delivery by providing faster diagnoses, personalized care, and improved patient outcomes. However, addressing ethical considerations, ensuring responsible development, and fostering collaboration between healthcare professionals and AI specialists are crucial to unlocking its full potential. As point-of-care AI evolves, its impact on patient care and healthcare systems will continue to unfold, leading to a more personalized, efficient, and accessible healthcare experience.

CHAPTER

25

AI Across the Pharmaceutical Value Chain

From Discovery to Commercialization

The transformative power of AI extends far beyond pharmaceutical marketing. Its impact ripples across the entire pharmaceutical value chain, from the initial spark of drug discovery to the final stages of post-marketing surveillance. This chapter explores how AI is revolutionizing each step of this intricate process, highlighting the potential for a more efficient, data-driven, and patient-centric approach to pharmaceutical development and commercialization.

1. **Drug Discovery and Development:**
   - **Accelerating Molecule Identification**: AI algorithms can analyze vast chemical databases to identify potential drug candidates with desired properties, significantly reducing the time and resources required for traditional discovery methods.
   - **Optimizing Clinical Trial Design**: AI can help design more efficient clinical trials by simulating patient responses, identifying optimal dosing regimens, and predicting potential outcomes, leading to faster drug development timelines.
   - **Predicting Patient Responses**: AI-powered analytics can analyze genetic and clinical data to predict how individuals might respond to specific treatments, paving the way for personalized medicine approaches.

2. **Pharmacovigilance and Risk Management:**
   - **Proactive Safety Signal Detection**: AI can analyze real-world data from electronic health records and social media to identify potential safety concerns and adverse events associated with medications, allowing for early intervention and risk mitigation strategies.
   - **Personalized Risk Assessment**: AI algorithms can leverage patient data to assess individual risk factors for potential side effects, enabling more informed treatment decisions and improved patient safety.
3. **Supply Chain Optimization:**
   - **Demand Forecasting and Inventory Management**: AI can analyze market trends, predict drug demand, and optimize inventory levels, reducing the risk of stockouts and ensuring the timely delivery of essential medications.
   - **Streamlining Logistics and Manufacturing**: AI-powered automation can improve logistics processes, optimize manufacturing workflows, and minimize production delays, leading to greater efficiency and cost savings.
4. **Personalized Medicine:**
   - **Tailoring Treatments**: AI can analyze a patient's genetic information, medical history, and lifestyle factors to recommend personalized treatment plans and predict the most effective course of therapy for individual needs.
   - **Genomic Drug Discovery**: AI can analyze vast genomic datasets to identify potential drug targets and develop treatments tailored to individual genetic profiles.
5. **Commercialization:**
   - **Pricing and Market Access Strategies**: AI can analyze market data, competitor landscape, and payer preferences to inform pricing strategies and optimize reimbursement processes, ensuring broader patient access to essential medications.

- **Sales Force Optimization**: AI-powered tools can provide sales representatives real-time data on healthcare professional preferences, treatment guidelines, and patient demographics, enabling more targeted and effective interactions.
- **Patient Adherence and Engagement**: AI-powered platforms can deliver personalized medication reminders, support groups, and educational resources, improving patient adherence to treatment plans and ultimately leading to better health outcomes.

Remembering that AI is not a replacement for human expertise is crucial. Its true value lies in its ability to augment human capabilities. By leveraging AI's analytical prowess alongside human judgment, creativity, and ethical considerations, the pharmaceutical industry can unlock the full potential of this transformative technology. As AI continues to evolve, its impact on the pharmaceutical value chain will only become more profound, paving the way for a future of more effective, efficient, and patient-centered healthcare.

CHAPTER

26

The Human Factor in AI-Powered Pharma Marketing

A Delicate Duet

As Artificial Intelligence (AI) waltzes into the pharma marketing world, a crucial partner remains on the stage: the human element. While AI's potential to personalize engagement, optimize campaigns, and glean insights is undeniable, it cannot and should not replace the essential role of humans in this complex ecosystem. To truly unlock the potential of AI-powered pharma marketing, we must understand and nurture the delicate duet between these two forces.

The Chorus of Concerns

Before delving into the harmony, let's acknowledge the concerns surrounding AI's intrusion:

- **The Empathy Vacuum**: Can AI truly understand patients' nuanced emotions and experiences? Will its cold calculations drown out the vital need for human empathy and compassion in healthcare communication?
- **The Creativity Conundrum**: AI thrives on data and logic, but can it replace the spark of human creativity? Will formulaic campaigns generated by algorithms eclipse the power of storytelling and emotional connection in patient engagement?
- **The Ethical Enigma**: Who is ultimately responsible for AI algorithms' decisions? How can we ensure fairness,

transparency, and accountability in a world fueled by data and driven by black boxes?

The Human Counterpoint:

These concerns highlight the irreplaceable value of the human factor in AI-powered pharma marketing:

- **Empathy and Ethics**: Healthcare is fundamentally about people and their stories. Human expertise can ensure AI algorithms are trained on diverse data, mitigating bias and fostering fairness. Human intervention remains vital in interpreting AI outputs, applying ethical considerations, and ensuring personalized care remains at the heart of communication.
- **Creativity and Connection**: While AI can analyze data and predict trends, human creativity breathes life into campaigns. Human storytellers can craft compelling narratives, design engaging experiences, and forge emotional connections with patients that resonate beyond algorithms.
- **Accountability and Responsibility**: Ultimately, the decisions made in pharma marketing, driven by AI or not, rest with humans. Human leadership must set ethical boundaries, establish clear processes, and ensure responsible implementation of AI technology.

The Harmonious Duet:

The future of AI-powered pharma marketing lies not in pitting humans against machines but in orchestrating a harmonious duet where both play complementary roles:

- **AI as the Analyst**: Providing data-driven insights, optimizing campaigns, and identifying hidden trends, freeing human resources for more strategic tasks.
- **Humans as Artists**: Interpreting AI outputs, weaving narratives, and injecting empathy and creativity into patient engagement.

- **Humans as Guardians**: Setting ethical boundaries, ensuring transparency, and upholding accountability throughout the AI-powered marketing process.

Composing a Future in Harmony:

To ensure this harmonious duet flourishes, we must:

- **Invest in Human and AI Skills**: Equip healthcare professionals and marketing teams with the skills to effectively understand, utilize, and collaborate with AI technology.
- **Foster Open Communication**: Encourage dialogue between AI developers, pharma companies, healthcare professionals, and patients to address concerns, share best practices, and ensure ethical implementation.
- **Prioritize Transparency and Explainability**: Demystify AI algorithms, explain decision-making processes, and offer patients meaningful control over their data.
- **Focus on Patient Value**: Remember that AI and humans are tools for a higher purpose, improving patient care, promoting health outcomes, and building trust in the healthcare system.

By prioritizing the human factor and nurturing its interplay with AI, we can unlock the true potential of AI-powered pharma marketing. When played in harmony, this duet promises a future where technology empowers healthcare professionals, personalizes patient experiences, and ultimately contributes to a healthier world.

So, let the human voice and the AI symphony resonate together, composing a future where healthcare thrives on the harmonious collaboration between its most powerful instruments.

The Irreplaceable Duet: Human Creativity and Empathy in a Technological Symphony

As the world embraces the transformative power of technology, a fascinating paradox emerges: the enduring importance of human creativity and empathy. In a landscape increasingly populated by algorithms and AI, these uniquely human qualities stand out as irreplaceable, playing a vital role in shaping our experiences, driving innovation, and navigating the complexities of human connection.

The Symphony of Machines:

AI and automation undeniably offer a dazzling array of advantages. They analyze data with superhuman speed, predict trends with uncanny accuracy, and tirelessly automate tasks. Imagine AI orchestrating logistics, composing personalized music, or translating languages in real-time. These feats, once relegated to the realm of science fiction, are now woven into the fabric of our daily lives.

However, amidst this symphony of machines, a disquieting note arises. Can cold calculations and algorithmic patterns truly replace the magic of human creativity? Can sterile data processing ever mirror the depth of human empathy? The answer, resounding and clear, is no.

The Indelible Mark of Creativity:

Human creativity is not merely a technical skill; it is a spark, a leap of imagination, a dance of the mind that births the new and unexpected. It fuels artistic expression, scientific breakthroughs, and the very essence of human innovation. Imagine the captivating brushstrokes of a painting, the stirring melody of a symphony, or the revolutionary idea that disrupts an entire industry. These are testaments to the irreplaceable power of human imagination, a force that any algorithm cannot duplicate.

Creativity is not confined to grand artistic gestures; it permeates every corner of human experience. It is the child crafting a fantastical universe from building blocks, the surgeon devising a novel surgical technique, and the entrepreneur envisioning a solution to a pressing social problem. In these instances, humans go beyond the predictable, forging new paths and weaving possibilities from the threads of imagination.

The Unquantifiable Depth of Empathy:

Empathy, the cornerstone of human connection, transcends mere data analysis. It is the ability to step into another's shoes, feel their emotions, and understand their perspective. It fuels compassion, guides ethical decision-making, and forms the bedrock of strong relationships. Imagine the comforting hand on a shoulder in times of grief, the patient listener offering solace, or the selfless act of kindness that uplifts another. These are expressions of empathy, qualities that bind us together and make us human.

While AI can process vast amounts of data and recognize patterns in human behavior, it cannot truly understand the nuances of human emotions. It cannot offer a shoulder to cry on or grasp the complex tapestry of emotions that weaves through our lives. Empathy is a uniquely human faculty, a bridge of understanding that connects us at the deepest level.

The Collaborative Chorus:

Therefore, the future lies not in pitting humans against machines but in creating a harmonious duet where technology amplifies both strengths. Imagine AI processing data to create personalized learning experiences while human teachers ignite a passion for discovery in their students. Or envision AI analyzing healthcare trends to predict disease outbreaks while human doctors offer patients personalized care and emotional support. In these cases, technology and human qualities join forces, amplifying the impact of both.

This collaborative approach requires fostering a culture that values and nurtures creativity and empathy. We must:

- **Invest in Education**: Cultivate creative thinking skills, critical thinking, and emotional intelligence from a young age. Encourage exploration, imagination, and the arts, building a future generation equipped to thrive in a technology-driven world.

- **Empower Empathy**: Promote social-emotional learning programs that foster empathy, compassion, and ethical decision-making. Encourage open communication, active listening, and understanding of diverse perspectives.
- **Design with Humans in Mind**: When developing technology, prioritize human needs and values. Ensure AI algorithms are fair and unbiased, and design interfaces that are user-friendly and accessible to all.
- **Celebrate the Human Spark**: Recognize and reward human creativity and empathy in all its forms. Showcase stories of innovators, artists, and everyday heroes who demonstrate the power of these qualities to make a difference in the world.

By cherishing our irreplaceable human qualities and harnessing the power of technology responsibly, we can compose a future where machines amplify our capabilities but never replace the essential spark of creativity and empathy that makes us human. This is the true symphony of progress, a harmonious blend of technological marvel and the irreplaceable magic of the human spirit.

So, let the instruments of technology and humanity play together, not in competition, but in a beautiful and powerful collaboration. Together, we can craft a future where innovation flourishes, compassion thrives, and the unique song of humanity continues to resonate throughout the ages.

Optimizing Your Marketing Efforts with AI: Key Points to Remember and Reflect

Step 1: Define Your Goals and Objectives:

- **AI-Powered Goal Setting**: Analyze historical data and past campaigns to suggest realistic and achievable goals based on industry benchmarks and your company's performance.
- **Automate KPI Selection**: Recommend relevant KPIs aligned with your goals, taking into account your industry and target audience.

Step 2: Collect Data and Establish Benchmarks:

- **Automated Data Collection**: Utilize AI-powered tools to automatically collect and organize data from various sources (e.g., website analytics, social media platforms, surveys) into a centralized platform.
- **Real-Time Performance Dashboards**: Generate dynamic dashboards displaying key metrics and identifying potential areas for improvement in real time.

Step 3: Implement Your Optimization Strategy:

- **AI-Powered A/B Testing**: Design and run complex A/B tests with multiple variables, automatically analyzing results and suggesting the most effective combinations for optimization.
- **Personalization**: Leverage AI to personalize your optimization strategies based on individual user behavior and preferences, tailoring experiences and messaging for better engagement.

Step 4: Analyze and Interpret Results:

- **Advanced Data Analytics**: Utilize AI models to analyze large datasets, identify hidden patterns, and uncover deeper insights from your test results.
- **Predictive Analytics**: Forecast future performance based on historical data and current trends, helping you anticipate potential outcomes and adjust your strategy accordingly.

Step 5: Refine and Optimize:

- **Automated Recommendations**: Based on data analysis and AI insights, receive automated recommendations for future A/B tests, personalization strategies, and overall campaign optimization.
- **Adaptive Learning**: AI algorithms can learn from past successes and failures, continuously refining your optimization approach and leading to faster improvement cycles.

Additional Benefits of AI Optimization:

- **Scalability**: Handle large volumes of data efficiently, supporting complex marketing campaigns and dynamic testing environments.
- **Efficiency**: Automate repetitive tasks like data collection and analysis, freeing up resources for strategic decision-making.
- **Objectivity**: Eliminate human bias and subjective interpretations, leading to data-driven decisions based on concrete evidence.

Remember:

- **AI is a Tool**: While powerful, AI cannot replace human expertise and judgment. Utilize it to enhance your decision-making, not replace it completely.
- **Ethical Considerations**: Ensure responsible data collection, use, and privacy practices when optimizing AI.
- **Transparency and Explainability**: Choose AI models that clearly explain their outputs, fostering trust and understanding within your team.

Integrating AI responsibly and effectively can significantly enhance your ability to measure, analyze, and optimize your marketing efforts. This can lead to better results and a more data-driven approach to achieving your goals.

CHAPTER

27

AI+Human Collaboration: A Symphony of Success in Pharma Sales and Promotion

The pharma sales and promotion world is undergoing a transformative shift orchestrated by the delicate duet of Artificial Intelligence (AI) and human expertise. While AI brings unparalleled data analysis, automation, and predictive capabilities, the human touch continues to be irreplaceable in building trust, fostering empathy, and navigating the nuances of healthcare communication. So, how can this collaboration optimize pharma sales and promotion and bring forth a future where technology empowers success?

The AI Conductor:

AI in pharma sales and promotion plays a powerful role, conducting an orchestra of data and insights:

- **Hyper-Personalized Engagement**: AI analyzes vast pools of patient data, segmenting audiences and tailoring marketing messages to individual needs and preferences. Imagine targeted campaigns addressing specific disease burdens, medication adherence challenges, or treatment preferences.
- **Data-Driven Optimization**: AI crunches sales data, identifying trends, predicting customer behavior, and optimizing promotion strategies. Imagine real-time insights suggesting adjustments to sales calls, allocating resources to high-potential markets, or refining marketing content based on audience engagement.

- **Automation of Mundane Tasks**: AI automates repetitive tasks like scheduling appointments, preparing sales reports, and analyzing competitor activities. This frees up valuable human time for more strategic pursuits, enabling personalized interactions and relationship building.

The Human Virtuoso:

The human element, however, remains the irreplaceable soloist in this performance:

- **Empathy and Trust**: Building trust with healthcare professionals and patients is paramount. Humans excel at empathy, emotional intelligence, and active listening, fostering meaningful connections and addressing individual concerns.
- **Creative Storytelling**: Compelling narratives resonate deeply with audiences. Humans weave stories that connect emotionally, build brand loyalty, and inspire healthcare professionals and patients to engage with new treatments.
- **Ethical Decision-Making**: AI may present insights, but humans apply ethical judgment and expertise. Balancing commercial goals with patient well-being, navigating regulatory concerns, and ensuring responsible communication are crucial roles that demand human intervention.

Harmony in the Duet:

This powerful collaboration demands a harmonious blend of AI and human strengths:

- **Symbiotic Integration**: AI should not replace humans but augment their capabilities. Imagine AI providing real-time patient data during sales calls, enabling personalized dialogues, and offering relevant scientific evidence.
- **Humans in the Loop**: Don't let AI dictate decisions. Humans should interpret insights, set strategic direction, and consider ethical implications.

- **Upskilling and Reskilling**: Equip sales teams and marketing professionals with AI literacy, data analysis skills, and the ability to collaborate effectively with technology.

Examples of Success:

Imagine these scenarios:

- AI generates tailored patient profiles for sales reps, highlighting medication history, treatment preferences, and potential adherence challenges. With this information, reps personalize their approach, build rapport, and effectively address patient concerns.
- AI analyzes social media conversations to identify rising concerns about a specific drug. The marketing team quickly develops and deploys targeted communication campaigns addressing these concerns transparently and ethically.
- AI monitors clinical trial data in real-time, identifying promising new drugs and potential safety concerns. With this insight, the sales team prioritizes the promotion of effective and safe treatments, improving patient outcomes.

Ultimately, AI and human collaboration in pharma sales and promotion promises a future where:

- Sales and marketing efforts are targeted, personalized, and data-driven, maximizing campaign effectiveness and return on investment.
- Patient engagement is meaningful and empathetic, improving adherence, treatment satisfaction, and health outcomes.
- Ethical considerations are prioritized to ensure responsible communication, fair access to medication, and the well-being of patients above all else.

By orchestrating this powerful duet, we can unlock AI's true potential in pharma sales and promotion, composing a symphony of success that resonates with business goals and the vital mission of improving human health.

AI-Driven Lead Generation and Sales Forecasting

AI and Human Collaboration: A Duet for Lead Generation and Sales Forecasting Harmony

The business world is increasingly serenaded by the powerful duet of Artificial Intelligence (AI) and human expertise. This collaboration promises improved efficiency, accuracy, higher lead generation, and sales figures forecasting. But how can each partner contribute and harmonize to achieve optimal results?

The AI Conductor:

AI brings to the stage its impressive technical prowess:

- **Data-Driven Prospecting:** AI sifts through vast troves of data, identifying potential leads with uncanny accuracy. Imagine AI analyzing website visitors, social media activity, and industry trends to identify individuals with a high likelihood of conversion.
- **Lead Scoring and Prioritization:** AI assigns scores to leads based on their specific characteristics and predicted buying behavior. This helps sales teams prioritize their efforts and focus on the most promising opportunities.
- **Predictive Analytics:** AI analyzes historical data and market trends to forecast future sales accurately. This empowers companies to allocate resources effectively and anticipate shifts in customer demand.

The Human Virtuoso:

However, it's the human element that injects warmth and understanding into the performance:

- **Relationship Building:** Building potential customers is essential for conversion. Humans excel at active listening, empathy, and personalized communication, qualities that AI cannot replicate.
- **Qualifying Leads:** Not all leads are created equal. Humans possess the unique ability to assess the suitability of a lead

beyond the data, uncovering deeper motivations and tailoring their approach accordingly.

- **Ethical Consideration and Bias Mitigation:** AI algorithms can perpetuate bias if not carefully monitored. Humans bring ethical judgment and critical thinking to ensure fair and responsible lead generation and sales practices.

Harmonizing the Duet:

To achieve a truly successful performance, AI and humans must collaborate seamlessly:

- **Symbiotic Integration:** AI should not replace human interaction but rather empower it. Imagine AI providing sales reps real-time insights about potential customers, enabling them to personalize their conversations and address specific needs.
- **Human Oversight:** Humans must interpret AI output, identify potential biases, and set strategic direction.
- **Continuous Learning and Adaptation:** Both AI and humans need to evolve. AI models should be continuously updated with new data, while humans need to upskill to utilize AI tools and collaborate with technology effectively.

Examples of Success:

Imagine these Scenarios:

- AI analyzes website traffic and suggests potential leads based on specific page visits and browsing patterns. Sales reps then reach out to these warm leads with personalized messages, significantly increasing conversion rates.
- AI forecasts a potential drop in demand for a particular product. The sales team proactively adjusts its marketing strategy and customer outreach, effectively mitigating the impact on sales.

- AI identifies key decision-makers within a target company (payer). The sales team uses this information to tailor their pitches and increase the likelihood of successful engagement.

Ultimately, AI and human collaboration in lead generation and sales forecasting promise a future where:

- Leads are identified and qualified more efficiently and accurately, leading to a higher return on investment for marketing and sales efforts.
- Sales forecasting becomes more precise, allowing companies to make data-driven decisions about resource allocation and product development.
- The human touch remains central to building meaningful relationships and closing deals, ensuring ethical and responsible engagement with potential customers.

By orchestrating this powerful duet between AI and human expertise, we can compose a symphony of success that transcends individual notes and resonates with the entire sales process, leading to a crescendo of profitability and long-term business success.

Data-Driven Prospecting:

AI can drive data for effective prospecting in several ways, acting as a powerful engine for identifying and prioritizing high-potential leads:

1. **Uncovering Hidden Patterns:**
    - **Data Analysis:** AI sifts through mountains of data from various sources, including company websites, social media platforms, public records, and industry reports.
    - **Pattern Recognition:** Using sophisticated algorithms, AI identifies hidden patterns and correlations humans might miss. This could reveal untapped markets, emerging trends, or specific characteristics of ideal customers.

- **Predictive Modeling:** Based on the uncovered patterns, AI can develop predictive models that estimate the likelihood of conversion for individual leads. This helps prioritize outreach efforts and optimizes sales resources.

2. **Tailoring Lead Profiles:**
   - **Lead Scoring:** AI assigns scores to leads based on various factors such as company size, industry, firmographics, website behavior, and online engagement. This score indicates the lead's potential value and likelihood of converting.
   - **Behavioral Segmentation:** AI analyzes website clickstream data, social media activity, and email interactions to segment leads based on their behavior and interests. This enables personalized outreach based on individual needs and preferences.
   - **Dynamic Profiling:** AI continuously updates lead profiles as new information becomes available, ensuring outreach remains relevant and aligned with the lead's evolving situation.

3. **Identifying New Lead Sources:**
   - **Web Crawler Technology:** AI-powered web crawlers scour the internet for relevant data such as industry news, job postings, and conference registrations, uncovering potential leads not found through traditional channels.
   - **Social Media Listening:** AI monitors social media conversations to identify individuals expressing interest in specific products or services, expanding the pool of potential leads.
   - **Industry Trend Analysis:** AI analyzes industry trends and market forecasts to identify promising sectors and emerging customer needs, helping businesses tailor their prospecting efforts to future opportunities.

4. **Optimizing Campaign Performance:**
   - **Real-Time Insights:** AI provides real-time data on campaign performance, allowing for on-the-fly adjustments and optimizing messaging, channels, and targeting strategies.
   - **A/B Testing:** AI facilitates A/B testing of different lead generation tactics, such as landing page designs or ad copy, to determine the most effective approach for specific audiences.
   - **Conversion Tracking:** AI tracks the progression of leads through the sales funnel, identifying points of friction and drop-off, allowing for targeted interventions and improved conversion rates.

Overall, AI plays a crucial role in driving data for effective prospecting by:

- **Automating Time-Consuming Tasks:** Freeing up human resources for more strategic efforts.
- **Expanding the Reach of Prospecting:** Uncovering new lead sources and identifying hidden opportunities.
- **Enhancing Targeting Accuracy:** Reaching the right individuals with the right message at the right time.
- **Increasing Conversion Rates:** Optimizing campaigns and improving lead nurturing strategies.

By leveraging these capabilities, businesses can transform their prospecting efforts from a scattershot approach to a data-driven and personalized journey, ultimately driving higher sales and achieving sustained growth.

Lead Scoring and Prioritization:

The Symphony of Scores: AI Lead Scoring and Prioritization

As the world embraces AI's power, lead scoring and prioritization have become a harmonious duet between human intuition and data-driven insights. But how exactly does AI compose this melody, assigning numerical values to prospects and guiding sales teams toward the most promising opportunities?

The Algorithmic Maestro:

Imagine an orchestra of data points conducted by a sophisticated AI algorithm. Each instrument represents a relevant factor about a potential lead:

- **Firmographics:** Company size, industry, location, and other business-related details.
- **Website Behavior:** Time spent on specific pages, downloaded content, and engagement metrics.
- **Social Media Activity:** Interactions with brand channels, expressions of interest, and industry discussions.
- **Marketing Interactions:** Email opens, clicks, and campaign responses.
- **Public Records:** Financial data, legal filings, and news mentions.

Each instrument plays its melody, and the AI maestro, powered by machine learning, analyzes and harmonizes them into a single score: the lead score.

Composing the Score:

This score reflects the *likelihood of conversion*, factoring in:

- **Data Strength:** Importance and accuracy of each data point.
- **Predictive Power:** Historical results from similar leads with specific characteristics.
- **Industry Benchmarks:** Average scores for comparable businesses in the market.

By understanding the underlying melody of each data point, AI can identify patterns and correlations that humans might miss. This empowers businesses to:

- **Prioritizing High-Potential Leads:** Focus sales efforts on prospects with the highest scores, maximizing the return on investment of limited resources.
- **Filter out Unqualified Leads:** Removing low-scoring leads from the sales funnel saves time and energy.
- **Identify Hidden Gems:** Unearth seemingly average leads with high hidden potential based on subtle data patterns.

Beyond the Numbers:

While AI plays a powerful role in composing the lead score melody, the human ear remains essential for discerning its meaning. Sales teams must:

- **Understand the Score Breakdown:** Analyze the individual data points contributing to the score to tailor their approach and identify optimal engagement strategies.
- **Apply Human Judgment:** For a more nuanced evaluation, consider factors beyond the data, such as market trends, specific customer needs, and personal intuitions.
- **Monitor and Adapt:** Regularly evaluate the effectiveness of the lead scoring system and adjust the algorithm data points as needed to ensure its relevance and accuracy.

Tracking Website Behavior for Lead Scoring

In pharmaceutical sales, AI can analyze website traffic and page visits to identify potential leads, but it's not a straightforward process like counting website visitors. Here is how AI can be used for lead scoring and qualification in pharma sales:

1. **Tracking Website Behavior:**
    - AI monitors website traffic and analyzes visitor behavior, including:
    - **Pages Visited:** AI tracks which pages visitors view, particularly those related to specific drugs, treatment areas,

or clinical trials. This indicates potential interest in a particular product or therapy.

- **Time Spent on Pages:** AI measures the time spent on specific pages. Visitors lingering on drug information pages or downloading white papers suggest deeper interest than skimming product overviews.
- **Downloads Form Submissions:** AI tracks downloads of brochures, case studies, or white papers related to specific drugs. Filling out contact forms requesting information or demos indicates a strong lead.

2. **User Profiling and Lead Scoring:**
    - AI analyzes visitor data (if available), like demographics, job titles, and previous website interactions.
    - AI assigns each visitor a "lead score" based on pre-defined criteria. These criteria are established by analyzing patterns in visitor behavior and demographics. This score reflects the visitor's potential value as a lead. For example, an oncologist visiting a page on new cancer treatment would have a higher score than a student researching a general health topic. This process is automated and based on data-driven insights, ensuring objectivity and accuracy in lead qualification.
3. **Segmentation and Targeting:**
    - AI segments website visitors based on their behavior and lead scores.
    - High-scoring leads with relevant demographics (e.g., doctors specializing in the drug's treatment area) are categorized as high-priority leads.
    - Pharma sales representatives can focus on these high-potential leads with targeted outreach and relevant information.

Examples:

- A cardiologist downloads a white paper on a new drug for heart failure and lingers on the clinical trial page. AI assigns a high lead score, and the pharmaceutical company sends the doctor targeted information about the trial.
- A general practitioner visits the company website but only skims the product overview page and leaves quickly. AI assigns a low lead score, and the pharma company might not prioritize outreach to this visitor.

Benefits of AI-Powered Lead Scoring:

- **AI Efficiently identifies High-Quality Leads,** allowing sales reps to focus on the most promising opportunities, improving efficiency and conversion rates. This provides a sense of reassurance about the process's effectiveness.
- **Personalization of Outreach:** AI allows targeted communication based on the lead's interests and needs.
- **Improved Resource Allocation:** Sales teams can prioritize their efforts with data-driven insights.

Limitations to Consider:

- **Data Quality:** The effectiveness of AI depends on the quality and accuracy of website tracking data.
- **Privacy Concerns:** Balancing data collection with user privacy is crucial. Transparent data practices are essential.

While AI provides valuable insights, it is important to remember that human expertise is crucial in building relationships and closing deals. This makes the audience feel valued and integral to the success of the sales strategy. AI is a valuable tool for pharma sales, but it should be used alongside human expertise to analyze website traffic and quality leads and ultimately improve sales success.

Conclusion:

Website personalization is no longer a luxury but a necessity for pharmaceutical companies. By leveraging AI and data insights, pharma companies can create a dynamic and user-centric website experience that caters to the specific needs of patients, HCPs, and other stakeholders. This leads to a more effective online presence, improved brand perception, and contributes to better patient care.

The Future of Lead Scoring

The world of lead scoring is constantly evolving, with AI playing a leading role in its orchestration:

- **Advanced Algorithms:** Deep learning and natural language processing will enable even more granular analysis and precise scores based on unstructured data like emails and social media interactions.
- **Real-Time Updates:** Scores will dynamically adjust with every new interaction, ensuring an accurate reflection of a lead's evolving potential.
- **Predictive Intelligence:** AI will predict conversion likelihood and suggest optimal campaign strategies and next steps for specific leads.

By mastering the delicate duet of AI and human expertise, businesses can transform lead scoring from a static number to a dynamic symphony of data and intuition, guiding sales teams towards a crescendo of qualified leads and higher conversion rates. So, let the data points sing, the algorithms conduct, and the human judgment lead the way, and together, compose a future where lead scoring becomes a powerful tool for success, ensuring every note resonates with business growth and profitability.

CHAPTER 28

Reskilling and Upskilling for Human+AI Collaboration

The rise of artificial intelligence (AI) is rapidly transforming the workforce, demanding a shift from traditional skills to a collaborative approach where humans and AI work together. This necessitates reskilling and upskilling initiatives on a large scale. Here's a detailed look at this crucial transition:

1. **Why Reskilling and Upskilling are Essential:**
   - **Automation and Job Displacement**: AI automates various tasks and creates new opportunities. Individuals need adaptable skillsets to navigate this shifting landscape.
   - **Evolving Job Requirements**: Existing jobs are changing as AI augments human capabilities. Workers need to update their skills to remain relevant and competitive.
   - **Closing the Skills Gap**: The demand for AI-related skills is surging, while many need more expertise. Reskilling and upskilling address this gap.
2. **Key Skills for the Human+AI Collaborative Future:**
   - **Technical Skills**: Data analysis, AI literacy, programming basics, data visualization, and automation tools.
   - **Soft Skills**: Critical thinking, problem-solving, communication, collaboration, creativity, and emotional intelligence.

- **Human-centered Design** involves understanding user needs, designing AI systems for ethical and equitable use, and mitigating potential biases.
- **Adaptability and Lifelong Learning**: Continuous learning and skill development are crucial in this dynamic environment.

3. **Implementing Reskilling and Upskilling Programs:**
   - **Government Initiatives**: Public-private partnerships can provide funding and resources for training programs.
   - **Educational Institutions**: Universities and colleges can offer AI-related courses and certifications.
   - **Private Companies**: Businesses can invest in employee training and development programs focused on AI and emerging technologies.
   - **Online Learning Platforms**: Accessible and diverse online resources can cater to individual learning styles and schedules.
4. **Challenges and Considerations:**
   - **Equity and Access:** Ensure training programs are accessible to diverse populations, including marginalized communities.
   - **Financial Constraints:** Provide affordable training options to address budgetary limitations.
   - **Motivation and Engagement:** Design engaging learning experiences that foster motivation and knowledge retention.
   - **Monitoring and Evaluation:** Track the effectiveness of training programs and adapt them based on outcomes.
5. **Examples of Successful Initiatives:**
   - **Amazon Career Choice:** Provides funding for employees to pursue high-demand skills, including AI and cloud computing.

- **Google AI Education:** Offers online courses and training materials on AI for developers, educators, and researchers.
- **IBM SkillsBuild:** Equips individuals with digital skills through free online courses and certificate programs.

Reskilling and upskilling are not just optional; they are essential for individuals and the workforce to thrive in the human+AI collaborative future. By embracing continuous learning, developing relevant skills, and fostering a culture of adaptability, we can ensure that AI works alongside us, empowering humanity to achieve new heights of progress and well-being.

Risk of Job Losses: A Deeper Dive

The rise of AI in pharmaceutical marketing is a double-edged sword. While it automates tasks and optimizes campaigns, it can also lead to job losses in certain areas. While quantifying the exact number of job losses attributable to AI in pharma marketing is challenging due to a lack of comprehensive data, here's a breakdown of potential impact across different areas:

High Risk of Job Losses

- **Data Entry and Administrative Roles**: Repetitive tasks like data entry, scheduling social media posts, and basic reporting are prime AI automation targets. Here are some examples of how this might happen:

Example 1: **Clinical Trial Data Management**: AI can automate data entry of patient demographics, treatment information, and adverse events reported during clinical trials.

Example 2: **Social Media Calendar Management**: AI-powered scheduling tools can automate the scheduling of social media posts based on pre-defined parameters and audience targeting.

Example 3: Generating Basic Reports: AI can generate routine reports on website traffic, social media engagement metrics, or email campaign performance, freeing human resources for in-depth analysis and strategic decision-making.

- **Traditional Media Buying**: AI-powered programmatic advertising platforms can automate ad buying processes, potentially reducing the need for large media buying teams.

Example 1: Media Buying and Ad Placement: Programmatic advertising platforms use AI algorithms to analyze audience data, identify optimal ad placements across various websites and apps, and automate the bidding process for ad space in real time.

Example 2: Campaign Performance Monitoring: AI can continuously monitor the performance of ad campaigns across different channels, providing insights on impressions, clicks, and conversions. This allows for automated adjustments to budget allocation and targeting strategies.

Example 3: Basic Media Relations Tasks: AI can automate tasks like sending out press releases or scheduling media interviews, although human interaction remains essential for building relationships with journalists and securing media coverage.

- **Content Creation (to an extent)**: AI can generate basic ad content like ad copy, social media posts, or email newsletters. This could impact entry-level content creation tasks involving formulaic content formats.

Example 1: Generating Ad Copy Variations: AI can create multiple variations of ad copy with different headlines, body text, and calls to action, allowing for A/B testing to identify the most effective versions for specific audience segments.

Example 2: Social Media Post Drafts: AI can generate social media post drafts based on pre-defined templates and audience targeting criteria. Human content creatives can then review and edit these drafts for tone, brand voice, and adherence to regulatory guidelines.

Example 3: Email Personalization: AI can personalize email content for marketing campaigns by inserting recipient names, referencing past interactions, or including product recommendations based on user data (with consent)).

Key Points to Remember:

- AI excels at automating repetitive tasks and data-driven processes.
- While AI can generate content, human creativity and editorial oversight are still crucial.
- The focus is shifting from data entry to data analysis and interpretation.

The impact of AI will vary depending on the specific role and company structure. However, pharma companies and marketing professionals can prepare for the future by developing the necessary skills to thrive in a data-driven and AI-powered marketing landscape by understanding the areas most susceptible to automation.

Medium Risk of Job Losses

- **Sales Representatives (Specific Functions)**: AI can automate tasks like scheduling appointments, qualifying leads, and providing basic product information. However, the human touch remains crucial for building relationships with HCPs and closing deals. Sales reps might need to adapt their roles to focus more on strategic relationship management and consultative selling. Here is a breakdown of these areas and functions:
- **Task Automation**: AI-powered tools can automate tasks like
  - **Lead Qualification**: AI can analyze customer data and online behavior to identify and score potential leads based on pre-defined criteria. This can streamline identifying high-value leads for sales reps to focus on.
  - **Appointment Scheduling**: AI-powered scheduling assistants can automate appointment scheduling with HCPs based on their availability and preferences.
  - **Basic Product Information Delivery**: AI chatbots can answer routine questions about products or provide basic

product information to HCPs, freeing up sales reps for more in-depth discussions and demonstrations.

- **Shifting Focus**: Sales reps will likely adapt their roles to focus more on the following:
- **Building Relationships**: AI can't replicate the human touch in building trust and rapport with HCPs. Sales reps will need to excel at relationship management and foster long-term partnerships.
- **Consultative Selling**: Understanding HCP's specific needs and challenges and offering customized solutions will become even more crucial.
- **Strategic Negotiation and Deal Closing**: AI might assist with initial outreach and lead qualification, but closing deals and negotiating contracts will remain within the domain of experienced sales reps.

Example: An AI-powered lead scoring system identifies a cardiologist who has recently downloaded white papers on a new heart failure medication. The system flags this as a high-value lead and automatically schedules a preliminary meeting with a sales rep. However, the sales rep takes the lead, building rapport with the cardiologist, understanding their specific patient population, and tailoring a presentation on how the new medication can benefit their practice.

- **Market Research Analysts (Specific Tasks)**: AI can analyze vast amounts of market data and identify trends, which might reduce the need for certain data collection and analysis tasks performed by market research analysts. However, human expertise remains valuable for interpreting data, drawing insights, and developing strategic recommendations.
- **Task Automation**: AI can automate some aspects of market research, such as:
  - **Data Collection and Analysis:** AI can gather vast market data from online sources, social media sentiment analysis, and healthcare databases.

  - **Identifying Trends and Patterns**: AI algorithms can analyze data and identify trends in disease prevalence, treatment preferences, and competitor activities.
- **Shifting Focus**: Market research analysts will likely need to focus more on the following:
  - **Interpreting Data and Drawing Insights**: AI provides the data, but human expertise is crucial for interpreting its meaning, drawing actionable insights, and identifying underlying trends.
  - **Developing Strategic Recommendations**: Based on the insights from data analysis, market research analysts will play a vital role in developing strategic recommendations for product development, marketing campaigns, and market positioning.
  - **Conducting Qualitative Research**: While AI can analyze quantitative data, qualitative research methods like focus groups and in-depth interviews with HCPs and patients will remain valuable for understanding nuanced perspectives and unmet needs.

Example: An AI system analyzes social media data and identifies a growing conversation among patients about a specific side effect of a common medication class. It presents this data to a market research analyst. The analyst interprets this as a potential market opportunity and recommends further research to understand the scope of the issue and explore potential solutions. This might involve conducting focus groups with patients to gather more qualitative data on their experiences and preferences. By leveraging AI for data collection and analysis, pharma companies can free upmarket research analysts to focus on higher-level strategic thinking and provide valuable insights to guide future marketing and product development efforts.

Lower Risk of Job Losses

In pharmaceutical marketing, AI will likely impact certain roles less. Here's a closer look at these roles and examples of why they might face a reduced risk of job losses.

- **Marketing Managers and Directors**: These roles require strategic thinking, creativity, and leadership skills that are difficult to automate with AI. However, AI can support these roles by providing data-driven insights and automating routine tasks, allowing them to focus on higher-level strategies.
- **Strategic Thinking and Leadership**: These roles require critical thinking, strategic planning, and the ability to lead and inspire teams. These skills are difficult to automate with AI.
- **Decision-Making**: Marketing leaders need to make complex decisions based on data analysis, market insights, and an understanding of customer needs. While AI can provide valuable data and insights, the final decisions will remain with human leaders.
- **Managing and Motivating Teams**: Creating a positive and productive work environment, fostering collaboration, and motivating teams are all crucial aspects of leadership that AI cannot replicate.

Example: An AI system analyzes market research data and identifies a growing demand for patient education materials on chronic diseases. However, the marketing director decides these materials' format, content, and distribution strategy. They might leverage AI to personalize the content based on patient demographics, but the overall strategic direction and leadership remain human-driven.

- **Creative Directors and Copywriters**: While AI can generate basic content, crafting compelling and emotionally relevant brand messaging still requires human creativity and storytelling skills. These skills will become even more valuable in the age of AI.

- **Creativity and Storytelling**: Crafting compelling and emotionally resonant brand messaging requires human creativity and the ability to tell stories that resonate with the target audience. AI can assist with generating content variations, but human expertise is crucial for crafting impactful messaging.
- **Understanding Brand Voice and Tone**: Maintaining a consistent brand voice and tone across all marketing materials is essential. While AI can analyze existing content, it takes human understanding to ensure that new content aligns seamlessly with the brand's overall voice and personality.
- **Adherence to Regulations**: Pharma marketing is heavily regulated. Creative directors and copywriters must ensure all marketing materials comply with complex regulations. This requires a deep understanding of the legal landscape, which AI cannot easily replace.

Example: A pharma company launches a new medication for a rare genetic disorder. The creative director works with a team of copywriters to develop a public awareness campaign. They might use AI to generate different slogan options but ultimately select the one that best captures the emotional impact of the disease and the hope offered by the new medication while ensuring all materials adhere to relevant advertising regulations.

- **Medical Science Liaisons (MSLs):** The human element is irreplaceable for building trust and relationships with HCPs. MSLs will continue to play a vital role in medical education and scientific exchange.
- **Building Trust and Relationships**: Building trust and rapport with HCPs is critical to an MSL's role. This requires strong interpersonal skills, active listening, and an understanding of individual HCPs' needs and challenges. AI cannot replicate these human qualities.

- **Scientific Expertise and Medical Knowledge**: MSLs act as scientific liaisons between the company and HCPs. They need a deep understanding of the science behind the company's products and the ability to answer complex medical questions. This level of expertise is difficult to automate.
- **Educational Outreach and Medical Affairs**: MSLs are vital in educating HCPs about the company's products, providing scientific data, and facilitating investigator-sponsored clinical trials. This requires real-world interaction and scientific communication skills that AI cannot replace.

Example: An MSL meets with an oncologist to discuss a new cancer treatment option. The MSL leverages its scientific knowledge to answer the oncologist's specific questions about the drug's mechanism of action, clinical trial results, and potential side effects. They build trust and rapport by actively listening to the oncologist's concerns and addressing them personally. While AI can be a valuable tool for marketing tasks requiring data analysis, automation, or content generation, the human element remains irreplaceable in areas like strategic leadership, creative storytelling, building trust with HCPs, and scientific communication. Pharmaceutical marketing professionals thrive in the evolving marketing landscape by focusing on these core strengths and embracing AI as a collaborator.

Important Considerations

- **Job Transformation, not Elimination**: While some tasks might be automated, AI will likely transform existing roles rather than eliminate them. Upskilling and Reskilling initiatives are crucial to preparing the workforce for these changes.
- **Impact on Different Company Sizes**: Larger pharma companies with bigger marketing budgets might be more likely to adopt AI faster, potentially impacting workforce size more significantly. Smaller companies might integrate AI gradually, with less immediate job losses.

- **Evolving Regulatory Landscape**: Regulations governing data privacy and marketing practices influence how AI is implemented in pharma marketing, potentially impacting the extent of job losses.

Overall, the rise of AI in pharmaceutical marketing requires a nuanced approach. While some roles might be directly impacted, the focus should be on reskilling and upskilling the workforce to leverage AI as a powerful tool. This human-AI collaboration will be key to success in the future of pharmaceutical marketing.

Mitigating Job Losses:

The rise of AI in pharma marketing poses a challenge, but proactive measures can help mitigate job losses and prepare the workforce for the future. Here's a breakdown of strategies:

1. **Upskilling and Reskilling Programs**:
    - **Importance**: Equipping marketing teams with the skills to work alongside AI is crucial. Companies can invest in training programs that focus on:
    - **Data Analysis and Interpretation**: Understanding how to analyze AI-generated data and translate insights into actionable marketing strategies.
    - **AI Literacy**: Gaining a basic understanding of AI capabilities and limitations to foster better collaboration with AI tools.
    - **Digital Marketing Skills**: Developing skills in search engine optimization (SEO), content marketing automation, and social media analytics to complement AI capabilities.

    Example: A pharma company partners with an online learning platform to offer courses on data visualization, marketing analytics, and understanding AI in marketing. They also provide internal workshops on interpreting AI-generated reports and using AI tools for campaign optimization.

2. Emphasis on Strategic Marketing:

- **Importance**: With AI automating routine tasks, human talent can focus on higher-level strategic activities such as:
- **Developing and Implementing Overall Marketing Plans** involves setting goals, identifying target audiences, and crafting integrated marketing campaigns.
- **Building Relationships with HCPs and Patient Advocacy Groups**: Fostering trust and collaboration with key stakeholders in the healthcare landscape.
- **Supervising and Optimizing AI-Powered Marketing Campaigns**: Humans oversee AI tools, analyze data, and make strategic adjustments for optimal campaign performance.

Example: A marketing team uses AI to automate social media ad targeting. However, human marketers develop the overall social media strategy, create compelling ad creatives, and analyze campaign performance to identify areas for improvement. They leverage AI insights to refine targeting and optimize ad spending for maximum reach and engagement.

3. Job Rotation and Redeployment:

- **Importance:** Providing opportunities for employees in potentially impacted roles to transition to other areas within the marketing department can help minimize job losses.

Example: A data entry specialist whose role is being automated might be offered training in data analysis to transition into a role focused on implementing AI-generated reports and identifying marketing opportunities.

4. Early Retirement and Attrition Programs:

- **Importance**: In some cases, offering voluntary early retirement or severance packages with outplacement services can be a way to manage workforce reductions.

Example: A pharma company facing significant job losses due to AI adoption might offer eligible employees an attractive early retirement package. Outplacement services can help these individuals with resume writing, interviewing skills, and job search strategies.

5. **Collaboration Between HR and Marketing Teams:**

   Importance: Open communication and collaboration between HR and marketing teams are crucial for anticipating AI's impact, developing reskilling programs, and effectively managing the transition.

   Example: The HR department and marketing leadership work together to identify potential skill gaps and develop a comprehensive training program to address them. They also collaborate on communication strategies to inform employees about changes and support them through the transition.

By adopting a proactive approach that prioritizes upskilling, reskilling, and strategic redeployment, pharma companies can mitigate job losses and ensure their marketing teams have the skills and knowledge needed to thrive in the AI-powered future.

Upskilling and Reskilling Programs for Pharma Marketing in the Age of AI

The rise of AI in pharma marketing necessitates a shift in skillsets for marketing professionals. Here's a detailed look at upskilling and reskilling programs:

Upskilling:

- **Focus**: Equipping existing marketing professionals with the skills to leverage AI effectively alongside their current expertise.
- **Examples**:
  - **Data Analysis and Visualization**: Training programs can teach marketing teams to use data analysis tools like Excel or Google Data Studio to interpret AI-generated data for campaign performance insights, audience trends, and competitor analysis. Additionally, courses in data

visualization can equip them with the skills to present complex data clearly and compellingly to stakeholders.

- **AI for Marketing Specialization Courses**: Online platforms like Coursera or edX offer specialized courses on how AI is transforming marketing. These courses can provide a foundational understanding of AI concepts, machine learning algorithms used in marketing automation, and the ethical considerations surrounding AI use.
- **Understanding AI-Powered Marketing Tools**: Workshops or in-house training sessions can familiarize marketing teams with specific AI tools used in pharma marketing, such as programmatic advertising platforms, social media listening tools, or AI-powered content generation software. This can help them understand how these tools work, how to utilize them effectively, and how to interpret the data they generate.

Reskilling:

- **Focus**: Equipping marketing professionals with new skills to transition into different roles within the marketing department or even a related field that leverages AI.
- **Examples**:
  - **Data Analyst Bootcamps**: These intensive programs can equip individuals with the skills to clean, analyze, and interpret large datasets. This newfound expertise can be applied to support AI-powered marketing initiatives by providing data analysis skills to complement the insights generated by AI.
  - **Content Marketing Certification Programs**: As AI automates basic content creation, the focus shifts towards crafting high-quality, strategic content. Reskilling programs focusing on content marekting strategy, SEO optimization, and copywriting can equip individuals to create compelling content that resonates with target audiences.

- **Digital Marketing Project Management Courses**: With AI automating tasks, marketing professionals can focus on managing and overseeing AI-powered campaigns. Project management courses can equip individuals with the skills to effectively plan, execute, and monitor marketing campaigns that leverage AI tools.

Additional Considerations:

- **Micro-Learning Opportunities**: Bite-sized learning modules or online tutorials can provide quick and focused training on specific AI-related skills, keeping marketing teams up-to-date with the latest advancements.
- **Mentorship Programs**: Pairing experienced marketing professionals with individuals undergoing upskilling or reskilling can provide valuable guidance and support during the transition.
- **Focus on Soft Skills**: While technical skills are important, soft skills like critical thinking, problem-solving, and communication remain crucial for success in AI-powered marketing. Training programs emphasizing these skills can ensure that marketing professionals are well-rounded and adaptable to evolving industry demands.

By implementing a combination of upskilling and reskilling programs tailored to the specific needs of the pharma marketing teams, companies can create a future-proof workforce equipped to leverage AI's capabilities and achieve marekting goals effectively.

How Pharma Can Address These Challenges

Here's how pharmaceutical companies can address the challenges in the age of AI-powered marketing:

Strategic Planning and Leadership:

- **Develop A Clear AI Adoption Strategy**: Define the specific goals for AI implementation in marketing. This might involve automating repetitive tasks, optimizing campaign performance, or gaining deeper audience insights.

- **Invest in Responsible AI Practices**: Implement ethical guidelines for AI use in marketing, ensuring data privacy, avoiding algorithm bias, and maintaining brand strategy.
- **Change Management and Communication**: Openly communicate the rationale behind AI adoption and its potential impact on the workforce. Develop training programs and support structures to help employees adapt and thrive in the new landscape.

Workforce Development:

- **Upskilling and Reskilling Programs**: Invest in training initiatives to equip marketing teams with the skills to work alongside AI. Focus on data analysis, AI literacy, digital marketing skills, and content creation for the AI age.
- **Career Development Opportunities**: Offer career counseling and support for employees whose roles might be impacted by AI. Reskilling for new opportunities in the marketing department or related fields.
- **Building Agile Marketing Teams**: Foster a culture of continuous learning and adaptation. Encourage experimentation with AI tools and embrace a data-driven approach to marketing decision-making.

Collaboration and Integration:

- **Breakdown Silos**: Promote collaboration between marketing, IT, and data science teams. This ensures effective integration of AI tools within the marketing workflow and efficient data management practices.
- **Partnerships with AI Experts**: Consider partnering with AI solution providers or consultants to gain expertise in implementing and utilizing AI tools for marketing purposes.

- **Focus on Human+AI Collaboration:** View AI as a tool to augment human capabilities, not replace them. Leverage human creativity, strategic thinking, and relationship-building skills alongside AI's data analysis and automation capabilities.

Addressing Ethical Considerations:

- **Data Privacy and Security**: Implement robust data security measures and ensure compliance with relevant data privacy regulations, such as HIPAA and GDPR.
- **Transparency and Explainability**: Ensure transparency in how AI tools are used for marketing. Be able to explain the rationale behind AI-driven decisions and avoid "black box" algorithms.

By adopting a comprehensive approach that addresses these challenges, pharma companies can harness the power of AI in pharma marketing while mitigating risks and ensuring a smooth transition for their workforce. This will allow them to develop effective marketing strategies that reach the right audience with the right message at the right time, ultimately improving patient outcomes and achieving their business goals.

CHAPTER

29

The Future of Pharma Marketing in the AI Age

The future of pharma marketing will be a dynamic landscape shaped by the increasing integration of AI and a focus on patient-centricity. Here is a closer look at some potential trends:

1. **Hyper-Personalized Marketing**:
   - **Leveraging AI**: AI will enable highly targeted marketing campaigns based on a deeper understanding of individual HCP and patient needs. To create personalized messaging and content, machine learning algorithms can analyze vast amounts of data, including demographics, medical history, treatment preferences, and online behavior.

   Example: An AI-powered platform analyzes a patient's medical records and identifies them as a good candidate for new medication. The platform personalizes email content for the patient, highlighting the medication's benefits for their specific condition and providing educational resources tailored to their needs.

2. **Precision Targeting and Programmatic Advertising**:
   - **AI for Audience Segmentation**: AI can analyze HCP and patient data to create highly targeted audience segments based on specific demographics, disease states, and treatment pathways.

- **Programmatic Ad Buying**: AI algorithms can automate the ad buying process, dynamically identifying the most relevant online platforms and publications to reach target audiences with laser focus and optimize ad spending for maximum reach and engagement.

Example: A pharmaceutical company launches a new diabetes medication. It uses AI to create targeted ad campaigns for different audience segments, such as HCPs specializing in diabetes management or patients recently diagnosed with Type 2 diabetes. The AI platform programmatically buys ad space on relevant medical websites, patient forums, and social media platforms frequented by its target audience.

3. **The Rise of AI-Powered Content Creation**:

- **AI for Content Generation and Optimization**: AI can assist with content creation by generating drafts, suggesting headlines, and optimizing content for specific keywords. This frees up human content creators to focus on the strategic aspects of content development.

Example: A pharma company uses an AI tool to generate different blog post variations about a new medication. Human content creators then edit the drafts, ensuring accuracy, brand voice consistency, and compliance with regulatory guidelines.

4. **Patient Education and Engagement Through AI Chatbots**:

- **AI-Powered Chatbots for 24/7 Support:** Pharma companies can leverage AI chatbots to provide patients with 24/7 medication information, answer routine questions about side effects, and offer medication adherence reminders.

Example: A patient with high blood pressure can use a chatbot to ask questions about their medication dosage, potential side effects, and interactions with other medications. The chatbot provides relevant information and encourages patients to consult their doctor for specific concerns.

5. **The Growing Importance of Influencer Marketing**:
    - **Identifying Key Opinion Leaders (KOLs)**: AI can analyze social media data to identify HCPs or patient advocacy groups with significant influence within their communities.
    - **Partnering with KOLs**: Pharma companies can collaborate with these KOLs to develop educational content, participate in social media campaigns, and reach a wider audience with trusted information about their products.

Example: A pharma company uses AI to identify a prominent cardiologist who actively educates patients about heart disease on social media. They partner with the cardiologist to develop a series of educational videos about a new heart failure medication, leveraging their expertise and influence to reach a large audience of patients.

Overall, the future of pharma marketing will be data-driven, personalized, and patient-centric. AI will be a powerful tool for automation, content generation, and audience insights. However, human expertise in creativity, strategic thinking, and building trust with stakeholders will remain crucial for success.

PART VI

Launching into the Future: The Rise of AI-Powered Product Launches

Chapter 30. AI-Powered Product Launches

Chapter 31. AI-Powered Content Creation and Personalized Marketing

Chapter 32. Human Oversight and Control of AI-Driven Messaging and Targeting

The product launch landscape is undergoing a seismic shift. Gone are the days of relying solely on intuition and traditional marketing tactics. Today, a new breed of launches is emerging, powered by the transformative potential of Artificial Intelligence (AI). This chapter delves into the exciting world of AI-powered product launches, exploring how this cutting-edge technology is revolutionizing every stage of the launch process, from pre-launch market research to post-launch customer engagement.

We'll witness how AI empowers companies to gain deeper market insights, personalize marketing campaigns with laser focus, and optimize sales strategies for maximum impact. Prepare to discover the secrets behind crafting successful AI-driven launches – a roadmap to navigating the exciting future of bringing innovative products to market and exceeding customer expectations in a dynamic and competitive environment.

CHAPTER
30

AI-Powered Product Launches

The world of pharmaceutical marketing is on the cusp of a revolution. Raising awareness of a new drug is no longer enough. Today's patients, healthcare professionals (HCPs), and other stakeholders demand a more nuanced and targeted approach. This is where the powerful synergy between human expertise and artificial intelligence (AI) comes into play.

In this chapter, we delve into the transformative role of human collaboration during the critical phase of product development and launch. We will explore how AI empowers data-driven decision-making, personalizes communication, and optimizes the customer journey for all stakeholders in bringing a new medication to market.

The Challenges of Traditional Launch Strategies:

- **Information Overload**: HCPs are bombarded with marketing messages for new drugs, making it difficult to differentiate and identify medications that truly benefit their patients.
- **Unmet Patient Needs**: Traditional marketing approaches often need help understanding the specific needs, anxieties, and information requirements of patients with a particular condition.
- **Missed Opportunities**: Pharmaceutical companies might miss out on valuable insights from real-world data, hindering their ability to tailor communication strategies and optimize post-launch marketing efforts.

The Promise of Human+AI Synergy:

By leveraging the strengths of both humans and AI, pharmaceutical companies can revolutionize product development and launch strategies.

AI-Powered Product Launch in Pharma: A Multifaceted Approach

The launch of a new pharmaceutical product is a complex and critical endeavor. AI (Artificial Intelligence) is rapidly transforming this process, offering pharma companies a powerful toolkit to streamline tasks, gain deeper market insights, and achieve successful product launches. Here is a breakdown of the key aspects of AI-powered product launches in pharma:

Pre-Launch Activities:

1. **Market Research and Target Audience Identification**:
   - **Leveraging AI for Data Analysis**: Imagine a pharma company developing a new diabetes medication. Traditionally, market research might involve surveys and focus groups. However, AI can analyze vast datasets like:
     - **Electronic Health Records (EHRs)**: This anonymized data can reveal disease prevalence, treatment patterns, and potential unmet needs in the diabetic population.
     - **Social Media Conversations**: AI can analyze online discussions about diabetes, for example, to understand patient concerns, preferred treatment options, and potential anxieties related to medication use.
     - **Claims Data**: By analyzing insurance claims data, AI can identify the economic burden of diabetes on healthcare systems and pinpoint patient segments with high medication utilization.
   - **AI-Powered Persona Development**: Based on the data analysis, AI can help create detailed profiles (personas) of target audiences. Here's an example:

- **Persona 1: Busy Endocrinologists**: They prioritize concise, evidence-based information on the medication's efficacy, safety profile, and cost-effectiveness compared to existing treatments.
- **Persona 2: Patients with Newly Diagnosed Type 2 Diabetes**: They might experience information overload and require clear explanations of the disease, treatment options, and potential side effects, delivered in an empathetic and easy-to-understand manner.

2. **Clinical Trial Optimization:**
   - **Patient Recruitment with AI**: Traditionally, recruiting for clinical trials can be time-consuming and expensive. AI can analyze patient data and medical records to identify individuals with a high probability of being eligible for the trial based on inclusion/exclusion criteria. This can significantly accelerate the recruitment process and reduce costs.
   - **Predictive Analytics for Informed Decisions**: AI models can analyze ongoing clinical trial data in real time. This allows for:
   - **Early Identification of Safety Concerns**: If the AI detects potential adverse events associated with the medication, the trial can be paused or adjusted to mitigate risks.
   - **Predicting Trial Outcomes**: AI models can analyze data to predict the medication's potential efficacy and inform decisions about trial design or dosage optimization.

By leveraging AI in these pre-launch activities, pharma companies can gain deeper market insights, identify the most promising patient segments, and optimize clinical trials for faster and more efficient product development. This ultimately paves the way for a successful launch of the new medication.

Launch Activities:

1. **Targeted Marketing and Communication**:
   - **Personalized Messaging Across Channels**: With the help of AI, pharma companies can craft personalized marketing messages and content tailored to resonate with specific HCPs (Healthcare Professionals) and patient segments. Here is how:
     - **Email Marketing**: AI can personalize email subject lines, content, and CTAs (calls to action) based on the recipient's persona (e.g., highlighting cost-effectiveness for endocrinologists vs. focusing on improved quality of life for patients).
     - **Social Media Ads**: AI can identify relevant online communities frequented by target audiences and create targeted social media ad campaigns with messaging that addresses their specific needs and concerns.
     - **Website Landing Pages**: AI can personalize landing pages with dynamic content based on the user's browsing history or previous interactions. For example, a patient who has downloaded a white paper on the disease might see a landing page emphasizing the medication's efficacy. In contrast, a new visitor might see a more general overview.
   - **Programmatic Ad Buying and Optimization**: Gone are the days of static ad placements. AI automates the ad-buying process:
     - **Identifying Optimal Platforms**: AI analyzes vast amounts of data to identify the most relevant medical websites, publications, and social media platforms for reaching target audiences with laser focus.
     - **Real-Time Optimization**: AI can monitor real-time campaign performance, dynamically adjusting ad spending and targeting parameters to maximize reach

and engagement with the most relevant audience segments. This ensures the marketing budget is used efficiently and delivers the best return on investment (ROI).

2. **Sales Force Enablement:**
    - **AI-Powered Sales Tools for HCP Engagement**: AI can equip sales reps with powerful tools to enhance their interactions with HCPs:
        - **Targeted HCP Identification**: AI can analyze data to identify HCPs who specialize in treating the disease the new medication addresses and are likely to prescribe it.
        - **Predictive Analytics for Personalized Sales Pitches**: AI can analyze HCPs' past prescribing habits and preferences to predict their potential interest in the new medication. This allows sales reps to tailor their presentations to address specific needs and anticipated questions.
        - **Content Recommendations**: AI can suggest the most relevant sales collateral and educational resources for HCPs based on their specialty and the specific product being launched. This empowers sales reps to deliver data-driven presentations and answer HCP questions effectively.

These launch activities, powered by AI, help pharma companies deliver targeted and personalized communication to HCPs and patients, ultimately influencing prescribing decisions and increasing medication adoption.

Post-Launch Activities:

1. **Pharmacovigilance and Safety Monitoring**:
    - **Real-Time Data Analysis for Early Detection**: Traditionally, pharmacovigilance relies on passive reporting of adverse events. AI can analyze data from various sources in real-time, including:

    - **Electronic Health Records (EHRs)**: AI can identify potential adverse events associated with the new medication much faster than traditional methods by analyzing physician reports of side effects.
    - **Social Media Conversations**: AI can monitor social media platforms for medication mentions and potential side effects. While unreliable as a diagnostic tool, it can raise flags for further investigation.
    - **Spontaneous Reporting Systems**: AI can analyze data from spontaneous reporting systems where patients or healthcare professionals report adverse events directly to regulatory bodies.
- **Predictive Modeling for Proactive Risk Management**: AI models can be built based on historical data to predict potential safety risks associated with the medication. This allows for:
    - **Targeted Interventions**: If AI identifies a potential risk for a specific patient population, targeted warnings or dosage adjustments can be implemented to mitigate risks.
    - **Proactive Communication with HCPs**: Pharma companies can proactively communicate potential safety concerns to HCPs based on AI-driven insights, ensuring informed prescribing decisions.

2. **Customer Relationship Management (CRM)**:
    - **AI-Powered Chatbots for 24/7 Patient Support**:
        - **Medication Adherence Reminders**: Chatbots can send automated reminders to patients to take their medication as prescribed, improving adherence rates and treatment outcomes.
        - **Answering Routine Questions**: Chatbots can answer frequently asked questions about the medication's side effects, dosage, and potential interactions with other medications, freeing pharmacists and nurses for more complex queries.

    - **Offering Emotional Support**: Chatbots can provide basic emotional support and resources for patients managing chronic conditions.

- **Sentiment Analysis for Continuous Improvement**: AI can analyze online reviews, social media posts, and patient surveys to understand patient perceptions of the new medication:
    - **Identifying Areas for Improvement**: AI can analyze patient feedback to identify potential issues with the medication, such as side effects not previously reported or difficulties with using the medication delivery system.
    - **Tailoring Future Marketing Messages**: Pharma companies can better adjust marketing messages to address patient needs and concerns by understanding patient sentiment.

These post-launch activities ensure the medication's safety and efficacy while fostering positive patient experiences. AI empowers pharmaceutical companies to address potential issues and improve patient care proactively.

Benefits of AI-Powered Product Launch:

- **Increased Efficiency and Cost Savings**: AI automates repetitive tasks, streamlines processes, and optimizes marketing efforts, leading to cost savings and faster time to market.
- **Deeper Market Insights**: AI provides data-driven insights into market trends, competitor activity, and patient needs, allowing for more informed decision-making.
- **Improved Patient Targeting and Engagement**: Personalized marketing messages and content resonate better with target audiences, improving patient engagement and medication adherence.
- **Enhanced Safety Monitoring**: AI facilitates real-time safety monitoring and allows for proactive risk mitigation strategies.

Challenges and Considerations:

- **Data Privacy and Security**: Strict regulations govern patient data privacy. Pharma companies must ensure all AI applications comply with these regulations and prioritize data security.
- **Algorithmic Bias**: AI algorithms can perpetuate biases in the data they are trained on. Careful training data selection and monitoring is crucial to ensure fair and unbiased AI use.
- **Human Expertise Remains Essential**: While AI is a powerful tool, human expertise in areas like strategic planning, building trust with HCPs, and understanding the nuances of disease states remains irreplaceable. AI should augment human capabilities, not replace them.

Overall, AI offers a transformative approach to pharma product launches. By leveraging AI's data analysis, automation, and personalization capabilities, pharma companies can achieve greater efficiency, gain deeper market insights, and ultimately bring life-changing medications to patients faster and more effectively.

CHAPTER 31

AI-powered Content Creation and Personalized Marketing

The digital landscape is abuzz with the potential of AI to revolutionize content creation and personalized marketing. But remember, it's not AI versus humans; it's about *human+AI collaboration*, where their unique strengths combine to create a symphony of success. Here's how they can work together:

Human Strengths:

- **Creativity and Storytelling**: Humans excel at crafting compelling narratives, visuals, and experiences that resonate with audiences on an emotional level.
- **Strategic Thinking and Campaign Planning**: Humans define campaign goals, identify key channels, and orchestrate different elements for maximum impact.
- **Domain Expertise and Audience Understanding**: Deep knowledge of the target audience, industry trends, and market opportunities ensures relevant and impactful content and messaging.
- **Ethical Considerations and Responsible Marketing**: Humans safeguard data privacy, ensure transparency, and prioritize responsible communication throughout all marketing efforts.

AI Strengths:

- **Data Analysis and Segmentation**: AI analyzes vast datasets of customer demographics, behavior, and online interactions to create precise audience segments for laser-targeted marketing.
- **Personalized Content Creation and Optimization**: AI generates content like emails, ads, and website experiences tailored to individual preferences and needs, fostering deeper engagement.
- **Real-time Analytics and Performance Tracking**: AI continuously monitors campaign performance, offering instant insights for optimizing messaging, content, and targeting strategies.
- **Automation and Efficient Content Generation**: AI can automate repetitive tasks like content scheduling, data analysis, and A/B testing, freeing human resources for strategic thinking and creative pursuits.

Synergy in Action:

Imagine this:

- AI segments audiences based on demographics, interests, and online behavior.
- Humans develop overarching campaign themes and content strategies, ensuring brand alignment and emotional resonance.
- AI personalizes email content, ad variations, and website experiences for individual audience members, showcasing relevant information and product benefits.
- Real-time analytics reveal how segments respond to different variations to different variations, allowing humans to refine messaging, optimize targeting, and adapt to changing audience preferences.
- Ethical considerations remain paramount, with humans ensuring data privacy, transparency, and responsible communication at every stage.

Challenges and Considerations:

- **Data Quality and Privacy**: Ensure accuracy and completeness of data used by AI and prioritize responsible data collection and utilization.
- **Interpretability and Explainability of AI Models**: Understand how AI algorithms reach their conclusions to avoid black-box decision-making and facilitate human oversight.
- **Upskilling and Workforce Development**: Equip marketing teams with the necessary skills to collaborate effectively with AI and interpret its insights.
- **Over-reliance on AI and Neglecting Human Skills**: Remember that AI is a tool, not a replacement for human creativity, empathy, and ethical intuition.

By harmonizing human ingenuity and storytelling with the analytical power of AI, we can craft personalized marketing campaigns that truly resonate with audiences. This synergy fosters deeper connections, drives engagement, and leads to successful market results. But remember, ethical considerations are paramount. We must ensure responsible data use and transparency and prioritize building genuine connections with consumers, always keeping sight of the human element at the heart of every marketing effort.

This is not a static story. As AI technology evolves and our understanding of its ethical implications deepens, the possibilities for content creation and personalized marketing will continue to expand. By nurturing a culture of continuous learning, prioritizing ethical responsibility, and maintaining a deep commitment to human-centered marketing, we can turn this powerful synergy into a force for good, transforming the marketing landscape and driving the success that positively impacts everyone involved.

Content Creation and a Personalized Campaign: An Example

Scenario: Anti-diabetic drug launch— Human+AI synergy in content creation and personalized campaign.

Target Audience: Adults aged 50+ with prediabetes or type 2 diabetes who are concerned about managing their condition and living a healthy life.

Campaign Goal: Increase awareness and adoption of a new anti-diabetic drug called GlucoBalance.

Human Contribution:

- **Campaign Strategy**: Develop a campaign theme emphasizing "Empowering you to thrive with diabetes," focusing on positive control, healthy living, and improved quality of life.
- **Storytelling**: Craft engaging narratives of people with diabetes who successfully manage their condition with GlucoBalance, showcasing real-life experiences and emotional connections.
- **Content Formats**: Create diverse content like informative articles, video testimonials, blog posts, recipes, and social media infographics, addressing varied preferences and learning styles.
- **Ethical Considerations**: Ensure sensitive portrayals of people with diabetes, transparency about drug information, and accessibility to different abilities.

AI Contribution:

- **Audience Segmentation**: Analyze health data and online behavior to identify distinct audience segments like newly diagnosed, active seniors, and individuals struggling with lifestyle changes.
- **Personalized Content Creation**: Generate tailored email greetings, website recommendations, and social media feeds that address each segment's needs and concerns.

- **Dynamic Ad Targeting**: Show relevant variations of video ads across platforms based on user demographics, interests, and online activity.
- **Real-time Performance Tracking**: Monitor engagement metrics across channels, providing insights to optimize content, messaging, and targeting strategies.

Synergy in Action:

1. Humans develop a video series featuring diverse individuals with diabetes who share their stories and success with GlucoBalance.
2. AI analyzes viewer demographics and engagement to identify resonating themes and preferred video formats for each audience segment.
3. Humans create personalized video snippets from the series, highlighting relevant testimonials and tips tailored to each segment's needs.
4. AI delivers these personalized video snippets across platforms through targeted ads and social media feeds.
5. Real-time analytics reveals the effectiveness of different variations, allowing humans to refine content further and optimize targeting for maximum impact.

Ethical Considerations:

- **Data Privacy**: Ensure informed consent for data collection and responsible use throughout the campaign.
- **Algorithmic Bias**: Monitor and mitigate potential biases in AI algorithms to ensure fair representation and equal access to information across diverse segments.
- **Transparency and Accessibility**: Communicate about data use, provide options for opting out of personalization, and make content accessible for people with disabilities.

Expected Outcome:

- Increased awareness and adoption of GlucoBalance among targeted audience segments.
- Deeper engagement with personalized content leads to a positive perception of the drug and its impact on quality of life.
- A successful launch campaign showcases human+AI collaboration's power in personalized healthcare intervention marketing.

Remember, this is just one example. The possibilities for personalized content creation and marketing in the healthcare field are endless. By prioritizing ethical considerations, continuing learning, and leveraging the unique strengths of both humans and AI, we can create future campaigns that empower individuals to manage their health, improve their well-being, and thrive.

CHAPTER 32

Human Oversight and Control of AI-Driven Messaging and Targeting

In dynamic pharma marketing, AI promises powerful tools for personalized messaging and targeting. However, it's crucial to remember that human oversight and control remain paramount. Here's how we can ensure the responsible AI in this sensitive domain:

Human Oversight Strategies:

- **Defining Ethical Guidelines**: Establish clear guidelines for data collection, use, and responsible messaging to ensure patient privacy, transparency, and adherence to regulatory requirements.
- **Curating Training Data**: Humans curate and review training data for AI algorithms to avoid biases and ensure accurate representation of target audiences.
- **Setting Guardrails for Algorithms**: Define parameters and limitations for AI-generated content and targeting to prevent unintended consequences or offensive messaging.
- **Ongoing Monitoring and Evaluation**: Monitor AI-driven campaigns for potential biases, ethical violations, and effectiveness, making necessary adjustments.
- **Maintaining Human Control over Key Decisions**: Humans retain ultimate control over campaign strategy, messaging, and targeting decisions, leveraging AI insights to inform, not dictate, these choices.

Control Mechanisms:

- **Human-in-the-Loop Systems**: Implement systems where humans review and approve AI-generated content before dissemination, ensuring accuracy, ethical alignment, and brand consistency.
- **Explainable AI Models**: Utilize AI models that provide clear explanations for their recommendations, allowing humans to understand the reasoning behind targeting and messaging decisions.
- **A/B Testing and Human Evaluation**: Conduct A/B testing with alternative content and targeting approaches, incorporating human evaluation alongside AI metrics to assess the effectiveness and ethical implications.
- **Regular Audits and Risk Assessments**: Conduct audits of AI systems and data practices to identify and mitigate potential risks associated with bias, discrimination, or privacy violations.

Benefits of Human Oversight:

- **Ethical Considerations and Responsible Marketing**: This ensures patient well-being is prioritized, and that accurate and truthful marketing materials and messaging align with professional codes of conduct.
- **Avoiding Unintended Consequences**: Mitigates risks associated with algorithmic bias, stereotyping, or offensive content, protecting vulnerable populations and maintaining brand reputation.
- **Effective Communication and Patient Trust**: Human involvement fosters empathy, understanding, and trust in patient communication, leading to more effective engagement and positive brand perception.
- **Maintaining Creative Control and Brand Identity**: Humans safeguard brand voice, messaging consistency, and overall campaign strategy, ensuring alignment with marketing goals and brand values.

Challenges and Considerations:

- **Upskilling and Workforce Development**: Equip pharma marketing teams with the necessary skills to understand AI capabilities, limitations, and ethical implications.
- **Transparency and Communication**: Communicate to patients and healthcare professionals how AI is used in marketing campaigns, ensuring informed consent and building trust.
- **Finding the Right Balance**: Leveraging AI's power for personalization while maintaining essential human oversight to avoid ethical pitfalls and ensure responsible communication.

By embracing human oversight and control alongside the power of AI, we can unlock the full potential of personalized marketing in pharma. This synergy allows us to deliver targeted messages that resonate with patients, navigate ethical considerations with nuance, and build trust while achieving marketing goals.

Remember, AI is a tool, not a replacement for human judgment, empathy, and ethical responsibility. By harnessing the unique strengths of both, we can create a future of pharma marketing that is both effective and deeply human-centered.

PART VII

AI-Powered Pharma Brand Management: Optimizing Your Brand in the Digital Age

Chapter 33. Market Research and Insights with AI: Unleashing Pharma Brand Power

Chapter 34. Optimizing Your Sales and Distribution with AI: A Step-by-Step Guide

Chapter 35. Optimizing Clinical Trials and Patient Recruitment with AI: A Step-by-Step Guide

Chapter 36. Building Trust and Connections: A Step-by-Step Guide to Brand Communication and Reputation Management

Chapter 37. Unveiling the Impact: A Step-by-Step Guide to Measuring Marketing Performance

Chapter 38. Beyond the Typed Word: Generative AI and Conversational AI Revolutionize Brand Communication and Reputation Management

Chapter 39. Orchestrating Reputation in Pharma: Leveraging AI for Trustworthy Brand Symphony

Chapter 40. The Synergy of Minds in Brand Management and Customer Engagement

Chapter 41. The Synergy of Human+AI Collaboration for Customer Interaction

Chapter 42. Conducting the Audience: Market Research and Analysis for Pharma Branding Step by Step

Chapter 43. From Insights to Impact: Translating Your Pharma Branding Symphony into Action

44. Symphony of Applications: Expanding the Reach of Brand Communications

45. Composing Compelling Content: Content Creation and Optimization for Pharma Branding

46. Harmonizing Communication: Personalized Marketing and Engagement in Pharma Branding

47. AI in Regulatory Compliance and Risk Management

48. Optimizing the Sales and Distribution Symphony: A Step-by-Step Guide

49. AI's Harmonious Symphony: Enhancing Brand Communication and Reputation Management

50. Roles Humans and AI Play in Building Trust and Emotional Connections

The pharmaceutical industry is transforming, driven by the rapid integration of artificial intelligence (AI) across various disciplines. Brand managers require innovative tools and strategies to navigate this dynamic landscape as competition intensifies and patient expectations evolve. Enter AI: A powerful partner equipped to unlock unique insights, personalize patient experiences, and optimize brand-building activities across the entire marketing value chain. This chapter delves into the exciting world of AI-powered pharma brand management, empowering you with the knowledge and tools to elevate your brand strategy. We will explore how AI can be harnessed to:

- **Gain Unprecedented Market Intelligence**: Uncover hidden patterns and trends in vast datasets, identifying promising patient segments and predicting market shifts with unmatched accuracy.
- **Craft Personalized Patient Engagement**: Deliver bespoke content, recommendations, and support tailored to individual needs and preferences, fostering deeper connections and trust.
- **Revolutionize Content Creation**: Generate targeted marketing materials, educational resources, and creative assets, optimizing message effectiveness and resonating with diverse audiences.
- **Navigate Regulations with Confidence**: Navigate complex regulatory landscapes with AI-powered compliance tools, minimizing risks and ensuring ethical, transparent communication.
- **Optimize Sales and Distribution**: Streamline sales force activities, target healthcare professionals with greater precision, and optimize logistics for efficient distribution.
- **Accelerate Clinical Trials**: Identity eligible patients faster, streamline communication, and manage recruitment efforts effectively, bringing life-saving treatments to market sooner.

Part VII: AI-Powered Pharma Brand Management:... 353

- **Protect and Enhance Brand Reputation**: Monitor online conversations, identify potential reputational threats, and proactively manage brand communications to safeguard your brand image.
- **Measure and Analyze Performance**: Gain deeper insights into marketing campaigns, quantify ROI in real-time, and make data-driven decisions for future success.

This chapter guides you to unlocking AI's vast potential in pharmaceutical brand management. By embracing these innovative solutions, you can build stronger brands, deliver optimal patient experiences, and thrive in the ever-evolving healthcare landscape.

Remember, AI is not a replacement for human expertise but a powerful collaborator, enhancing your judgment and amplifying your ability to connect with patients on a deeper level. So, let's embark on this exciting journey together and discover how AI can empower you to build brands that inspire, heal, and make a difference in patients' lives worldwide.

CHAPTER 33

Market Research and Insights with AI: Unleashing Pharma Brand Power

In the competitive world of pharma brand management, gaining accurate and actionable market insights is no longer just a *nice to have*— it's a necessity for building successful brands. Enter AI, revolutionizing how pharma companies unearth valuable information and transform it into strategic advantages. Let's dive into how AI empowers market research and insights:

1. **Identifying Hidden Patient Segments:**
   - **Challenge**: Traditional market research often relies on broad demographics, needing more specific patient needs and preferences.
   - **AI Solution**: Text analysis of social media conversations, online forums, and patient surveys can uncover hidden patient segments based on shared experiences, language patterns, and emotional sentiment.

   Example: Analyzing online discussions about a specific disease can reveal sub-groups facing unique challenges. Imagine identifying a segment of young adults struggling with a rare side effect, allowing you to tailor marketing and support programs specifically for them.

2. **Predicting Market Trends with Foresight:**
   - **Challenge**: Predicting future market trends can take time and effort, leading to missed opportunities or reactive strategies.

- **AI Solution**: AI algorithms can analyze vast amounts of historical data, competitor actions, and social media trends to predict future market shifts and patient needs.

Example: By analyzing sales data, competitor launches, and patient advocacy group discussions, AI can predict a surge in demand for a specific type of medication, allowing you to increase production and marketing efforts proactively.

3. **Mining Patient Experiences for Deeper Insights:**
   - **Challenge**: Traditional surveys often need to pay more attention to the nuances of patient experiences, failing to capture emotional aspects and real-world challenges.
   - **AI Solution**: Natural Language Processing (NLP) can analyze patient narratives from surveys, support groups, and online reviews, extracting deeper insights into their experiences, concerns, and unmet needs.

Example: Analyzing patient narratives about a specific medication can reveal hidden side effects, unexpected benefits, or emotional burdens beyond clinical data, informing you about how to improve the patient experience.

4. **Going Beyond Demographics with Psychographic Targeting:**
   - **Challenge**: Targeting solely on demographics can be inefficient, missing specific patient mindsets and motivations.
   - **AI Solution**: AI can analyze social media activity, purchase patterns, and online content consumption to understand patient psychographics, values, and preferred communication styles.

Example: By understanding the preferred online channels and content types of specific patient segments, you can create targeted marketing campaigns that resonate deeply and drive engagement.

5. **Real-Time Sentiment Analysis for Proactive Response:**
   - **Challenge**: Traditional methods of understanding patient sentiment lag, preventing timely responses to concerns or negative perceptions.
   - **AI Solution**: AI-powered sentiment analysis tools can monitor online conversations, news articles, and social media mentions in real-time, identifying emerging trends and potential reputational risks.

Example: Proactively address patient concerns about a medication's side effects by launching an informative campaign based on real-time social media sentiment analysis, mitigating potential damage and building trust.

Remember:

- **Ethical Considerations**: Ensure responsible data collection, anonymization, and transparent communication regarding AI usage.
- **Human+AI Collaboration**: AI excels at analyzing vast data, but human expertise remains crucial for interpreting insights and making strategic decisions.
- **Focus on Patient Value**: Ultimately, AI-powered market research should serve patients by identifying their needs and guiding brand strategies that improve their lives.

By harnessing the power of AI, pharma brands can move beyond basic demographics and delve into the rich tapestry of patient experiences, motivations, and preferences. This deeper understanding fosters targeted marketing and trust and allows brands to make a meaningful difference in the lives of the patients they serve.

Unveiling the Invisible: Step-by-Step Guide to Identifying Hidden Patient Insights with AI

Understanding patient needs and preferences in the pharma industry goes beyond surface-level demographics. Hidden insights reside within vast data — narratives, social media conversations, online forums, and patient surveys — waiting to be unlocked. With its data-crunching prowess, AI opens doors to these elusive gems, empowering brands to build deeper connections and deliver impactful solutions. Let's embark on a step-by-step journey of uncovering hidden patient insights:

1. **Define Your Objective:** What specific questions do you have about your target audience? Are you seeking to understand unmet needs, identify specific patient segments, or predict treatment preferences? Clearly defining your goals guides your data collection and analysis approach.
2. **Data Gathering:** Cast your net wide. Utilize surveys, social media platforms, online communities, customer service conversations, and public health databases. Ensure ethical data collection and patient consent practices are in place.
3. **Data Preprocessing:** Clean and standardize your data. This involves removing irrelevant information, correcting errors, and formatting it for AI analysis. Consider anonymizing data to comply with privacy regulations.
4. **Choose Your AI Weapon:** Different AI techniques excel at different tasks. Here are some popular options:
    - **Text Analysis:** Uncover sentiment, themes, and emerging topics from patient narratives.
    - **Natural Language Processing (NLP):** Extract hidden meaning and nuances from patient language, understanding emotions and unspoken needs.
    - **Clustering Algorithms:** Group patients with similar characteristics to discover hidden segments based on behavior, experiences, or preferences.
    - **Predictive Analytics:** Forecast future patient needs and treatment preferences based on historical data and emerging trends.

5. **Train and Optimize Your AI Model:** Feed your chosen AI technique with the preprocessed data and let it learn. Monitor its performance, refine its parameters, and ensure it aligns with your objectives.
6. **Analyze and Interpret Results:** AI provides insights, but human expertise is crucial for interpretation. Look for patterns, connections, and anomalies that reveal hidden aspects of your target audience.
7. **Validate and Apply Insights:** Don't jump to conclusions. Validate your findings with additional data sources or qualitative research. Once confident, integrate these insights into your marketing strategy, product development, or patient support initiatives.

Examples in Action:

- **Identifying a Previously Unknown Patient Segment:** Analyzing online support groups, AI reveals a community of young adults struggling with a rare side effect of your medication. You develop targeted educational resources and support programs specifically for them.
- **Predicting the Rise of a Specific Treatment Preference:** AI, analyzing social media discussions and clinical trial data, predicts a surge in demand for a personalized medicine approach. You adjust your production and marketing efforts to meet this anticipated need.
- **Uncovering Emotional Barriers to Medication Adherence:** NLP analysis of patient narratives reveals hidden anxieties and concerns associated with medication. You create an empathy-driven campaign to address these concerns and improve adherence rates.

Remember, AI is a powerful tool, but only a tool. Ethical considerations, human expertise, and a patient-centric approach are crucial for transforming hidden insights into meaningful actions that truly benefit patients and elevate your brand.

Predicting Market Trends with Foresight: A Step-by-Step Guide for Pharma Brands

Navigating the dynamic pharma market requires proactive planning and understanding of future trends. AI serves as your crystal ball, analyzing vast amounts of data to predict shifts in patient needs, competitor actions, and regulatory landscapes. Let's unveil a step-by-step process for harnessing AI's predictive power:

1. **Define Your Scope:** Identify the specific trends you want to anticipate. Is it predicting demand for new disease treatment, forecasting competitor drug launches, or understanding changes in patient preferences for specific drug classes?
2. **Data Gathering:** Collect relevant data from various sources, such as historical sales, clinical trial results, competitor filings, social media conversations, patient surveys, and economic indicators. Ensure data quality and ethical acquisition practices.
3. **Data Preprocessing:** Clean and organize your data, removing inconsistencies and formatting for AI analysis. This might involve data imputation, standardization, and feature engineering to extract meaningful insights.
4. **Choose Your AI Technique:** Different AI algorithms excel at different tasks. Here are some common choices:
    - **Time Series Forecasting:** Analyze historical data patterns to predict future demand for specific medications or drug classes.
    - **Regression Analysis:** Identify relationships between factors (e.g., economic trends, disease prevalence) and predict their impact on specific market segments.
    - **Natural Language Processing (NLP):** Analyze social media, news articles, and online forums to extract insights about emerging trends and patient sentiment.
    - **Machine Learning:** Train algorithms on existing data to recognize patterns and predict future market shifts based on new information.

5. **Train and Optimize Your Model:** Feed your chosen technique with the preprocessed data and let it learn. Monitor its performance, adjust parameters, and ensure it aligns with your prediction goals.
6. **Validate and Interpret Results:** Don't rely solely on AI predictions. Compare results with expert opinions, benchmark against other forecasting models, and consider potential biases in the data or algorithms.
7. **Actionable Insights:** Translate your predictions into actionable plans. Optimize production and distribution for anticipated demand surges, adjust marketing strategies to address patient trends, or prepare for potential regulatory changes.

Examples in Action:

- **Predicting a Rise in Personalized Medicine:** By analyzing clinical trial data, patient forums, and news articles, AI predicts a growing demand for personalized medicine approaches in cancer treatment. Your pharma brand proactively invests in developing personalized therapies and targeted marketing campaigns.
- **Forecasting Drug Shortages:** AI, analyzing global supply chain data and social media discussions, predicts a potential shortage of a critical medication. You can alert healthcare providers, stockpile the medication, or advocate for alternative solutions.
- **Anticipating Regulatory Shifts:** NLP analysis of government documents and industry publications helps you prepare for upcoming regulatory changes that may impact drug approval processes or marketing restrictions.

Remember, AI predictions are not absolute truths but rather informed probabilities. Ethical data practices, human evaluation of results, and a flexible approach are crucial for making the most of AI's foresight and navigating the ever-evolving pharma landscape.

Unveiling the Patient Narrative: Step-by-Step Guide to Mining Deeper Insights

Patient experiences hold a treasure trove of valuable insights waiting to be mined. Traditional surveys often scratch the surface, missing the nuances and rich tapestry of emotions, frustrations, and unmet needs. Enter AI, your powerful pickaxe, to uncover the hidden gems and translate them into actionable intelligence. Let's embark on a step-by-step journey:

1. **Define Your Focus:** What specific aspects of the patient experience do you want to explore? Are you interested in understanding treatment adherence challenges, uncovering side effect anxieties, or identifying unmet support needs? Clearly defining your goals guides your data collection and analysis approach.
2. **Gather Patient Narratives:** Cast your net wide beyond traditional surveys. Consider:
   - **Qualitative Interviews:** Conduct in-depth interviews to capture detailed experiences and emotional nuances.
   - **Patient Support Groups:** Analyze online forum discussions and group conversations, revealing unfiltered insights and peer-to-peer support dynamics.
   - **Social Media Posts:** Examine relevant conversations, reviews, and comments on platforms where patients openly share experiences.
   - **Customer Service Interactions:** Analyze calls and online chat transcripts, uncovering pain points and unmet needs expressed directly to your brand.
3. **Prepare the Data:** Clean and prepare your textual data for AI analysis. This involves:
   - **Transcription:** Extract text from audio/video interviews if needed.

- **Anonymization:** Ensure patient privacy by removing identifying information.
- **Normalization:** Standardize language, correct typos, and remove irrelevant information.
- **Sentiment Analysis:** Label data with positive, negative, or neutral sentiment for easier analysis.

4. **Choose Your AI Weapon:** Different AI techniques excel at different tasks:
   - **Natural Language Processing (NLP):** Extract entities, emotions, and relationships from text, uncovering hidden themes, concerns, and unmet needs.
   - **Topic Modeling:** Identify recurring themes and topics across patient narratives, revealing broader trends and shared experiences.
   - **Text Clustering:** Group similar patient experiences based on content or sentiment, uncovering sub-segments with unique needs and challenges.
5. **Train and Optimize Your Models:** Feed your chosen techniques with the prepared data and let them learn. Monitor their performance, adjust parameters, and ensure they align with your objectives.
6. **Analyze and Interpret Results:** AI provides insights, but human expertise is crucial for interpretation. Look for patterns, connections, and hidden emotions within the extracted themes, topics, and sentiment clusters.
7. **Actionable Insights:** Don't let insights gather dust. Translate them into meaningful actions:
   - **Develop Empathy-Driven Marketing Campaigns:** Address patient concerns and anxieties revealed in the narratives.
   - **Improve Product Design or Support Services:** Address usability issues and unmet needs identified from patient experiences.

- **Personalize Patient Support Programs:** Cater to specific needs and challenges identified within different patient segments.

Examples in Action:

- **Uncovering Hidden Side Effect Anxieties:** Analyzing patient support group discussions, NLP identifies hidden anxiety about a rare side effect of your medication. You develop educational resources and support programs specifically addressing this concern.
- **Understanding Medication Adherence Challenges:** Text clustering in customer service transcripts reveals specific reasons for non-adherence. You tailor interventions and reminder programs to address these identified barriers.
- **Identifying Unmet Support Needs:** Topic modeling in social media posts reveals a need for emotional support in managing a chronic condition. To address this unmet need, you launch a peer-to-peer support program.

Remember, AI is a tool for amplifying human empathy and understanding. Ethical data practices, responsible interpretation, and a patient-centric focus are crucial for transforming patient narratives into meaningful actions that improve lives and elevate your brand's impact.

Unveiling the Mind Behind the Click: Psychographic Targeting with AI: A Step-by-Step Guide

Understanding patient demographics is merely the starting point in today's pharma landscape. Emotions, values, lifestyles, and motivations — the world of psychographics— are key to truly resonating with your target audience. AI, your powerful magnifying glass, unveils these hidden aspects, enabling you to craft targeted, impactful marketing campaigns that connect on a deeper level. Let's embark on a step-by-step journey:

1. **Define Your Objective:** What specific psychographic insights do you seek? Are you trying to understand patient attitudes toward treatment options, identify lifestyle factors impacting medication adherence, or segment your audience based on values and motivations? Clearly defining your goals guides your data collection and analysis approach.
2. **Data Gathering:** Go beyond traditional demographics. Consider:
   - **Social Media Activity:** Analyze platform usage, content interactions, and online communities to understand values, interests, and lifestyle choices.
   - **Online Surveys and Quizzes:** Design surveys that delve into patient preferences, motivations, and emotional responses to specific topics.
   - **Customer Support Interactions:** Analyze transcripts for clues about personality traits, communication styles, and emotional triggers related to your brand.
   - **Website Engagement:** Track user journeys, content preferences, and time spent on specific sections to understand cognitive styles and information needs.
3. **Prepare the Data:** Clean and structure your data for AI analysis:
   - **Textual Data:** Standardize language, extract relevant keywords, and categorize responses based on sentiment and emotion.
   - **Behavioral Data:** Segment user interactions and website activity based on specific metrics and patterns.
4. **Choose Your AI Technique:** Different AI algorithms excel at different tasks:
   - **Machine Learning:** Train algorithms on combined demographics and behavioral data to predict psychographic profiles and segment audiences based on shared values, motivations, and lifestyles.

- **Natural Language Processing (NLP):** Extract emotional undertones and personality traits from textured data, uncovering hidden attitudes and preferences.
- **Clustering Algorithms:** Group patients with similar online behavior, interests, and content consumption patterns, revealing psychographic segments with unique characteristics.

5. **Train and Optimize Your Models:** Feed your chosen techniques with the prepared data and let them learn. Monitor performance, adjust parameters, and ensure the models align with your objectives.
6. **Analyze and Interpret Results:** AI provides insights, but human expertise is crucial for interpretation. Look for patterns, connections, and correlations between diverse data points to understand underlying psychographic factors.
7. **Actionable Insights:** Translate insights into targeted actions:
   - **Craft Personalized Marketing Messages:** Develop campaigns that resonate with specific psychographic segments' values, motivations, and preferred communication styles.
   - **Design Content that Resonates:** Create informational materials, videos, and social media posts that cater to the interests, emotional needs, and learning styles of your target audience.
   - **Offer Tailored Support Programs:** Develop interventions and resources that address the specific challenges and concerns identified within different psychographic groups.

Examples in Action:

- **Identifying the "Health Enthusiast" Segment:** Using online engagement data and social media activity analysis, AI reveals a segment of patients highly motivated by preventative health and holistic wellness. You develop targeted campaigns emphasizing your medication's lifestyle benefits and natural ingredients.

- **Understanding the "Treatment Skeptics" Segment:** NLP analysis of customer support interactions identifies a segment anxious about potential side effects. You create personalized reassurance messages and offer educational resources addressing their specific concerns.
- **Segmenting Patients Based on Decision-Making Styles:** Machine learning, survey responses, and online behavior reveal different patient segments: information-seekers, convenience-driven, and emotionally guided decision-makers. You personalize communication and marketing channels accordingly.

Remember, AI-powered psychographic targeting is not about manipulation but understanding and connecting with patients more deeply. Ethical data practices, responsible use of insights, and a commitment to patient well-being are crucial for building trust and achieving meaningful outcomes.

Listening & Researching in Real-Time: Step-by-Step Guide to Proactive Sentiment Analysis

In the fast-paced pharma world, understanding and responding to patient sentiment in real time is crucial for building trust, managing reputation, and fostering positive brand perception. AI-powered sentiment analysis empowers you to become a listening ear, proactively engaging with patients and addressing concerns swiftly. Let's delve into a step-by-step guide:

1. **Define Your Scope:** What do you want to monitor? Identify relevant online channels like social media platforms, patient forums, news articles, or customer service interactions. Determine specific topics or keywords related to your brand, medications, or disease areas.
2. **Data Collection:** Utilize real-time data streaming tools to capture relevant conversations and content as they happen. Ensure ethical data practices and user content where applicable.

3. **Data Processing:** Clean and Prepare the Data for Analysis:
    - **Text Cleaning:** Remove noise like symbols, emojis, and irrelevant mentions.
    - **Normalization:** Standardize language (e.g., slang, typos).
    - **Entity Recognition:** Identify key figures, brands, and medications mentioned in the text.
4. **Choose Your AI Technique:** Different algorithms excel at specific tasks:
    - **Sentiment Analysis:** Classify text as positive, negative, or neutral, revealing overall sentiment towards your brand or specific topics.
    - **Entity-Level Sentiment:** Analyze sentiment towards specific entities (e.g., brand, medication) within the text, providing granular insights.
    - **Opinion Mining:** Extract patients' specific opinions, concerns, and suggestions in their own words.
5. **Train and Optimize Your Models:** Fine-tune your chosen algorithms with relevant training data to ensure accurate sentiment classification and filter out irrelevant noise.
6. **Real-Time Analysis and Alerts:** Set up real-time monitoring dashboards to visualize sentiment trends and identify emerging issues or concerns. Configure alerts to notify you of spikes in negative sentiment or mentions of specific keywords.
7. **Take Proactive Action:** Don't just monitor; respond!
    - **Address Negative Sentiment:** Acknowledge concerns, provide factual information, and offer support where necessary.
    - **Engage with Positive Mentions:** Thank patients for sharing their experiences, fostering loyalty and trust.
    - **Identify and Address Misinformation:** Correct inaccurate online information, promoting clarity and trust.
    - **Refine Marketing and Communication Strategies:** Use sentiment insights to improve messaging, content, and overall brand communication.

Examples in Action:

- **Identify and Address a Medication Side Effect Concern:** Real-time sentiment analysis detects a surge in negative mentions about a potential side effect of your medication. You proactively issue a statement clarifying the issue, offering support to affected patients, and demonstrating transparency.
- **Engage with Patients Expressing Gratitude:** You identify heartwarming stories and positive sentiments towards your brand on social media. You thank these patients, fostering loyalty and encouraging further positive engagement.
- **Debunk Misinformation About Your Brand:** You detect false claims about your medication's safety. You swiftly issue a fact-based response, clarifying the issue and protecting your brand perception.

Remember, AI-powered sentiment analysis is powerful, but responsible use is paramount. Be transparent about your monitoring practices, respect user privacy, and focus on genuine engagement to build meaningful connections with patients and effectively navigate the dynamic online landscape.

Tailoring the Experience: A Step-by-Step Guide to Personalized Marketing and Engagement with AI

In today's saturated healthcare market, one-size-fits-all tactics no longer resonate. Patients crave personalized experiences that cater to their unique needs and preferences. AI unlocks the power of personalization, enabling you to craft targeted messages, deliver relevant content, and foster deeper patient engagement. Let's embark on a step-by-step journey:

1. **Define Your Goals:** What do you want to achieve with personalization? Increase medication adherence? Drive awareness of a new service? Improve patient satisfaction? Clearly define your objectives to guide your data collection and strategy.

2. **Gather Patient Data:** Collect diverse data points to build detailed patient profiles:
   - **Demographic:** Age, location, medical history, diagnosis, treatment stage.
   - **Behavioral:** Website interactions, app usage, content preferences, engagement patterns.
   - **Psychographic:** Values, lifestyle, communication style, information needs (derived from surveys, social media activity).
3. **Data Segmentation:** Group patients based on shared characteristics, needs, or behaviors. AI-powered clustering algorithms can help identify relevant segments automatically.
4. **Choose Your AI Technique:** Different AI techniques excel at different tasks:
   - **Recommendation Engines:** Suggest relevant medications, educational resources, or support programs based on individual patient profiles and preferences.
   - **Adaptive Content:** Generate personalized website content, email newsletters, or social media posts tailored to specific segments or individual needs.
   - **Chatbots:** Offer patients personalized support, answer questions, and guide them through specific journeys based on their unique situations.
5. **Model Training and Optimization:** Use the collected data to train your chosen AI techniques, refining their ability to make accurate predictions and generate personalized recommendations or content.
6. **Real-Time Personalization:** Deliver personalized experiences across various touchpoints:
   - **Dynamic Website Content:** Display relevant information and offers based on user behavior and interests.
   - **Targeted Email Campaigns:** Segment audiences and send emails with personalized messaging and recommendations.
   - **Conversational AI:** Train chatbots to adapt their responses and provide information specific to each patient's needs.

7. **Measure and Improve:** Track the impact of your personalized campaigns on key metrics like engagement, conversions, and patient satisfaction. Use these insights to refine your strategies and personalize further.

Examples in Action:

- **Recommend Personalized Medication Reminders:** Based on a patient's medical history and behavior, an AI-powered app suggests personalized reminders and educational content to improve adherence.
- **Deliver Targeted Content After Diagnosis:** Following a diagnosis, patients receive a website experience tailored to their specific disease, offering relevant support groups, articles, and treatment information.
- **Chatbot Provides Emotional Support:** A chatbot identifies a patient experiencing anxiety and offers personalized coping mechanisms and resources based on individual preferences.

Remember:

- **Ethical Considerations:** Be transparent about data collection and usage, prioritize patient privacy, and avoid perpetuating bias.
- **Human+AI Collaboration:** AI assists with personalization, but human expertise remains crucial for interpretation, ethical considerations, and ongoing strategy refinement.
- **Focus on Patient Value:** Personalization should not be intrusive but focused on delivering genuine value, addressing individual needs, and improving patient lives.

By embracing these steps and considerations, AI-powered personalization can transform your marketing and engagement strategies, fostering deeper connections with patients and achieving positive outcomes that truly matter.

CHAPTER

34

Optimizing your Sales and Distribution with AI: A Step-by-Step Guide

In the competitive pharma world, efficient sales and distribution are critical for getting life-saving treatments to patients who need them. AI presents a powerful tool to optimize these processes, leading to increased reach, improved efficiency, and better patient outcomes. Let's delve into a step-by-step guide:

1. **Define Your Optimization Goals**:
   - **What Specific Areas Do You Want to Improve?** Is it targeting high-potential healthcare professionals, optimizing inventory management, or streamlining logistics and delivery?
   - **Identify Key Metrics**: Choose relevant metrics (e.g., sales volume, cost-efficiency, patient access) to track your progress and measure the impact of AI-driven optimizations.
2. **Gather and Analyze Data**:
   - **Sales Data**: Analyze past sales records to identify trends, top-performing regions, and purchasing patterns of healthcare professionals.
   - **Market Data**: Gather information about disease prevalence, competitor activity, and healthcare provider demographics in the target market.
   - **Logistics Data**: Analyze distribution networks, inventory levels, and delivery lead times to identify potential bottlenecks and areas for improvement.

3. **Choose Your AI Techniques**: Different AI algorithms excel at distinct tasks:
    - **Predictive Analytics**: Forecast future drug demand in specific regions, allowing for optimized production and inventory management.
    - **Machine Learning**: Identify high-potential healthcare professionals based on past prescribing patterns and patient demographics, enabling targeted marketing efforts.
    - **Route Optimization**: Optimize delivery routes for medical couriers to reduce transportation costs and ensure timely delivery of critical medications.
    - **Demand Forecasting**: Predict potential supply chain disruptions and drug shortages, enabling proactive preparations and risk mitigation.
4. **Model Training and Implementation**:
    - Train your AI models on the gathered data, ensuring accuracy and alignment with your optimization goals.
    - Integrate AI outputs into your existing sales and distribution processes via dashboards, automated recommendations, or decision-support systems.
5. **Continuous Monitoring and Improvement**:
    - Track key metrics to assess the impact of AI-driven optimizations and identify areas for further improvement.
    - Utilize AI to analyze ongoing data, refine your models, and adapt your strategies to changing market conditions and patients:
    - Ensure responsible data collection and usage, respecting patient privacy and adhering to industry regulations.
    - Avoid biases in AI models by using diverse datasets and transparent algorithms.

- Prioritize patient access to medications over solely profit-driven optimization strategies.

Examples in Action:

- **Predicting Drug Demand**: AI forecasts a surge in demand for a new medication in a specific region. The manufacturer adjusts production and distribution accordingly, ensuring timely availability for patients.
- **Targeting High-Value Healthcare Professionals**: AI identifies key doctors with high prescribing potential for a specific therapy. The sales team focuses its efforts on these individuals, leading to increased market penetration.
- **Optimizing Delivery Routes**: AI-powered delivery routes for medical couriers, reducing travel time and fuel costs while ensuring medications arrive quickly and efficiently.
- **Proactive Inventory Management**: AI forecasts potential supply chain disruptions and drug shortages, allowing the company to secure alternative sources or increase production in advance, mitigating stockouts and ensuring patient access.

Remember:

- **Human+AI Collaboration**: AI empowers with insights and recommendations, but human expertise remains crucial for strategic decision-making and ethical considerations.
- **Focus on Patient Value**: Ultimately, AI-driven sales and distribution optimization should serve patients by ensuring medication access, affordability, and timely delivery.
- **Continuous Adaptation**: The healthcare landscape is dynamic. Regularly assess your goals, data, and AI models to adapt to changing conditions and optimize for long-term success.

By integrating AI thoughtfully and ethically into your sales and distribution strategies, you can achieve greater efficiency, reach more patients, and fulfill your mission of delivering life-saving treatments to those who need them most.

CHAPTER

35

Optimizing Clinical Trials and Patient Recruitment with AI: A Step-by-Step Guide

Clinical trials are crucial for developing new life-saving treatments, but they can be costly and time-consuming and face significant challenges in patient recruitment. AI brings promising tools to optimize these processes, leading to faster research, better data quality, and improved patient care. Let's embark on a step-by-step journey:

1. **Define Your Optimization Goals:**
   - **What specific aspects of your clinical trial do you want to improve?** Is it identifying qualified patient candidates, predicting enrollment rates, optimizing trial design, or streamlining data collection?
   - **Prioritize Key Metrics**: Choose Relevant Metrics (e.g., recruitment rate, completion rate, data quality) to track your progress and measure the impact of AI-driven changes.
2. **Gather and Analyze Data:**
   - **Historical Trial Data**: Analyze past trials of similar treatments to identify successful treatment strategies, common challenges, and patient drop-out factors.
   - **Patient Data**: Gather medical records and demographic information to understand patient characteristics and potential eligibility for specific trials.

- **External Data**: Collect industry data on disease prevalence, patient demographics, and social media sentiment to understand broader patient populations and potential recruitment pools.

3. **Choose Your AI Techniques**:

   Different AI algorithms excel at various tasks:

   - **Machine Learning**: Identify ideal patient candidates based on medical history, genetic data, and lifestyle factors, predicting their eligibility and suitability for specific trials.
   - **Natural Language Processing (NLP)**: Analyze social media platforms and online forums to understand patient sentiment towards specific diseases and potential interest in participating in trials.
   - **Predictive Analytics**: Forecast enrollment rates and potential challenges, allowing for proactive adjustments to the trial design and recruitment strategies.
   - **Virtual Screening**: Utilize image recognition and AI-powered analysis of medical scans to access patient eligibility and reduce screening burdens remotely.

4. **Model Training and Implementation**:

   - Train your AI models on the gathered data, ensuring accuracy and alignment with your optimization goals.
   - Integrate AI outputs into your clinical trial platform or patient recruitment strategy (e.g., targeted advertising, chatbots for eligibility screening, virtual trial participation options).

5. **Continuous Monitoring and Improvement:**

   - Track key metrics to assess the impact of AI-driven optimizations and identify areas for further improvement.
   - Utilize AI to analyze ongoing data, refine your models, and adapt your strategies to changing patient demographics, evolving recruitment trends, and emerging ethical considerations.

6. **Ethical Considerations**:
   - Prioritize patient privacy and informed consent throughout data collection and AI development.
   - Ensure fairness and inclusivity in AI models, avoiding biases that might exclude certain patient groups from participating in trials.
   - Maintain transparency about AI usage and its role in patient recruitment, fostering trust and understanding.

Examples in Action:

- **Predicting Trial Enrollment**: AI forecasts a lower-than-expected enrollment rate for a specific trial. Researchers adjust eligibility criteria and target recruitment efforts to specific patient demographics, ensuring sufficient participation.
- **Virtual Screening for a Rare Disease**: AI analyzes medical scans from a large patient database, remotely identifying potential candidates for a rare disease trial, overcoming geographical limitations, and accelerating recruitment.
- **Chatbot-Powered Pre-screening**: A chatbot guides patients through eligibility criteria and answers basic questions, streamlining the initial screening process and improving recruitment efficiency.
- **Social Media Sentiment Analysis**: AI analyzes online discussions about a specific disease, identifying communities interested in potential treatments and targeting them with relevant trial information.

Remember:

- **Human+AI Collaboration**: AI empowers with insights and predictions, but human expertise remains crucial for ethical considerations, clinical decision-making, and ensuring patient well-being throughout the trial process.

- **Focus on Patient Benefit**: Ultimately, AI-driven optimization should serve patients by facilitating their participation in relevant trials, accelerating research, and leading to the development of better treatments.
- **Continuous Adaptation**: The clinical trial landscape is dynamic. Regularly assess your goals, data, and AI models to adapt to changing regulations, ethical considerations, and patient needs.

Integrating AI thoughtfully and ethically into your clinical trial and patient recruitment strategies can contribute to more efficient research, broader patient access, and the faster development of life-saving treatments for all.

CHAPTER

36

Building Trust and Connections: A Step-by-Step Guide to Brand Communication and Reputation Management

In today's digital age, where information travels fast, and opinions spread like wildfire, brand communication, and reputation management are more crucial than ever. It's not just about pushing out messages; it's about fostering genuine connections with stakeholders, building trust, and navigating the ever-changing online landscape. Let's delve into a step-by-step guide:

1. **Define Your Brand Identity**:
   - **What are your core values, mission, and vision?** Clearly articulate who you are as a brand, what you stand for, and what makes you unique.
   - **Identify Your Target Audience**: Who are you trying to reach? Understand their needs, preferences, and communication channels.
2. **Craft a Compelling Narrative:**
   - **Develop a Strong Brand Story**: What journey are you taking with your audience? Be genuine and authentic, and connect with their emotions.
   - **Define Your Key Messages**: What do you want people to know and remember about your brand? Ensure they are consistent, clear, and resonate with your audience.

3. **Choose the Right Channels:**
    - **Where does your target audience spend their time?** To reach them effectively, utilize a mix of online (social media, website, email) and offline (events, in-person or (Face-to-face visits, PR) channels.
    - **Be Mindful of Channel-Specific Best Practices:** Tailor your communication style and content to each platform's unique characteristics.

4. **Listen and Engage:**
    - **Openly Listen to Your Audience**: Monitor social media mentions, customer reviews, and online conversations to understand their feedback and concerns.
    - **Respond Promptly and Authentically**: Address positive and negative feedback, demonstrating your commitment to communication and transparency.

5. **Build Relationships:**
    - **Cultivate Relationships with Key Stakeholders**: Media, influencers, and industry experts can amplify your brand voice and help reach new audiences.
    - **Participate in Relevant Conversations**: Join online communities, forums, and discussions to share your expertise and build trust.

6. **Measure and Adapt:**
    - **Track Key Metrics**: Monitor engagement, reach, sentiment analysis, and brand mentions to understand the impact of your communication efforts.
    - **Be Ready to Adapt**: Be open to feedback, learn from data insights, and continuously refine your strategies based on the evolving landscape.

7. **Reputation Management:**
   - **Proactively Monitor Your Online Reputation**: Identify and address potential crises or negative mentions before they escalate.
   - **Be Truthful and Transparent**: Always communicate honestly for mistakes, building trust even in challenging situations.
   - **Demonstrate Commitment to Positive Change**: Show how you address concerns and work to improve.

Remember:

- **Authenticity is Key**: People crave genuine connections. Be true to your brand identity and avoid sounding robotic or overly promotional.
- **Focus on Value**: Provide your audience with valuable information, resources, and experiences that enrich their lives.
- **Ethics Matter**: Be responsible with data, respect privacy, and avoid misleading or harmful communication practices.

By following these steps and prioritizing trust, transparency, and genuine connection, you can build a strong brand communication and reputation management strategy that fosters loyalty, advocates for you, and fuels your long-term success.

AI's Role in Brand Communication

AI plays a multi-faceted role in brand communication and reputation management, serving as a powerful tool to enhance your efforts and achieve greater Impact. Here is how:

1. **Deepening Audience Understanding**:
   - **Social Listening and Sentiment Analysis**: AI tools can scan vast amounts of data from social media forums and online reviews to gain valuable insights into audience sentiment, preferences, and brand perception. This helps you tailor your communication and address emerging concerns proactively.

- **Identifying Influencers and Potential Brand Advocates**: AI can analyze online conversations and identify individuals with high reach and positive influence regarding your brand or industry. Engaging with these individuals can expand your reach and amplify your message.

2. **Crafting Compelling Content**:
   - **AI-Powered Writing Assistants**: These tools can generate draft content, suggest headlines and formats, and even provide basic fact-checking. This can streamline content creation and free up your team's time for more strategic tasks.
   - **Personalization and Targeted Messaging**: AI can analyze audience data and preferences to personalize messages and content, making them more relevant and engaging for specific groups or individuals. This can improve overall engagement and conversions.
3. **Building Relationships and Engaging Authentically**:
   - **Chatbots and Virtual Assistants**: AI-powered chatbots can handle basic customer inquiries, provide instant support, and even engage in simple conversations. This can improve customer satisfaction and create a more personalized brand experience.
   - **Social Media Monitoring and Engagement**: AI tools can help you track brand mentions, respond to comments and messages in real-time, and identify opportunities for meaningful engagement with your audience. This fosters a sense of community and strengthens relationships.
4. **Reputation Management and Crisis Response**:
   - **Identify Potential Crises and Negative Sentiments**: AI can scan online conversations and news sources to detect early signs of negative PR or potential crises, allowing for proactive responses and mitigation strategies.

- **Monitoring Brand Mentions and Sentiment Analysis**: AI can track how public perception of your brand evolves, helping you gauge the effectiveness of your communication efforts and identify areas for improvement.

5. **Continuous Improvement and Measurement**:
    - **Analyzing Campaign Performance and Tracking Key Metrics**: AI can analyze data from various channels to understand what content resonates most with your audience and measure the effectiveness of your communication efforts. This helps you refine your strategies and optimize your return on investment.
    - **Identifying Emerging Trends and Adapting Communication Style**: AI can help you stay ahead by analyzing social media trends and adapting your communication style to resonate with evolving preferences and expectations.

Remember:

- **Human Oversight is Crucial**: AI should be a tool to empower your team, not replace it. Human expertise in communication strategy, ethical considerations, and nuanced messaging remains essential.
- **Transparency and Responsible Use**: Be transparent about using AI and prioritize responsible data collection and usage to maintain trust and ethical brand practices.
- **Focus on Human Connection:** Ultimately, AI should drive communication efforts that foster genuine connections with your audience, build trust, and create a positive brand image.

Integrating AI thoughtfully and ethically into your brand communication and reputation management strategies allows you to gain deeper audience insights, personalize your approach, and build stronger relationships with your stakeholders. This will lead to a more successful and impactful brand.

CHAPTER

37

Unveiling the Impact: A Step-by-Step Guide to Measuring and Analyzing Marketing Performance

In today's data-driven marketing landscape, understanding the effectiveness of your efforts is crucial. Measuring and analyzing your marketing performance allows you to optimize campaigns, allocate resources wisely, and achieve your business goals. Let's embark on a step-by-step journey:

1. **Define Your Goals and Objectives:**
   - **What do you want to achieve with your marketing efforts?** Is it increasing brand awareness, driving website traffic, generating leads, or boosting sales? Clearly defined goals provide a foundation for selecting relevant metrics and analyzing results.
   - **Identify Your Target Audience**: Understanding who you're trying to reach helps you choose the right metrics and track progress specific to their behavior and engagement.
2. **Establish Your Measurement Framework**:
   - **Select Key Performance Indicators (KPIs)**: These quantifiable metrics align with your goals. Examples include website traffic, conversion rates, cost per lead, and return on investment (ROI).
   - **Choose Data Sources**: Determine where you will gather your data, such as website analytics, social media platforms, email marketing tools, and CRM systems.

- **Set Up Tracking Tools**: Implement tracking pixels, conversion tracking codes, and analytics platforms to capture relevant data from your marketing activities.

3. **Collect and Analyze Data:**
   - **Regularly Gather Data**: Monitor your chosen KPIs and track how they evolve.
   - **Use Data Visualization Tools**: Charts, graphs, and dashboards can help you visualize trends, identify patterns, and gain insights from your data.
   - **Perform Deeper Analysis**: Utilize statistical tools and analysis techniques to understand the relationships between your marketing efforts and outcomes.
4. **Interpret and Evaluate Findings:**
   - **Compare Results to Benchmarks**: Compare your performance to industry averages or historical data.
   - **Identify High-Performing and Underperforming Campaigns**: Isolate factors contributing to success or failure to inform future strategies.
   - **Evaluate ROI**: Calculate the return on investment for your marketing initiatives to assess their financial effectiveness.
5. **Take Action and Optimize:**
   - **Refine Your Marketing Mix**: Based on your analysis, adjust your strategies, allocate resources differently, and test new approaches.
   - **Optimize Campaigns**: Improve performance by experimenting with different ad copy, landing pages, or content formats.
   - **Set New Goals and KPIs**: As your marketing evolves, refine your objectives and measurement framework to remain focused and adaptable.

Additional Tips:

- **Multi-Channel Attribution**: Track how users interact with your brand across different touchpoints before conversion to understand the full customer journey.
- **Qualitative Data**: To better under audience perception, complement quantitative feedback from surveys, customer interviews, and social media sentiment analysis.
- **A/B Testing**: Conduct controlled experiments to compare campaign elements and identify the most effective approaches.
- **Stay Informed**: Learn new measurement tools, analytics techniques, and industry best practices to remain competitive.

Remember:

- **Measurement is an Ongoing Process**: Regularly tracking and analyzing your performance is crucial for continuous improvement.
- **Focus on What Matters**: Choose KPIs that directly align with your business goals and avoid vanity metrics that don't reflect true impact.
- **Actionable Insights**: Don't get lost in data. Use your findings to make informed decisions and optimize your marketing efforts for success.

By implementing a structured approach to measuring and analyzing your marketing performance, you can gain valuable insights, optimize your strategies, and ultimately achieve your marketing goals in a data-driven and impactful way.

AI's Transformative Role

AI plays a transformative role in measuring and analyzing marketing performance, offering powerful tools and techniques that elevate your efforts from basic data collection to insightful, actionable intelligence. Here's how AI can supercharge your measurement game:

1. **Automating Data Collection and Cleaning**:
   - **Say Goodbye to Manual Data Entry**: AI tools automatically collect data from diverse sources, such as websites, social media platforms, email marketing tools, and CRM systems, streamlining the process and eliminating human error.
   - **Data Cleaning and Normalization**: AI pre-processes your data, handling missing values, outliers, and inconsistencies, ensuring data quality and accuracy for reliable analysis.
2. **Advanced Analytics and Insights**:
   - **Predictive Modeling**: AI can forecast future marketing performance, customer behavior, and campaign outcomes based on historical data and trends, empowering proactive decision-making.
   - **Attribution Modeling**: AI goes beyond last-click attribution, revealing the complex journey users take before conversion and providing insights into the true impact of each touchpoint.
   - **Customer Segmentation and Personalization**: AI can identify distinct customer segments based on behavior and preferences, enabling personalized marketing campaigns with higher engagement and conversion rates.
3. **Real-Time Optimization and Campaign Management**:
   - **A/B Testing at Scale**: AI automates A/B testing of different ad copy, landing pages, or campaign elements, identifying the most effective real-time variations, leading to faster performance optimization.
   - **Dynamic Bidding and Budget Allocation**: AI optimizes ad spend across platforms and campaigns in real-time, ensuring you reach the right audience at the right price for maximum ROI.
   - **Chatbots and Virtual Assistants**: AI-powered chatbots can answer customer inquiries, provide support, and gather valuable feedback, improving customer experience and generating data for analysis.

4. **Enhanced Reporting and Visualization:**
    - **Automated Reporting**: AI tools automatically generate reports, dashboards, and visualizations, saving time and providing clear insights into your marketing performance.
    - **Interactive Dashboards**: Explore data interactively, drill down into specific segments, and identify trends at a glance, enabling data-driven decision-making in real-time.
    - **Natural Language Generation**: AI can translate complex data into easy-to-understand summaries and reports, making insights accessible to everyone in your team.

Remember:

- **Human+AI Collaboration**: While AI empowers with insights and automation, human expertise remains crucial for interpreting data, setting goals, and making strategic decisions based on ethical considerations.
- **Data Privacy and Security**: Ensure responsible data collection, storage, and usage, comply with regulations, and respect user privacy.
- **Transparency and Explainability**: Understand how AI models work and be transparent about how they are used in your analyses to maintain trust and ethical marketing practices.

By thoughtfully and ethically integrating AI into your marketing performance measurement and analysis, you can unlock deep insights, automate tedious tasks, optimize campaigns in real time, and achieve superior marketing results with data-driven confidence.

CHAPTER

38

Beyond the Typed Word: Generative AI and Conversational AI Revolutionize Brand Communication and Reputation Management

The landscape of brand communication and reputation management is undergoing a profound transformation. No longer solely confined to carefully crafted press releases and meticulously controlled messaging, today's brands must navigate a dynamic, interactive digital environment where every interaction shapes reputation. In this evolving world, Generative AI and Conversational AI (prompt engineering) emerge as powerful tools, offering exciting possibilities for brands to connect with audiences in personalized, engaging, and ultimately reputation-enhancing ways.

Generative AI, with its ability to create human-quality text, images, and even video, unlocks a new era of content creation. Imagine crafting personalized marketing campaigns that resonate with individual preferences, developing real-time responses to customer inquiries, or generating engaging social media content that sparks meaningful conversations.

Conversational AI, powered by chatbots and virtual assistants, goes beyond scripted interactions, fostering natural, two-way dialogues that build customer trust and understanding. While rapidly evolving, these technologies hold immense potential to reshape how brands communicate, build relationships, and, ultimately, manage their reputation in the digital age.

Let's delve deeper into these transformative tools, exploring their specific applications in brand communication and reputation management, their potential benefits and considerations, and how they can empower brands to thrive in the ever-evolving digital landscape. So, fasten your seatbelts, for we are about to embark on a journey into the future of communication, where AI-driven interaction holds the key to forging deeper connections and building stronger brand reputations.

1. **The Power of Personalization and Connection:**
    - Traditionally, brand communication relied on standardized messages broadcast to large audiences. However, AI allows for personalized and nuanced communication, making it feel more human and relatable. Imagine Chatbots that naturally converse with customers and answer questions, fostering genuine connection.
    - Social media content tailored to individual preferences, sparking dialogue and engagement.
    - Marketing campaigns that speak directly to specific needs and aspirations, resonating on a deeper level.
2. **Evolving Brand Script and Automation:**
    - The "human voice" implies more than just words. It's about understanding intent, responding with empathy, and adapting to a conversation's flow. When used thoughtfully, AI can go beyond scripted interactions and create dynamic dialogues that mimic human conversational nuances. This fosters trust and builds stronger relationships with your audience.
3. **Authenticity and Emotional Intelligence:**
    - A major concern with AI is the potential for robotic communication that needs more authenticity. However, advanced AI technologies are starting to incorporate emotional intelligence, allowing them to understand and respond to human emotions. This ability to convey empathy

and understanding makes AI-powered communication more sincere and human-like.

4. **Transparency and Ethical Considerations:**
    - It's crucial to remember that AI communication still originates from machines. Transparency is key. Be upfront about using AI and ensure it aligns with your brand values and ethical standards. Focus on using AI to enhance human communication, not replace it.

By "unveiling the human voice of AI," we emphasize the potential of AI to transcend automation and scripted interactions. It can become a powerful tool for brands to connect with their audience on a more personal and authentic level, ultimately leading to stronger relationships and a positive brand reputation.

It's important to note that this technology is still evolving, and ethical considerations remain paramount. Responsible use and transparency are crucial to ensure AI serves as a force for good in brand communication.

Orchestrating Brand Communication with AI: Generative and Conversational Tools in Action

Human ingenuity and AI synergy present exciting possibilities for brands to reimagine communication and cultivate meaningful connections with their audiences. Let's explore how Generative AI and Conversational AI can be applied step-by-step to enhance brand communication and reputation:

1. **Understanding Your Audience:**
    - **AI-Powered Social Listening:** Tools like Brandwatch or Sprout Social analyze vast online conversations, uncovering audience preferences, sentiment, and emerging trends. Imagine identifying brand advocates and tailoring communication accordingly, like a conductor understanding the strengths of each musician.

- **Chatbot Interactions:** Interactive chatbots gather first-hand data through conversations, providing insights into customer needs and pain points. Think of this as direct feedback from the audience, informing the composition of future performances.

2. **Crafting Personalized Content:**
   - **Generative AI Writing Assistants:** Platforms like ShortlyAI or Rytr assist in generating personalized website copy, marketing emails, and social media posts based on audience segments and data. Each audience member receives a unique 'verse" within the overall brand message, similar to individual instruments playing their parts.
   - **Dynamic Ad Creation:** AI tools like Google's Performance Max automatically generate personalized copy and visuals based on user profiles and interests. Imagine crafting unique ads for each audience member, like custom sheet music tailored to their musical sensibilities.

3. **Engaging in Real-Time Conversations:**
   - **Chatbots and Virtual Assistants:** AI-powered chatbots answer customer questions, provide support, and personalize interactions based on previous conversations. This creates a sense of ongoing dialogue, like the back-and-forth between the conductor and the orchestra during a performance.
   - **Interactive Video Experiences:** Platforms like InVideo allow the creation of personalized video messages, where the CEO or spokesperson directly addresses different audience segments with tailored content, fostering a deeper connection like a soloist engaging the audience directly.

4. **Building Relationships and Fostering Trust:**
   - **Sentiment Analysis and Feedback Integration:** AI tools analyze customer reviews and social media mentions, identifying areas for improvement and opportunities to

address concerns. This feedback loop, like audience applause guiding the conductor, allows for continuous improvement and refinement of communication strategies.

- **Personalized Recommendations and Product Suggestions:** AI-powered recommendation engines suggest relevant product content based on past interactions and preferences, nurturing individual relationships like a conductor tailoring the music to resonate with each audience member.

Remember:

- **Human+AI Collaboration Remains Key:** AI empowers with personalization and insights, but human expertise steers the creative direction, ensures ethical considerations, and infuses communication with authenticity.
- **Start Small and Experiment:** Explore different AI tools and applications, analyze their effectiveness, and refine your approach based on learnings.
- **Prioritize Data Privacy and Transparency:** Be responsible with data collection and usage, clearly communicate how AI is used, and maintain trust with your audience.

By strategically integrating Generative AI and Conversational AI into your brand communication strategy, you can orchestrate personalized experiences, cultivate deeper audience connections, and ultimately compose a winning performance in the ever-evolving symphony of brand communication.

The Future of Pharma Communication: Where AI Meets Personalized Healthcare

While ethical considerations and regulatory compliance demand careful navigation, the pharmaceutical industry holds immense potential for leveraging Generative AI and Conversational AI in responsible and impactful ways. Here are some specific examples:

1. **Patient Education and Empowerment:**
   - **Interactive Patient Journey Platforms:** Imagine chatbots guiding patients through medication adherence programs, answering questions, and addressing concerns in a personalized and empathetic manner, similar to a virtual health coach.
   - **AI-Powered Symptom Checkers:** Platforms like *Buoy Health* utilize AI to analyze user-reported symptoms and provide potential causes, empowering patients with the knowledge and facilitating informed conversations with healthcare providers.
   - **Personalized Medication Reminders:** AI-powered apps like *Mango Health* send timely reminders tailored to individual medication schedules and preferences, improving adherence and treatment outcomes.

2. **Clinical Trial Recruitment and Engagement:**
   - **Targeted Social Media Campaigns:** AI can identify potential trial participants based on specific demographics and medical conditions, enabling more efficient and targeted recruitment efforts.
   - **Chatbots for Informed Consent:** Conversational AI can guide potential participants through consent forms, answer questions, and address concerns, improving transparency and informed decision-making.
   - **Virtual Assistants for Data Collection:** AI-powered assistants can help patients accurately report symptoms and side effects during trials, improving data quality and reducing participant burden.

3. **Drug Safety and Pharmacovigilance:**
   - **AI-Powered Analysis of Social Media and Online Forums:** Tools like *Scio Health* can detect potential adverse drug reactions by analyzing online conversations, enabling proactive pharmacovigilance and timely interventions.

- **Chatbots for Patient Reporting:** AI chatbots can facilitate patient reporting of adverse events in a user-friendly and confidential manner, improving data collection and early detection of safety concerns.
- **Predictive Modeling for Risk Assessment:** AI algorithms can analyze patient data and identify individuals at higher risk of adverse reactions, allowing for personalized safety monitoring and targeted interventions.

4. **Personalized Marketing and Communication:**
   - **Disease Awareness Campaigns:** AI-powered content creation can generate targeted campaigns based on specific demographics and disease states, raising awareness and educating patients about relevant treatment options.
   - **Tailored Patient Support Programs:** AI chatbots can offer personalized support to patients based on their specific needs and concerns, ranging from medication adherence to managing side effects.
   - **Interaction Medication Guides:** Generative AI can create dynamic medication guides tailored to individual patient literacy levels and preferred learning styles, improving medication understanding and adherence.

It's Crucial to Remember:

- **Data privacy and patient confidentiality are paramount:** Ensure compliance with regulations and prioritize informed consent data collection and usage transparency.
- **AI should complement, not replace, human expertise**. Healthcare professionals remain central to diagnosis, treatment, and patient care. AI acts as a tool to empower patients, enhance communication, and augment healthcare delivery.
- **Ethical consideration and responsible development are essential**. Prioritize fairness, transparency, and responsible

AI development that benefits patients and upholds trust in the pharmaceutical industry.

By using AI thoughtfully and ethically, the pharmaceutical industry can unlock a future of personalized communication, empowered patients, and improved healthcare outcomes for all. Remember, this is just the beginning of a promising journey, and the potential for AI to revolutionize pharma communication and patient care is limitless.

CHAPTER 39

Orchestrating Reputation in Pharma: Leveraging AI for a Trustworthy Brand Symphony

In the fast-paced and information-rich pharma world, reputation management is more significant. Generative AI and Conversational AI offer innovative tools to navigate this complex landscape, build trust with stakeholders, and proactively manage your brand's perception. Let's explore their applications step-by-step:

1. **Monitoring and Identifying Issues:**
   - **Social Media Listening**: AI platforms like Brandwatch or Meltwater scan vast online conversations, identifying brand mentions, sentiment analysis, and potential emerging crises. Imagine having an early warning system that detects negative mentions about a specific drug or clinical trial, allowing for a swift and proactive response.
   - **Real-Time News Monitoring**: Tools like NewsGuard track news articles and identify misinformation or inaccurate reporting that could impact your brand reputation. Think of this as having a dedicated team constantly scanning the news landscape for potential threats.
2. **Proactive Engagement and Communication:**
   - **Chatbots for Customer Service**: AI-powered chatbots can answer basic questions, address concerns, and direct users to relevant resources 24/7, fostering trust and demonstrating responsiveness. Imagine offering immediate

support to patients experiencing side effects or having medication-related inquiries.

- **Personalized Communications**: AI can analyze customer data and preferences, crafting targeted email outreach or social media messages that address specific concerns and build relationships. Send personalized messages to healthcare professionals addressing their questions or concerns about your product.

3. **Transparency and Crisis Response:**
   - **AI-Powered Fact-Checking**: Platforms like *Snopes Fact Check* utilize AI to analyze information and identify misinformation, allowing for timely and accurate counter-narratives during crises. Picture having a real-time tool fact-checking negative claims about a product launch, ensuring accurate information reaches stakeholders quickly.
   - **Sentiment Analysis During Crises**: AI tools can analyze public sentiment toward your brand during sensitive situations, providing valuable insights to guide communication strategies and mitigate reputational damage. Imagine understanding the emotional undercurrents of a product recall in real time, enabling more empathetic and effective communication.

Examples:

- Pfizer utilizes AI-powered chatbots to answer patient questions about COVID-19 vaccines, providing trusted information and building brand trust during a critical period.
- Merck leverages social media listening tools to identify early mentions of potential drug side effects, allowing for proactive communication and patient support.
- Novartis employs AI-powered sentiment analysis to understand public perceptions of its clinical trials. This information informs its communication strategies and allows it to address concerns transparently.

Remember:

- Transparency and ethical AI use are paramount. To build trust and uphold ethical standards, maintain data privacy, avoid misleading information, and use AI responsibly.
- Human Oversight remains crucial. AI provides insights and automates tasks, but human expertise guides strategic decisions, ensures ethical communication, and fosters genuine connections.
- Tailor your approach. When selecting and implementing AI-powered solutions, consider your specific audience, communication goals, and regulatory landscape.

By strategically integrating Generative AI and Conversational AI, pharma companies can move beyond reactive reputation management and build a proactive, transparent, and trustworthy image. In this dynamic symphony of reputation, AI is a powerful instrument. Still, the conductor — the human expertise and ethical considerations— remains in control, orchestrating a performance that resonates with all stakeholders.

Weighing the Notes: Benefits and Considerations of AI for Pharma Reputation Management

While Generative AI and Conversational AI offer exciting possibilities for pharma reputation management, it's crucial to carefully consider the benefits and potential drawbacks before embarking on this journey:

Benefits:

- **Enhanced Efficiency and Scalability:** AI automates tasks like social media monitoring, sentiment analysis, and basic customer service interactions, freeing human teams to focus on strategic initiatives. Imagine analyzing vast amounts of online data for potential issues in minutes instead of relying on manual processes.

- **Personalized Communication and Engagement:** AI tools can tailor messages to specific stakeholders, addressing their unique concerns and needs. Picture sending targeted communications to healthcare professionals with relevant product information, fostering deeper relationships and trust.
- **Proactive Crisis Response:** AI can detect emerging issues early on, enabling brands to respond swiftly and mitigate reputational damage. Imagine identifying negative social media trends about a product launch and developing counter-narratives before they escalate.
- **Data-Driven Insights and Decision-Making:** AI provides valuable insights into public sentiment, brand perception, and potential threats, empowering data-driven communication strategies. Picture understanding how different audiences perceive your brand, allowing for tailored communication approaches.
- **24/7 Availability and Global Reach:** AI-powered chatbots and virtual assistants offer support and answer questions around the clock, regardless of location, ensuring accessibility and building trust with global audiences. Imagine offering multilingual support to patients worldwide, even in regions with limited healthcare resources.

Considerations:

- **Data Privacy and Security:** Pharmaceutical brands handle sensitive health data. Ensure compliance with regulations and prioritize data privacy in all AI implementations. Trust is paramount in this industry, and data breaches could significantly damage your reputation.
- **Transparency and Explainability:** Be transparent about using AI and explain how it informs your communication strategies. Avoid misleading information and ensure human oversight in decision-making processes. Remember, patients and healthcare professionals deserve clear and trustworthy communication.

- **Ethical Considerations and Algorithmic Bias:** Carefully assess potential biases in AI algorithms and ensure they align with ethical principles and the fair representation of diverse stakeholders. Biased AI can lead to inaccurate insights and discriminatory practices, severely damaging your reputation.
- **Human Expertise Remains Crucial:** AI complements human expertise but doesn't replace it. Ensure your team possesses the skills to interpret AI insights, develop ethical communication strategies, and build genuine stakeholder relationships. Remember, AI is a tool, and humans guide its utilization.
- **Regulatory Landscape and Compliance:** The pharma industry operates within a complex regulatory framework. Ensure your AI solutions comply with all relevant regulations and data privacy laws to avoid legal complications and reputational harm.

Remember, integrating AI into pharma reputation management requires a nuanced approach. Consider the benefits and potential drawbacks, prioritize ethical considerations and data privacy, and leverage human expertise alongside AI tools. By conducting thorough due diligence and prioritizing responsible implementation, you can harness the power of AI to build a stronger, more trustworthy brand image within the ever-evolving landscape of the pharmaceutical industry.

The future of communication holds immense potential, where AI is an empowering tool to create personalized experiences, build meaningful connections, and ultimately cultivate a reputation worthy of the trust in its hands. Now, the curtain rises, and the performance begins. Are you ready to orchestrate a brand symphony that resonates with the world?

CHAPTER

40

The Synergy of Minds in Brand Management and Customer Engagement

The pharma marketing world is transforming, where AI and human collaboration create a powerful synergy to improve brand management and customer engagement. This synergy unlocks deeper connections with patients, fosters loyalty, and builds trust in the brand. Here is how it works:

Human Strengths:

- **Empathy and Understanding:** Humans can empathize with patients, understanding their needs, anxieties, and aspirations, enabling the creation of authentic and compassionate brand experiences.
- **Strategic Thinking and Brand Storytelling**: Humans excel at formulating brand strategy, weaving compelling narratives, and ensuring brand consistency across touchpoints.
- **Creativity and Innovative Content**: Humans can develop engaging formats like patient dairies, interactive infographics, and emotional video testimonials, fostering deeper patient connections.
- **Ethical Considerations and Patient Privacy**: Humans prioritize responsible data use, ensure transparency in communication, and safeguard patient well-being throughout brand-building efforts.

AI Strengths:

- **Data Analysis and Customer Insights**: AI can analyze vast datasets of patient demographics, behavior, and online interactions to identify key customer segments and preferences.
- **Personalized Brand Experiences**: AI can tailor website content, email marketing, and patient support communications to specific needs and interests, ensuring relevance and resonance.
- **Real-time Feedback and Performance Tracking**: AI continuously monitors customer engagement metrics, providing real-time insights for optimizing brand messaging and tactics.
- **Automated Tasks and Efficient Communication**: AI can automate tasks like appointment reminders, medication adherence support, and chatbots, freeing human resources for more strategic activities.

Synergy in Action:

Imagine this:

- AI segments patients based on disease stage, treatment needs, and online behavior.
- Humans develop a branded patient support program with educational resources, interactive tools, and peer-to-peer forums, addressing specific needs identified by analysis.
- AI personalizes each segment's email marketing and website content, showcasing relevant information, product features, and testimonials from satisfied patients.
- Real-time analytics reveal how patients engage with different content and brand communications, allowing humans to refine messaging, optimize user experience, and adapt to evolving needs.

- Ethical considerations remain paramount, with humans ensuring informed consent, data privacy, and responsible communication in brand interactions.

Challenges and Considerations:

- **Data Privacy and Ethical Concerns**: Ensure adherence to strict data privacy regulations and prioritize responsible data collection and use, building patient trust.
- **Interpretability and Explainability of AI Models**: Understand how AI algorithms reach their conclusions to avoid black-box decision-making and ensure transparency in brand messages.
- **Upskilling and Workforce Development**: Equip marketing teams with the necessary skills to collaborate effectively with AI and interpret its insights to inform strategy.
- **Over-reliance on AI and Ignoring Human Intuition**: Remember that AI is a tool, not a replacement for human creativity, empathy, and ethical considerations.

By harmonizing human empathy and brand expertise with the analytical power of AI, we can revolutionize brand management and customer engagement in pharma marketing. This synergy has the potential to build genuine connections with patients, address their evolving needs, and improve their lives. It's not just about selling products; it's about building trust, fostering loyalty, and creating a positive brand experience that empowers patients on their health journey.

Remember, this is a continuous dance. As AI technology evolves and our understanding of ethical implications deepens, the possibilities for brand management and customer engagement in pharma will continue to expand. By nurturing a culture of continuous learning, prioritizing ethical responsibility, and maintaining a deep commitment to patient well-being, we can turn this powerful synergy into a force for good, transforming the pharma landscape and fostering true partnerships with patients.

AI-Powered Chatbots and Virtual Assistants for Customer Interaction

In customer interaction, AI-powered chatbots and virtual assistants are making waves. But to truly excel, they need more than just AI muscle. Enter the magic of human+AI collaboration, where strengths combine to create chatbots that understand, engage, and delight customers. Here is how it unfolds:

Human Strengths:

- **Empathy and Emotional Intelligence**: Humans can perceive customer emotions, read between the lines, and respond with compassion and understanding, fostering trust and positive interactions.
- **Creativity and Problem-Solving**: Humans excel at thinking outside the box, crafting witty conversation flows, and devising solutions to unexpected customer queries, ensuring satisfaction even in complex situations.
- **Domain Expertise and Brand Voice**: Humans understand the intricacies of the represented domain, ensuring chatbots communicate accurately, consistently, and in line with the brand's overall tone and personality.
- **Ethical Considerations and Responsible Communication**: Humans prioritize responsible data use, transparent communication, and adherence to ethical guidelines, protecting consumer privacy and building trust.

AI Strengths:

- **Data Analysis and Personalization**: AI can analyze vast customer data to personalize interactions, tailoring responses to individual needs and preferences and creating a more relevant and engaging experience.
- **Real-time Learning and Improvement**: AI can continuously learn from customer interactions, improving its ability to

understand nuances, address queries accurately, and anticipate future needs.

- **24/7 Availability and Multilingual Support**: AI-powered chatbots provide consistent service around the clock and across languages, ensuring immediate response and global reach.
- **Automation of Repetitive Tasks**: AI can handle routine inquiries and tasks, freeing human agents for more complex and strategic interactions and improving overall efficiency and customer satisfaction.

Synergy in Action:

- Humans create conversation flows for various customer scenarios, incorporating empathy, humor, and personalized greetings based on customer data.
- AI analyzes customer responses and adapts the conversation in real-time, identifying frustrations, suggesting solutions, and escalating to human agents when needed.
- Real-time customer feedback allows humans to refine the chatbot's responses and identify areas for improvement, ensuring continuous learning and evolution.
- Ethical considerations are baked into AI training data and monitored for biases, ensuring fair and respectful communication with all customers.

Challenges and Considerations:

- **Data Privacy and Security**: Ensure stringent data protection measures and transparent communication about data collection and usage to build customer trust.
- **Interpretability and Explainability of AI Models**: Understanding how AI reaches its conclusions to avoid black-box decision-making and ensure transparency in chatbot responses.

- **Upskilling and Workforce Development**: Equip customer service teams with the necessary skills to collaborate with AI and effectively manage chatbot interactions.
- **Maintaining Human Oversight and Control**: Humans should stay in the loop, reviewing chatbot interactions, providing feedback, and ensuring AI is a tool to enhance, not replace, human customer service.

By harmonizing human empathy and expertise with the analytical power of AI, we can craft chatbots and virtual assistants that truly enhance customer interactions. This synergy leads to improved satisfaction, loyalty, and brand perception. Ultimately, it's not just about automation; it's about humanizing technology, forging emotional connections, and delivering memorable experiences for every customer interacting with the brand.

Remember, this is an ongoing journey of innovation and learning. As AI technology evolves and our understanding of ethical considerations deepens, the possibilities for AI-powered chatbots and virtual assistants will continue to expand. By fostering a culture of collaboration, prioritizing responsible AI use, and keeping the human touch at the heart of every interaction, we can usher in a future where technology serves as a bridge, not a barrier, to building meaningful customer relationships.

Example of a Chatbot and Virtual Assistant for Patient Support

Scenario: **Virtual Patient Support Team: Human AI Synergy in Action**

Meet "Clara," the AI-powered virtual assistant, and "Sam," the human patient advocate.

Together, they form the virtual patient support team for "Hopewell Health," a leading cancer treatment center.

Clara's Strengths:

- **24/7 Availability**: Answers basic questions, schedules appointments, and provides medication reminders anytime.
- **Real-time Symptom Monitoring**: Analyzes user-reported symptoms and suggests actionable steps based on pre-programmed protocols.
- **Multilingual Support**: Provides information and support in different languages, catering to diverse patient needs.
- **Data Analysis and Personalized Recommendations**: Based on patient data and preferences, the doctor recommends relevant educational resources, support groups, and wellness tips.

Sam's Strengths:

- **Empathy and Emotional Intelligence**: Provides compassionate support, listens actively, and addresses patient concerns with understanding and warmth.
- **Domain Expertise**: Deep knowledge of cancer treatment protocols, side effects, and patients' emotional challenges.
- **Creativity and Problem-Solving**: Thinks outside the box to address complex concerns, connect patients with appropriate resources, and navigate unexpected situations.
- **Ethical Considerations and Responsible Communication**: Prioritizes patient privacy, transparency, and informed consent in all interactions.

Synergy in Action

- Clara monitors a patient's reported fatigue and suggests stretching exercises.
- Sam follows up with the patient via video call the next day, assessing their well-being, offering emotional support, and addressing any anxieties they might have about the fatigue.

- Clara analyzes patients' medication records and reminds them to take them on time, providing educational information about potential side effects.
- Sam follows up with the patient a week later to inquire about any side effects, provide reassurance, and answer any lingering questions about the medication.
- Clara identifies a patient struggling with social isolation and recommends joining an online support group for people with similar diagnoses.
- Sam welcomes the patient to the online support group, introduces them to other members, and facilitates their integration Into the community.

Expected Outcomes:

- Improved patient satisfaction and well-being through 24/7 support, personalized recommendations, and compassionate interactions.
- Enhanced adherence to treatment regimens and decreased anxiety with access to timely information and expert guidance.
- Increased patient empowerment and sense of control over their health journey through personalized resources and social support.

Ethical Considerations:

- **Data Privacy and Security**: Adhere to strict data protection regulations and communicate transparently about data collection and usage.
- **Human Oversight and Control**: Sam remains available to escalate complex situations, prioritizes urgent needs, and always provides essential human connection.
- **Avoiding Bias and Discrimination**: Train AI models with diverse datasets and monitor for potential biases to ensure fair and equitable treatment of all patients.

The synergy between Clara's AI capabilities and Sam's human expertise creates a powerful team for patient support. This integrated approach allows *Hopewell Health* to provide holistic care that addresses patients' physical, emotional, and social needs. Ultimately, it's about empowering patients on their journey, delivering compassionate support, and demonstrating that they are not alone in their fight.

Remember, this is just one example. The possibilities for human-AI collaboration in patient support are endless if we nurture a culture of continuous learning, prioritize ethical responsibility, and maintain a deep commitment to patient well-being. We can turn this powerful synergy into a force for good, transforming healthcare and improving the lives of countless individuals.

Example of a Chatbot and Virtual Assistant for HCPs

Scenario: Dr. AI and Ally: the HCP Powerhouse

Meet Dr. AI, a cutting-edge virtual assistant, and Ally, a knowledgeable human research librarian, working together to empower Dr. Taylor, a busy family physician. Here's how their synergy elevates healthcare:

Dr. AI's Strengths:

- **Real-time Medical Information Access**: Dr. AI scans vast databases and clinical trial results to provide the latest evidence-based information on medications, diagnoses, and treatment options.
- **Differential Diagnosis Assistance**: Analyzes patient symptoms and suggests potential diagnoses with supporting data and relevant research articles.
- **Medication Interaction Checks**: Flags potential adverse interactions between prescribed medications and alert Dr. Taylor to safer alternatives.

- **24/7 Availability**: Assists Dr. Taylor anytime, anywhere, even after hours or during emergencies.

Ally's Strengths:

- **Critical Appraisal and Knowledge Curation**: Evaluate the quality and relevance of Dr. AI's findings, ensuring trustworthy information for Dr. Taylor's clinical decisions.
- **Personalized Research Support**: Tailors information searches to Dr. Taylor's specific patient cases and clinical interests, providing in-depth insights and context.
- **Human Understanding and Empathy**: Connects with Dr. Taylor personally, understands his thought process, and anticipates his needs beyond data retrieval.
- **Ethical Considerations and Patient Privacy**: Prioritizes responsible data use, ensures informed consent for research participation, and safeguards patient confidentiality.

Synergy in Action:

- Dr. Taylor consults Dr. AI about a patient with complex symptoms. Dr. AI suggests several possible diagnoses with supporting research articles.
- Ally reviews the articles, identifies the most relevant and reliable sources, and summarizes key findings for Dr. Taylor.
- Dr. Taylor discusses the diagnoses with Ally, considering the patient's medical history and unique circumstances.
- Together, they formulate a differential diagnosis plan and order targeted tests to confirm the most likely diagnosis.
- Dr. AI assists in finding the latest treatment guidelines and potential clinical trials relevant to the patient's condition.
- Ally helps Dr. Taylor interpret the guidelines, considering their applicability to the patient and potential ethical implications.
- Dr. Taylor makes informed treatment decisions and is confident in the information provided by the human-AI duo.

Expected Outcomes:

- Improved time efficiency for Dr. Taylor, allowing him to focus on patient care and spend less time searching for information.
- Enhanced quality of care through access to the latest medical knowledge and evidence-based practice.
- Reduced medical errors and improved patient safety through medication interaction checks and accurate diagnoses.
- Increased job satisfaction for Dr. Taylor with the support and expertise provided by Dr. AI and Ally.

Ethical Considerations:

- **Transparency and Informed Consent**: Ensure patients understand how AI uses their data and that they have control over their research participation.
- **Avoiding Bias and Discrimination**: Train Dr. AI with diverse datasets and monitor for potential biases in information retrieval to ensure fair and equitable treatment of all patients.
- **Maintaining Human Oversight and Control**: Dr. Taylor retains ultimate decision-making authority, leveraging AI and Ally's insights to inform, not dictate, their clinical judgment.

By combining Dr. AI's analytical powers with Ally's human expertise, this dynamic duo empowers Dr. Taylor to deliver exceptional patient care. This synergy unlocks a new era of healthcare, where AI augments human capabilities, elevates clinical decision-making, and ultimately leads to better health outcomes for all.

Remember, this is just a glimpse into the future. As AI technology evolves and our understanding of its ethical implications deepens, the possibilities for HCP support will continue to expand. By nurturing a culture of continuous learning, prioritizing ethical responsibility, and maintaining a deep commitment to patient well-being, we can turn this powerful synergy into a force for good, transforming healthcare and empowering HCPs to become even more effective healers.

Patient Education and Disease Awareness Campaigns

The world of patient education and disease awareness campaigns is ripe for an explosion of power thanks to the synergy between human empathy and AI's analytical muscle. Here's how this collaboration fuels meaningful connections, empowers patterns, and ultimately positively impacts health outcomes.

Human Strengths:

- **Storytelling and Emotional Intelligence**: Humans excel at creating compelling narratives, using humor, analogies, and real-life experiences to resonate with patients on an emotional level and make information impactful.
- **Cultural Sensitivity and Inclusivity**: Understanding diverse needs and tailoring messaging to resonate with different communities ensures broad reach and effectiveness.
- **Ethical Considerations and Responsible Communication**: Humans prioritize accurate information, transparency, and respect for patient privacy, building trust and encouraging engagement.
- **Strategic Planning and Management**: Defining campaign goals, selecting appropriate channels, and monitoring performance allow for continuous optimization and impact assessment.

AI Strengths:

- **Personalized Content Creation and Targeting**: AI can tailor educational materials and outreach to individual needs, interests, and health literacy levels, ensuring relevance and accessibility.
- **Real-time Data Analysis and Feedback**: AI can track engagement with educational materials, identify areas of confusion, and adapt future content based on audience responses.

- **Multilingual Support and Global Reach**: AI can translate materials into multiple languages and disseminate them across diverse channels, overcoming language barriers and reaching wider audiences.
- **Interactive Quizzes and Assessment**: AI can generate engaging quizzes and self-assessment tools to reinforce learning, monitor progress, and empower patients to manage their health proactively.

Synergy in Action

Imagine this:

- Humans develop a series of short video testimonials featuring diverse patients sharing their experiences with a specific disease.
- AI personalizes video distribution, showcasing stories relevant to individuals based on their demographics, diagnosis, and preferred language.
- Short quizzes embedded within the videos assess viewers' understanding and provide personalized learning recommendations based on their responses.
- Real-time analytics reveal which video segments and topics resonate most effectively with different audience segments.
- Humans utilize these insights to refine the campaign, create targeted content variations, and optimize messaging for maximum impact.
- Ethical considerations remain paramount, with humans ensuring informed consent, data privacy, and transparent communication throughout the campaign.

Challenges and Considerations:

- **Data Privacy and Security**: Ensure adherence to strict data protection regulations and transparent communication about data collection and usage.

- **Interpretability and Explainability of AI Models**: Understand how AI algorithms personalize content and avoid black-box decision-making to build trust and confidence.
- **Upskilling and Workforce Development**: Equip healthcare professionals and patient advocacy groups with the necessary skills to collaborate effectively with AI and interpret its insights.
- **Over-reliance on AI and Neglecting Human Touch**: Remember, AI is a tool, not a replacement for human empathy, cultural sensitivity, and ethical considerations.

By harmonizing human creativity and storytelling with the analytical power of AI, we can revolutionize patient education and disease awareness campaigns. This synergy leads to personalized, accessible, and culturally sensitive information that empowers patients, fosters active engagement, and improves health outcomes.

Remember, this is an ongoing journey of discovery and innovation. As AI technology evolves and our understanding of its ethical implications deepens, the possibilities for patient education and disease awareness campaigns will continue to expand. By fostering a culture of continuous learning, prioritizing ethical responsibility, and maintaining a deep commitment to patient well-being, we can leverage this powerful synergy to create a future where everyone can access the information and support they need to live healthy lives.

CHAPTER

41

The Synergy of Human+AI Collaboration for Customer Interaction

The pharma marketing landscape is undergoing a revolution driven by the powerful synergy between human expertise and artificial intelligence (AI). While AI excels at data analysis and personalization, the human touch remains irreplaceable in building trust, navigating ethical considerations, and crafting emotionally resonant communication. This chapter explores how this human+AI collaboration transforms customer interaction across the entire spectrum of pharma marketing stakeholders—healthcare professionals (HCPs), patients, payers, regulators, and investors.

Understanding the Customer Journey:

The first step in leveraging human+AI synergy is mapping the customer journey for each stakeholder group. Here is a glimpse into how this might look:

1. **Healthcare Professionals (HCPs):**
    - **Awareness:** HCPs might first become aware of a new medication through conferences, medical journals, or pharmaceutical company representatives.
    - **Education and Research**: They then delve deeper into research data, clinical trial results, and potential applications within their specific practice area.
    - **Evaluation and Adoption**: They evaluate the medication's safety profile, efficacy data, cost-effectiveness, and

potential integration into their treatment protocols.

- **Ongoing Engagement**: HCPs might seek additional information, request samples, or participate in educational webinars hosted by the pharmaceutical company.

2. **Patients:**

- **Diagnosis and Initial Information Gathering**: Patients often begin their journey after diagnosis. They might use online resources, consult with patient support groups, or talk to their doctor to learn more about their condition.
- **Treatment Options and Research**: Patients explore available treatment options, researching medication side effects, drug interactions, and potential lifestyle adjustments.
- **Prescriptions and Adherence**: They receive a prescription from their doctor, and their journey continues with medication adherence, managing side effects, and potentially seeking additional support or information.
- **Long-Term Management**: The patient journey becomes an ongoing process of managing their condition, monitoring progress, and potentially adjusting treatment plans in consultation with their healthcare providers.

3. **Payers:**

- **Market Analysis and Cost Evaluation**: Payers analyze market trends, disease burden, and potential cost implications of covering a new medication.
- **Reimbursement Negotiations**: They negotiate reimbursement rates with pharmaceutical companies based on cost-effectiveness data and potential impact on healthcare budgets.
- **Coverage Decisions and Monitoring**: Payers determine whether to cover the new medication and establish specific criteria for patient access. They might also monitor medication utilization and treatment outcomes.

4. **Regulators:**
   - **Pre-Clinical and Clinical Trial Review**: Regulators assess the safety and efficacy data from pre-clinical studies and clinical trials to ensure ethical development and patient safety.
   - **Approval Process**: They review the drug's application package, including manufacturing processes, quality control measures, and potential risks and benefits.
   - **Post-Market Surveillance**: Regulators monitor the medication's safety profile once it is on the market, investigating potential adverse events and ensuring ongoing compliance with regulations.

5. **Investors:**
   - **Market Research and Opportunity Identification**: Investors analyze market trends, disease areas with unmet needs, and the potential for new drug discoveries.
   - **Company Evaluation and Due Diligence**: They assess a pharmaceutical company's pipeline, research and development (R&D) capabilities, leadership team, and overall financial health.
   - **Investment Decisions and Portfolio Management**: Investors decide whether to invest in the company based on their risk tolerance and potential ROI. They might also track the company's progress and adjust their portfolio holdings accordingly.

The Power of Customer Journey Mapping:

By mapping the customer journey for each stakeholder group, pharma companies can identify key touchpoints where human+AI collaboration can have the highest impact. This allows for targeted communication strategies that address each customer segment's needs and information requirements at every stage of their journey.

The Power of AI in Personalization:

In pharmaceutical marketing, AI's power in personalization goes beyond simply tailoring content or messages. It unlocks deeper understanding and engagement with each customer segment, leading to more effective communication and improved outcomes. Here is a breakdown of how AI personalizes the customer journey across various stakeholders:

1. **HCP Personalization:**
    - **Targeted Information Delivery:** AI analyzes an HCP's research interests, publication history, and practice area to deliver relevant clinical trial data, educational materials, and updates on new medications most suited to their patient needs.
    - **Adaptive Learning Modules**: AI can create personalized online learning modules for HCPs, focusing on specific disease areas or treatment options relevant to their practice.
    - **Virtual Case Studies**: AI can personalize case studies showcasing how other HCPs have successfully used a new medication in their practice settings, catering to the physician's area of expertise.
2. **Patient Personalization:**
    - **Content Curation Based on Diagnosis**: AI analyzes a patient's diagnosis and medical history to curate educational content, such as infographics or explainer videos, focusing on their specific condition and treatment options.
    - **Interactive Risk Assessment Tools**: AI-powered tools can personalize risk assessments for potential side effects, considering a patient's medical history and other medications they might be taking.
    - **Personalized Support Chatbots**: AI-powered chatbots can answer patients' specific questions about medication adherence and potential side effects and offer emotional support throughout their treatment journey.

3. **Payer Personalization:**
    - **Cost-Effectiveness Analysis at Scale**: AI can analyze vast datasets to generate personalized cost-effectiveness reports for payers, considering factors like patient demographics, potential treatment duration, and disease burden within their region.
    - **Predictive Modeling for Budgeting**: AI can leverage historical data and market trends to create predictive models that help payers budget for potential medication utilization and healthcare costs associated with new drug therapies.
    - **Real-World Data Analysis**: AI can analyze real-world data on medication usage and treatment outcomes, allowing payers to personalize reimbursement strategies based on patient response and cost-effectiveness in specific populations.
4. **Regulator Personalization:**
    - **Streamlined Clinical Trial Review**: AI can analyze pre-clinical and clinical trial data to identify potential safety concerns or irregularities, allowing regulators to focus their review on critical areas and personalize their requests for additional information from pharmaceutical companies.
    - **Predictive Risk Assessment for Adverse Events**: AI can analyze historical data on adverse events associated with similar medications to predict potential risks for new drugs, allowing regulators to implement personalized monitoring and mitigation strategies.
    - **Tailored Post-Market Surveillance**: AI can personalize post-market surveillance of a medication based on its potential risks and side effects, focusing regulatory resources on areas of greatest concern.
5. **Investor Personalization:**
    - **Dynamic Investment Opportunity Analysis**: AI can analyze market trends, competitor pipelines, and potential

regulatory hurdles to provide investors with personalized insights into the potential return on investment (ROI) for a specific pharmaceutical company or drug discovery.

- **Risk Assessment and Portfolio Management**: AI can personalize risk assessments for investors, considering their risk tolerance and investment goals. It can also recommend adjustments to its portfolio based on real-time market data and the performance of pharmaceutical companies it has invested in.

The Benefits of AI-Powered Personalization:

By leveraging AI for personalization, pharma companies achieve several benefits:

- **Increased Customer Engagement**: Personalized communication resonates deeply with each stakeholder group, increasing engagement and receptivity to information.
- **Improved Patient Outcomes**: Tailored educational content and support can empower patients to manage their health more effectively and adhere to treatment plans.
- **Enhanced Decision-Making**: Personalized data insights empower HCPs, payers, regulators, and investors to make informed decisions regarding treatment options, coverage strategies, approvals, and investment opportunities.

Overall, AI empowers pharma companies to move beyond a one-size-fits-all approach. By personalizing the customer journey for each stakeholder group, human+AI collaboration fosters trust, optimizes communication, and ultimately drives success in today's dynamic pharma marketing landscape.

The Human Touch: Building Trust and Empathy:

The human touch remains irreplaceable in pharma marketing, where complex medical information meets human health and well-being. While AI excels at data analysis and personalization, the human element fosters trust, builds empathy, and creates genuine customer connections. Here is a deeper dive into how the human touch strengthens customer interactions across various stakeholders in pharma marketing:

1. **Building Trust with HCPs:**
   - **Addressing Specific Needs:** Beyond delivering data points, human representatives can engage in open conversations with physicians, addressing their questions and concerns about a new medication. This personalized approach builds trust and fosters a sense of partnership.
   - **Navigating Ethical Considerations**: Human interaction allows for nuanced discussions about a medication's potential benefits and risks, addressing ethical considerations and aligning with a physician's values and treatment philosophy.
   - **Building Rapport and Long-Term Relationships**: Human representatives can build rapport with physicians over time, fostering a sense of trust and open communication beyond a single product launch or clinical trial.
2. **Empathy for Patients:**
   - **Understanding Emotional Concerns**: Human interaction allows a deeper understanding of a patient's emotional state beyond their medical history. A compassionate representative can address anxieties, fears, and hopes related to their condition and treatment options.
   - **Personalized Support and Guidance**: Human support goes beyond pre-programmed responses in a chatbot. Humans can empathize with a patient's challenges and provide personalized guidance on medication adherence, managing side effects, and connecting them with relevant resources.
   - **Active Listening and Emotional Support**: Patients often need a listening ear and emotional support throughout

treatment. Human interaction allows for active listening, validating their concerns, and fostering a sense of empowerment in managing their health.

3. **Investor Relations:**
   - **Vision and Leadership Insights**: AI can analyze financial data, but human interaction allows investors to delve deeper into a company's vision, leadership team's capabilities, and long-term strategy. This fosters trust and confidence in the company's future.
   - **Addressing Concerns and Building Confidence**: Human interaction allows for directly addressing investor concerns and clarifying any uncertainties about the company's pipeline, research capabilities, or potential roadblocks to the market. This builds confidence and strengthens investor relations.
   - **Authentic Storytelling and Building Relationships**: Human interaction facilitates authentic storytelling about the company's mission and impact on patient lives. This emotional connection goes beyond financial data and strengthens investor relationships.

The Human Advantage in Ethical Considerations:

- **Navigating Sensitive Topics**: Human judgment is crucial in navigating sensitive topics such as data privacy and potential biases in AI algorithms. Humans ensure responsible use of patient data and transparent communication with all stakeholders.
- **Upholding Ethical Principles**: Human interaction allows for a nuanced understanding of ethical considerations in drug development and marketing. Humans ensure all communication and practices align with the highest ethical standards.
- **Building Trust Through Transparency**: Humans play a vital role in fostering trust through transparency. This involves

openly addressing medications' potential risks and side effects while communicating their benefits accurately and ethically.

The Synergy of Human Touch and AI

AI provides a powerful foundation for personalization and data-driven insights, but the human touch breathes life into communication and builds genuine connections. By leveraging this synergy, pharmaceutical companies can create a customer-centric marketing approach that fosters trust and empathy, ultimately leading to improved outcomes for all stakeholders in the healthcare landscape.

Here is how human+AI collaboration can create a powerful customer-centric marketing strategy:

1. **Data-Driven Audience Segmentation**: AI analyzes customer data to segment audiences and identifies their needs and preferences.
2. **Personalized Content Creation**: Humans collaborate with AI to create targeted content (blog posts, educational videos, social media messages) tailored to each segment.
3. **Multichannel Communication**: AI orchestrates communication across various channels (email, social media, healthcare portals) to reach customers where they are.
4. **Human-Led Relationship Building**: Human representatives build trust and rapport with customers through ongoing interactions, addressing specific questions and concerns.
5. **Continuous Optimization:** AI tracks customer engagement and feedback, allowing humans to refine communication strategies further and personalize content.

Examples of Human+AI Synergy in Action:

- A pharmaceutical company launches a new medication for a chronic condition. AI personalizes email campaigns for patients while human representatives manage a dedicated helpline to address patient concerns and medication adherence challenges.

- A clinical trial sponsor leverages AI to identify potential participants based on specific criteria. Human research coordinators then contact these individuals, explaining the trial details and addressing any questions or anxieties.

The future of pharma marketing is not about AI replacing humans but rather about humans and AI working together in a powerful synergy. By leveraging AI's analytical capabilities and human expertise in communication, empathy, and ethics, pharma companies can create a customer-centric marketing approach that fosters trust, improves patient outcomes, and drives success in the ever-evolving healthcare landscape.

The Synergy of Human Oversight and AI Capabilities in Navigating Ethical Considerations

Navigating ethical considerations is paramount in pharma marketing, where innovation and progress often intersect with sensitive patient data and complex medical realities. Here is a detailed exploration of how human oversight and AI capabilities can work together to ensure responsible and ethical marketing practices:

Key Ethical Considerations in Pharma Marketing:

- **Data Privacy**: Pharma companies collect vast amounts of data from patients and HCPs. Ensuring this data is collected, stored, and used responsibly by regulations like HIPAA (Health Insurance Portability and Accountability Act) in the US or GDPR (General Data Protection Regulation) in the EU is crucial.
- **Transparency and Bias Detection**: AI algorithms can perpetuate biases in the data they are trained on. Humans must oversee these algorithms to identify and mitigate potential biases in communication or targeting strategies.
- **Truthful and Balanced Communication**: Marketing materials should accurately represent a medication's benefits and risks, avoiding misleading claims or cherry-picking data to paint an overly positive picture.

- **Responsible Promotion and Avoiding Off-Label Marketing**: Pharma companies must promote medications only for their approved uses, avoiding the temptation to market them for unapproved conditions or to downplay potential side effects.

The Human Role in Ethical Oversight:

- **Developing Ethical Guidelines**: Human leadership plays a crucial role in developing clear ethical guidelines for data collection, AI usage, and overall marketing practices within the company.
- **Data Governance and Compliance**: Humans ensure data privacy regulations are followed throughout the data lifecycle, from collection to storage and use in marketing campaigns.
- **Monitoring and Auditing**: Humans oversee AI algorithms and marketing campaigns to identify and address potential ethical issues, ensuring ongoing compliance and responsible practices.

The Power of Mitigating Ethical Risks:

- **Data De-Identification**: AI can be used to de-identify patient data while still allowing valuable insights to be extracted for marketing purposes. This protects patient privacy while allowing for personalized communication.
- **Bias Detection and Mitigation**: AI can analyze marketing materials and identify potential biases in language or imagery, allowing humans to address them before communication is disseminated.
- **Transparency Reporting and Audit Trails**: AI can track data usage, create transparent and responsible data handling practices for regulators, and build stakeholder trust.

The Synergy of Human and AI in Navigating Ethical Challenges:

The true power lies in the synergy between human oversight and AI capabilities. Humans bring ethical frameworks, empathy, and critical thinking, while AI offers data analysis, bias detection, and transparency tools. Here is how they work together:

- **Humans Define Ethical Boundaries**: Leadership establishes clear guidelines for data usage, AI application, and overall marketing communication that adhere to the highest ethical standards.
- **AI Identifies Potential Pitfalls**: AI algorithms analyze data and marketing materials to identify potential biases, privacy concerns, or misleading language.
- **Humans Address and Rectify Issues**: Human judgment comes into play to address any ethical concerns flagged by AI, ensuring responsible marketing practices and patient privacy.

In today's data-driven pharma marketing landscape, navigating ethical considerations requires a multifaceted approach. By leveraging the strengths of human oversight and AI capabilities, pharma companies can ensure responsible communication, build trust with stakeholders, and contribute to a future where innovation in healthcare goes hand in hand with ethical practices.

Building a Customer-Centric Foundation

In the ever-evolving pharma marketing world, the synergy between human expertise and AI unlocks a powerful approach to customer-centric marketing. This approach prioritizes understanding and addressing the specific needs of each stakeholder group— HCPs, patients, payers, regulators, and investors. Here is a breakdown of how this human+AI collaboration translates into real-world action:

1. **Data-Driven Audience Segmentation**: AI analyzes vast datasets from various sources, such as patient demographics, HCP prescribing habits, and online behavior. Based on this data, AI segments customers into distinct groups with similar needs, preferences, and information requirements.

2. **Understanding the Customer Journey**: Humans collaborate with AI to map the customer journey for each stakeholder group. This journey encompasses touchpoints, pain points, and information needs throughout the customer's interaction with a specific medication or pharmaceutical company.

Tailoring Communication with Human+AI Synergy:

- **Personalized Content Creation**: Leveraging Audience Segmentation and customer journey insights, humans and AI work together to create targeted content (e.g., blog posts, social media messages, educational videos) tailored to each segment's needs. AI might generate initial drafts or identify trending topics, while humans refine the content for clarity, emotional resonance, and brand voice.
- **Multichannel Communication**: AI orchestrates communication across various channels (email, social media, healthcare portals, targeted online advertising) to reach customers where they are most likely to engage with the content.
- **Human-Led Relationship Building**: Human representatives can be crucial in building customer rapport and trust. They can address questions, concerns, or requests that AI-powered chatbots might not easily address.

Optimizing the Customer Experience

1. **Real-Time Feedback and Analytics**: AI tracks customer engagement metrics such as content click-through rates, video completion rates, and social media interactions. This real-time data allows humans to analyze the effectiveness of communication strategies and continuously refine approaches based on audience response.
2. **Agile Content Iteration**: Human+AI teams can iterate on content and communication strategies based on feedback and analytics data. This ensures that messages remain relevant, address evolving needs, and resonate more deeply with each customer segment.

Examples of Human+AI Synergy in Action:

Example #1: A pharmaceutical company launches a new medication for a chronic respiratory condition.

- **AI Segmentation**: AI segments patients based on disease severity, medication history, and online behavior.
- **Targeted Content Creation**: Humans and AI collaborate to create educational videos explaining the medication's benefits and potential side effects, tailored for newly diagnosed patients versus those managing the condition for several years.
- **Multichannel Communication**: The videos are disseminated through social media ads, patient support group forums, and healthcare provider portals.
- **Human-Led Support**: Nurses or respiratory therapists answer patient questions through a dedicated helpline, providing additional support and addressing individual concerns.

Example #2: A clinical trial sponsor needs to recruit participants for a new oncology treatment:

- **AI Targeting**: AI analyzes patient databases to identify individuals with specific cancer types and genetic profiles that meet the trial criteria.
- **Personalized Outreach**: Humans craft targeted email strategies explaining the trial details and addressing potential anxieties about research participation.
- **Ongoing Communication**: Human representatives manage a dedicated phone line to answer questions and guide potential participants through enrollment.

Example #3: AI-Powered Chatbots with Human Oversight:

- **Scenario**: A pharmaceutical company launches a new medication for a complex neurological condition. Patients might have questions and concerns about its side effects, interactions with other medications, and potential impact on their daily lives.

- **Human+AI Synergy**:
  - **AI**: An AI-powered chatbot is integrated into the company's website and patient support app. The chatbot can answer frequently asked questions about the medication, dosage instructions, and potential side effects. It can also schedule appointments with healthcare providers or direct patients to relevant educational resources.
- **Human**:
  - Pharmacists or trained medical professionals monitor the chatbot interactions and intervene when necessary.
  - They can address complex or nuanced questions that the AI might not be able to handle.
  - They can also analyze chatbot data to identify emerging trends in patient concerns and use this information to develop more targeted educational content.

Example #4: AI-Driven Market Research with Human Analysis

- **Scenario**: A pharmaceutical company is developing a new drug for a rare genetic disease. Traditional methods can be challenging when gathering patient insights for such a niche population.
- **Human+AI Synergy**:
  - **AI:** Social media listening tools powered by AI can be used to identify online communities and forums where patients with rare diseases discuss their experiences and challenges. AI can analyze these conversations to understand patient needs, unmet medical needs, and language used to describe their condition.
  - **Human**: Market research professionals then analyze the AI-generated data to identify key themes and insights.
- They can then conduct targeted outreach to patient advocacy groups or patient interview sessions to gain a deeper understanding of the patient experience and inform the development of the new drug.

Example #5: AI-Powered Content Personalization with Human Curation

- **Scenario**: A pharmaceutical company has a portfolio of medications targeting various therapeutic areas. They want to create educational content for HCPs but ensure it is relevant to their specific area of practice.
- **Human+AI Synergy**:
    - **AI** can analyze HCPs' online profiles, research publications, and past interactions with the company's website to understand their areas of expertise and interests.
- **Human**: Medical writers and content creators leverage AI insights to curate personalized educational content for HCPs. This might include summaries of recent clinical trial data, case studies relevant to their practice, or upcoming webinars focused on specific disease areas.
- Humans ensure the content is accurate, evidence-based, and adheres to ethical marketing guidelines.

Benefits of Customer-Centric Marketing with Human+AI Synergy

- **Increased Customer Engagement**: Targeted communication resonates more deeply with each stakeholder group, leading to higher engagement and receptivity to information.
- **Improved Patient Outcomes**: Personalized education and support can empower patients to manage their health more effectively and adhere to treatment plans.
- **Enhanced Decision-Making**: Data-driven insights empower HCPs, payers, regulators, and investors to make informed decisions regarding treatment options, coverage strategies, approvals, and investment opportunities.
- **Stronger Brand Reputation**: A customer-centric approach prioritizes trust, transparency, and ethical communication, fostering a stronger brand reputation in the pharmaceutical industry.

The Importance of Trust and Transparency

These examples highlight the importance of trust and transparency in the human+AI synergy for pharma marketing. Patients, HCPs, and other stakeholders must know how AI is used and feel confident that their data is handled responsibly.

Here are some additional points to be considered:

- **Communicate the Role of AI**: Inform customers about how AI is used in communication and content creation.
- **Provide Options for Human Interaction**: Ensure there are always avenues for patients and HCPs to connect with human representatives for more complex questions or concerns.
- **Uphold Ethical Data Practices**: Be transparent about data collection practices and ensure data is used responsibly by regulations.

By fostering a human+AI collaboration built on trust, transparency, and ethical considerations, pharma companies can leverage this synergy to create a customer-centric marketing approach that benefits patients, healthcare providers, and the industry.

CHAPTER 42

Conducting the Audience: Market Research and Analysis for Pharma Branding, Step-by Step

In the dynamic world of pharma branding, crafting a message that resonates requires understanding your audience like a maestro understands their orchestra. Market research and analysis are essential to gather insights, identify opportunities, and build a strategy that resonates with patients, healthcare professionals, and other key stakeholders.

Here's a step-by-step guide to navigating the research symphony featuring illustrative examples from the pharma landscape:

1. **Define Your Objectives and Stakeholders**:
    - **Start with the "Why"**: What specific questions do you have about your brand, target audience, or market landscape? Are you launching a new drug, targeting a new patient segment, or assessing brand awareness?
    - **Identify Your Audience**: Who are you trying to reach? This could include patients, healthcare professionals (HCPs), investors, or the general public. Each group has unique needs and perspectives.

    Example: A pharmaceutical company launching a new diabetes medication might want to understand patient attitudes toward treatment options, preferred communication channels, and concerns about potential side effects. Additionally, they might target HCPs to gather insights on prescribing habits, perceptions of new medication, and potential barriers to adoption.

2. **Choose Your Research Instruments:**
   - **Quantitative Research:** Collects numerical data through surveys, polls, and market share analysis. It is used to understand general trends, the prevalence of conditions, and brand awareness levels.
   - **Qualitative Research**: Uncovers deeper insights through focus groups, interviews, and social media listening. This helps understand motivations, perceptions, and emotional responses to your brand or product.

Example: For the diabetes medication example, quantitative research might involve surveys to understand the size and demographics of the target patient population and market share analysis to assess competitor offerings. Qualitative research could involve focus groups with patients to understand their experiences with existing medications, concerns about diabetes management, and preferred information sources.

3. **Analyze and Interpret Data**:
   - **Quantitative Data**: Analyze statistics, identify trends, and segment your audience based on demographics or other relevant factors.
   - **Qualitative Data**: Identify key themes, recurring emotions, and common pain points from interviews and focus groups. Look for patterns and insights that paint a holistic picture of your audience.

Example: Analyzing quantitative data might reveal that a specific age group of patients with diabetes are dissatisfied with current treatment options and prefer online patient communities for information gathering. Qualitative research might uncover patient anxieties about managing side effects, a desire for personalized treatment plans, and a preference for clear and concise information from healthcare professionals.

4. **Translate Insights into Actionable Strategies**:
   - **Develop Messaging that Resonates**: Use your understanding of your audience's needs, preferences, and

concerns to craft targeted messaging that effectively communicates your brand's value perception.

- **Identify Effective Communication Channels**: Align your chosen channels (e.g., social media, patient support groups, targeted advertising) with your audience's preferred information sources and communication styles.

Example: Based on the research, the company might develop patient education materials that address specific concerns about side effects and offer personalized treatment plan examples. They might also engage with patient communication online and provide clear, concise information tailored to their preferred communication styles. For HCPs, they might develop targeted marketing materials highlighting the medication's unique benefits and address potential prescribing barriers.

5. **Continuously Monitor and Adapt**:

- Regularly evaluate the effectiveness of your strategies and refine them based on ongoing research and market feedback.
- Stay up-to-date on industry trends, competitor activity, and evolving patient needs to ensure your message remains relevant and impactful.

Example: The company might track patient engagement with their online materials, monitor social media sentiment towards the brand, and conduct periodic surveys to assess brand awareness and perceptions. By continuously monitoring and adapting their strategies, they can ensure their messaging remains relevant and resonates with their evolving audience.

Remember, market research and analysis are not a one-time event but an ongoing process. By consistently conducting research, analyzing data, and translating insights into action, pharmaceutical brands can ensure their communication resonates with their audience, builds trust, and ultimately achieves their marketing objectives. This is the true symphony of market research—where data becomes the melody, insights guide the harmony, and actionable strategies create a performance that resonates with your audience.

Defining Your Objectives and Stakeholders: A Roadmap for Pharma Brand Understanding

The first step in conducting your pharma brand market research symphony is akin to tuning the instruments— understanding your "why" and identifying your "who." Here's a detailed approach to defining your objectives and stakeholders:

1. **Clarify Your Brand Goals:**
   - **Are You Launching a New Drug?** Understanding patient needs, competitor offerings, and prescribing potential among HCPs becomes crucial.
   - **Rebranding an Existing Product?** Assessing brand awareness, patient perceptions, and competitor landscape helps guide strategic repositioning.
   - **Targeting a New Patient Segment?** Identifying their demographics, preferred communication channels, and information needs is paramount.
   - **Building Brand Loyalty?** Analyzing patient satisfaction, engagement with your brand, and potential areas for improvement becomes key.

   Example: A company launching a new cholesterol medication might aim to understand patient concerns about side effects, preferred treatment options, and information sources. For an HCP-focused research objective, they should assess prescribing habits, potential barriers to adoption, and prescriptions of existing cholesterol medication options.

2. **Identify Your Key Stakeholders:**
   - **Patients:** Segmenting by demographics, disease stage, and medication adherence patterns offers deeper insights.

- **Healthcare Professionals (HCPs):** Consider different specialties, prescribing habits, and information needs within target therapeutic areas.
- **Investors:** Understanding their expectations and concerns about your brand and the broader market landscape is vital.
- **Payers and Policymakers:** Examining reimbursement requirements, pricing strategies, and regulatory influences is important.
- **Media and Influencers:** Identifying key publications, journalists, and online communities relevant to your brand is crucial.

Example: Patients with different risk factors and adherence levels, cardiologists, primary care physicians, healthcare investors, pharmacy benefit managers, medical journalists, and patient advocacy groups are the most likely target audience for cholesterol medication.

3. **Dive Deeper into Stakeholder Needs and Perceptions:**
   - **What are their Motivations, Preferences, and Pain Points?** Conduct surveys, focus groups, and social media listening to uncover their challenges and unmet needs.
   - **How do they Perceive Your Brand and Competitors?** Analyze brand awareness, sentiment analysis, and competitive benchmarking to understand their perceptions.
   - **What are their Preferred Communication Channels and Information Sources?** Identify where they seek information and tailor your outreach strategies accordingly.

Example: Patient focus groups might reveal concerns about managing cholesterol levels, anxieties about potential side effects, and a desire for personalized treatment plans. HCP interviews might uncover prescribing preferences, perceived benefits of new medication compared to competitors, and information gaps they want to address.

Remember:

- **Specificity is Key:** Clearly define your research objectives and identify the stakeholder groups you want to understand.
- **Go Beyond Demographics:** Segment your audience based on relevant factors like disease stage, treatment experience, and information needs.
- **Consider the Broader Context:** When defining your research scope, consider industry trends, competitor activity, and regulatory landscape.

By clearly defining your objectives and stakeholders, you set the stage for a market research symphony that resonates with your audience and provides valuable insights to guide your pharma branding efforts. This is the first act in your quest for understanding—a vital step in composing a brand message that connects with your audience and builds a lasting reputation.

Choosing Your Research Instruments: The Orchestra of Data Collection in Pharma Branding

With your objectives and stakeholders clearly defined, selecting the instruments that will help you gather valuable data and compose your market research symphony is time. Here's a step-by-step guide:

1. **Align Instruments with Objectives:**
    - **Quantitative Research:** Best for measuring prevalence, brand awareness, market share, and general trends.
    - **Qualitative Research:** Deeper insights into motivations, perceptions, and emotional responses.

   Example: To understand patient preferences for cholesterol medication delivery methods (e.g., pills, injections), for example, a quantitative survey with multiple-choice questions could be used. However, to uncover underlying anxieties about injections, focus groups or in-depth interviews would provide richer qualitative data.

2. **Consider Your Stakeholders:**
   - **Patients:** Surveys, focus groups, online patient communities, social media listening.
   - **HCPs:** Surveys, interviews, advisory boards, medical conferences, and social media analysis.
   - **Investors:** Investor surveys, financial reports, industry analysis.
   - **Payers and Policymakers:** Interviews, government reports, industry conferences.
   - **Media and Influencers:** Media monitoring tools, interviews, and social media analysis.

Example: Pain specialists could be interviewed to gauge HCP perceptions of new pain medication. Additionally, tracking online discussions among HCPs on medical forums and social media would offer real-time insights into their opinions.

3. **Explore Quantitative Options:**
   - **Surveys:** Structured questionnaires to gather data from large, representative samples.
   - **Market Share Analysis:** Tracks sales data to understand competitor performance and market trends.
   - **Website Analytics:** Monitors website traffic and user behavior to assess brand awareness and online engagement.
   - **Web Scraping:** Collects publicly available online data for competitor or sentiment analysis.

Example: A survey of patients with chronic pain could quantify medication adherence rates and satisfaction levels with existing treatment options. Market share analysis could identify emerging competitors and track the market penetration of specific pain medication categories.

4. **Delve into Qualitative Methods:**
   - **Focus Groups:** Moderate small group discussions to explore shared experiences and opinions.

- **In-depth Interviews:** One-on-one conversations to dive deeper into individual motivations and perceptions.
- **Ethnography:** Observing people in their natural environments to understand their behavior and decision-making processes.
- **Social Media Listening:** Analyzing online conversations to understand brand sentiment, patient concerns, and emerging trends.

Example: Focus groups with patients with diabetes could uncover unmet needs in managing their condition and identify communication gaps related to specific medications. Ethnographic research could observe how patients interact with medication reminders and other tools to gain insights into their daily routines.

5. **Consider Emerging Techniques:**
   - **Mobile Surveys:** Gather real-time data from patients using their smartphones.
   - **Social Media Sentiment Analysis:** Use AI-powered tools to analyze the emotional tone of online conversations.
   - **Eye-tracking Studies:** Understand how patients visually navigate websites and marketing materials.
   - **Virtual Reality (VR) Research:** Immerse patients in simulated scenarios to assess their reactions to new products or treatment options.

Example: A mobile survey app could track patients' pain levels in real-time and collect feedback on medication side effects. AI-powered sentiment analysis of online patient communities could detect emerging safety concerns or identify influential patient advocates.

Remember:

- **Mix and Match Methods:** Combine quantitative and qualitative approaches for a holistic understanding.

- **Pilot Test Your Instruments:** Ensure they are appropriate for your research objectives and target audience.
- **Ethical Considerations are Paramount:** Respect data privacy, obtain informed consent, and anonymize data when necessary.

Choosing the right research instruments and carefully aligning them with your objectives and stakeholders allows you to collect valuable data that resonates with your audience and forms the melodic core of your pharma branding research symphony. So, pick your instruments, tune them carefully, and prepare to conduct a research performance that yields actionable insights for your brand.

Analyzing and Interpreting Data: Harmonizing Insights in Your Pharma Branding Symphony

Having gathered your research instruments and collected valuable data, you're now ready to transform it into meaningful insights. This, like interpreting a complex musical score, requires careful analysis and thoughtful interpretation. Let's delve into this critical step:

1. **Organize and Clean Your Data:**
    - **Quantitative Data:** Use statistical software to organize and clean datasets, checking for missing values and outliers.
    - **Qualitative Data:** Transcribe interviews and focus groups, categorize responses by themes, and identify recurring patterns.

    Example: Using statistical software to analyze survey responses about preferred delivery methods for cholesterol medication research. Transcribe and categorize focus group discussions to identify patient concerns about side effects and information needs.
2. **Analyze Quantitative Data:**
    - **Descriptive Statistics:** Summarize key data points like averages, percentages, and correlations.
    - **Hypothesis Testing:** Test specific predictions about your audience or your brand's performance.

- **Segmentation:** Divide your audience into groups based on shared characteristics for deeper analysis.

Example: Calculate the average of patients who prefer injections and compare it to those who prefer pills. Test your hypothesis that patients with higher anxiety levels are more likely to express concerns about side effects. Segment patients by disease stage and analyze their preferred information sources.

3. Interpret Qualitative Data:

- **Thematic Analysis:** Identify recurring themes, ideas, and emotions participants express.
- **Narrative Analysis:** Understand the stories and experiences shared by participants.
- **Content Analysis:** Examine participants' language to uncover implicit meanings and biases.

Example: Identify key themes from patient focus groups around side effects, such as fear of needles, concerns about long-term impacts, and desire for transparent information. Analyze patient narratives to understand their struggles and motivations for managing cholesterol. Examine the language HCPs use during interviews to uncover potential biases towards specific medication types.

4. Triangulate Data Sources:

- Combine insights from different research methods to gain a more complete picture.
- Look for consistency and inconsistencies across data sources to identify robust findings.

Example: Compare survey data on preferred delivery methods with qualitative insights from focus groups to better understand patient perspectives. Look for consistency between patient concerns about side effects expressed in individual interviews and broader themes identified in social media listening data.

5. **Interpret Data in Context:**
   - **Data Analysis is an Iterative Process:** Continuously re-evaluate your interpretations as you gather more information.
   - **Prioritize Validity and Reliability:** Ensure your findings are accurate, trustworthy, and representative of your target audience.
   - **Seek Expert Advice:** Consider involving data analysts or researchers with pharma branding and market research expertise.

Following these steps and carefully analyzing your data can transform collected information into actionable insights that resonate with your audience. This is the true art of data interpretation—harmonizing diverse notes into a coherent melody that forms the backbone of your pharma branding strategy.

Remember, these insights are the foundation for building your brand message, ensuring it resonates with your stakeholders' unique needs and perspectives. So, conduct your analysis carefully and prepare to orchestrate a symphony of understanding that elevates your brand to new heights.

CHAPTER 43

From Insights to Impact: Translating Your Pharma Branding Symphony into Action

The data has been collected, analyzed, and interpreted. The crucial step is transforming valuable insights into actionable strategies that resonate with your stakeholders. This, like translating a musical score into a captivating performance, requires creativity, strategic thinking, and mindful tailoring. Let's explore this crucial step:

1. **Define Your Strategic Objectives**:
    - **Align Insights with Your Overall Brand Goals**: Research serves your broader marketing and branding strategy.
    - **Set Specific, Measurable, Achievable, Relevant, and Time-bound (SMART) Goals**: Ensure your strategy translates into tangible outcomes.

    Example: Based on research revealing patient anxieties about a new diabetes medication's side effects, a pharma company might set the SMART objective to increase patient understanding of side effects by 20 percent within six months, measured through surveys and website engagement with educational materials.

2. **Prioritize Insights and Opportunities**:
    - **Not All Insights are Created Equal**: Focus on findings with the highest impact potential for the brand and audience.
    - **Identify Opportunities to Address Unmet Needs or Differentiate Your Brand**: Leverage research to stand out from competitors.

Example: The company might prioritize addressing patient concerns about needle size based on research highlighting this as a significant anxiety trigger. Additionally, they might leverage qualitative insights about preferred information channels to develop engaging online educational videos about side effects.

3. **Develop Targeted Messaging and Content**:
   - **Craft Messages that Resonate with Your Audience's Needs, Preferences, and Concerns**: Speak their language, address their pain points, and offer solutions.
   - **Tailor Content to Different Stakeholder Groups**: HCPs require different information than patients, for example.

Example: The company might develop patient-friendly infographics and animated videos explaining potential side effects, their management, and when to seek medical attention. For HCPs the company might create detailed presentations with clinical trial data and prescribing guidelines addressing common concerns.

4. **Choose Effective Communication Channels**:
   - **Deliver Targeted Messages Through Preferred Channels:** Leverage research findings to reach your audience where they are.
   - **Consider a Multi-channel Approach**: Combine online content, social media engagement, healthcare professional outreach, and patient support groups.

Example: The company might launch an educational campaign on its website and social media, partnering with patient advocacy groups for wider reach. They might also conduct webinars for HCPs and provide educational materials for patient consultations.

5. **Measure and Adapt**:
   - **Track Progress Towards Your SMART Objectives**: Monitor website traffic, engagement with educational materials, and surveys to assess impact.
   - **Be Prepared to Adapt Your Approach Based on Feedback and Data**: Continuous improvement is key.

Example: The company might track website visits to educational content, monitor social media mentions and sentiment, and conduct follow-up surveys to gauge patient understanding of side effects. Based on the results, they might refine their content, expand to new channels, or address emerging concerns.

Remember:

- **Collaboration is Key**: Involve marketing communication and medical teams in translating insights into action.
- **Ethical Considerations Remain Paramount**: Ensure transparency, data privacy, and responsible communication practices.
- **Long-term Commitment is Essential**: Building trust and brand loyalty takes time and effort.

You can orchestrate a pharma branding symphony that delivers impact and trust by translating your research insights into actionable strategies and tailoring your approach to resonate with your audience. Remember, this is not a one-time performance but an ongoing journey of understanding, adaptation, and continuous improvement. So, pick your baton, lead your stakeholders on a journey of informed communication, and watch your brand's reputation flourish in the ever-evolving landscape of pharma marketing.

The Never-Ending Symphony: Continuously Monitoring and Adapting Your Pharma Branding Strategies

In the dynamic world of pharma branding, success isn't just about composing a beautiful and impactful message; it's about ensuring it resonates with your audience over time. This requires continuous monitoring, adaptation, and refinement, akin to fine-tuning your orchestra to maintain a harmonious performance. Here's how to approach this crucial step:

1. **Establish Monitoring Mechanisms:**
   - **Track Key Performance Indicators (KPIs):** Metrics aligned with SMART objectives, like website traffic, engagement with educational materials, social media sentiment, and brand awareness surveys.
   - **Utilize Market Research Tools:** Monitor industry trends, competitor activity, and evolving patient needs through ongoing surveys, social media listening, and competitor analysis.
   - **Gather Stakeholder Feedback:** Conduct regular surveys, focus groups, and online discussions to understand evolving needs and perceptions.

Example: A company promoting a new diabetes medication might track website visits to patient education materials, monitor social media sentiment toward the brand, and conduct follow-up surveys to gauge patient understanding of treatment benefits. They might also track competitor marketing campaigns and emerging industry trends in diabetes management.

2. **Analyze and Interpret Data:**
   - **Regularly Review Your KPIs and Market Research Data:** Identify trends, areas of improvement, and potential threats.
   - **Evaluate the Effectiveness of Your Communication Strategies:** Assess whether your message resonates with your audience and achieves your objectives.
   - **Consider External Factors:** Analyze how industry changes, regulatory updates and competitor activity might impact your brand perception.

Example: The company might discover that while website traffic to educational materials is high, patient completion rates are low. Analyzing social media sentiment could reveal concerns about potential side effects not adequately addressed in their messaging. They might also identify a competitor launching a similar medication with a different communication strategy.

3. **Adapt and Refine Strategies:**
   - **Modify Your Messaging:** Address identified concerns, personalize content based on feedback, and ensure it remains aligned with evolving needs and trends.
   - **Optimize Communication Channels:** Experiment with new channels, adjust content formats based on engagement data, and tailor your approach to different stakeholder groups.
   - **Continuously Learn and Iterate:** Never stop seeking new insights, conduct ongoing research, and be willing to adjust your strategy based on data and feedback.

   Example: The company might develop shorter, more engaging educational videos to improve patient completion rates. They might address messaging and utilize patient testimonials to build trust. Additionally, they might explore influencer marketing partnerships to reach new patient segments.

4. **Be Agile and Responsive:**
   - **Stay Attuned to Emerging Trends and Unexpected Events:** Respond quickly to crises, address negative feedback, and leverage new opportunities.
   - **Be Flexible in Your Approach:** Don't be afraid to experiment, test new strategies, and adapt to changing audience preferences.
   - **Prioritize Continuous Improvement:** View adaptation as an ongoing process, not a one-time fix.

   Example: The company might quickly address negative social media comments about potential side effects with transparent communication and factual information. Following new regulatory guidance on managing potential risks, they might adapt new messaging and content.

Remember:

- **Data-driven Decision-making is Key:** Base your adaptations on concrete evidence and insights, not intuition.

- **Transparency and Ethical Communication are Paramount:** Be upfront about any changes, address concerns openly, and maintain responsible information practices.
- **Collaboration is Crucial:** Involve relevant teams in monitoring, analysis, and adaptation to ensure alignment and effectiveness.

By continuously monitoring your impact, adapting your strategies based on data and feedback, and remaining agile in a dynamic environment, you can ensure your pharma brand's message continues to resonate with your audience, building trust and achieving long-term success. Remember, the most beautiful symphony requires constant adjustments and fine-tuning. So, conduct your monitoring with diligence, adapt with agility, and watch your brand's voice evolve into a harmonious melody that resonates with stakeholders throughout the ever-changing healthcare landscape.

CHAPTER

44

Symphony of Applications: Expanding the Reach of Communications

Artificial Intelligence (AI) can play a crucial role in expanding the reach of marketing communication to all stakeholders within the pharmaceutical industry. Here is how:

1. **Hyper-Targeting and Personalization:**
   - AI can analyze vast patient demographics, medical history, and online behavior datasets to identify and target specific patient groups with relevant information about new treatments or disease awareness campaigns.
   - Chatbots powered by AI can answer patient questions 24/7 in a personalized manner, catering to individual needs and concerns.

Hyper-Targeting:

Imagine a net cast so fine it only catches specific fish. Hyper-targeting with AI in pharma marketing works similarly. AI can analyze a vast data pool to identify highly specific patient groups most likely to benefit from a particular drug or treatment. Here is how it breaks down:

- **Data Sources**: AI gathers data from various sources, including electronic health records (EHRs), pharmacy dispensing records, online surveys, social media activity, and wearables (with patient consent).

- **Advanced Analytics**: AI algorithms analyze this data to identify patterns and segment patients based on factors like:
    - Demographics (age, gender, location)
    - Medical history (diagnoses, medications, allergies)
    - Online behavior (searches for medical information, participation in online health communities)
    - Socioeconomic factors (income, education level)

By creating these highly granular patient segments, pharma companies can target their marketing communication with laser precision.

Hyper-Targeting Example:

- **Disease Awareness Campaign**: A pharmaceutical company developing a new migraine medication utilizes AI to target its awareness campaign. AI analyzes data points like online searches for "migraine symptoms" and prescription history for migraine medications. It then identifies specific segments like:
    - Women aged 25-45 with a history of frequent headaches.
    - People who live in high-stress urban areas searched for information about alternative migraine treatments. With this hyper-targeted approach, the company can reach individuals most likely interested in learning about their new medication.

Personalization:

Once AI identifies the right audience, it personalizes the communication to resonate with each individual. This goes beyond just using a name in an email. Here are some examples:

- **Content Tailoring**: AI can personalize the content of messages based on the patient's needs and medical history. For example, a message about a new diabetes medication might highlight different benefits for a newly diagnosed patient compared to someone who has been managing the condition for years.

- **Channel Selection**: AI can determine each patient's most effective communication channel. For instance, some patients prefer educational videos, while others respond better to text messages with medication reminders.
- **Language Optimization**: AI can analyze past campaign data to understand which language and tone resonate best with different demographics. This ensures the message is clear, culturally appropriate, and emotionally relevant.

Personalization Example:

- **Post-Diagnosis Support**: After a patient is diagnosed with a chronic condition like high blood pressure, they receive a series of personalized emails from the pharmaceutical company that developed a new blood pressure medication. AI tailors the content based on the patient's specific situation:
  - The first email might be an educational video explaining high blood pressure and its management.
  - Subsequent emails could address concerns based on the patient's age and medical history. For example, an email for a younger patient might focus on lifestyle changes, while an email for an older patient might discuss potential medication interactions.
  - These emails could also prompt the patient to sign up for a medication adherence program or connect with a support group.
  - These are just a couple of examples, but they showcase the power of AI in hyper-targeting and tailoring communication for maximum impact.

Benefits of Hyper-Targeting and Personalization:

- **Increased Engagement**: Highly relevant and personalized messages are more likely to grab attention and lead to action, such as visiting a doctor, attending a webinar, or signing up for a clinical trial.

- **Improved Patient Outcomes**: Patients receiving targeted information about medications tailored to their specific condition are more likely to adhere to treatment plans and experience better health outcomes.
- **Enhanced Brand Reputation**: Personalized communication demonstrates that pharma companies understand individual patient needs, fostering trust and loyalty.
- **Resource Optimization**: Hyper-targeting avoids bombarding irrelevant audiences with generic messages, allowing for more focused marketing efforts that maximize returns on investment (ROI).

Ethical Considerations:

It's important to emphasize that data privacy and ethical considerations are paramount. Patient data must be collected and used by regulations and with the patient's consent. Transparency about data collection practices is key to building trust.

By leveraging AI for hyper-targeting and personalization, pharma companies can create a win-win situation: patients receive the information they need to make informed healthcare decisions, and companies can reach the right audience with the right message at the right time.

2. Multichannel Communication Management:

Multichannel communication management with AI in pharma marketing involves orchestrating a seamless and coordinated flow of information across various channels to reach target audiences effectively. Here is a breakdown:

- AI can manage and orchestrate communication across various channels like email, social media, SMS, and healthcare provider portals.
- It can personalize messages for each channel, audience, and platform, ensuring the right message reaches the right person at the right time.

Challenges of Multichannel Communication:

Traditionally, managing multichannel communication across different channels like email, social media, healthcare provider portals, and SMS can take time and effort. Issues include:

- **Inconsistent Messaging**: Maintaining a consistent brand voice and message across diverse platforms can take time and effort.
- **Channel Overload**: Bombarding audiences with messages on every channel can lead to information overload and disengagement.
- **Data Silos**: Data from different channels might be siloed, making it difficult to understand audience behavior and tailor communication accordingly.

How AI Can Help:

AI brings the power of automation and intelligence to multichannel communication management:

- **Unified Platform**: AI-powered platforms can integrate with various communication channels, creating a centralized hub for managing content creation, scheduling, and performance monitoring.
- **Personalized Content Delivery**: AI can personalize messages based on audience data and channel specifics. For instance, emails might be longer and more detailed, while social media posts might be concise and visually engaging.
- **Dynamic Scheduling**: AI can analyze real-time data to schedule messages strategically. For example, an email about a new medication might be sent after a patient has watched a relevant educational video on the company's website.

Examples of Multichannel Communication Management with AI:

- **Disease Awareness Campaign**: A pharmaceutical company launches a campaign to raise awareness about a new diabetes medication. AI manages communication across various channels.

- **Social Media**: Posts with infographics and patient testimonials are scheduled on platforms like Facebook and Twitter (X, now).
- **Email Marketing**: Personalized emails with targeted information about the disease and treatment options are sent to individuals identified as pre-diabetic through AI analysis.
- **Healthcare Provider Portals**: Secure healthcare provider portals deliver targeted messages with clinical trial data and educational resources to relevant doctors.
  - **Post-Surgical Pain Management**: A company launches a new pain medication after surgery. AI manages communication:
  - **Pre-Surgery**: Patients receive informative SMS messages about the medication and potential side effects a few days before surgery.
  - **Post-Surgery**: A series of personalized emails are sent with tips on managing pain and medication adherence reminders.
  - **Mobile App**: Patients can access an educational app with video tutorials and medication dosage information integrated with the AI communication platform.

These examples showcase how AI can create a cohesive and personalized communication experience across different channels, maximizing reach and engagement with target audiences.

3. Language Optimization and Content Creation:

Language optimization and content creation with AI in pharma marketing is all about using AI's analytical power to craft compelling messages that resonate with target audiences. Here is a deeper dive:

Understanding Your Audience:

The first step is understanding your target audience's needs, preferences, and communication styles. Traditionally, this might involve market research surveys or focus groups. AI, however, can analyze vast troves of existing data to gain deeper insights:

- **Social Media Analysis**: AI can analyze social media conversations to understand patients' language to discuss their conditions, concerns, and preferred information sources.
- **Website Analytics**: AI can analyze website visitor behavior to understand what type of content resonates best with different audience segments (e.g., short explainer videos vs. in-depth research articles).
- **Customer Reviews**: Analyzing customer reviews of existing medications or treatments can reveal pain points, misunderstandings, and preferred communication styles.

AI-Powered Language Optimization:

Once you understand your audience, AI can help you optimize your language for maximum impact:

- **Readability Score**: AI can analyze content to ensure it is written at an appropriate reading level for the target audience. This is crucial, especially for complex medical information.
- **Sentiment Analysis**: AI can analyze existing marketing materials to identify which language evokes positive emotions, trust, and a sense of understanding in your audience.
- **Cultural Nuances**: AI can help identify culturally appropriate language and avoid misunderstandings in global marketing campaigns.

AI-Assisted Content Creation:

AI can be a powerful tool for creating targeted and engaging content:

- **Blog Posts and Articles**: AI can suggest relevant topics, generate headlines, and even draft initial blog posts that human editors can refine with their expertise.
- **Social Media Content**: AI can analyze trending topics and suggest engaging social media posts tailored to specific patient segments (e.g., young adults vs. older demographics).

- **Personalized Video Scripts**: AI can analyze patient data and generate personalized video scripts that address their concerns about a medication or health condition.

Examples of Language Optimization and Content Creation with AI:

- **Campaign for a New Asthma Medication**: AI analyzes social media conversations to understand how patients describe their asthma symptoms. The campaign uses this language to create relatable and informative content like:
  - **Blog Post**: "Tired of Struggling to Breathe? Understanding and Managing Asthma."
  - **Social Media Video**: A short animation explaining how the new medication works, narrated clearly and concisely.
- **Educational Materials for Diabetes Medication**: AI analyzes website data to determine which type of content resonates best with newly diagnosed patients. The company creates:
  - **Interactive infographics**: Visually engaging infographics explaining blood sugar levels and management techniques.
  - **Simple Explainer Videos**: Short, clear videos using language appropriate for patients unfamiliar with diabetes terminology.

These examples show how AI can help pharma companies go beyond dry medical jargon and create content that resonates with patients on an emotional and infomrational leve. AI empowers pharma companies to deliver clear, informative, and engaging communication by optimizing language and tailoring content to specific needs.

4. Physician Engagement and Education:

Physician engagement and education are crucial aspects of pharma marketing, and AI can significantly enhance these efforts. Here's a detailed explanation:

- AI can be used to create targeted educational content for physicians about new medications, treatment options, and clinical trial opportunities.

- Chatbots can answer doctors' specific questions about a drug's mechanism of action, side effects, or dosage recommendations.

Challenges in Physician Engagement:

Traditionally, engaging physician often involves:

- **Time-Consuming In-Person Meetings**: Physicians have busy schedules, making scheduling regular face-to-face meetings with pharma representatives challenging.
- **Generic Information Overload**: Physicians receive constant information from various sources. Generic product presentations might not resonate with their specific needs and patient population.
- **Difficulty Staying Updated**: The medical field constantly evolves, and keeping physicians informed about the latest research and treatment options can take time and effort.

How AI Can Help:

AI offers innovative solutions to these challenges:

- **Personalized Learning Experiences**: AI can analyze physicians' prescribing habits, research interests, and patient demographics. It can then curate personalized educational content like:
  - **Targeted Online Module**: Focused on specific disease areas or treatment options relevant to the physician's practice.
  - **Case Studies**: Real-world case studies showcasing how the physician's peers use the new medication in their practice.
  - **Microlearning Opportunities**: AI can deliver bite-sized educational content in various formats like:
  - **Short Video Tutorials**: Concise videos explaining a new medication's mechanism of action and clinical benefits.
  - **Interactive Infographics**: Engaging infographics summarizing key clinical trial data in an easily digestible format.

- **24/7 Virtual Assistants**: AI-powered virtual assistants can answer physicians' specific questions about a drug's safety profile, dosage recommendations, or potential drug interactions.

Examples of Physician Engagement and Education with AI:

- **Launch of a New Oncology Drug**: A pharmaceutical company leverages AI to engage oncologists:
  - **Personalized Learning Portal**: Physicians receive access to a secure online portal with curated content based on their practice area (e.g., lung cancer vs. breast cancer).
  - **Interactive Case Studies**: The portal features real-world case studies showcasing how other oncologists have successfully used the new drug in their patients.
  - **AI-Powered Chatbot**: Physicians can access a 24/7 chatbot to ask specific questions about the drug's side effects or potential interactions with other medications they frequently prescribe.
  - **Continuing Medical Education (CME) Programs**: A pharma company collaborates with a medical association to develop AI-powered CME programs:
  - **Adaptive Learning Modules**: The CME programs use AI to adapt to the physician's learning pace and knowledge gaps, focusing on improvement areas.
  - **Interactive Quizzes**: AI-powered quizzes reinforce key takeaways from the CME modules and personalize the learning experience.

By providing physicians with relevant, accessible, and personalized educational experiences, AI fosters deeper engagement and empowers them to make informed patient treatment decisions. This ultimately benefits both the pharmaceutical company and patient care.

5. Investor and Partner Communication:

AI can transform investor and partner communication in the pharmaceutical industry by streamlining processes, delivering targeted information, and enhancing transparency. Here's a breakdown:

- AI can generate reports and presentations summarizing clinical trial data, market trends, and financial performance for investors and partners.
- It can personalize communications highlighting key information relevant to each stakeholder group.

Challenges in Investor and Partner Communication:

Traditionally, communication with investors and partners can be:

- **Time-Consuming and Labor-Intensive**: Preparing reports, presentations, and responding to inquiries can significantly burden management teams.
- **Generic and One-Size-Fits-All**: Generic communication might not cater to the specific information needs of different investor groups or partners.
- **Lack of Real-Time Data Access**: Investors and partners might not have immediate access to the latest data on clinical trials, financial performance, or market trends.

How AI Can Help:

AI offers innovative solutions to these challenges, fostering more efficient and effective communication:

- **Automated Report Generation**: AI can analyze vast amounts of data to generate comprehensive reports on clinical trial progress, financial performance, and market analysis. These reports can be customized based on the audience (e.g., investors vs. potential licensing partners).
- **Dynamic Presentations and Q&A Support**: AI can generate dynamic presentations with data visualizations and key takeaways tailored to the specific interests of investors or partners. Additionally, AI-powered chatbots can answer questions during presentations, freeing executives for more in-depth discussions.

- **Real-Time Data Dashboards**: AI can create secure online dashboards that give investors and partners real-time access to key metrics like stock performance, clinical trial enrollment numbers, and upcoming milestones. This fosters transparency and builds trust.

Examples of Investor and Partner Communications with AI:

- **Quarterly Earnings Reports**: A pharmaceutical company leverages AI to automate the creation of its quarterly earnings reports:
    - **Financial Analysis**: AI analyzes financial data and generates charts and graphs highlighting key performance indicators (KPIs) relevant to investors.
    - **Market Trends**: AI incorporates market research data into the report, providing investors with insights into the competitive landscape and potential growth opportunities.
    - **Executive Summary**: AI generates a concise and informative executive summary that key investors can quickly digest.
- **Partnership for a New Drug Delivery System**: A pharmaceutical company partners with a biotech company to develop a novel drug delivery system. AI facilitates communication:
    - **Collaborative Platform**: AI powers a secure online platform where both companies can share research data, track project progress, and communicate seamlessly.
    - **Milestone Tracking**: The platform uses AI to track project milestones and automatically generate reports for both companies' leadership teams.

Using AI to streamline communication and provide real-time data access, pharmaceutical companies can build stronger relationships with investors and partners. This fosters trust and transparency and ultimately drives the success of new drug development and commercialization efforts.

6. **Building Trust and Transparency:**

Building trust and transparency is paramount in the pharmaceutical industry, and AI can be a powerful tool in achieving this goal. Here is how:

- AI-powered chatbots can provide real-time customer service and answer patient questions about potential side effects or drug interactions, fostering trust and transparency.
- AI can analyze social media sentiment to identify and address concerns early, mitigating potential reputational risks.

Challenges in Building Trust and Transparency:

- **Past Controversies**: The pharmaceutical industry has been criticized for practices like high drug prices or selecting reporting of clinical trial data, which has eroded public trust.
- **Complex Medical Information**: Communicating complex medical information to patients clearly and understandably can be challenging.
- **Misinformation and Negative Bias**: Negative media coverage or online misinformation can create a climate of distrust.

How AI Can Help:

AI offers innovative solutions to these challenges by promoting open communication and addressing concerns:

- **Proactive Patient Education**: AI can personalize educational content for patients about their conditions, potential treatment options, and side effects. This empowers patients to make informed decisions about their healthcare.
- **Real-Time Monitoring and Addressing Concerns**: AI can monitor social media conversations and online forums to identify patient concerns about a drug's safety or efficacy. This allows for prompt responses and proactive management of potential reputational risks.
- **Transparency in Clinical Trials**: AI can be used to create interactive platforms where patients can access information

about ongoing clinical trials, including inclusion/exclusion criteria and preliminary results. This fosters transparency and builds trust in the research process.

Examples of Building Trust and Transparency with AI:

- **Addressing Medication Side Effects**: A pharmaceutical company leverages AI to:
  - **Monitor Social Media**: AI monitors social media platforms for mentions of the company's medication and potential side effects.
  - **AI-Powered Chatbot Support**: A 24/7 AI-powered chatbot answers patient questions about the medication, including potential side effects and how to manage them.
  - **Targeted Educational Resources**: The chatbot can direct patients to personalized educational resources based on their concerns.
- **Transparency in a New Pain Medication Launch**: A pharmaceutical company utilizes AI for transparency throughout the launch of a new pain medication:
- **Interactive Clinical Trial Platform**: An online platform provides patients with clear explanations of the ongoing clinical trial process, including participant demographics and key metrics.
- **Real-Time Data Updates**: The platform allows patients to access real-time progress updates on the clinical trial, fostering trust and engagement.
- **Open Communication with Media**: AI helps analyze media inquiries and identify potential concerns. The company can then proactively address these concerns with clear and factual information.

By fostering open communication, addressing concerns promptly, and empowering patients with information, AI can be a valuable tool for building trust and transparency in the pharmaceutical industry. This not only benefits the companies themselves but also fosters a more informed and empowered patient population.

The Synergy with Humans

While AI excels at data analysis and content personalization, human expertise remains crucial. Here is where the magic of "Human+AI" comes in:

- **Strategic Direction**: Humans set the overall communication strategy, define target audiences, and determine the brand voice.
- **Creative Content Development**: Humans craft compelling narratives and emotionally engaging content that resonates with audiences.
- **Ethical Considerations**: Humans ensure AI-generated communication adheres to ethical guidelines and regulations.

By combining human creativity and strategic oversight with AI's data-driven capabilities, pharmaceutical companies can achieve a new level of targeted, personalized, and effective communication with all stakeholders. This *Synergy of Minds* will be a critical driver of the pharmaceutical marketing revolution. Here is how this synergy plays out in pharmaceutical marketing:

AI's Strengths:

- **Data Analysis and Insights**: AI can analyze vast datasets to identify trends, segment audiences, and predict patient behavior with unmatched accuracy.
- **Personalization at Scale**: AI can simultaneously personalize communication for thousands or even millions of patients, ensuring relevant and targeted messages.
- **Content Creation Efficiency**: AI can generate drafts, identify trending topics, and automate content creation tasks, freeing human time for more strategic work.

Human Strengths:

- **Strategic Thinking and Creativity**: Humans set the overall communication strategy, define brand voice, and develop compelling narratives that resonate with audiences on an emotional level.

- **Ethical Considerations and Transparency**: Humans ensure AI-generated communication adheres to ethical guidelines and data privacy regulations and fosters trust with patients.
- **Emotional Intelligence and Empathy**: Humans understand the emotional aspects of healthcare and can craft communications that address patients' anxieties, hopes, and concerns.

The Synergy in Action:

Imagine a team of marketing professionals working alongside AI. Here is how they can leverage each other's strengths:

1. **Human Strengths Define Goals**: The marketing team defines the communication goals, target audiences, and brand messaging.
2. **AI Analyzes Data**: AI analyzes patient data, social media conversations, and market trends to identify opportunities and refine the target audience segments.
3. **Humans Craft Compelling Content**: The marketing team creates compelling content (blog posts, videos) based on AI insights and tailors it to specific audience segments.
4. **AI Personalizes Communication**: AI personalizes each patient's content and delivery channels (email, social media), ensuring maximum reach and engagement.
5. **Humans Monitor and Adapt**: The marketing team monitors campaign performance and uses AI data to continuously optimize and adapt communication strategies.

This synergy between human vision and AI execution creates a powerful and effective marketing approach.

Benefits of the Human+AI Synergy:

- **More Effective Communication**: By combining AI's data-driven insights with human creativity and emotional intelligence, pharma companies can create communication that resonates more deeply with patients.

- **Improved Patient Outcomes**: Personalized communication can empower patients to make informed decisions about their healthcare and adhere to treatment plans more effectively.
- **Enhanced Brand Reputation**: The human+AI approach fosters transparency, trust, and patient-centric communication, which can strengthen brand reputation in the pharmaceutical industry.

The future of pharmaceutical marketing lies in the power of synergy between human and artificial intelligence. By leveraging AI's analytical capabilities and human expertise in strategy, creativity, and ethics, pharmaceutical companies can orchestrate a marketing revolution that benefits patients, healthcare providers, and the industry.

CHAPTER 45

Composing Compelling Content

A Step-by-Step Guide to Content Creation and Optimization in Pharma Branding

In pharma branding, where trust and information are paramount, crafting captivating content is analogous to composing a symphony that resonates with your audience. Here is a step-by-step guide to navigating this musical journey:

1. **Define Your Content Objectives**:
   - **Align with your Overall Brand Strategy**: Is your goal to raise awareness, educate patients, build trust with HCPs, or establish thought leadership?
   - **Set SMART Objectives**: Define measurable, achievable, and relevant goals for each content piece, such as increasing website traffic, video completion rates, or social media engagement metrics.

Example: A company launching a new diabetes medication might aim to educate patients about treatment options, increase brand awareness among HCPs, and establish its expertise in diabetes management. Their content objectives could be to increase website traffic to patient education materials by 20 percent, achieve a 70 percent completion rate for HCP-targeted explainer videos, and secure the publication of two thought leadership articles in major medical journals within a year.

2. **Understand Your Audience**:
    - **Segment Your Audience**: Identify different stakeholder groups (patients, HCPs, investors, etc.) and their unique needs, preferences, and information consumption habits.
    - **Conduct Audience Research**: Utilize surveys, focus groups, and social media listening to gain deeper insights into their pain points, language preferences, and preferred content formats.

Example: The company might segment patients by disease stage, treatment experience, and preferred information sources. Research could reveal that patients prefer short, visually engaging content, while HCPs favor evidence-based articles and webinars.

3. **Choose the Right Content Format**:
    - **Align format with objectives and Audience**: Use infographics for quick data overviews, explainer videos for complex topics, blog posts for in-depth discussions, and social media posts for community engagement.
    - **Consider Emerging Formats**: Experiment with interactive content, podcasts, or virtual reality experiences for a more immersive learning experience.

Example: For patients, the company might develop visually appealing infographics about managing diabetes, create short animated videos explaining medication benefits, and publish blog posts addressing common patient concerns. For HCPs, they might produce webinars with clinical trial data, develop interactive case studies, and collaborate with KOLs on podcast interviews.

4. **Craft Compelling Content**:
    - **Focus on Value and Relevance**: Deliver valuable information, address audience needs, and offer solutions to their problems.
    - **Maintain Transparency and Accuracy**: Ensure content is factually accurate, cites credible sources, and complies with regulatory guidelines.

- **Tell Stories and Evoke Emotions**: Use storytelling techniques, data visualizations, and patient testimonials to connect with your audience emotionally.

Example: Patient education materials might use relatable stories of individuals managing diabetes successfully, while HCP-targeted data might showcase patient outcomes and expert opinions. Both formats should prioritize clear, concise language and transparency about potential risks and benefits.

5. **Optimize for Search Engines and Distribution**
   - **Conduct Keyword Research**: Identify relevant keywords and optimize your content titles, meta descriptions, and website structure for search visibility.
   - **Promote Your Content**: Utilize social media channels, email marketing, influencer partnerships, and industry publications to reach your target audience.
   - **Monitor and Track Performance**: Analyze website traffic, social media engagement, and content download rates to track progress and identify areas of improvement.

Example: The company might optimize website content for relevant diabetes-related keywords and promote educational materials through patient advocacy group partnerships and social media advertising. They might also track website traffic sources and adjust their distribution strategy based on performance data.

Remember:

- **Content Creation is an Ongoing Process**: Regularly refresh existing content, create new formats, and experiment with different approaches.
- **Collaboration is Key**: Involve subject matter experts, communication teams, and digital marketing specialists for content development and optimization.
- **Always Prioritize Ethical Considerations**: Maintain data privacy, avoid misleading information, and ensure transparency in all content creation efforts.

By following these steps and tailoring your content to resonate with your audience, you can compose an impactful symphony of information that builds trust, educates stakeholders, and propels your pharma brand to new heights in the competitive healthcare landscape. Compelling content is the lifeblood of your brand communication, so keep composing, optimizing, and refining your message to leave a lasting impression on your audience.

AI's Role in Content Creation

In pharma branding, AI is emerging as a powerful tool to enhance and even revolutionize content creation and optimization. Here's how AI can play a role in each stage of the process.

1. **Defining Content Objectives**:
    - **AI-Powered Sentiment Analysis**: Analyze vast amounts of online data to understand audience needs, concerns, and emerging trends, which will inform your content objectives.
    - **Predictive Analytics**: Forecast potential content performance based on past successes and industry benchmarks, aiding in setting SMART objectives.

   Examples: AI might analyze social media discussions about different diabetes treatment options to identify topics patients are most interested in or concerned about. It could also predict the reach and engagement of different content formats based on historical data.

2. **Understanding Your Audience**:
    - **AI-Driven Audience Segmentation**: Automatically segment audiences based on demographics, online behavior, and social media interactions, providing deeper insights into their needs and preferences.
    - **Natural Language Processing (NLP)**: Analyze unstructured data, such as customer reviews and social media comments, to understand your audience's emotional undertones and hidden pain points.

Example: AI might segment patients based on their online discussions about specific disease management challenges, such as medication adherence or managing side effects. NLP could analyze patient reviews to identify recurring concerns and phrases that reveal emotional aspects of their experiences.

3. **Choosing the Right Content Format**:
    - **AI-Powered Content Recommendations**: Utilize AI to suggest optimal content formats based on audience preferences, industry trends, and the performance of similar content.
    - **Automated Content Personalization**: AI can personalize content delivery, suggesting specific articles, videos, or resources based on user profiles and interests.

Example: AI might recommend creating an infographic to explain a complex medication mechanism based on high engagement with similar visual content in the past. It could also personalize patient education materials by suggesting resources relevant to their disease stage or treatment concerns.

4. **Craft Compelling Content**:

- **AI-Powered Copywriting**: Utilize AI tools to generate creative headlines, draft content outlines, and suggest relevant keywords, helping with brainstorming and overcoming writer's block.
- **AI-Powered Storytelling**: Leverage AI to analyze successful storytelling trends and recommend narrative structures, character archetypes, and emotional hooks to enhance your content.

Example: AI might help craft compelling headlines for patient education materials or suggest storylines for explainer videos based on best practices in healthcare communication. However, remember that human oversight and ethical considerations are crucial to ensure factual accuracy and adherence to regulatory guidelines.

5. **Optimize for Search Engines and Distribution**:

- **AI-Powered SEO Optimization**: Suggest relevant keywords, optimize title tags and meta descriptions, and identify target audiences for improved search engine ranking.
- **AI-Driven Content Promotion**: Analyze past campaign data and recommend optimal distribution channels and target audiences for each piece of content.

Example: AI might recommend promoting a specific blog post on relevant patient forums or suggest partnering with specific influencers based on their reach and audience demographics. Remember, responsible use and ethical marketing practices are paramount in pharma communication.

Thus, AI can be a valuable tool for content creation and optimization, boosting efficiency, generating new ideas, and personalizing content for your audience. However, it is crucial to remember that AI does not replace human judgment, creativity, and ethical considerations. Use AI strategically and human expertise to ensure your pharma branding content remains informative, trustworthy, and impactful.

CHAPTER

46

Harmonizing Communication: Personalized Marketing and Engagement in Pharma Branding

In pharma branding, where trust and individual needs are paramount, personalized marketing and engagement are no longer options but necessary. Here's a step-by-step guide to orchestrating a symphony of personalized communication:

1. **Define Your Personalization Objectives**:
   - **Align with Your Overall Brand Strategy**: Are you aiming to improve patient adherence, build brand loyalty, or drive specific treatment adoption?
   - **Set SMART Objectives**: Define measurable, achievable, and relevant goals for your personalized approach, like increased engagement with personalized email campaigns or higher medication refill rates among targeted patient segments.

Example: A company managing a diabetes medication might aim to personalize patient communication to improve medication adherence, leading to better health outcomes. Their personalized marketing objectives could be to increase the open rate of medication reminder emails by 15 percent and achieve a 20 percent reduction in missed refills within six months.

2. **Understand Your Audience on a Deeper Level**:
   - **Segment by Relevant Factors**: Go beyond demographics and segment patients based on disease stage, treatment history, medication adherence patterns, and preferred communication channels.

- **Gather Individual Data**: Utilize patient surveys, medical records (with informed consent), and website interactions to understand individual needs, concerns, and preferences.

Example: The company might segment patients by risk of complications and adherence challenges based on refill data and preferred communication channels (email, SMS, or mobile app notifications). They also gather feedback through surveys about patient concerns and preferred information formats.

3. **Develop Personalized Content and Messaging**:
    - **Tailor Content to Individual Needs**: Offer educational materials for their specific disease stage, address their identified concerns, and suggest resources relevant to their medication adherence challenges.
    - **Craft Personalized Messages**: Use their name, acknowledge their specific situation, and offer targeted support or encouragement based on their data.

Example: The company might develop personalized email campaigns reminding patients about upcoming refills, offer educational videos relevant to their specific risk factors, and send motivational messages based on their adherence history. They might also use their preferred name and acknowledge their recent challenges or successes in managing diabetes.

4. **Utilize Personalized Marketing Channels**:
    - **Leverage Multiple Channels**: Utilize emails, SMS, mobile apps, social media, and even targeted online advertising to reach patients on their preferred channels.
    - **Personalize Delivery**: Adapt the timing and frequency of messages based on individual preferences and medication schedules.

Example: The company might send medication reminders via SMS a few hours before the patient's usual dose time, push personalized educational content for their mobile app based on their recent interactions, and use targeted social media ads with messages relevant to their concerns.

5. **Measure and Adapt**:
   - **Track Engagement and Impact**: Monitor open rates, click-throughs, website traffic, and medication refill rates to assess the effectiveness of your personalized approach.
   - **Continuously Refine Your Strategy**: Use data-driven insights to optimize segmentation, personalize content more effectively, and adapt communication channels based on patient preferences and engagement patterns.

   Example: The company might analyze which personalized email formats have the highest engagement rates and adjust their content strategy accordingly. They might also experiment with different reminder frequencies and channels based on patient feedback and adherence data.

Remember:

- **Privacy and Transparency are Paramount**: Obtain informed consent for data collection, ensure data security, and be transparent about how their information is used.
- **Ethical Considerations are Crucial**: Avoid stigmatizing language, prioritize patient well-being over sales goals, and respect individual communication preferences.
- **Personalization is an Ongoing Journey**: Continuously gather feedback, experiment with new approaches, and adapt your strategy to maintain relevance and effectiveness.

By following these steps and prioritizing ethical considerations, you can orchestrate a personalized marketing and engagement strategy that resonates with your audience individually. This, in turn, fosters trust, builds loyalty, and ultimately leads to better health outcomes for patients— the true symphony of success in pharma branding.

AI's Role in Personalized Marketing and Engagement in Pharma Branding

In personalized marketing and engagement in pharma branding, AI is becoming a transformative force by automating tasks, extracting insights, and delivering individualized experiences to patients. Here's how AI can play a crucial role in each stage of the process:

1. **Define Personalization Objectives:**
   - **AI-Powered Predictive Analytics:** Forecast the potential impact of personalized campaigns on medication adherence, brand loyalty, or treatment adoption, aiding in setting achievable and relevant objectives.
   - **AI-Driven Sentiment Analysis:** Analyze data from social media, patient forums, and surveys to understand patients' broader concerns and unmet needs, which will inform your overall personalization strategy.

   Example: AI might predict the potential increase in refill rates based on the success of similar personalized email campaigns in the past. It could also analyze patient discussions on social media to identify emerging concerns or preferences that could be addressed through personalized communication.

2. **Understanding your Audience on a Deeper Level:**
   - **AI-Powered Customer Segmentation:** Automatically segment patients based on vast datasets, including medical records (with informed consent), website interaction data, and social media behavior, revealing deeper patterns and hidden groups.
   - **Natural Language Processing (NLP):** Analyze unstructured data, such as patient feedback and online reviews, to identify individual concerns, emotional undertones, and nuanced language that might reveal specific needs or preferences.

   Example: AI might segment patients based on their online discussions about specific medication side effects, uncovering hidden groups experiencing unique challenges. NLP could analyze patient feedback on different healthcare apps to identify recurring concerns and personalize future versions to address them more effectively.

3. **Develop Personalized Content and Messaging:**
   - **AI-Powered Content Generation:** Utilize AI to personalize headlines, draft email subject lines, and suggest relevant content snippets based on individual patient data and preferences.
   - **AI-Driven Storytelling:** Leverage AI to analyze successful personalized content and recommend narrative structures or emotional hooks that resonate with specific patient segments.

Example: AI might personalize email subject lines with the patient's name and a reference to their recent medication refill history. It could also suggest educational videos tailored to their disease stage and preferred learning style. Human oversight and ethical considerations are crucial to ensure accuracy and compliance.

4. **Utilize Personalized Marketing Channels:**
   - **AI-Powered Channel Optimization:** Based on each patient's engagement history and preferred platforms, recommend optimal communication channels (email, SMS, mobile app notifications).
   - **Real-Time Personalization:** Utilize AI to adapt message timing and frequency based on individual behavior, such as sending medication reminders closer to their usual dose time if they historically tend to forget.

Example: AI might recommend switching patients from email to SMS notifications if they show higher engagement with mobile messages. It could also adapt the timing of reminders based on their past refill behavior, sending prompts earlier if they miss refills.

5. **Measure and Adapt:**
   - **AI-Powered Analytics Dashboards:** Use AI-powered dashboards to monitor engagement metrics, track impact on desired outcomes, and identify areas for improvement in real-time.

- **Automated Optimization:** Utilize AI to automatically adjust personalized messaging content, delivery channels, and campaign frequency based on real-time performance data.

Example: AI might identify specific email formats that lead to higher medication refills for a particular patient segment and automatically adjust future campaigns accordingly. It could also experiment with different reminder timings and analyze their impact on adherence rates, recommending optimal approaches for each patient.

Remember:

- **AI is a Tool, not a Replacement:** Human expertise and ethical considerations remain crucial for responsible data handling, crafting authentic messages, and ensuring patient privacy.
- **Transparency and Trust are Keys:** Be transparent about how AI is used, inform patients about data collection, and prioritize their well-being.
- **Continuous Learning and Adaptation:** AI constantly evolves, so stay updated on its capabilities, experiment with new applications, and refine your strategy based on emerging insights and ethical considerations.

By integrating AI responsibly and strategically, you can orchestrate a symphony of personalized marketing and engagement that truly resonates with your patients, building trust, improving health outcomes, and achieving a connection previously unimaginable in pharma branding.

CHAPTER

47

AI in Regulatory Compliance and Risk Management

In the intricate world of pharma branding, where strict regulations and patient safety reign supreme, ensuring regulatory compliance and risk management is not just a step— it's the foundation upon which success is built. Here's a step-by-step guide to navigating this complex maze and exploring the potential of AI to enhance your journey:

1. **Understand the Regulatory Landscape**:
   - **Identify Relevant Regulations**: Familiarize yourself with the regulatory bodies applicable to your area (FDA, EMA) and their pharma marketing and branding guidelines.
   - **Stay Updated on Changes**: Regulations evolve, so subscribe to regulatory body updates and industry publications to stay informed about potential changes and emerging requirements.

Examples: A US-based company launching a new diabetes medication must be well-versed in FDA regulations governing drug advertising and promotion. They must stay updated on ongoing discussions or revisions on specific claims or labeling requirements.

2. **Conduct Risk Assessments**:
   - **Identify Potential Risks**: Analyze your branding activities for non-compliance issues, misleading claims, or safety

concerns. Consider risks associated with content creation, distribution channels, and promotional campaigns.

- **Prioritize and Mitigate Risks**: Assess the probability and severity of each risk, prioritize based on potential impact, and implement mitigation strategies like internal training, pre-approval processes, and legal review.

Example: The company might identify risks of overstating the medication's efficacy or failing to disclose relevant side effects in its promotional materials. They might mitigate these risks by developing internal review processes, involving legal counsel, and ensuring all claims are factually accurate and compliant with regulations.

3. **Implement Compliance Measures**:
   - **Develop Clear Policies and Procedures**: Establish internal policies and procedures for content creation, review, and approval that align with regulatory requirements.
   - **Train Your Team**: Educate your marketing, branding, and communication teams on regulatory guidelines and relevant compliance best practices.

Example: The company might develop a brand compliance policy defining acceptable claims, requiring pre-approval for all marketing materials, and mandating training for employees involved in content creation.

4. **Monitor and Track Compliance**:
   - **Conduct Regular Audits**: Conduct internal audits to assess compliance with your policies and procedures and identify potential deviations.
   - **Track Industry Developments**: Stay appraised of regulatory enforcement actions and industry trends to address emerging compliance challenges proactively.

Example: The company might conduct regular audits of marketing materials and campaigns to ensure adherence to its policies and address any identified issues promptly. It might also track ongoing regulatory discussions and adapt its compliance practices accordingly.

AI's Role in Regulatory Compliance and Risk Management

While AI cannot replace human expertise and judgment in this critical area, it can be a valuable tool for enhancing efficiency, accuracy, and risk identification:

- **Automating Data Analysis:** AI can analyze vast regulatory documents and industry publications to identify relevant updates and potential compliance risks.
- **Detecting Non-Compliant Language:** AI-powered natural language processing (NLP) can scan marketing materials for potentially misleading claims or off-label promotion, flagging areas for human review.
- **Predictive Risk Assessment:** AI algorithms can analyze historical data and identify patterns to predict potential compliance risks associated with specific content or marketing strategies.

Remember:

- **Ethical Considerations are Paramount:** Ensure AI aligns with regulatory requirements and prioritizes patient safety and transparency.
- **Human Oversight Remains Crucial:** Regulatory experts with deep domain knowledge should always carefully review and interpret AI recommendations.
- **Compliance is an Ongoing Journey:** Continuously learn, adapt, and leverage innovative tools to navigate the evolving regulatory landscape.

By diligently following these steps and exploring the potential of AI responsibly, you can navigate the intricate maze of regulatory compliance and risk management, building a solid foundation for your pharma branding strategy that prioritizes safety, transparency, and ethical considerations. Remember, ensuring compliance is not just a requirement; it's a commitment to building trust and protecting the well-being of your patients, the true north star in the world of pharma branding.

CHAPTER

48

Optimizing the Sales and Distribution Symphony: A Step-by-Step Guide

In pharma branding, where reaching the right healthcare professionals (HCPs) and ensuring smooth medication access is crucial for success, sales and distribution optimization play a central role in the overall melody. Here's a step-by-step guide to orchestrating a harmonious distribution symphony and exploring how AI can enhance your efforts:

1. **Understand Your Landscape**:
   - **Identify Target Audience**: Segment HCPs by specialty, practice setting, and prescribing habits to tailor your sales and distribution approach.
   - **Analyze Market Dynamics**: Assess competitor strategies, emerging trends, and regulatory landscape to identify opportunities and challenges.

   Example: A company promoting a new diabetes medication might segment HCPs by endocrinologists, primary care physicians, and pharmacists, recognizing that each group has different prescribing needs and information preferences. The company might also analyze competitor marketing strategies and upcoming regulatory changes to adjust its distribution approach.
2. **Optimize Your Sales Team**:
   - **Train and Equip Your Team**: Ensure representatives have deep product knowledge, understand HCP needs, and effectively navigate regulatory restrictions.

- **Leverage Technology**: Utilize digital tools for territory management, data analysis, and targeted messaging to increase sales team efficiency.

Example: The company might provide in-depth training on the new medication's mechanism of action and clinical data. They might equip representatives with mobile apps for presenting clinical trial results and managing patient data while adhering to privacy regulations.

3. **Build Robust Distribution Channels**:
   - **Choose the Right Partners**: Select distributors with a strong reach, expertise in your therapeutic area, and compliance with regulations.
   - **Ensure Fair Pricing**, efficient delivery timelines, and effective inventory management practices to negotiate optimal terms.

Example: The company might partner with specialty distributors focusing on diabetes medications with key HCP groups. They might negotiate terms that incentivize timely delivery to pharmacies and ensure transparent pricing throughout the distribution chain.

4. **Utilize Effective Sales Tools**:
   - **Develop Impactful Marketing Materials**: Create evidence-based materials tailored to HCPs, highlighting the medication's benefits and addressing potential concerns.
   - **Embrace Digital Engagement**: Use webinars, online portals, and interactive tools to educate HCPs and conveniently offer valuable resources.

Example: The company might develop clinical case studies demonstrating the medication's effectiveness in different patient populations. They might also design interactive online tools for HCPs to assess patient eligibility and calculate optimal dosages.

5. **Track and Analyze Performance**:
   - **Monitor Key Metrics**: Track sales figures, market share, HCP engagement, and patient access rates to measure progress and identify areas for improvement.
   - **Conduct Regular Evaluations**: Analyze data to identify successful strategies, address underperforming channels, and refine your approach based on insights.

Example: The company might monitor the number of prescriptions written by different HCP groups and track which distribution channels offer the fastest delivery times. They might analyze engagement data from online tools to identify topics of interest for future educational materials.

AI's Role in Sales and Distribution Optimization

While AI cannot replace the human touch in HCP interactions, it can be a powerful tool for increasing efficiency, gaining insights, and optimizing your sales and distribution strategy:

- **Predictive Analytics:** AI can analyze data to predict HCP prescribing behavior, identify high-potential customer segments, and optimize resource allocation for sales representatives.
- **Marketing Automation:** AI-powered tools can personalize marketing messages to HCPs based on their specialty and past interactions, delivering relevant information efficiently.
- **Demand Forecasting:** AI algorithms can analyze sales data and external factors to predict future medication demand, helping optimize inventory management and distribution channels.

Remember:

- **Ethical Considerations are Paramount:** Ensure AI-driven targeting and marketing comply with regulations and respect HCP privacy.

- **Transparency and Trust are Key:** Be transparent about how AI is used and prioritize building trust with HCPs through ethical interactions and valuable information.
- **Continuous Learning and Adaptation:** Stay updated on emerging AI applications, experiment with new possibilities, and adapt your strategies based on data and HCP feedback.

By following these steps and utilizing AI responsibly, you can orchestrate a symphony of sales and distribution optimization that resonates with HCPs, ensures patients have access to essential medications, and strengthens your position in the competitive pharma landscape. Remember, a well-optimized sales and distribution strategy is not just about reaching doctors and pharmacies; it's about building relationships, providing essential support, and ultimately contributing to better patient outcomes.

AI's Symphony of Optimization: Step-by-Step Implementation in Sales and Distribution

AI is rapidly transforming the world of sales and distribution, offering tools to enhance efficiency, gain valuable insights, and optimize strategies across the entire process. Here's a deeper dive into how AI can empower each step:

1. **Understanding Your Landscape:**
   - **Target Audience Segmentation:** AI-powered customer segmentation tools can analyze vast datasets (prescription data and online behavior) to reveal hidden patterns and identify high-potential HCP segments beyond basic demographics.
   - **Market Dynamics Analysis:** AI algorithms can process news articles, social media discussions, and regulatory documents to predict emerging trends, identify potential competitors, and inform strategic decision-making.

Example: A pharma company launching a new drug can utilize AI to segment HCPs by their prescribing habits for similar medications, uncovering previously unknown groups with high potential adoption rates. Additionally, AI can analyze competitor marketing campaigns and regulatory discussions to predict potential market shifts and adjust their distribution strategy accordingly.

2. **Optimizing Your Sales Team:**
   - **Predictive Performance Evaluation:** AI algorithms can analyze historical data to predict the potential sales performance of individual representatives, enabling targeted training and coaching programs to maximize their effectiveness.
   - **Personalized Coaching and Feedback:** AI-powered tools can analyze call recordings and interactions with HCPs, providing real-time personalized feedback and coaching suggestions to individual representatives.

Example: A pharmaceutical company can leverage AI to identify top-performing representatives and analyze their successful communication patterns. These insights can then be used to develop personalized coaching programs for other representatives, improving their communication skills and ultimately increasing sales effectiveness.

3. **Building Robust Distribution Channels:**
   - **AI-Driven Partner Selection:** AI can analyze past performance data and market trends to suggest optimal distribution partners based on reach, expertise, and compliance history.
   - **Dynamic Pricing and Inventory Management:** AI algorithms can analyze real-time demand data and predict future needs, optimizing pricing strategies and ensuring efficient inventory management across the distribution chain.

Example: A drug manufacturer can use AI to identify distributors with a proven track record of efficiently delivering medications to specific regions. Additionally, AI can predict fluctuations in demand based on seasonal changes or disease outbreaks, allowing for proactive pricing and inventory allocation adjustments to avoid shortages or wasted stock.

4. **Utilizing Effective Sales Tools:**
   - **Personalized Content Generation:** AI can analyze HCP profiles and engagement data to personalize marketing materials, tailoring language, examples, and case studies to resonate with specific interests and needs.
   - **Interactive and Adaptive Presentations:** AI-powered tools can generate interactive presentations that adapt to real-time HCP responses, addressing specific concerns and providing relevant information dynamically.

Example: A pharma company can use AI to personalize email marketing campaigns to HCPs highlighting the new drug's benefits relevant to their specific patient population. Furthermore, AI can develop interactive presentations that adjust content based on the HCP's questions and feedback, creating a more engaging and informative experience.

5. **Tracking and Analyzing Performance:**
   - **Real-Time Performance Dashboards:** AI-powered dashboards can analyze sales data, HCP engagement metrics, and distribution channel performance in real time, providing actionable insights for immediate optimization.
   - **Predictive Sales Forecasting:** AI algorithms can analyze historical data and external factors to predict future sales trends, enabling proactive resource allocation and marketing campaign adjustments.

Example: A pharmaceutical company can utilize AI to monitor sales figures across different regions and identify underperforming areas in real-time. They can then analyze distribution channel data to pinpoint potential bottlenecks and take immediate corrective actions. Additionally, AI can predict future demand for the new drug based on market trends and competitor activity, allowing the company to optimize production and distribution planning.

Remember:

- **Human Oversight Remains Crucial:** While AI-driven insights are valuable, human judgment and ethical considerations are essential to ensure fair targeting, transparent communication, and responsible practices.
- **Data Quality is Paramount:** AI thrives on high-quality data. Invest in data governance and ensure data used for AI initiatives is accurate, complete, and unbiased.
- **Continuous Learning and Adaptation:** The AI landscape is rapidly evolving. Stay updated on new developments, experiment with various applications, and refine your strategies based on performance data and ongoing ethical considerations.

By thoughtfully integrating AI into each step of your sales and distribution processes, you can orchestrate a symphony of optimization that improves efficiency, strengthens relationships, and ultimately drives market success. Remember, AI is a powerful tool, but human ingenuity and responsible decision-making remain the conductors of the success story.

CHAPTER

49

AI's Harmonious Symphony: Enhancing Brand Communication and Reputation Management

In the ever-evolving realm of brand communication and reputation management, AI emerges as a powerful conductor, enhancing effectiveness while ensuring the melody of trust and transparency remains the core focus. Here's a step-by-step exploration of how AI can harmonize each stage.

1. **Defining Your Brand Identity and Values:**

   AI offers valuable tools for defining and refining your brand identity and values within the competitive pharma landscape.

   - **AI-Powered Sentiment Analysis**: Go beyond traditional surveys and delve into real-world conversations. Analyze vast amounts of patient testimonials, medical forum discussions, and social media mentions related to your therapeutic area. This can help uncover:
   - **Unconscious Patient Anxieties and Needs**: Beyond reported side effects, AI can identify recurring concerns, emotional responses to treatments, and unmet needs patients express online.
   - **Industry Perception of Your Brand**: Analyze how healthcare professionals, competitors, and media outlets discuss your brand and its competitors. This can reveal strengths, weaknesses, and opportunities for differentiation.
   - **Competitive Analysis**: Don't just research competitor products— understand their brand narratives. Use AI to

analyze competitors' language in marketing materials, patient interactions, and social media engagement. This can inform your own:

- **Unique Value Proposition**: Identify gaps in the market where your brand can offer a distinct emotional connection or address unmet needs discovered through sentiment analysis.
- **Messaging and Tone of Voice**: Understand how competitors position themselves emotionally and tailor your language to resonate with your target audience differently.

Example: A pharmaceutical company developing a new asthma medication can analyze online patient forums and social media discussions to uncover the following:

- **Undisclosed Patient Anxieties**: Beyond traditional side effect complaints, AI might reveal emotional burdens like stigma or fear of dependence, informing messaging that addresses these unspoken concerns.
- **Competitor Brand Narratives**: Analyzing how competitors position themselves might reveal an opportunity to emphasize patient empowerment or a specific quality-of-life benefit not yet addressed by others.

By leveraging AI for deeper insights and competition analysis, you can define a brand identity and values that truly resonate with your target audience, building a strong foundation for successful pharma branding.

2. **Understanding Your Audience: AI-Powered Insights for Pharma Engagement**

   Understanding your audience is critical for effective communication and brand building in the complex pharma world. AI can offer unique insights and predictive capabilities to enhance your audience's understanding:

   - **AI-Driven Audience Segmentation**: Go beyond traditional demographics. Leverage AI algorithms to segment your audience based on a wider range of factors, including:

- **Medical Conditions and Treatment Journey Stage**: Segment patients based on specific diagnoses, medication adherence, and online discussions about their condition. This allows for targeted messaging relevant to their unique needs and concerns.
- **Digital Health Behavior**: Analyze platform usage, online research patterns, and engagement with disease communities to understand patient information preferences and preferred communication channels.
- **Psychographic Factors**: Uncover underlying attitudes, values, and motivations related to health and treatment decisions. This allows you to craft messaging that resonates emotionally and aligns with their health perspectives.

Predictive Modeling: Don't just guess how your audience will react. Utilize AI to predict:

- **Patient Sentiment Towards New Treatment Options**: Analyze online discussions and social media reactions to similar medications to anticipate potential concerns and proactively address them in your communication.
- **Impact of Disease Awareness Campaigns**: Predict the reach and engagement of different campaign messages within specific patient segments, allowing for data-driven optimization and resource allocation.
- **Adherence Likelihood for Different Patient Profiles**: Based on historical data and online behavior, identify patients at risk of non-adherence and develop targeted interventions or support programs.

Example: A pharmaceutical company launching a new diabetes medication can use AI to:

- Segment patients based on their online discussions, identifying groups struggling with specific challenges like managing side effects or navigating complex dosing schedules. This allows them to tailor product information and support resources accordingly.

- Predict potential affordability or medication effectiveness concerns based on social media sentiment analysis of similar drugs. This allows them to proactively address these concerns in pre-launch communication and marketing materials.
- Identify patients at risk of non-adherence based on online behavior patterns and digital health tool usage. This allows them to offer targeted interventions and personalized reminders to improve adherence rates.

By leveraging AI for audience segmentation and predictive modeling, you can gain deeper insights into your target audience, craft more relevant and impactful communication, and ultimately improve patient engagement and brand loyalty within the pharma landscape.

3. **Developing A Multi-Channel Communication Strategy: AI-Powered Precision in Pharma**

   In the competitive pharma world, reaching the right audience with the right message across the right channels is important. AI can empower you to create personalized content and optimize your multi-channel communication strategy for maximum impact:

   - **AI-Powered Content Creation**: Go beyond generic messaging. Utilize AI tools to generate:
   - **Personalized Patient Education Materials**: Create targeted content based on individual diagnoses, treatment stages, and preferred learning styles. This ensures information is relevant, accessible, and resonates with each patient's specific needs.
   - **Disease Awareness Campaigns**: Tailor messaging and creative assets for patient segments and healthcare professionals based on online behavior, interests, and information consumption patterns. This ensures your campaign resonates with diverse audiences and achieves maximum reach within specific communities.

- **Interactive Patient Support Tools**: Develop AI-powered chatbots or virtual assistants that offer personalized guidance, answer frequently asked questions, and address patient concerns in real time.

Channel Optimization: Don't waste resources on ineffective channels. Leverage AI analytics to:

- **Identify the Preferred Communication channels of Different Patient Segments**: Analyze engagement data across email, social media platforms, mobile apps, and patient portals to understand where each audience is most receptive to your message.
- **Predict the Most Effective Channels for Specific Campaign Goals**: Using historical data and audience insights, AI can predict where different messages will achieve the highest reach, engagement, and conversion rates (medication adherence reminders, appointment bookings).
- **Optimize Campaign Performance in Real Time:** Use AI to monitor campaign performance across different channels and make data-driven adjustments to messaging, targeting, and budget allocation for continuous improvement.

Example: **A pharmaceutical company launching a new medication can use AI to**:

- Develop personalized patient education videos targeted to different age groups and preferred learning styles, ensuring maximum comprehension and engagement.
- Tailor disease awareness campaigns for specific patient segments identified through online behavior analysis, addressing their unique concerns and information needs within relevant online communities.
- Implement an AI-powered chatbot on their patient portal to answer frequently asked questions about the medication, providing personalized support and improving medication adherence rates.

By leveraging AI-powered content creation and channel optimization, you can develop a multi-channel communication strategy that resonates with diverse audiences, maximizes message reach, and fosters stronger patient engagement and brand loyalty within the pharma landscape.

4. **Creating Authentic and Engaging Content: Crafting Compelling Narratives in Pharma**

   In the pharmaceutical industry, building trust and engagement requires informative content that resonates with individual patient experiences. AI can empower you to create valuable content, personalize interactions, and craft authentic narratives that foster deeper connections with your audience.

   - **AI-Powered Content Curation**: Go beyond generic information sharing. Utilize AI to:
   - **Aggregate and Personalize Patient Education Materials**: Curate content based on individual diagnoses, medical history, and learning styles. Recommend articles, videos, and infographics that address their specific needs and concerns, fostering patient empowerment and informed decision-making.
   - **Identify and Promote Patient Stories**: Leverage AI to surface authentic patient testimonials and success stories from online communities or social media platforms. Share these narratives responsibly and ethically, showcasing your brand's real-world impact and building trust with potential patients.
   - **Curate Disease Awareness Content Based on Real-Time Trends**: Utilize AI to identify emerging topics, concerns, and questions with online patient communities related to your therapeutic area. Curate and share relevant content that addresses these concerns promptly and informally, demonstrating your brand's commitment to patient well-being and thought leadership.

Chatbots for Personalized Interactions: Offer personalized support and engagement beyond traditional channels. Implement AI-powered chatbots to:

- **Answer Frequently Asked Questions About Medications and Treatment Options**: Provide patients with readily available information and address common concerns, reducing the burden on healthcare professionals and improving patient satisfaction.
- **Offer Personalized Medication Reminders and Adherence Support**: Leverage AI to tailor reminders and educational content based on individual medication schedules and potential adherence challenges, improving treatment outcomes and patient well-being.
- **Facilitate Emotional Support and Connection**: Utilize AI-powered chatbots to offer basic emotional support resources or encourage patients to connect with relevant support groups, fostering a sense of community and belonging for individuals managing chronic conditions.

Example: **A pharmaceutical company developing a new diabetes medication can use AI to:**

- Curate personalized patient educational materials, recommending articles and videos based on their disease stage, treatment regimen, and preferred learning style.
- Identify and share patient stories of successful blood sugar management on social media, showcasing the medication's impact in a relatable and authentic manner.
- Implement an AI-powered chatbot on their patient portal to answer medication-related questions, offer personalized reminders, and connect patients with relevant support groups. This will foster ongoing engagement and improve medication adherence.

By leveraging AI for content curation and personalized interactions, you can create informative, engaging, and patient-centric content that builds trust, fosters meaningful connections, and ultimately strengthens your brand within the competitive pharma landscape.

5. **Monitoring and Responding to Feedback: Building a Two-Way Dialogue in Pharma**

   In the pharma industry, where patient trust and satisfaction are paramount, effectively monitoring and responding to feedback is crucial. AI can empower you to analyze sentiment, streamline customer service, and foster a two-way dialogue that strengthens your brand.

   AI-Powered Sentiment Analysis:

   Go beyond traditional surveys and delve deeper. Utilize AI to:

   - **Analyze Real-Time Patient Feedback Across Diverse Channels**: Monitor online forums, social media platforms, patient portals, and healthcare professional review sites to identify emerging concerns, medication side effect discussions, and unmet needs.
   - **Track Brand Sentiment and Competitor Comparisons**: Analyze how patients perceive your brand and compare it to competitors, identifying areas for improvement and opportunities for differentiation.
   - **Real-Time Sentiment Analysis**: Monitor online mentions and social media conversations, identifying potential crises or negative feedback early on. This allows for prompt and proactive responses, mitigating reputational damage.
   - **Predict and Proactively Address Potential Crises**: Leverage AI to identify early warning signs of negative sentiment or potential public relations issues, allowing swift and strategic communication to mitigate risks.
   - **AI-Driven Reporting**: Generate comprehensive reports with actionable insights from sentiment analysis and social media activity, allowing for effective reputation management strategies.

Chatbot-Assisted Customer Service: Offer responsive and accessible support. Integrate AI-powered chatbots to:

- **Provide 24/7 Support for Basic Inquiries and Medication Questions**: Address frequently asked questions about product information, side effects, and dosage instructions, offering patients immediate assistance and reducing the burden on healthcare professionals.
- **Gather and Categorize Patient Feedback**: Utilize chatbots to collect patient feedback on their experience, medication adherence challenges, or suggestions for improvement, providing valuable insights to inform product development and communication strategies.
- **Escalate Complex Issues to Human Representatives Seamlessly**: Train AI chatbots to identify situations requiring human intervention and connect patients with live support agents for personalized assistance.
- **Chatbots for Crisis Communication**: Utilize AI-powered chatbots to address basic customer concerns during a crisis, providing initial support and reducing pressure on human teams.

Example: **A pharmaceutical company developing a new chronic pain medication can use AI to:**

- Monitor online patient forums and social media discussions to identify emerging concerns about potential side effects or medication effectiveness. This will allow them to address these concerns and provide accurate information proactively.
- Analyze patient reviews on healthcare professional platforms to compare their brand sentiment against competitor medications, identifying areas where they excel and opportunities to improve patient satisfaction.
- Utilize AI-powered chatbots on their patient portal to answer basic medication questions, gather feedback on adherence challenges, and seamlessly connect patients with live support agents for personalized guidance on complex issue resolution.

By leveraging AI for sentiment analysis and chatbot-assisted support, you can foster a continuous feedback loop with patients, proactively address their concerns, and ultimately build stronger brand loyalty and trust within the pharma landscape.

6. **Measuring and Adapting: Continuous Improvement in Pharma Branding**

   Adaptability and data-driven decision-making are crucial for maintaining a strong brand and competitive edge in the dynamic pharma world. AI can empower you to measure performance effectively, predict future trends, and continuously adapt your strategies for ongoing success:

   - **AI-Powered Performance Dashboards**: Go beyond traditional metrics. Utilize AI-powered dashboards to track:
   - **Patient Engagement Across Channels**: Monitor website traffic on patient education materials, social media engagement with disease awareness campaigns, and app usage for medication adherence support programs. Gain real-time insights into the effectiveness of different communication strategies and content formats.
   - **Brand Sentiment and Competitor Comparisons**: Track changes in patient sentiment towards your brand over time, compare it to competitors and identify emerging areas of concern or opportunities for differentiation.
   - **Medication Adherence Rates and Patient Outcomes**: Leverage AI to analyze data from connected devices or patient portals to track medication adherence rates, identify patient groups struggling with adherence, and measure the impact of your patient support programs on health outcomes.

Predictive Analytics: Anticipate challenges and optimize your approach. Utilize AI to predict:

- **Future Patient Needs and Treatment Trends**: Based on market research and online behavior analysis, predict emerging disease areas, evolving patient preferences, and potential shifts in treatment demands. This allows you to proactively develop new medications, tailor communication strategies, and stay ahead of the curve.

- **Potential Patient Safety Concerns and Medication Side Effects**: Leverage AI to analyze historical data and social media discussions to identify early warning signs of potential safety issues or negative side effects, allowing for proactive risk mitigation and communication strategies.
- **The Effectiveness of Planned Marketing Campaigns**: Based on historical data and competitor analysis, use AI to predict the reach engagement and potential impact of planned marketing campaigns before they launch, allowing for data-driven optimization and resource allocation.

Example: A pharmaceutical company launching a new diabetes medication can use AI to:

- Track patient engagement with their website, social media campaigns, and educational app, identifying content formats and communication channels that resonate best with patient segments.
- Compare brand sentiment towards their medication with competitor offerings, identifying areas where they excel and opportunities to improve patient perception.
- Analyze data from connected insulin pumps and blood sugar monitors to predict potential adherence challenges in specific patient groups and design targeted interventions to improve medication adherence rates.

By leveraging AI-powered performance dashboards and predictive analytics, you can gain deeper insights into your audience, measure the effectiveness of your strategies, and continuously adapt your approach to build a successful and evolving pharma brand. This allows you to anticipate future needs, address patient concerns proactively, and ultimately contribute to improved patient outcomes within the dynamic healthcare landscape.

AI in Brand Communication: Unveiling the Symphony of Benefits and Considerations

AI has emerged as a powerful conductor in brand communication, promising both a harmonious melody of benefits and a need for thoughtful considerations. Let's delve deeper into both aspects:

Benefits:

1. **Enhanced Efficiency and Scalability**:
    - **Automate Repetitive Tasks**: Free your team's time from data analysis, content creation, and basic customer service inquiries, allowing them to focus on strategic initiatives.
    - **Reach and Wider Audiences**: Leverage AI to personalize content and target specific demographics across diverse channels, reaching new audiences and maximizing your brand's footprint.
    - **Optimize Campaign Performance**: Use AI algorithms to analyze real-time data and adjust campaigns for better performance, maximizing ROI and minimizing wasted resources.
2. **Personalized Communication and Engagement**:
    - **Segment Audience Effectively**: AI can identify patterns and segment your audience based on demographics, interests, and behaviors, enabling highly personalized messaging and offers.
    - **Tailor Content and Recommendations**: Create content and product recommendations that resonate with individual customer preferences, fostering engagement and building stronger relationships.
    - **24/7 Customer Support**: Implement AI-powered chatbots to answer basic questions and address concerns around the clock, providing continuous support and improving customer satisfaction.

3. **Improved Data Insights and Decision-Making**:
    - **Gather and Analyze Vast Amounts of Data**: AI can collect data from diverse sources, uncovering hidden trends and patterns that human analysis might miss.
    - **Predict Future Trends and Challenges**: Leverage AI to predict customer behavior, market shifts, and potential issues, allowing for proactive planning and strategy adjustments.
    - **Measure Campaign Effectiveness Actively**: Utilize AI-powered dashboards and reports to track key metrics and gain deeper insights into campaign performance, optimizing future efforts.

Considerations:

1. **Ethical Implications and Transparency**:
    - **Avoid Biased Algorithms**: Ensure your AI tools are built and trained on diverse data sets to avoid discriminatory or offensive outputs.
    - **Be Transparent About AI Usage**: Inform your audience about how AI is used in your communications and marketing activities, building trust and avoiding ethical concerns.
    - **Maintain Human Oversight**: AI should be a tool to support human expertise, not replace it. Ensure human judgment and ethical considerations guide AI implementation.
2. **Data Privacy and Security**:
    - **Comply with Data Privacy Regulations**: Ensure your data collection and usage practices comply with relevant regulations and respect user privacy.
    - **Implement Robust Security Measures** to protect sensitive customer data against breaches and unauthorized access, maintaining data integrity and user trust.
    - **Be Clear About Data Usage**: Inform users how their data is collected, used, and stored, allowing them to make informed choices.

3. **Explainability and Interpretability**:
   - **Understand How AI Models Work**: Choose AI tools that offer transparency into their decision-making processes to ensure responsible and explainable outcomes.
   - **Address Potential Biases**: Identify and mitigate potential biases within your AI models to ensure fair and ethical treatment of all customers.
   - **Prioritize Human Understanding**: Focus on AI solutions that provide clear explanations and insights humans can easily understand and act upon.

By harmonizing AI's benefits with careful consideration of ethical, privacy, and interpretability concerns, you can orchestrate a brand communication symphony that resonates with your audience, builds trust, and drives your business forward.

AI is a powerful tool, but ethical considerations, human oversight, and responsible data handling remain crucial for a sustainable and successful brand communication strategy.

AI-Powered Brand Management: A Human-Centered Revolution in Pharma Marketing

As we have explored, AI presents a transformative force in pharmaceutical marketing, offering powerful tools to enhance brand building, communication, and engagement. Yet, amidst technological advancements, one crucial element remains constant: the **human touch**.

AI is at its best when it is a synergistic partner, amplifying human strengths and creativity. By leveraging AI for data analysis, personalized content creation, and real-time insights, marketers can craft authentic messages, cultivate deeper connections with patients, and build brands that resonate on an emotional level.

However, the ethical and responsible use of AI is paramount. Transparency, data privacy, and a deep understanding of human values must guide every step of the AI-powered branding journey.

Remember, AI is not a replacement for human expertise and empathy. It's a collaborative tool that empowers marketers to become more strategic, data-driven, and patient-centric. As we embrace this human-AI synergy, we unlock the true potential of AI-powered branding, ushering in a new era of patient engagement and meaningful brand connection in the pharma industry.

This future holds immense promise for improving health outcomes, fostering trust, and ultimately empowering patients to make informed decisions about their well-being. Let us leverage the power of AI responsibly, ethically, and with a human-centered approach, co-creating a brighter future for pharma marketing and patient care.

Remember, the synergy of minds— human and AI— truly orchestrates the pharma marketing revolution.

CHAPTER 50

Roles Humans and AI Play in Building Trust and Emotional Connections

Humans and AI: Weaving Trust and Emotional Connections

Building trust and forging emotional connections are intricate dances— and humans and AI have roles to play, each with their strengths and limitations.

Humans:

- **Masters of Empathy**: Our ability to read unspoken cues, understand emotions, and respond with genuine care is unmatched. We can tailor our communication and actions to individual needs, building rapport and trust through shared experiences and vulnerability.
- **Ethical Navigators**: Humans possess the judgment and discernment to navigate complex ethical dilemmas, prioritize informed consent, and communicate transparently. This fosters trust by respecting individual well-being and privacy.
- **Cultural Chameleons:** Cultural sensitivity is ingrained in humans. We can adapt our communication and actions to diverse values, beliefs, and experiences, ensuring inclusivity and respect.

AI:

- **Data Analyst and Optimizer**: AI analyzes data and tailors content to individual preferences. This creates a sense of being understood and valued, strengthening trust and connection.

- **Connection Facilitator**: AI can overcome barriers to connection by organizing online communities, providing translation services, and connecting people with shared interests.
- **Tireless Supporter**: AI-powered chatbots and virtual assistants can offer basic emotional support 24/7, particularly where human resources are limited.

Synergy in Action

The real magic happens when humans and AI collaborate:

- **Human Storytellers and AI Personalization**: Imagine captivating narratives tailored to individual experiences and emotions, using AI to analyze data and choose the most impactful elements.
- **Human Support Groups + AI Moderators**: Envision online communities empowered by AI to manage logistics and translation while humans provide compassionate guidance and individual attention.
- **Human Cultural Experts + AI Communication**: Consider experts training AI systems on the nuances of different cultures, ensuring respectful and inclusive interactions.

Challenges and Considerations

- **Over-reliance on AI**: Humans must remain central to building trust and emotional connections. AI should augment, not replace, human interaction.
- **Ethical Consideration**: Ensure transparency, informed consent, and responsible data use in AI-driven interactions.
- **Human Oversight and Control**: Humans must maintain responsibility for ethical decision-making and ensure AI doesn't reinforce biases or perpetuate misinformation.

The Future of Trust and Control

As AI technology evolves, its role will likely expand. However, remember:

- AI is a tool, not a replacement for human empathy and connection.
- Building trust and emotional connections requires *synergy*, leveraging the strengths of both humans and AI.
- The future of trust lies in a human-centered approach, where AI empowers, amplifies, and protects humans' unique capabilities to connect and empathize.

By working together, humans and AI can create a world where trust and emotional connections thrive, paving the way for a more inclusive and empathetic future.

Humans: Masters of Empathy and Emotional Resonance

Building trust and emotional connections is an inherently human endeavor. Our ability to empathize, read emotions, and respond with genuine care and understanding sets us apart from machines. In fostering deep connections, humans play several crucial roles:

1. **Emotional Intelligence and Shared Experiences**: Humans excel at reading and responding to non-verbal cues, facial expressions, and tone of voice. This allows us to understand the subtle nuances of emotional communication and tailor our responses accordingly. AI, while advancing emotional recognition, still struggles to grasp the full complexity of human emotions.
2. **Storytelling and Shared Experiences**: Humans use narratives, anecdotes, and humor to connect with others on a deeper level. We share our vulnerabilities, fears, and joys, creating a sense of humanity and understanding. AI can generate scripts and personalize content, but it lacks the lived experience and genuine emotional involvement that brings stories to life.

3. **Cultural Sensitivity and Inclusivity**: Humans can tailor their communication and actions to different cultural contexts and individual backgrounds. This builds trust and rapport by respecting diverse values, beliefs, and experiences. AI systems, trained on large datasets, can struggle with cultural nuances and biases, potentially leading to misrepresentations and misunderstandings.
4. **Ethical Considerations and Responsible Communication:** Humans can navigate complex ethical dilemmas, prioritize informed consent, and ensure transparency in communication. This builds trust by respecting personal privacy, autonomy, and well-being. AI systems, while programmed with ethical guidelines, may still encounter situations requiring human judgment and ethical discernment.

AI: A Complementary Tool

While humans hold the key to trust and emotional connections, AI can play a valuable supporting role:

1. **Personalized Interactions**: AI can analyze data and tailor communications to individual needs and preferences. This creates a sense of being understood and valued, furthering trust and rapport.
2. **Facilitating Connections**: AI can connect people with similar interests, organize online communities, and provide translation services, breaking down barriers and fostering broader connections.
3. **Augmenting Human Capabilities**: AI can automate repetitive tasks, analyze vast amounts of data, and provide insights that help humans build stronger relationships. For instance, AI can recommend relevant resources for personal development or identify individuals who might need support.
4. **Scaling Emotional Support**: AI-powered chatbots or virtual assistants can offer basic emotional support to a wider range

of people, particularly in cases where human resources are limited. However, this support should always be complemented by human interaction when needed.

Synergy: Humans and AI Working Together

By combining human strengths with AI's capabilities, we can build even stronger trust and emotional connections:

- **Human Storytellers Working with AI Personalization**: Imagine creating captivating narratives tailored to individual experiences and emotions, using AI to analyze data and choose the most impactful elements.
- **Human Support Groups Facilitated by AI Moderators**: Envision online communities empowered by AI to manage logistics and translation while humans provide compassionate guidance and individual attention.
- **Human Cultural Experts Guiding AI Communication**: Consider experts training AI systems on the nuances of different cultures, ensuring respectful and inclusive interactions.

As AI technology evolves, its role in building trust and emotional connections may become more significant. However, it will always be a tool, supplementing and amplifying the unique capabilities of humans to empathize, connect, and build meaningful relationships.

Remember, AI should never replace human interaction but rather enhance it. The future of trust and emotional connection lies in humans and AI working together, leveraging their strengths to create a more connected and empathetic world.

PART VIII

Harmonizing Technology and Humanity

Chapter 51. Prompt Engineering: Whispering to the AI in Pharmaceutical Marketing

Chapter 52. Chain Prompting: Orchestrating a Symphony of Content

Chapter 53. The Game of *Exquisite Corpse* and Chain Prompting

Chapter 54. AI's Symphony in Pharma Marketing: Harmonizing Technology with Humanity

Harmonizing Technology and Humanity - The Future of Pharma Marketing

The pharmaceutical marketing landscape stands at a crossroads. As artificial intelligence (AI) continues to revolutionize the industry, a critical question emerges: can technology and humanity work harmoniously to drive a more effective and ethical approach? This chapter delves into the heart of this question, exploring the delicate dance between human expertise and AI capabilities.

We'll navigate the potential pitfalls of technology overreach, emphasizing the irreplaceable value of human empathy, trust-building, and ethical considerations in pharma marketing. Here's a taste of what you'll discover:

- **The Power of AI in Pharma Marketing:** Unveiling how AI empowers data-driven decision-making, personalized communication, and optimized customer journeys across all stakeholder groups.
- **The Human Touch: A Differentiator:** Exploring the irreplaceable role of human empathy, emotional intelligence, and storytelling in building trust with patients, HCPs, and other stakeholders.
- **Navigating Ethical Considerations:** Delving into potential ethical concerns surrounding data privacy, bias in AI algorithms, and ensuring responsible marketing practices in a data-driven world.
- **The Synergy of Minds:** Unveiling the power of human+AI collaboration in creating a future-proof pharma marketing ecosystem, where technology amplifies human expertise and ethical marketing principles.

This chapter is your call to action. We'll challenge you to move beyond the simplistic narrative of technology replacing humans in pharma marketing. Instead, we'll advocate for a future where technology and humanity work harmoniously, leading to a more patient-centric, ethical, and ultimately, successful pharma marketing revolution.

CHAPTER 51

Prompt Engineering: Whispering to the AI in Pharmaceutical Marketing

The Whisper in the Machine: Prompt Engineering and the Future of Pharma Marketing

Imagine a conversation not held in hushed boardrooms or sterile labs but within the humming circuits of a digital mind. A conversation where human intent and artificial intelligence intertwine, whispering possibilities into existence. This is the realm of **prompt engineering**, and its arrival in the pharma marketing world marks a watershed moment.

This chapter delves into the intricate dance between humans and machines, exploring how **crafting the right prompts** can unlock a new era of personalized outreach, groundbreaking content creation, and a deeper connection with patients. We'll shed light on the **synergy of minds** unleashed when marketers partner with AI, not as a replacement but as an amplifier, magnifying their voice and tailoring their message to resonate with individual needs and motivations.

No longer shackled by one-size-fits-all campaigns, we'll discover the power of crafting prompts that **dance with data, doctor, patient, and payer**. We'll witness how the right words, whispered into the ear of an AI model, can generate content that speaks directly to the anxieties of a cancer patient, the information needs of a busy HCP, or the concerns of a cost-conscious payer.

This is not a story of technology replacing humanity but of **humanity harnessing technology** to reach further, understand deeper, and connect more meaningfully. It's a story of **unleashing creativity fueled by data**, of empathy amplified by algorithms, and of a future where the whispers in the machine become a symphony of care, understanding, and, ultimately, a healthier world.

So, turn the page, dear reader, and prepare to step into the future of pharma marketing, where **the synergy of minds** powered by prompt engineering paints a brighter picture for every patient, every HCP, and every stakeholder in the intricate healthcare ecosystem. This is the whisper in the machine, a song worth listening to.

Before we begin, let's understand the basics of prompt engineering: what prompt engineering is and how it works.

What is Prompt Engineering?

It's the art of crafting specific instructions that guide AI models to generate desired outputs, like text, images, or code. Think of it as giving the AI clear directions on what you want to create.

How Does it Work?

You provide a prompt and let the AI model do the magic. The prompt type and specific model you use will influence the result.

What are the Benefits of Prompt Engineering to Pharma Marketing?

There are endless possibilities! From personalized patient education to innovative content creation, prompt engineering can streamline workflows, boost patient engagement, and tailor marketing efforts to specific needs.

Types of Prompts:

- **Informative Prompts**: Provide factual information and ask the AI to generate related content, like summarizing clinical trial results or creating engaging product descriptions.

- **Creative Prompts**: Describe a desired style or tone and let the AI generate creative outputs, like crafting patient testimonials in a friendly, relatable voice or writing blog posts with a humorous touch.
- **Personalization Prompts**: Incorporate individual patient data or demographics to generate personalized content, like educational modules tailored to specific health conditions or medication needs.

Practical Applications in Pharma Marketing:

- **Generating Effective Ad Copy**: Craft targeted ad copy for different platforms and patient segments, ensuring clarity, relevance, and emotional resonance.
- **Personalizing Patient Education**: Create custom educational materials based on individual patient needs and reading levels, improving understanding and engagement.
- **Developing Social Media Content**: Generate engaging posts and captions that spark conversation and build brand awareness.
- **Automate Repetitive Tasks**: Use AI to answer frequently asked patient questions, freeing time for more complex interactions.
- **Analyzing Marketing Data**: Leverage AI to identify patterns and trends in customer behavior, informing future marketing campaigns.

Examples:

- **Prompt**: "Write a blog post summarizing the benefits of the new diabetes medication in a friendly and relatable tone."
- **Output**: "Living with diabetes can be tough, but hope exists! This new medication helps you manage your sugar levels and live a fuller life. Let's dive into how it works and answer your questions."

- **Prompt**: "Generate social media captions for videos showcasing patient testimonials about their experience with the new drug."
- **Output**: "Caption 1: "I used to feel limited by my diabetes, but now I can conquer anything!" - John, a grateful patient. #LiveLimitless #NewDrugName"
- **Prompt**: "Develop a personalized educational module for a patient with high blood pressure, incorporating their medication regimen and lifestyle preferences."
- **Output**: "Interactive module with educational videos, diet tips tailored to your preferences, and reminders to take your medication."

Remember, this is just a glimpse into the world of prompt engineering for pharmaceutical marketing. In this chapter, you will discover more ways to leverage this powerful tool to transform your marketing efforts.

Now let us explore further how we can get the most out of the art and science of prompt engineering:

Prompt Engineering: Whispering to the AI in Pharma Marketing

Imagine you're writing a letter to a friend. You wouldn't just start with "Dear...," right? You'd choose specific words, weave in shared memories, and tailor the tone to your friend's personality. Prompt engineering in pharma marketing works similarly, but instead of a pen, you're using code as your brush, and the recipient is a powerful AI mode.

Think of a prompt as *a set of instructions or cues* you give the AI to guide its output. It's like whispering in the machine's ear, telling it what you want to create. In pharma marketing, this translates to crafting prompts that instruct the AI to generate things like:

- **Targeted Social Media Posts**: Imagine prompts like "Write a Facebook post for HCPs highlighting the benefits of our new diabetes medication, focusing on its efficacy and side-effect profile."

- **Personalized Patient Education Materials**: Prompts like "Generate a brochure explaining the potential side effects of our cancer treatment, written in clear, concise language for anxious patients."
- **Data-Driven Marketing Reports**: Prompts like "Analyze our customer data and generate a report identifying key trends in physician prescribing patterns to our cardiovascular drugs."

But Why Use AI for These Tasks? Here is where the synergy of minds kicks in:

- **Personalization at Scale**: AI can analyze vast datasets and customize content to specific audiences, something human marketers can't always do efficiently.
- **Creative Spark and Efficiency**: AI can uncover hidden patterns and trends in data, leading to more targeted and effective marketing campaigns.
- **Data-Driven Insights**: AI can uncover hidden patterns and trends in data, leading to more targeted and effective marketing campaigns.

Of course, with great power comes responsibility. Prompt engineering in pharma marketing needs to be done ethically and responsibly considering the following:

- **Bias and Misinformation**: Carefully crafted prompts avoid biased language and ensure factual accuracy.
- **Transparency and Human Oversight**: AI is a tool, not a replacement. Humans must set parameters, analyze outputs, and ensure ethical communication.
- **Patient Privacy and Data Security**: Data used for AI models must be handled responsibly and securely, adhering to strict regulations.

Ultimately, prompt engineering is not about replacing human creativity or marketing expertise. It's about adding a powerful tool to the marketing toolbox, enabling pharma companies to:

- More impactful and personalized messages.
- Reach the right audiences with the right content at the right time.
- Gain deeper insights into customer behavior and market trends.
- Focus on strategic planning and creative direction, leaving repetitive tasks to AI.

So, when you whisper the right prompts into the AI's ear, you're not generating content or reports. You're building bridges of understanding, fostering trust with patients and HCPs, and ultimately contributing to a healthier future.

Remember, prompt engineering is not a magic bullet but a powerful tool that can unlock a new era of personalized communication and impact in pharmaceutical marketing when used responsibly and strategically.

Whispering with Precision: Prompt Engineering's Potential for Personalization and Connection in Pharma Marketing

Imagine standing backstage at a grand theater, not with actors and spotlights, but with algorithms and data sets. Pharma marketers wield new artistry in this digital stage: **prompt engineering**. Unlike the one-size-fits-all monologues of the past, this allows crafting personalized whispers tailored to individual needs and aspirations, forging deeper connections than ever before.

Let's explore how prompt engineering unlocks the potential for personalization and connection in pharma marketing:

1. **Tailored Messages for Diverse Audiences**:
    - **HCPs**: Imagine prompts generating research summaries targeted to specific medical specialists, highlighting relevant

data, and addressing individual interests. This personalized approach fosters deeper engagement and informed decision-making.

- **Patients**: Craft prompts to generate educational materials addressing patients' unique worries and uncertainties about a new treatment. This personalized information empowers patients and builds trust.
- **Payers**: Develop prompts to create cost-effective analyses customized to payer concerns and budget constraints. This targeted communication fosters collaboration and ensures value-driven healthcare solutions.

2. **Beyond Words: Building Emotional Resonance:**
   - **Empathy-Driven Prompts**: Craft prompts that instruct AI to analyze patient testimonials and social media discussions, generating content that resonates with their experiences and emotional journeys. This emotional connection fosters trust and brand loyalty.
   - **Data-Driven Storytelling**: Use prompts to analyze patient data and weave insights into compelling narratives. Imagine generating personalized stories of patients overcoming challenges with your treatment, creating a powerful emotional impact.
3. **Dynamic Engagement Across Channels:**
   - **Social Media Whispers**: Design prompts to generate personalized social media posts tailored to individual preferences and online behavior. This targeted engagement sparks conversations and builds genuine connections with HCPs and patients.
   - **Interactive Responses**: Craft prompts to create AI-powered chatbots that answer patient questions and offer personalized support. This dynamic engagement fosters trust and empowers patients to take control of their health.

4. **Ethical Considerations and Human Oversight:**
    - Remember, personalization isn't manipulation. Ensure prompts avoid bias, respect patient privacy, and prioritize factual accuracy. Human oversight remains crucial to guiding AI, analyzing outputs, and ensuring ethical communication.

In conclusion, prompt engineering isn't about replacing human empathy but about amplifying it with the power of data and creativity. By whispering the right cues into the ear of AI, pharma marketing can:

- Break through the noise with personalized messages that resonate.
- Forge deeper connections built on trust and understanding.
- Empower patients, engage HCPs, and collaborate with payers.
- Ultimately, it contributes to a future where healthcare is as individual as the people it serves.

So, let's embrace the possibilities of prompt engineering, not as a technological gimmick but as a new artistic language for pharma marketing. By whispering with precision and empathy, we can create a symphony of understanding and a healthier future, one personalized note at a time.

Diversity of Prompts

The world of prompts in pharma marketing is as diverse as the audiences it aims to reach. Here is a breakdown of different types of prompts and their suitability for specific needs:

1. **Information Prompts**:
    - **Goal**: Deliver factual information and data-driven insights.
        - **Examples**: "Analyze our customer data and generate a report identifying key trends in physician prescribing patterns for our cardiovascular drug."

- "Write a factual and concise blog post summarizing the latest research findings on the efficacy of our new oncology treatment."
- "Create a data visualization illustrating the cost-effectiveness of our diabetes medication compared to competitors."

2. **Creative Prompts:**
   - **Goal**: Spark creative content, generate engaging narratives, and evoke emotions.
     - **Examples**: "Write a patient testimonial video script that captures the journey of overcoming challenges with our medication, focusing on hope and resilience."
     - "Develop a social media campaign concept targeting HCPs, using humor and relatable scenarios to highlight the benefits of our new diagnostic tool."
     - Craft a personalized email to a specific patient, addressing their concerns and offering tailored support resources.
3. **Interactive Prompts:**
   - **Goal**: Foster dialogue, answer questions, and provide personalized experiences.
     - **Examples:** "Develop a chatbot script for our website that guides patients through symptom assessments and offers relevant health information based on their responses."
     - "Create an AI-powered tool that allows HCPs to input their specific patient details and receive personalized treatment recommendations."
     - "Design an interactive infographic that allows patients to explore the mechanism of action of our medication and its potential side effects in a visually engaging way."

Choosing the Right Prompt Type

Choosing the best prompt type depends on the specific marketing objective and target audience:

- **For Targeted HCP Communications**: Informative prompts and interactive tools deliver data-driven insights and personalized recommendations.
- **For Patient Education and Support**: Creative prompts and interactive tools excel at building empathy, providing personalized information, and fostering patient engagement.
- **Creative Prompts:** Can spark audience interest in broader awareness campaigns and generate engaging content for social media and other channels.

Remember:

- **Clarity and Specificity are Keys**: The more detailed and precise your prompts, the better the AI can understand your intent and generate relevant outputs.
- **Experimentation is Encouraged**: Don't be afraid to try different prompt types and refine your approach to find what works best for your specific needs.
- **Always Prioritize Accuracy and Ethical Considerations**: Ensure your prompts avoid bias, misinformation, and manipulation, and focus on delivering factual and responsible communication.

By understanding the different types of prompts and choosing the right ones for your goals, you can unlock the full potential of prompt engineering in pharma marketing and create personalized, impactful communication that resonates with your audience.

Unleashing Creativity with AI: Effective Use of Prompts in Pharma Marketing

AI language models like Bard are powerful tools for pharma marketing, but maximizing their potential requires crafting well-defined prompts. Here are several prompt techniques for different marketing initiatives, with examples to spark your creativity:

1. **Persona-Driven Content Generation**:
   - **Technique**: Describe a detailed patient, HCP, patient, or payer persona, then prompt the AI to generate content tailored to their needs and preferences.

   Example: "Sarah is a 35-year-old tech-savvy diabetic struggling to manage her insulin injections at work discreetly. Create a series of interactive mobile app notifications offering practical tips and discreet reminders for managing her medication."

2. **Data-driven insights and Storytelling:**
   - **Technique**: Feed the AI relevant data sets and keywords, then prompt it to create a compelling narrative connecting the data to patient challenges or HCP interests.

   Example: "Analyze clinical trial data on a new cancer treatment targeting a specific gene mutation. Write a blog post for patients explaining the science behind the drug in an engaging and easily understandable way."

3. **Personalized Patient Support and Education:**
   - **Technique**: Describe a specific patient concern or question, then prompt the AI to craft personalized responses or educational materials aligned with their situation.

   Example: "John is a cancer survivor experiencing anxiety about recurrence. Generate a chatbot script offering empathetic support and personalized resources for managing anxiety and connecting with other survivors."

4. **HCP-Focused Knowledge Sharing and Collaboration:**
   - **Technique**: Describe a specific clinical scenario or treatment dilemma faced by HCPs, and then prompt the AI to generate case studies, research summaries, or collaborative discussion forums.

   Example: "Dr. Lee is interested in exploring personalized medicine approaches for managing heart failure. Create a case study showcasing how AI-powered data analysis helped guide treatment decisions for a complex patient."

5. **Payer-Oriented Value Demonstration and Cost Effectiveness Analysis:**
    - **Technique**: Provide data on a new medication or preventive program, then prompt the AI to generate reports or presentations for payers, highlighting cost savings and improved patient outcomes.

Example: "Analyze data on a medication adherence program for patients with respiratory conditions. Develop a presentation for Ms. Garcia demonstrating the program's cost-effectiveness in reducing hospital readmissions."

Encourage iterative refinement. Use the AI-generated content as a starting point, iteratively refine it with your human expertise, and provide feedback to the AI to improve its understanding of your brand voice and marketing goals.

CHAPTER

52

Chain Prompting: Orchestrating a Symphony of Content

Imagine composing a melody, not note by note, but by whispering the first few bars and letting the AI orchestra fill in the rest. This is the essence of chain prompting, a technique that takes prompt engineering to the next level, weaving together a symphony of interconnected content.

Chain prompting is a fascinating technique in prompt engineering that takes things further than creating single pieces of content. Imagine it as crafting a complex narrative, not by writing every sentence yourself, but by whispering the starting point and letting an AI orchestra fill in the rest, note by note, building a cohesive and intricate sequence. Here is what chain prompting is all about:

Concept:

- You provide an initial (seed prompt) for the AI, outlining the desired content's theme, tone, and general direction.
- The AI analyzes the seed prompt and generates an initial response.
- You then use the AI's generated response as a new prompt, adding further details or instructions to refine the direction.
- This process continues iteratively, with you feeding the AI's previous output as the next prompt, gradually building a chain of interconnected content.

Benefits:

- **Creating Multi-Touchpoint Campaigns:** Start with a social media post prompt and watch the AI cascade it into related tweets, blog posts, and personalized emails, all seamlessly connected.
- **Developing Interactive Narratives**: Craft an initial prompt for a patient education video, and the AI can spin it into a branching storyline, adapting to user choices for a dynamic learning experience.
- **Building Brand Ecosystems**: Start with a brand identity prompt, and the AI can generate a cascade of content across different channels, ensuring consistent messaging and tone throughout.

How Chain Prompting Works

1. **Start with a Seed Prompt**: This is your initial idea or question. It could be anything from a new medication to a challenge HCPs face in diagnosing a rare disease.
2. **Pass the Torch to AI**: Give the AI your seed prompt and ask it to respond. This response could be a solution, a new question, or content related to your initial ideas.
3. **Chain Reaction**: Build on the AI's response by asking another question, providing additional content, or adding your creative twist. This creates a back-and-forth exchange in which the AI and you fuel each other's ideas.
4. **Repeat and Refine:** Continue the chain with as many interactions as you like, each building upon the previous one. The more you interact with the AI, the more it understands your intent and the more intricate and insightful the chain becomes.

How To Do It

In pharma marketing, chain prompting holds immense potential for:

1. **Define Your Goal**: What type of content chain do you want to build? A campaign, a narrative, or something else?
2. **Craft a Clear Seed Prompt:** Be specific about the theme, tone, and target audience. The more detailed you are, the better the AI can understand your intent.
3. **Iterate and Refine:** Use the AI's output as a new prompt, adding details or instructions to guide the direction. Don't be afraid to backtrack and adjust if needed.
4. **Maintain Control**: Use stop words or specific instructions to set boundaries for the AI's creativity. Human oversight is crucial to ensure accuracy and ethical considerations.
5. **Invest in Data Quality**: The AI's performance depends on the data it's trained on. Ensure your data is clean, accurate, and representative.

Remember:

- Chain prompting is a collaborative process. It's about harnessing the power of AI to amplify human creativity, not replace it.
- Start small and experiment. Begin with simple chains and gradually increase complexity as you gain experience.
- Prioritize ethical considerations. Ensure your prompts and AI outputs are factual, unbiased, and respectful of privacy.

Remember, the possibilities are endless. Feel free to experiment with different prompts, styles, and techniques to unlock the full potential of AI in optimizing your pharma marketing initiatives. By embracing these prompt techniques and fostering a collaborative spirit between humans and AI, you can craft compelling content, personalize interactions, and ultimately, stronger relationships with HCPs and payers, paving the way for a future where pharma marketing is truly impactful and driven by a deep understanding of individual needs.

Careful Orchestration

However, chain prompting requires careful orchestration to avoid dissonance and ensure coherence:

- **Maintaining Control**: Define clear boundaries for the AI's creativity, using "stop words" or specific instructions to guide the generated content within relevant parameters.
- **Human Oversight is Crucial**: Monitor the AI's output at every stage, ensuring factual accuracy, ethical considerations, and alignment with desired messaging.
- **Data Quality is Key**: The AI's performance hinges on the data quality it's trained on. Invest in clean, accurate, representative data sets to fuel responsible and effective chain prompting.

Chain Prompting: A Hypothetical Example

Starting Prompt:

"Craft a series of personalized messages for a 35-year-old woman diagnosed with moderate-persistent asthma, focusing on education, support, and motivation."

Chain 1: Diagnosis and Understanding

AI Response:

Hello, (Patient Name). I understand you've recently been diagnosed with asthma. It's normal to feel overwhelmed, but you're not alone. Let's talk about what asthma is and how to manage it effectively.

User Feedback: "Great start! Can you offer specific resources for learning about asthma triggers and medications?"

AI Response:

Of course! Here are some reliable websites and infographics explaining asthma triggers and common medications. We can also explore interactive quizzes to personalize your understanding.

Chain 2: Daily Management and Triggers

User Prompt: "Fantastic! Now, help me identify potential triggers in my daily life and develop strategies to avoid them."

AI Response: Let's start with your home environment. Tell me about your dust exposure, pets, and any potential allergens you encounter at work or in your hobbies.

User Feedback: "I work in a bakery, and flour dust irritates my airways. I also have a cat at home."

AI Response: You are right; flour dust and cat allergens can be triggers. Here are tips for minimizing exposure at work and home, including wearing a mask at the bakery and regularly grooming your cat.

Chain 3: Support and Motivation

User Prompt: " This is helpful. How can I stay motivated to manage my asthma and stick to my treatment plan?"

AI Response: Let's connect you with a virtual support group specifically for people with asthma. You can share experiences, ask questions, and find inspiration from others facing similar challenges.

User Feedback: "That sounds great! Can you also create personalized reminders for taking my medication and tracking my symptoms?"

AI Response: Absolutely! I can set up alerts on your phone and generate weekly reports summarizing your symptoms and medication adherence.

This is just a small example, but it showcases how chain prompting can be used to:

- Personalize content based on individual needs and preferences.

- Provide comprehensive education and support across different phases of the patient journey.
- Motivate and empower patients to take control of their asthma management.
- Offer access to additional resources and support networks.

Remember, chain prompting is a flexible tool that can be adapted to various aspects of the patient journey and tailored to specific patient demographics and needs.

By fostering this collaborative dialogue between humans and AI, we can create a more engaging and effective experience for patients with chronic conditions, ultimately leading to better health outcomes and a more empowered patient population.

By skillfully wielding the baton of chain prompting, pharma marketers can orchestrate a symphony of personalized content, foster deeper engagement, and create a cohesive brand experience across every touchpoint. Remember, chain prompting is not about relinquishing control but about collaboration, harnessing the power of AI to amplify human creativity and create impactful pharma marketing narratives.

Remember, the future of pharma marketing lies in embracing innovative techniques and fostering collaboration between human and AI capabilities. Marketers can unlock new frontiers of creativity and connection with the healthcare landscape by drawing inspiration from traditional practices like the *Exquisite Corpse* and cutting-edge tools like chain prompting.

Pharma Marketing Applications

Here are some exciting ways to use the chain prompt technique in pharma marketing:

- **Patient-Journey Mapping**: Start with a patient's diagnosis and use the chain prompt to map their emotional journey, identifying challenges, potential interventions, and educational resources of each stage.

- **Brainstorming New Marketing Campaigns**: Start with a broad theme, "promoting healthy lifestyle choices for diabetes patients," and see where the AI takes you. Each iteration could generate new campaign ideas, content formats, or unexpected partnerships.
- **Developing Personalized Content**: Start with a patient persona and let the AI chain proceed through creating a personalized brochure or social media post addressing their specific needs and concerns.
- **Facilitating HCP collaboration:** Use the chain prompt to develop interactive case studies or online forums where HCPs can share experiences, discuss complex cases, and brainstorm innovative treatment approaches.
- **Generating Value Propositions for Payers**: Start with a specific medication or intervention and chain-prompt your way through demonstrating its cost-effectiveness, impact on patient outcomes, and potential for reducing healthcare costs.

Remember, the chain prompt technique is all about exploration and collaboration. Embrace the process's unpredictable nature, trust the AI's creative leaps, and be prepared to be surprised by the results. This technique can unlock a hidden reservoir of fresh ideas, personalized content, and innovative solutions for all your pharma marketing needs.

Unveiling the Palette: Prompting Techniques for Pharma Marketing

The pharma marketing world constantly evolves, and AI-powered prompting techniques offer exciting new possibilities to unleash creativity and craft impactful messages. Here are some diverse prompting techniques to fuel your marketing campaigns:

1. **Persona-Driven Prompts**:

   - **Step into the Shoes of Your Target Audience**: Imagine a specific patient profile, HCP, or payer persona facing a challenge. Prompt the AI to generate content tailored to their needs, preferences, and language style.

   Example: "John, a middle-aged businessman with type 2 diabetes, struggles to find healthy lunch options at work. Create a series of mobile app notifications with quick, delicious, and diabetic-friendly recipe suggestions."

2. **Data-Driven Insights and Storytelling**:

   - **Feed Your AI Data Treasure Trove**: Provide clinical trial data, patient surveys, or market research findings. Prompt the AI to analyze the data and weave informative narratives connecting it to patient challenges or HCP interests.

   Example: "Analyze data on a new cancer treatment targeting a specific genetic mutation. Write a blog post for patients explaining the science behind the drug in an engaging and easily understandable way."

3. **Personalized Patient Support and Education:**

   - **Describe a Specific Patient Concern or Question**: Prompt the AI to create personalized responses or educational materials that directly address the patient's situation and empower them with knowledge.

   Example: "Susan is anxious about potential recurrence after completing her cancer treatment. Generate a chatbot script offering empathetic support, personalized resources for managing anxiety, and connecting her with other survivor communities."

4. **HCP-Focused Knowledge Sharing and Collaboration:**

   - **Present a Clinical Dilemma or Treatment Challenges Faced by HCPs**: Prompt the AI to generate case studies, research summaries, or interactive discussion forums fostering collaborative problem-solving and knowledge sharing among healthcare professionals.

Example: "Dr. Lee wants to explore personalized medicine approaches for managing heart failure. Create a case study showcasing how AI-powered data analysis helped guide treatment decisions for a complex patient."

5. **Payer-Oriented Value Demonstration and Cost-Effectiveness Analysis:**
   - **Provide Data on Your New Medication or Preventive Program**: Prompt the AI to generate reports or presentations for payers, highlighting cost savings and improved patient outcomes, demonstrating the drug's value proposition.

Example: "Analyze data on a medication adherence program for patients with chronic respiratory conditions. Develop a presentation for Ms. Garcia demonstrating the program's cost-effectiveness in reducing hospital readmissions.

More Prompting Techniques

- **Emotional Targeting**: Create content that resonates emotionally, understanding your audience's fears, hopes, and aspirations.
- **Interactive Prompts**: Integrate quizzes, polls, and personalized assessments into your content, engaging your audience and tailoring the experiences to their needs.

Remember:

- Prompts are just the starting point. Your unique ideas, human expertise, and ethical considerations shape the outcomes.
- Experiment and refine! See what sparks your creativity and resonates with your target audience.
- Embrace collaboration! Use AI as a powerful tool to enhance your human-powered marketing efforts.

Chain Prompt Technique: More Examples

Example#1: Journey Map of a Hypertensive Patient

Here's an example of a hypertensive patient named Alex, exploring his challenges, opportunities for interventions, and personalized resources at each stage of his journey:

Seed Prompt: Alex, a 42-year-old busy professional, was recently diagnosed with hypertension. He feels overwhelmed and unsure of where to start.

AI Response: Alex might be struggling with understanding his diagnosis, managing medication adherence, and incorporating lifestyle changes into his hectic schedule.

Human Prompt: Let's explore Alex's initial diagnosis experience. How can we make it more informative and less intimidating?

AI Response: Consider personalized e-guides explaining hypertension in simple terms, highlighting potential risks and benefits of early intervention. Offer video consultations with approachable doctors to address anxieties and clarify doubts.

Human Prompt: Great! Now, let's focus on medication adherence. What tools and resources can help Alex integrate medication into his daily routine?

AI Response: Develop smart pill bottles with built-in reminders and adherence tracking. Offer gamified mobile apps with personalized medication schedules, educational quizzes, and rewards for consistent adherence.

Human Prompt: Interesting! What about dietary and lifestyle changes? How can we support Alex in adopting healthier habits without adding to his stress?

AI Response: Design AI-powered meal-planning tools that suggest delicious and healthy recipes based on Alex's preferences and dietary restrictions. Recommend convenient, short video workouts tailored to his fitness level and schedule.

Human Prompt: Brilliant! Let's also consider Alex's emotional well-being. How can we help him manage stress and anxiety related to his diagnosis?

AI Response: Integrate mindfulness and relaxation exercises into the mobile app, connect Alex with online support groups for hypertensive patients, and offer access to mental health professionals for personalized guidance.

Human Prompt: This is shaping beautifully! Finally, how can Alex stay engaged and on track throughout the journey?

AI Response: Implement a dynamic feedback system within the app, tracking the progress, celebrating milestones, and offering adaptive support based on Alex's changing needs and preferences.

This is just a glimpse into the potential of chain prompting for patient journey mapping. We've built a road map for Alex's journey by iterating on prompts and responses, offering informative resources, support tools, and personalized interventions at every critical step.

Example #2: Brainstorming with AI: Unveiling a Healthy Lifestyle Campaign for Diabetics

Let's unleash the power of prompting to brainstorm a captivating marketing campaign promoting healthy lifestyle choices for diabetic patients! Here's how the chain prompt technique can spark your creativity:

Seed Prompt: Create a campaign that inspires and supports diabetic patients adopting sustainable, healthy lifestyle changes.

AI Response: Consider focusing on "small wins" to avoid overwhelming patients. Break down healthy habits into bite-sized, achievable actions.

Human Prompt: Great idea! Let's personify these "small wins." How about a cartoon character named Sugar Savvy Sarah, who offers practical tips?

AI Response: Brilliant! Sarah could share recipes, exercise routines, and motivational boosters through a mobile app or social media.

Human Prompt: Let's add a gamified element to keep patients engaged. How about earning points for tracking progress and overcoming challenges?

AI Response: Absolutely! Points could unlock rewards like virtual badges, discounts on healthy products, or even participation in exclusive support groups.

Human Prompt: We need to personalize the experience. Can Sarah adapt her advice based on individual needs and preferences?

AI Response: Sure! Users could complete a short quiz to define their goals and challenges, and Sarah could tailor her tips accordingly.

Human Prompt: Let's make it interactive! How about live cooking demonstrations or fitness challenges with Sarah on social media?"

AI Response: Fantastic! User-generated content could be encouraged, showcasing patients' "small wins" and inspiring others.

Human Prompt: This is shaping up nicely! What about a catchy slogan to encapsulate the campaign's spirit?

AI Response: "Small Steps, Big Impact; Own Your Health with Sugar Savvy Sarah!"

Human Prompt: Perfect! Now, how can we reach patients beyond digital platforms?

AI Response: Partner with pharmacies and community centers to host workshops, cooking classes, and support groups led by healthcare professionals and Sarah's virtual presence.

This chain prompt journey has generated an engaging campaign blueprint focused on empowering diabetic patients with personalized, gamified support for adopting healthy lifestyle habits. Remember, this is just the beginning! Feel free to keep prompting:

- Explore different creative formats for Sarah's content (animated videos, podcasts, blog posts).
- Develop a partnership with fitness brands or healthy meal delivery services.
- Design incentives for healthcare providers to encourage campaign participation.
- Consider multilingual versions of the campaign to reach diverse patient populations.

Your campaign gains depth, dimension, and potential impact with each prompt. So, let's continue brainstorming, embrace the power of AI and human collaboration, and craft a campaign that inspires and empowers diabetic patients to take charge of their health and embrace a brighter future.

Example #3: Creating Personalized Content for a Diabetic Patient

Let's chain prompt our way to craft personalized content for a diabetic patient named Emily, keeping her unique needs and preferences in mind:

Seed Prompt: Emily is a 28-year-old tech-savvy diabetic struggling to stick to her meal plan at work. She loves Asian cuisine but finds healthy options limited around her office.

AI Response: Focus on convenience and quick recipe ideas. Offer meal prep tips and suggest portable containers for carrying lunch.

Human Prompt: Let's personalize further! How about a mobile app that recommends Asian-inspired diabetic-friendly meals based on Emily's location and dietary preferences?

AI Response: Excellent! The app could even suggest nearby restaurants with healthy options on their menu, complete with nutritional information.

Human Prompt: Cool! We can also gamify the experience. How about earning points for sticking to the meal plan and unlocking new recipe options or discounts at healthy restaurants?

AI Response: Absolutely! Points could even track progress toward personalized health goals, like maintaining blood sugar levels.

Human Prompt: Let's add a social element. In the app, could Emily connect with other tech-savvy diabetic patients to share recipe ideas and tips?

AI Response: Sure! A secure forum or private chat groups could foster a supportive community for sharing challenges and celebrating successes.

Human Prompt: How can we address Emily's emotional well-being? Can the app offer mindfulness exercises or stress management techniques for mealtime challenges?

AI Response: Definitely! Short guided meditations or breathing exercises help Emily manage stress and make healthier choices during busy workdays.

Human Prompt: This is shaping nicely! Let's make it visually appealing. Can the app integrate beautiful photos and engaging video tutorials for the recipes?

AI Response: Absolutely! User-generated content could also be encouraged, allowing Emily to share healthy Asian dishes and inspire others.

This chain prompt journey has built a framework for personalized content that caters to Emily's specific needs and preferences. Remember, the possibilities are endless:

- Refine the app features based on Emily's feedback, adding grocery list integration or personalized meal planning tools.
- Partner with local Asian restaurants to offer app users healthy menu options and discounts.
- Develop educational content within the app, demystifying diabetes management and sharing practical tips for managing blood sugar levels.
- Organize virtual cooking classes or fitness challenges for tech-savvy diabetic patients like Emily.

By enhancing the chain prompt technique and constantly refining your ideas, you can create personalized content that resonates with Emily's unique situation, empowers her to manage her diabetes confidently, and fosters a supportive community of like-minded individuals.

Example #4: An AI-Human Symphony: Collaborating with an HCP for Treating a Cancer Patient

Let's explore a hypothetical collaboration between an HCP, Dr. Lee, and AI to personalize Susan's cancer treatment journey.

Initial Diagnosis: Susan, a 35-year-old mother of two, receives a diagnosis of early-stage breast cancer. Dr. Lee utilizes AI-powered diagnostic tools to analyze scans and genomic data, revealing a specific gene mutation.

AI Prompt 1: Given Sarah's unique genetic profile, AI suggests a novel targeted therapy with promising clinical trial results.

Dr. Lee's Response: Intriguing! While conventional options exist, personalized therapy options offer the potential for enhanced efficacy and reduced side effects for Susan.

AI Prompt 2: Based on clinical trial data, the AI generates a personalized risk-benefit analysis, highlighting potential side effects and Susan's specific response probability.

Dr. Lee's Response: This detailed information is invaluable. I can discuss it with Susan to ensure she understands this novel therapy's potential benefits and risks.

Shared Patient Education: Dr. Lee leverages AI-generated visuals and patient-friendly summaries to explain the novel therapy to Susan. The AI personalizes the information based on Susan's age, background, and preferred communication style.

Treatment Decision Collaboration: Dr. Lee facilitates an open discussion with Susan, considering her values, family situation, and risk tolerance. AI presents alternative options and their respective outcomes, empowering Susan to participate actively in decision-making.

Treatment Monitoring and Optimization: Dr. Lee utilizes AI-powered tools to monitor Susan's response and potential side effects throughout the treatment course. The AI analyzes Susan's medical data and generates dynamic risk assessment, prompting Dr. Lee to adjust the treatment plan if needed.

Beyond Treatment: AI aids Dr. Lee in developing a personalized post-treatment plan for Susan, including follow-up schedules, wellness recommendations, and potential risk management strategies based on her unique risk profile.

The Power of Collaboration: This scenario highlights the synergy between AI and the HCP:

- AI provides advanced insights and personalized data analysis.
- Dr. Lee adds human empathy, ethical considerations, and clinical expertise.
- Susan benefits from a personalized treatment plan, informed decision-making, and ongoing support.

This is just one example, and the possibilities are endless. AI can:

- Help Dr. Lee identify relevant clinical trials for Susan based on her case.
- Facilitate secure communication between Dr. Lee and Susan through a personalized patient portal.
- Connect Susan with peer support groups for patients undergoing similar treatments.

By embracing AI as a collaborative tool, HCPs like Dr. Lee can elevate the standard of care, empowering patients like Susan to take charge of their journey and navigate the complexities of cancer treatment with personalized support and informed decision-making.

Remember, the human touch remains irreplaceable. Let's continue exploring ways to leverage AI's analytical power to empower HCPs like Dr. Lee, allowing them to focus on their best— building trust, providing compassionate care, and guiding patients like Susan toward a brighter future.

Example#5: Creating a Value Proposition for Payers

Let's prompt our way to a compelling value proposition for payers for our groundbreaking diabetes drug.

Seed Prompt:

Introducing "Empower": A revolutionary new drug tackling type 2 diabetes at its core, empowering patients and unlocking significant value for payers.

AI Response: AI has created the following multidimensional value proposition for payers.

Empower isn't just a new drug for type 2 diabetes; it's a paradigm shift in managing the disease. Empower offers payers a unique opportunity to:

Reduce Long-Term Costs:

- **Delay or prevent complications**: By effectively managing blood sugar levels at the source, Empower can help reduce the risk of costly downstream complications like cardiovascular disease, kidney failure, and amputations.
- **Minimize hospitalizations and readmissions**: Improved glycemic control can lead to fewer hospital stays and emergency room visits, significantly impacting healthcare spending.
- **Decrease disease burden**: Empower's potential to slow disease progression translates to lower healthcare costs for payers in the long run.

Improve Member Health Outcomes:

- **Enhanced quality of life**: Empower empowers patients to manage their diabetes better, improving overall health and well-being.
- **Increased productivity**: By effectively controlling their condition, patients are less likely to miss work due to illness, which increases productivity and economic benefits.
- **Reduced member dissatisfaction**: By offering a revolutionary treatment option, payers can demonstrate their commitment to providing members with the latest and most effective therapies.

Administrative Efficiency:

- **Simplified medication management**: Empower's potential for once-daily dosing can improve medication adherence and reduce the complexity of managing multiple medications.
- **Streamlined care coordination**: Empower's focus on addressing the root cause of type 2 diabetes can potentially streamline care coordination and reduce the need for multiple specialists.

- **Reduced administrative burden**: Fewer complications and hospitalizations can lower the administrative costs of managing complex chronic conditions.
- **Investing in the Future:**
    - **Future-proof your population health strategy**: Empower positions payers at the forefront of innovative diabetes management, demonstrating a commitment to long-term cost savings and improved member health.
    - **Attract and retain healthy members:** By offering a revolutionary treatment option, payers can position themselves as an attractive choice for health-conscious individuals.
    - **Contribute to a healthier society:** By effectively managing type 2 diabetes, Empower can help reduce the overall healthcare burden on society.

Empower is more than just a medication; it's a strategic partnership that allows payers to achieve significant cost savings, improve member health outcomes, and contribute to a healthier future. Let's unlock the true value of Empower together.

CHAPTER

53

The Game of *Exquisite Corpse* and Chain Prompts

The chain prompt is a fascinating technique for leveraging AI's creative power in pharma marketing. Imagine a game of *Exquisite Corpse*, where each player adds their part to a story, building it in an unpredictable and often delightful way. In the chain prompt technique, you do the same with AI, but instead of words, you use short prompts and responses to build a narrative or generate ideas.

The Game of *Exquisite Corpse*

The game of *Exquisite Corpse* or *Cadavre Exquis* in its original French is a collaborative drawing or writing game invented by the Surrealists in the 1920s. It's known for its unexpected and often humorous or absurd results.

Here's how it works:

1. **Folding and Concealment:** A piece of paper is divided into sections (usually three) and folded so only the last section is visible.
2. **Individual Contribution:** The first player draws or writes something in the visible section, keeping it secret from the others.
3. **Passing it on:** The paper is folded again, revealing the part of the first player's creation and concealing the rest. The second player adds to the drawing or writing based on what they see, without knowing what came before.

4. **Repeat and Reveal:** This process continues with as many players as you like, each adding their contribution without seeing the complete picture until the end.
5. **Unfolding the Masterpiece:** Finally, the paper is unfolded, revealing the full, collaborative creation— often a bizarre, nonsensical, and surprisingly amusing artwork or story.

Surrealists used the *Exquisite Corpse* to explore the limits of consciousness and creativity, encouraging spontaneity and collaboration. Today, it's still enjoyed as a fun and creative game, and variations have been developed for more than just drawing and writing.

Here are some additional facts about *Exquisite Corpse*:

- The name *Cadaver Equis* comes from a phrase that emerged in one of the first games. "Le Cadaver Equis bora le vin nouveau" (the Exquisite Corpse will drink the new wine).
- Famous Surrealists like André Breton, Salvador Dali, and Yves Tanguy played the game.
- The technique has also been used in music, film, and other art forms.

The game of *Exquisite Corpse*, popularized by the Surrealists, involves collaboratively creating a piece of art, typically a drawing or poem, sequentially and blindfolded. Each participant contributes a section without knowing what has come before, resulting in unexpected and often humorous or absurd creations. There are intriguing similarities between the exquisite corpse and chain prompting:

- **Collaborative Creativity**: Both rely on a collaborative approach, where humans and AI (or humans in the *exquisite corpse*) work together to build something creative.
- **Unforeseen Outcome**: Both embrace the element of surprise and the potential for unexpected, even nonsensical, outputs.

- **Iteration and Refinement**: Both involve a back-and-forth process of iteration and refinement, where each player (or prompt) builds upon the previous contribution.

However, there are also key *differences*:

- **Control and Guidance**: In chain prompting, the human holds more control, setting the initial direction and providing feedback to guide the AI's output. In *Exquisite Corpse*, blindness is central, leading to greater surprise and absurdity.
- **Purpose and Goal**: *Exquisite Corpse* is primarily associated with artistic expression and exploration. Meanwhile, chain prompting refers to a specific goal or purpose, such as generating marketing content or educational resources.
- **Application and Impact**: *Exquisite Corpse* has primarily remained within art and creative expression, while chain prompting is gaining traction in various fields, including pharma marketing.

Relevance to Pharma Marketing

The principles of the *Exquisite Corpse* adapted and incorporated into chain prompting, offer valuable potential for pharma marketing in several ways:

- **Breaking Creative Roadblocks**: Chain prompting can spark unexpected ideas and generate diverse content formats, helping marketers overcome creative inertia and develop engaging campaigns.
- **Personalized Content and Storytelling** allow for tailoring content to specific audiences and building unique narratives that resonate with individual needs and experiences.
- **Humorous and Engaging Messages**: By embracing the element of surprise, chain prompting can inject humor and lightheartedness into pharma marketing, making complex topics more accessible and engaging.

- **Collaborative Innovation:** Fosters collaboration between marketing teams and data scientists, leveraging human creativity and AI's data-driven insights for impactful campaigns.

Unleashing Creative Choas: *Exquisite Corpse* in Pharma Marketing

The world of pharma marketing often demands serious communication and scientific accuracy. But what if you could tap into *Exquisite Corpse's* playful absurdity to ignite a spark of creative energy within your brand team? This unconventional technique can help brainstorm new campaign ideas through creative roadblocks and foster a more playful and collaborative environment.

Imagine This:

Your brand team is stuck trying to devise a memorable campaign for a new medication to alleviate insomnia. The usual tactics feel tired and uninspired. So you decide to break out the metaphorical paper and scissors and play a round of *Exquisite Corpses*.

Here's How It Could Unfold:

Fold 1: Sarah, a copywriter, starts by writing a whimsical sentence on the hidden portion of the paper: "Dreaming sleep waltz beneath a moon made of cheese..."

Fold 2: David, the art director, peeks at the last word, "cheese," and draws a surreal landscape with a giant, glowing moon sculpted from cheddar.

Fold 3: The social media manager, Emily, glimpses the cheese moon and writes a humorous tagline: "Tired of counting sheep? Say cheese to restful nights!"

Unfolding the Masterpiece: The team unfolds the paper and bursts into laughter, surprised by the absurd yet strangely fitting combination of words and images. This unexpected spark becomes the seed for a campaign featuring cheese-themed sleep rituals, humorous social media memes, and partnerships with sleep clinics offering moonlit cheese meditation sessions.

The Magic of *Exquisite Corpse* Lies in its:

- **Unpredictability**: By hiding each other's contributions, you force your team to step outside their comfort zone and embrace the unknown.
- **Collaboration**: It builds on each other's ideas, fostering a sense of shared ownership and creative camaraderie.
- **Humor and Absurdism**: Injecting a dose of playful silliness can loosen creative inhibitions and lead to fresh, unexpected ideas.

Beyond Campaign Brainstorming, you can use *Exquisite Corpse* for:

- **Developing Patient Personas**: Each team member contributes personality traits, quirks, and challenges, resulting in a multifaceted and realistic patient profile.
- **Crafting Patient Education Materials**: Generate engaging narratives by combining scientific facts, unexpected metaphors, and humorous analogies.
- **Designing Clinical Trial Patient Recruitment Materials**: Avoid generic brochures by creating whimsical visuals and storylines that capture attention and spark curiosity.

Remember, the key is to embrace the playful spirit of the game and be open to the unexpected. Don't judge ideas too harshly; let the absurdity flow, and you might stumble upon your next groundbreaking pharma marketing campaign.

So, grab your team some paper and scissors, and unleash the creative chaos of *Exquisite Corpse* in your next brainstorming session. You might be surprised at the innovative and memorable ideas from this playful dance of words and images.

Let's break through the creative barriers and paint the canvas of pharma marketing with unexpected strokes of inspiration!

Example #1: *Exquisite Corpse* for Compassion: Building a Cancer Patient Persona

Imagine your brand team gathered around a table, paper, and scissors in hand, ready to play a round of *Exquisite Corpse*— this time, not for laughs, but for empathy. Their goal is to build a detailed, nuanced persona of a cancer patient, understanding their fears, hopes, and challenges.

Fold 1: Sarah, a nurse on the team, hides the first sentence: "Diagnosed at 32, fear hangs heavy, cloak.."

Fold 2: David, the marketing manager, peeks at the word "cloak" and sketches a portrait of a young woman wrapped in a swirling shawl, eyes filled with uncertainty.

Fold 3: The patient advocate, Emily, draws a hospital bedside table cluttered with pill bottles and a half-read copy of "Tuesdays with Morrie."

Fold 4: John, the research analyst, hides his growing persona with the following sentence: "Work hangs heavy too, a financial rope taut across hope."

Unfolding the Persona: Slowly, they reveal their contributions, piecing together the story of Anna, a passionate architect facing stage 2 breast cancer. Her vibrant career is on hold, replaced by doctor's appointments and chemotherapy sessions. The fear Sarah wrote about manifests in sleepless nights and the cloak David drew. Emily's bedside scene whispers of a disrupted life, while John's financial tension paints a picture of added burden.

This persona, born from playful chaos, becomes a valuable tool for the team:

- **Developing Marketing Materials**: Ads resonate with Anna's anxieties and aspirations, offering treatment options, community, and support.

- **Designing Patient Support Program**: The team prioritizes financial assistance and career guidance, recognizing Anna's unique concern.
- **Training Healthcare Professionals**: Doctors and nurses better understand Anna's emotional needs and everyday challenges.

Beyond Character on Paper:

Exquisite Corpse for patient personas goes beyond creating a character on paper. It fosters empathy, allowing the team to step into the shoes of someone like Anna, navigating the uncertainties and complexities of cancer. This shared experience leads to more compassionate, human-centered communication and support systems; in the competitive pharma marketing world, where data rules and science reign, the playfulness of *Exquisite Corpses* offers a surprising pathway to human connection. So gather your team, embrace the unconventional, and let the game guide you in building patient personas that resonate with empathy and understanding. You can unlock the key to creating meaningful experiences for those facing the greatest challenges.

Remember, creativity isn't just about catchy slogans and clever visuals. It's about using your imagination to build bridges of understanding and compassion. Start playing, and let's paint together a brighter future for patients, one creative fold at a time.

Example #2: Unleash the Power of *Exquisite Corpse* to Generate Marketing Materials that Speak Directly to Anna's Heart!

Fold 1: Sarah, the copywriter, starts with a tagline hidden on the paper: "Life is a blueprint, sometimes with unexpected revisions."

Fold 2: David, the art director, draws a dynamic image of Anna standing tall, her architect's tools transformed into cancer-fighting weapons— a pencil as a scalpel, a spray bottle as a chemotherapy pump.

Fold 3: Emily, the social media manager, glimpses the tools and writes a poignant tweet: "Building resilience, one brick at a time. You're the architect of your future, even when the plans change.#CancerWarriors"

Fold 4: John, the research analyst, adds a call to action: "Join our online community— share your blueprints, find support, and build a stronger foundation together."

Unfolding the Materials: The team reveals a cohesive campaign based on resilience and adaptability.

- **Print Ad**: The image of Anna with the tagline "Revisions, Welcome: Building a stronger future, one day at a time."
- **Social Media**: "Cancer may alter the blueprints, but your dreams stay strong. Share your story, find inspiration, and build a community with #CancerArchitects."
- **Website**: A resource hub offering practical tips for managing financial concerns, returning to work, and accessing support groups.

This campaign resonates with Anna's anxieties on multiple levels:

- **Acknowledging the Disruption**: The tagline and visuals validate her fear of change while emphasizing her power to adapt.
- **Celebrate her Strength:** The architect metaphor portrays her as a builder capable of crafting a new chapter in her life.
- **Offers Community and Support**: The online platform and hashtag connect her with others facing similar challenges, fostering a sense of belonging and shared strength.

Exquisite Corpse doesn't just generate text and images. It generates empathy, understanding, and a message that truly resonates. By stepping into Anna's shoes and letting the game guide their creativity, the team has crafted marketing materials beyond selling a product. They offer hope, connection, and a sense of shared journey. This is just one example, and the possibilities are endless. You can use Exquisite Corpse to:

- Develop video testimonials featuring patients like Anna, reliably sharing their stories and struggles.
- Create interactive online tools that help patients navigate treatment options and build personalized support plans.
- Organize workshops and events focused on coping with cancer's emotional and practical challenges, fostering connections, and building community.

Remember, the key is to let Anna's unique voice and experience guide your creativity. Embrace the playful spirit of the game, and you'll unlock the power of marketing to offer information, genuine connection, and support to those facing their toughest battles.

Let's keep playing, building empathy, and creating a marketing landscape that truly makes a difference in the lives of patients like Anna.

Example#3: Building Bridges of Support: Designing a Cancer Support Program for Anna with *Exquisite Corpse*!

Gather your team around the table, ready to play a round of *Exquisite Corpse* for a heartwarming cause: Crafting a comprehensive support program tailored for Anna, our young architect battling cancer.

Fold 1: Martha, the social worker, starts with a hidden sentence: "Lost in a maze of appointments longing for..."

Fold 2: David, the program coordinator, peeks "longing" and sketches a vibrant community garden, sunlight filtering through lush leaves onto smiling faces.

Fold 3: Emily, the financial counselor, sees the garden and writes: "Financial worries like weeds, choking hope. What if we offered..."

Fold 4: John, the patient advocate, hides the growing program with the following: "A helping hand to tend the soil, nurturing both body and spirit."

Unfolding the Program: Piece by piece, a supportive haven for Anna and others like her emerges:

- **The "Architect of Hope" Support Group**: A warm, welcoming space where patients can share experiences, exchange practical tips, and find solace in a shared understanding.
- **"Financial Gardeners' Counseling"**: Expert financial advisors help patients navigate insurance complexities, manage costs, and access financial aid, removing weeds of worry.
- **"Creative Sprout Workshops"**: These sessions include art therapy, journaling, and creative writing guided by qualified professionals. They allow patients to express their emotions and nurture their spirits.
- **"Career Compass Coaching"**: Career counselors help patients navigate work leave, explore alternative work options, and rebuild their professional trajectory.
- **"Building Bridges Community Outreach"**: Connecting patients with local resources, transportation assistance, and opportunities to volunteer and stay connected to their community.

This program addresses Anna's unique concerns on multiple levels:

- **Social Isolation**: The support group combats loneliness, fostering a sense of belonging and camaraderie.
- **Financial Burden**: Expert guidance alleviates financial worries, allowing Anna to focus on her well-being.
- **Professional Uncertainty**: Career coaching empowers her to explore various paths and maintain a sense of purpose.
- **Emotional Distress**: Creative therapies provide healthy outlets for expressing fears and anxieties, fostering emotional resilience.
- **Lack of Support**: Connection to resources and the community ensures Anna is not alone in her journey.

Exquisite Corpse doesn't just design programs. It builds bridges of empathy and understanding.

The team has crafted a support program that goes beyond providing services. By stepping into Anna's shoes and letting the game guide their creativity, they have created an ecosystem where Anna can flourish despite her challenges.

This is just one example, and the possibilities are endless. You can use the *Exquisite Corpse* to:

- Develop online modules focusing on nutrition, exercise, and managing side effects.
- Create mobile apps offering personalized reminders, educational materials, and connections to healthcare professionals.
- Organize volunteering opportunities for patients and survivors, fostering a sense of purpose and contribution.
- Partner with local businesses and organizations to provide discounts, services, and activities, promoting community integration.

Remember, the key is to let Anna's unique voice and needs guide your program design. Embrace the playful spirit of the game, and you'll unlock the power of support programs to offer resources, hope, empathy, and a helping hand through life's unexpected revisions.

Let's keep playing, building bridges, and creating support programs that empower patients like Anna to navigate their journeys with dignity and strength.

Example 4: Creating a Unique and Engaging Training Experience for HCPs

Let's unleash the power of Exquisite Corpse again, this time to create a unique and engaging training experience for HCPs, helping them connect with patients like Anna on a deeper level.

Fold 1: Eva, the medical educator, hides the first sentence: "Behind the diagnosis, a life...unfinished symphony, yearning to be heard."

Fold 2: David, the psychologist, peeks at "yearning" and sketches a split canvas— one side with a cold, sterile hospital room, the other with a vibrant landscape filled with vibrant colors and blooming flowers.

Fold 3: Emily, the patient associate, sees the contrasting images and writes: "Beyond protocols and charts, a human story... what if we..."

Fold 4: John, the oncologist, hides the growing exercise and writes: "Listened with open ears, not just stethoscopes, to the music of their hopes and fears?"

Unfolding the Training: We're no longer looking at a lecture outline. Here's a multifaceted training module for HCPs:

- **Empathy Workshop**: HCPs engage in guided visualization and role-playing exercises, stepping into the shoes of patients like Anna to understand their fears, hopes, and unspoken anxieties.
- **Holistic Patient Assessment**: The split canvas metaphor inspires a shift in patient evaluation and encourages HCPs to consider medical data and the patient's personal background, aspirations, and emotional well-being.
- **Communication Skills Training**: Interactive sessions focus on active listening, open-ended questions, and validating responses, helping HCPs build genuine connections with their patients and understand their unique stories.
- **Building Shared Decision-Making**: HCPs learn to translate complex medical information into understandable language, engage patients in treatment discussions, and respect their preferences and values.
- **Creating Support Networks**: The training emphasizes connecting patients with social workers, counselors, and community resources, ensuring holistic support beyond clinic walls.

Addressing Challenges

This training addresses key challenges HCPs face when treating cancer patients:

- **Compassion Fatigue**: Emphasizing empathy combats emotional burnout and reminds HCPs of the human beings behind the diagnosis.
- **Communication Gaps**: Training fosters effective communication strategies, ensuring informed choices and reducing patient anxieties.
- **Lack of Holistic Approach**: The split canvas metaphor encourages HCPs to consider the individual, not just the disease, leading to more personalized care.
- **Limited Understanding of Patient Needs**: Role-playing and patient stories bridge the gap, promoting genuine empathy and understanding.
- **Isolation and Lack of Suppor**t: Training underscores the importance of connecting patients with community resources and support networks.

Exquisite Corpse doesn't just train HCPs. It transforms them into empathetic guides and allies. By stepping into Anna's shoes and letting the game guide their learning, HCPs gain valuable insights into the patient experience. This fosters compassionate connections, empowers informed decision-making, and improves care for patients like Anna and beyond.

This is just one example, and the possibilities are endless. You can use the *Exquisite Corpse* to:

- Develop simulation scenarios where HCPs practice navigating challenging patient interactions and ethical dilemmas.
- Create interactive case studies incorporating multimedia elements like video testimonials and diary entries to bring patient stories to life.

- Organize workshops on topics like managing pain, coping with side effects, and communicating with difficult patients.
- Facilitate discussions with patient advocates and survivors to give HCPs firsthand insights into the patient experience.

Letting the patient's voice and needs guide your training design is key. Embrace the playful spirit of the game, and you'll unlock the power of HCP training to transform them into compassionate companions on the healing journey.

Let's keep playing, building empathy, and creating HCP training experiences that empower them to deliver patient-centered care that makes a difference.

Unleashing Creativity and Impact: Four Key Benefits of Prompt Engineering

The pharma marketing world constantly evolves, demanding innovative approaches to engage healthcare professionals, payers, and patients. This is where prompt engineering is a powerful tool to unlock creativity, refine communication, and maximize your marketing effort's impact.

Here are four major ways prompt engineering can benefit pharma marketing:

1. **Content Personalization:**
    - **Craft Targeted Messages for Specific Audiences**. Use prompts to generate content tailored to the needs and interests of HCPs, payers, or patient segments. Imagine crafting blog posts for HCPs addressing their clinical challenges or personalized video messages for patients offering encouragement and practical tips.
    - **Dynamic and Adaptable Content**: Prompts can adapt to real-time data and trends. Generate content that reflects the latest research findings, market updates, or patient concerns, ensuring your messaging remains relevant and impactful.

2. **Creative Idea Generation:**
   - **Break Through Creative Roadblocks**: Use prompts to spark new ideas for campaigns, brochures, or social media content. Overcome creative stalls by experimenting with different prompts and letting the AI help you explore unexpected avenues.
   - **Develop Compelling Narratives**: Create engaging stories that resonate with your audience. Provide prompts that set the scene, introduce characters, and establish the tone, allowing the AI to generate narratives that connect emotionally with your target audience.
3. **Enhanced Communication and Messaging:**
   - **Clarity and Conciseness**: Utilize prompts to refine your messaging, ensuring it's clear, concise, and impactful. Ask the AI to simplify complex medical terminology or translate dense research findings into understandable language for different audiences.
   - **Compelling Calls to Action**: Design effective calls to action that resonate with your target audience. Create prompts that inspire HCPs to learn more about a new treatment, encourage patients to adhere to their medical regimen, or motivate payers to consider the value proposition of your drug.
4. **Efficient Marketing Workflows:**
   - **Automation and Time-Saving**: Reduce repetitive tasks and save valuable time for your marketing team. Use prompts to automatically generate basic website copy, social media posts, or email drafts, allowing your team to focus on strategic planning and creative tasks.
   - **A/B Testing and Data-Driven Optimization**: Experiment with different prompts and analyze the results to see what resonates best with your audience. This data-driven approach allows you to refine your messaging and maximize the effectiveness of your marketing efforts.

Remember:

- Prompt engineering is a tool, not a magic bullet. The effectiveness relies on carefully crafted prompts and human oversight to ensure accuracy and ethical considerations.
- Combining AI-powered prompt engineering with human creativity and expertise is the key to achieving impactful and successful pharma marketing campaigns.

By embracing the power of prompt engineering, pharma marketing teams can break through creative barriers, personalize communication, and deliver messaging that resonates with their audiences. This leads to more effective outreach and helps build trust, understanding, and a healthier future for everyone.

So, are you ready to unleash the potential of prompt engineering and transform your pharma marketing game? Start crafting your prompts, engage your creativity, and let's unlock a world of possibilities in pharma marketing.

The Future of Prompt Engineering

The future of prompt engineering in pharma marketing is brimming with exciting possibilities, paving the way for deeper connections, hyper-personalization, and a fundamental shift in how we engage with our stakeholders:

1. **Beyond Text: Sensory Experiences**: Imagine crafting prompts that generate multi-sensory content, such as VR simulations for patient education or AI-composed music conveying the emotional journey of treatment. This immersive approach could revolutionize patient outreach and HCP training.
2. **Collaborative Co-creation**: Prompts will evolve to facilitate human+AI partnerships, allowing marketers to guide AI outputs with real-time feedback and continuous iteration. This collaborative approach promises more nuanced and impactful content tailored to specific needs.

3. **Contextual Awareness and Nuances**: AI models will become even more adept at understanding context and nuance, generating content that considers cultural sensitivities, ethical considerations, and individual patient circumstances. This level of sensitivity will be crucial for the responsible and effective use of communication.
4. **Adaptive Campaigns in Real Time:** Imagine campaigns that adjust on the fly based on real-time data and audience reactions. Prompts will enable us to dynamically personalize content and messaging, ensuring relevance and efficacy in a constantly evolving online landscape.
5. **Predictive and Preventative Care:** AI-powered analysis of vast data sets will inform prompts that generate personalized health insights and patient recommendations. This predictive approach could revolutionize preventative care and empower individuals to take ownership of their health.
6. **Democratization of AI Access:** Advancements in technology and cloud-based solutions will make AI tools like prompt engineering more accessible and affordable for smaller pharma companies, leveling the playing field and fostering innovation across the industry.
7. **Ethical Imperative and Transparency:** As AI influence grows, so will the need for robust ethical frameworks and transparent communication. Pharma marketers must ensure prompt engineering adheres to strict ethical guidelines and prioritizes patients' well-being over profit motive.
8. **Continuous Learning and Iteration:** The journey with prompt engineering is ongoing. Pharma companies must be ready to embrace continuous learning, adapt to new advancements, and constantly refine their approach to keep pace with the evolving AI landscape.

In conclusion, the future of prompt engineering in pharma marketing is about generating content and fostering genuine connections, empowering patients, and ultimately, shaping a more responsible and patient-centric healthcare system.

While challenges lie ahead, the potential of this transformative technology is undeniable. By embracing innovation, prioritizing ethics, and fostering collaboration, we can unlock a future where AI and human ingenuity work together to improve lives and create a healthier world.

Remember, the future is not written in stone; it's shaped by our choices today. Let's choose to use prompt engineering responsibly, ethically, and creatively, and together, we can write a copy of progress and positive change in the pharma marketing world.

CHAPTER

54

AI's Symphony in Pharma Marketing: Harmonizing Technology with Humanity

The landscape of pharma marketing is undergoing a paradigm shift. No longer are static ads and traditional channels enough to connect with patients and healthcare professionals (HCPs) meaningfully. This is where the symphony of human ingenuity and artificial intelligence (AI) orchestrate a powerful new performance.

This chapter delves into the diverse AI-powered technologies redefining how pharmaceuticals reach their audience. From digital twins mimicking complex biological systems to augmented reality experiences showcasing drug efficacy, AI is weaving its magic across various aspects of marketing. We'll explore the potential of gamification in driving engagement, the transformative power of natural language processing (NLP) in understanding patient sentiment, and the ethical considerations surrounding gene editing and robotics.

But this isn't just about technology for technology's sake. Each AI tool, from wearable data trackers to blockchain-powered supply chains, serves a critical purpose: empowering patients, informing HCPs, and ultimately improving health outcomes. We'll examine how these technologies harmonize with the human touch., ensuring transparency, ethical practice, and a patient-centric approach.

So, prepare to join the orchestra as we explore the melodies of AI in pharma marketing. Discover how this transformative force is composing a future where innovation and empathy collaborate to orchestrate healthier lives for all.

AI-Powered Technologies

1. **Natural Language Processing (NLP): Unlocking the Power of Words in Pharma Marketing**

   Natural language processing (NLP) revolutionizes how machines understand and manipulate human language. In pharma marketing, NLP promises to extract valuable insights from vast amounts of text data, empowering companies to personalize interactions, optimize campaigns, and gain a deeper understanding of patient needs and sentiments.

   Here are some ways NLP can impact pharma marketing:

   1. **Personalized Patient Engagement**:
      - **Analyze Patient Feedback and Social Media Conversations**: Identify patient concerns, preferences, and unmet needs to inform product development and marketing strategies.
      - **Generate Personalized Health Content**: Tailor educational materials and medication adherence reminders based on individual patient profiles and language preferences.
      - **Develop Chatbots for Patient Support**: Create AI-powered chatbots that answer questions, provide medication reminders, and offer personalized support to patients.

   2. **Optimized Marketing Campaigns**:
      - **Craft Targeted Marketing Messages:** Analyze patient demographics, medical history, and online behavior to segment populations and deliver relevant, personalized messages.

- **Optimize Website Content and Search:** Ensure website content is easily understood and searchable by patients, improving user experience and driving conversations.
- **Monitor Brand Sentiment and Reputation:** Track online mentions of your brand and products, identifying potential issues and opportunities for improvement.

3. **Deeper Understanding of Patient Data:**
   - **Analyze Clinical Trial Data:** Extract key insights from text-based reports and narratives to facilitate quicker data analysis and improved trial design.
   - **Automate Adverse Event Reporting:** Identify potential safety concerns from patient reports and social media, enabling proactive interventions and improved patient safety.
   - **Gain Insights From Scientific Literature:** Analyze research papers and publications to stay informed about the latest advancements and identify potential partnerships and collaborations.

Examples:

- **Novartis** uses NLP to analyze patient feedback and social media conversations to identify potential side effects of a new drug, leading to early intervention and improved patient safety.
- **Roche** leverages NLP to personalize educational content for patients with specific diseases, increasing patient engagement.
- **Pfizer** utilizes NLP to optimize its website content and search function, leading to a significant reduction in bounce rate and increased conversions.

Challenges and Considerations:

- **Data Privacy and Security**: Ethical data collection, storage, and use are paramount.
- **Model Bias and Accuracy**: Continuously monitor and mitigate potential biases in NLP models to ensure fair and accurate results.

- **Human Oversight and Control**: NLP should augment human expertise in marketing, not replace it.
- **Technological Infrastructure and Expertise**: Implementing NLP solutions requires specialized skills and resources.

NLP has the potential to revolutionize pharma marketing. By unlocking the power of language data, we can create a future where patient interactions are personalized, marketing campaigns are targeted and effective, and healthcare insights are deeper and more meaningful. It's a future where words become catalysts for better communication, improved patient care, and healthier lives.

2. **Robotics:**

   Robotics, the design and construction of machines capable of performing tasks autonomously, holds immense potential to reshape pharmaceutical marketing in diverse ways. From assisting patients to revolutionizing clinical trials, robots can enhance efficiency, personalize interaction, and improve brand perception.

   Here is how robotics can impact pharma marketing:

   1. **Enhanced Patient Support and Education**:
      - **Robotics-Powered Medication Reminders:** Robotics can remind patients to take their medication, answer basic dosage questions, and assist with medication management.
      - **Interactive Robots for Patient Education:** AI-powered chatbots can deliver personalized health information, answer patient queries, and offer emotional support.
      - **Telepresence Robots for Remote Consultations:** Healthcare professionals can utilize robots to examine patients remotely, conduct consultations, and offer support, overcoming geographical barriers.

2. **Automated Marketing Tasks and Research**:
   - **Robots for Personalized Marketing Campaign:** AI-powered robots can segment audiences, customize email content, and create targeted marketing campaigns for specific patient groups.
   - **Automated Data Analysis and Research:** Robots can process vast amounts of clinical trial data, identify trends, and predict patient outcomes, accelerating research and development.
   - **Robotic Drug Manufacturing and Packaging:** Automation can increase production efficiency, reduce costs, and ensure consistent quality control in pharmaceutical marketing.
3. **Improved Brand Perception and Innovation:**
   - **Robots Showcasing Innovation at Events and Conferences:** Utilizing robots to demonstrate new technologies and advancements can showcase your brand's commitment to innovation and attract stakeholders.
   - **Robotics in Patient Support Initiatives:** Partnering with organizations to provide robotic assistance to patients in underserved communities can enhance brand perception and position your company as socially responsible.
   - **Ethical Considerations and Responsible Implementation:** Emphasize the ethical use of robots in healthcare and prioritize patient safety, privacy, and transparency to build trust and positive brand association.

Challenges and Considerations:

- **Ethical Considerations**: Ensure ethical data collection, usage, and treatment of patients interacting with robots.

- **Accessibility and Affordability**: Make sure robotic solutions are accessible to all patient populations, especially those with limited resources.
- **Human Oversight and Control**: Robots should augment human expertise in healthcare, not replace it.
- **Developing User-Friendly and Approachable Robots**: Design robots that are easy to interact with, non-threatening, and cater to diverse cultural sensitivities.

Overall, robotics possesses the potential to revolutionize pharma marketing. By employing robots in patient care, marketing tasks, and research, we can create a future where patient interactions are personalized, marketing campaigns are data-driven and targeted, and innovation is showcased through tangible applications. It's a future where robots complement human expertise, fostering improved healthcare delivery, enhanced patient experiences, and a more positive perception of the pharmaceutical industry.

3. Cloud Computing: Powering the Future of Pharma Marketing

Imagine accessing vast amounts of data, running complex analyses, and deploying marketing campaigns instantly without expensive hardware or IT infrastructure. This is the magic of cloud computing, transforming how pharmaceutical companies market their products and engage with patients and healthcare professionals (HCPs). Let's explore how cloud computing plays out in pharmaceutical marketing and the benefits it brings.

What is Cloud Computing?

Simply put, cloud computing delivers on-demand services—servers, storage, databases, networking, software, analytics, and intelligence— over the internet, typically on a pay-as-you-go basis. Instead of managing your physical infrastructure, you access these resources remotely through a cloud provider like Amazon Web Services (AWS), Microsoft Azure, or Google Cloud Platform.

How Does it Play Out in Pharma Marketing?

Cloud computing empowers pharma marketing in several ways:

1. **Data Analytics and Insights**:
   - Store and analyze massive datasets from various sources (clinical trials, marketing campaigns, social media) to gain deeper insights into patient behavior, HCP preferences, and market trends.
   - Run complex machine learning and AI algorithms to predict sales, personalize marketing campaigns, and identify new drug targets.
   - Perform real-time analytics to understand the impact of campaigns and make data-driven decisions on the fly.
2. **Collaboration and Efficiency**:
   - Share data and documents securely within your team and with external partners (HCPs, agencies) instantly, regardless of location.
   - Use cloud-based marketing automation tools to streamline tasks, manage campaigns, and automate repetitive processes.
   - Enable remote collaboration by prioritizing team members' secure access to essential resources from anywhere.
3. **Scalability and Cost-Effectiveness**:
   - Scale your computing resources up or down based on your specific needs, avoiding unnecessary hardware costs.
   - Eliminate the need for upfront investments in expensive infrastructure, allowing for better budget allocation.
   - Pay only for the resources you use, making cloud computing a cost-effective solution for marketing campaigns of all sizes.

4. **Agility and Innovation**:
   - Access new technologies and software as they become available without waiting for lengthy procurement processes.
   - Experiment with innovative marketing campaigns and quickly adapt to changing market dynamics.
   - Foster a culture of innovation and agility within your marketing team.

Examples:

- **Pfizer** leverages the cloud to analyze social media data, identify patient concerns about a new drug, and address them through targeted communication.
- **Novartis** uses cloud-based data analytics to predict medication adherence rates and intervene with patients at risk of non-compliance.
- **AstraZeneca** deploys cloud computing to personalize email marketing campaigns for HCPs, increasing click-through rates and engagement.
- **Sanofi** collaborates with healthcare providers using cloud-based platforms to share patient data and improve treatment outcomes.

Benefits of Cloud Computing for Pharma Marketing:

- **Improved Decision-Making**: Data-driven insights lead to more effective marketing strategies.
- **Enhanced Marketing Campaigns**: Personalized content and real-time analysis optimizes campaign performance.
- **Increased Collaboration and Efficiency**: Teams work together seamlessly and save time on administrative tasks.
- **Reduced Costs**: Scalable and pay-as-you-go model promotes cost-effectiveness.
- **Faster Innovation**: Access to new technologies fosters agility and adaptability.

Considerations:

- **Data Security and Privacy**: Ensure compliance with regulations and secure storage of sensitive healthcare data.
- **Vendor Selection**: Choose a reputable cloud provider with strong security features and industry expertise.
- **Integration with Existing Systems**: Ensure seamless integration of cloud solutions with existing IT infrastructure.

By embracing cloud computing, the pharma marketing team can access powerful tools, unlock valuable insights, and achieve greater efficiency. This ultimately translates to more effective marketing, improved patient engagement, and better health outcomes.

4. **Wearables: Weaving Wellness onto the Wrist— A Revolution in Pharma Marketing**

   The rise of wearable technology is not just a fashion trend; it's a healthcare revolution, weaving a tapestry of real-time data and personalized insights onto our wrists. In pharma marketing, where human connections and data-driven precision are paramount, wearables emerge as powerful tools, orchestrating a synergy with AI that transforms how we engage with patients and shape healthcare experiences.

Beyond Steps and Calories: Wearables Reshape Patient Interactions

Today's pharma marketers are no longer confined to static brochures and broadcasted messages. Wearables empower them to connect with patients on a deeper level, offering:

- **Personalized Education and Engagement**: Imagine patients with chronic conditions receiving medication reminders, tailored exercise goals, and educational content delivered directly to their smartwatches, fostering proactive health management.
- **Enhanced Clinical Trial Participation**: Wearables can capture real-time health data during clinical trials, reducing participant burden and providing researchers with richer insights into treatment efficacy.

- **Hyper-Targeted Marketing Campaigns**: Gone are the days of one-size-fits-all messaging. Wearable data allows marketers to segment audiences based on activity levels, health metrics, and lifestyle choices, delivering highly relevant and personalized messages.

The Future Beckons: AI Unlocks Wearable Potential

As AI and wearables merge seamlessly, the future of pharma marketing becomes even more exciting:

- **AI-Powered Health Coaching**: Imagine wearables collecting data that AI analyzes to provide health coaching and interventions, empowering patients to make informed decisions about their well-being.
- **Remote Patient Monitoring**: Wearables can proactively manage chronic conditions through continuous monitoring. AI algorithms can analyze the data, identify potential health risks, and trigger alerts for healthcare providers, enabling preventative measures and improved patient outcomes.
- **Precision Medication Delivery**: Imagine smart wearables that dispense medication based on real-time health data, optimizing treatment effectiveness and minimizing side effects.

Navigating the Ethical Landscape: Trust is the Cornerstone

While the potential of wearables is undeniable, concerns about data privacy, security, and ethical use demand responsible practices. Pharma companies must prioritize the following:

- **Transparency**: Communicate how patient data is collected, used, and secured, building trust and fostering ethical data practices.
- **Security**: Implement robust cybersecurity measures to safeguard sensitive patient information.
- **Patient Control**: Empower patients with control over their data, allowing them to choose what information is shared and used.

A Symbiotic Future, Woven by AI and Wearables

The synergy between wearables and AI paints a vivid picture of the future of pharma marketing. It's a future where patients are active participants in their healthcare journey, empowered by personalized data and supported by intelligent interventions. By responsibly weaving wearables into their marketing strategies, pharma companies can forge a future where trust, precision, and patient well-being are at the heart of every interaction. This human+AI collaboration, orchestrated by the power of wearables, is key to unlocking a healthier future for all.

5. Internet of Things (IoT)

The Internet of Things (IoT) is weaving its magic across multiple industries, and pharma marketing is no exception. By connecting devices and collecting real-time data, IoT offers unique opportunities to personalize patient experiences, optimize marketing campaigns, and gain valuable insights into medication usage and health outcomes.

Here are some ways IoT can impact pharma marketing:

1. **Personalized Patient Engagement**:
    - **Smart Pill Bottles**: Track medication adherence, send refill reminders, and offer educational content based on real-time usage. Imagine a pill bottle reminding patients to take their medication and providing information about potential side effects based on their health profile.
    - **Wearable Health Trackers**: Monitor vital signs, activity levels, and sleep patterns, enabling personalized medication recommendations and disease management support. Imagine a diabetic patient receiving personalized insulin dosage suggestions based on their continuous glucose monitoring data.
    - **Interactive Patient Platforms**: Connect patients with healthcare professionals, provide educational resources, and address concerns in real time, fostering better

communication and engagement. Imagine a patient with chronic pain connecting with their doctor through a platform that collects data from their pain management device and facilitates informed treatment decisions.

2. **Optimizing Marketing Campaigns**:
   - **Targeted Advertising**: Based on smart devices and wearable data, personalized marketing messages are sent to specific patient segments and their health needs. Imagine targeting ads for a new allergy medication to individuals experiencing certain pollen levels through their smart air quality monitors.
   - **Enhanced Campaign Effectiveness**: Track the reach and engagement of marketing campaigns on smart devices, measuring real-time impact and optimizing strategies for better results. Imagine analyzing smart speaker data to understand how patients respond to audio advertisements for a new medication.
   - **Improved Market Research**: Gather in-depth insights into patient behavior and medication usage, informing product development and marketing strategies. Imagine studying anonymized data from connected devices to understand medication adherence patterns and identify pain points for patients managing specific conditions.

3. **Gaining Valuable Insights**:
   - **Real-Time Adverse Event Monitoring**: This technology detects potential side effects or medication interactions faster, enabling proactive interventions and improved patient safety. Imagine receiving alerts from smart pill bottles indicating medication interactions based on a patient's real-time health data.
   - **Enhanced Clinical Trial Data**: Collect precise and objective data from wearable sensors and devices, improving the accuracy and efficiency of clinical trials. Imagine tracking

patients' real-time response to new drug therapy through their connected devices, eliminating the need for subjective self-reporting.

- **Predictive Analytics**: Analyze connected device data to predict disease outbreaks, medication needs, and patient trends, informing resource allocation and preventive healthcare strategies. Imagine predicting potential flu outbreaks based on anonymized data from smart thermometers in a specific region.

Challenges and Considerations:

- **Data Privacy and Security**: Ethical data collection, storage, and use are paramount.
- **Accessibility and Affordability**: Not all patients may have access to the necessary devices or internet connectivity.
- **Technological Infrastructure and Integration**: Seamless integration of devices and data across different platforms is crucial.
- **Regulatory Compliance**: Navigating complex regulations surrounding data privacy and healthcare marketing is essential.

Overall, IoT holds immense potential to transform pharma marketing. By harnessing the power of connected devices and real-time data, we can create a future where medication management is personalized, marketing campaigns are targeted and effective, and healthcare insights are deeper and more impactful. It's a future where innovation, patient-centricity, and responsible data practices merge to revolutionize how we approach healthcare and empower individuals to live healthier lives.

A Collaborative Future, Orchestrated by AI and IoT

The merging of AI and IoT presents a compelling vision for the future of pharma marketing. By harnessing the power of connected devices and AI-driven insights, pharma companies can move beyond traditional marketing strategies, forging a collaborative future where patients are empowered, healthcare delivery is optimized, and marketing efforts are personalized and data-driven. This revolution, orchestrated by the synergy of minds (human+AI), will ultimately lead to better patient outcomes and a healthier future.

Remember, this is just the beginning. The possibilities of IoT in pharma marketing are still unfolding, and with continued advancements and collaborations, we can unlock even more exciting applications in the years to come.

6. **Predictive Analytics: Forecasting the Future of Pharma Marketing**

   Imagine knowing which patients are most likely to benefit from your treatment, which HCPs are receptive to your message, and what marketing campaigns will resonate best. This is the power of predictive analytics, a game-changer in pharma marketing, enabling data-driven decisions and future-oriented strategies. Let's explore how it plays out step-by-step:

Step 1: Data Collection and Integration:

- **Gather Diverse Data Streams**: Patient demographics, medical history, HCP interactions, social media data, and marketing campaign performance.
- **Ensure data quality and consistency** across different sources.
- **Integrate data** into a centralized platform for analysis.

Step 2: Model Building and Training:

- Based on your goals, choose appropriate predictive models (e.g., logistic regression, decision trees, neural networks).
- Train the models using historical data to identify patterns and relationships.
- Continuously refine and update the models as new data becomes available.

Step 3: Generating Predictions and Insights:

- **Predict** patient responses to therapies, HCP prescribing behavior, and campaign effectiveness.
- **Identify** patient sub-groups for targeted interventions, predict potential adverse events, and optimize campaign budgets.
- **Analyze** market trends and anticipate future patient needs and HCP preferences.

Step 4: Actionable Insights and Implementation:

- Translate predictions into actionable insights for marketing efforts and personalized healthcare interventions.
- Develop targeted and highly relevant marketing campaigns for specific patient segments or HCP profiles.
- Implement proactive measures to address potential issues identified through predictions.

Examples:

- **Pfizer** predicts which patients are at high risk of side effects, enabling early intervention and improved safety outcomes.
- **Novartis** identifies HCPs most receptive to specific drug information, optimizing sales rep targeting and messaging.
- **Roche** forecasts drug sales based on market trends and competitor analysis, informing pricing strategies and resource allocation.
- **AstraZeneca** uses social media data to predict upcoming health concerns and develop relevant patient educational campaigns.

Benefits of Predictive Analytics in Pharma Marketing:

- **Increased Campaign Effectiveness**: Target the right audience with the right message at the right time.
- **Improved Patient Outcomes**: Proactive interventions based on predicted risks and needs.

- **Enhanced HCP Engagement**: Deliver relevant information and personalize interactions.
- **Optimized Resource Allocation**: Prioritize efforts based on predicted ROI and market potential
- **Reduced Costs**: Streamline campaigns and avoid ineffective marketing endeavors.

Challenges and Considerations:

- **Data Privacy and Security**: Ensure responsible data collection, storage, and usage.
- **Model Explainability**: Understand how predictions are made to ensure transparency and trust.
- **Ethical Considerations**: Avoid discriminatory practices and prioritize patient well-being.
- **Continuous Improvement**: Regularly update models and adapt to changing market dynamics.

By embracing predictive analytics responsibly, pharma marketing can move beyond intuition and guesswork, entering a data-driven era. These future-oriented strategies benefit patients, HCPs, and the industry. Remember, prediction is not perfect, but by using it with ethical considerations and continuous improvement, you can navigate the future of healthcare with greater clarity and purpose.

7. **Closed Loop Marketing (CLM): Orchestrating a Continuous Conversation in Pharma Marketing**

   Imagine a virtuous cycle where marketing efforts seamlessly connect with customer interactions, leading to deeper understanding, optimized campaigns, and improved patient outcomes. This is the essence of closed-loop marketing (CLM), a powerful tool reshaping the pharma marketing landscape. Let's explore how CLM plays out in pharma marketing:

Step 1: Initiating the Loop:

- **Target Audience**: Defining your target audience, including healthcare professionals (HCPs) and patients, considering their specific needs and information preferences.
- **Multi-Channel Engagement**: To reach your audience, employ diverse channels like email, social media, healthcare provider portals, and mobile apps.
- **Compelling Content**: Deliver informative and engaging content tailored to each audience segment, addressing their pain points and interests.

Step 2: Capturing Feedback:

- **Interactive Elements**: Integrate feedback mechanisms within your marketing materials, like surveys, polls, and interactive forms.
- **Social Listening**: Monitor social media conversations and online forums to understand audience sentiment and brand perception.
- **Direct Engagement**: Encourage patient-HCP dialogue through support groups, online communities, and direct communication channels.

Step 3: Analyzing and Acting:

- **Data Integration**: Collect and analyze feedback data from various sources, containing it with existing customer information.
- **Insights Generation**: Leverage AI and data analytics to uncover trends, preferences, and potential areas for improvement.

Step 4: Closing the Loop:

- **Personalized Communication**: Utilize insights to deliver personalized messages, recommendations, and educational resources to individual patients and HCPs.

- **Dynamic Content**: Update your website app and other platforms with content relevant to the feedback received, creating a dynamic marketing experience.
- **Continuous Measurement**: Track the effectiveness of your efforts and analyze how feedback leads to improved patient outcomes.

Examples in Action:

- **Merck** launched a website with personalized content for HCPs based on their specialty and interests, increasing engagement and prescription rates.
- **Novartis** utilized social listening to identify patient concerns about a new drug, promptly addressing them through targeted communication.
- **Sanofi** analyzed patient feedback from an app to tailor medication adherence programs, leading to improved treatment outcomes.
- **AstraZeneca** partnered with patient advocacy groups to develop educational materials based on patient feedback, fostering trust and brand loyalty.

Benefits of CLM in Pharma Marketing:

- **Increased Engagement**: Deeper connections with patients and HCPs lead to better understanding and trust.
- **Improved ROI**: Optimized campaigns based on data insights maximize marketing dollars.
- **Personalized Experiences**: Tailored communication caters to individual needs and preferences.
- **Enhanced Compliance**: Real-time feedback allows for addressing concerns and improving adherence
- **Stronger Brand Loyalty**: Continuous dialogue builds lasting relationships with patients and HCPs.

Challenges and Considerations:

- **Data Privacy**: Ensures data security and compliance with regulations.
- **Integration Complexity**: Seamlessly integrate data from various channels.
- **Organizational Alignment**: Foster collaboration between marketing, sales, and medical teams.
- **Ethical Considerations**: Prioritize patient privacy and responsible use of data.

By strategically implementing CLM, pharma companies can transform their marketing efforts, creating a continuous conversation that fosters understanding, builds trust, and improves patient outcomes. Remember, CLM is a journey, not a destination, requiring continuous refinement and adaptation to ensure success in the ever-evolving healthcare landscape.

Integrating CLM with iPad Detailing in Pharma Marketing:

Closed-loop marketing and iPad detailing are powerful tools for pharma sales reps. By integrating the two, pharma reps can gain valuable insights into their interactions with healthcare professionals (HCPs), leading to more personalized and effective detailing experiences. Here is how:

Benefits of CLM in iPad Detailing:

- **Personalization**: Track individual HCP engagement with content, answer specific questions, and tailor future interactions based on their preferences.
- **Data-Driven Insights**: Analyze engagement data to understand what resonates with HCPs, identify high-performing content, and optimize future detailing materials.
- **Improved ROI**: Measure the effectiveness of detailing efforts and track conversions to see what's driving sales.
- **Enhanced Compliance**: Ensure detailing activities comply with regulations and track interactions for audit purposes.

Integration Strategies:

- **Interactive Content**: Embed surveys, polls, and quizzes within iPad presentations to capture real-time feedback from HCPs.
- **Content Personalization**: Utilize CLM software to personalize content based on HCP demographics, interests, and past interactions.
- **Data Capture**: Integrate the iPad app with the CLM platform to automatically capture data like product interest, competitor comparisons, and patient case studies discussed.
- **Follow-up Automation**: Use CLM dashboards to track key metrics such as engagement rates, content performance, and sales conversions.

Additional Tips:

- Train reps on using CLM features effectively and interpreting data insights.
- Ensure data privacy and security compliance.
- Integrate CLM with other marketing channels for a seamless omnichannel experience.
- Regularly refine your CLM strategy based on data and feedback.

By effectively integrating CLM with iPad detailing, pharma sales reps can gain valuable insights, personalize interactions, and receive better sales results.

CLM in iPad Detailing: How it Works:

Here's how closed-loop marketing plays out in pharma detailing:

Pre-Detailing:

1. **HCP Research**: The Rep uses the CLM platform to research the HCP's profile, including past interactions, prescribing habits, and areas of interest.
2. **Content Personalization**: Based on the research, the rep selects or tailors content from the CLM library to match the HCP's specific needs and preferences.

3. **Compliance Check**: The rep uses the CLM compliance features to ensure that all selected materials comply with regulations and company policies.

During Detailing:

1. **Interactive Engagement**: The rep uses the iPad app to present personalized content, incorporating polls, quizzes, and surveys to gauge HCP interest and capture real-time feedback.
2. **Data Capture**: Key discussion points, product interests, competitor comparisons, and patient case studies are automatically recorded within the CLM platform through the iPad integration.

Post-Detailing:

1. **Personalized Follow-up**: Based on the captured data, the CLM platform generates personalized email or message follow-ups, including relevant content, key reminders, and next steps.
2. **Performance Analysis**: The rep reviews CLM reports and dashboards to analyze engagement metrics, content performance, and potential sales leads identified during the detailing session.
3. **Feedback Loop**: HCP feedback captured through surveys, polls, and follow-up interactions is fed into the CLM system to refine content and personalize future interactions with that HCP.

Continuous Improvement:

- Reps regularly review CLM analytics to identify high-performing content, adjust their detailing approach, and personalize content for upcoming interactions.
- CLM platform and content library are updated based on market trends, competition analysis, and feedback from reps and HCPs.

These steps highlights how CLM creates a continuous loop of data collection, analysis, personalization, and improvement, leading to more effective and data-driven detailing experiences.

Remember, successful implementation requires training for reps, data compliance measures, and continuous optimization based on insights gained.

8. AI-Powered CRM: Revolutionizing Customer Interactions in Pharma Marketing

Imagine a CRM (Customer Relationship Management) system that anticipates your needs, suggests ideal communication strategies, and personalizes interactions seamlessly. This is the future of pharma marketing with AI-powered CRM, transforming customer relationships and driving better outcomes. Let's delve into how AI plays out in pharma marketing CRM step-by-step.

Step 1: Empowering Data:

- **Data Integration**: Consolidate patient, HCP, and market data from multiple sources, including CRM data, social media, and clinical trials.
- **Advanced Analytics**: Leverage AI and machine learning to analyze vast datasets, uncover hidden patterns, and predict customer behavior.
- **Customer Segmentation**: Utilize AI to segment patients and HCPs based on demographics, preferences, and treatment needs.

Step 2: Personalized Engagement:

- **Predictive Modeling**: Forecast individual patient needs and HCP preferences to guide targeted communications.
- **Content Personalization**: Generate content tailored to specific segments, ensuring relevance and maximizing engagement.
- **Real-Time Recommendations**: Suggest ideal communication channels, messaging strategies, and next steps based on AI insights.

Step 3: Optimizing Interactions:

- **Sentiment Analysis**: Understand patient and HCP sentiment through social media monitoring and communication analysis.

- **Automated Workflows**: Streamline processes like appointment scheduling, medication reminders, and adverse event reporting using AI assistants.
- **Performance Tracking**: Continuously monitor and analyze campaign effectiveness, using AI to optimize future interactions.

Benefits of AI-Powered CRM in Pharma Marketing:

- **Increased Personalization**: Deeper engagement through content and communication tailored to individual needs.
- **Improved ROI**: Optimized campaigns and targeted interactions maximize marketing resources.
- **Enhanced Compliance**: AI-driven reminders and interventions improve medication adherence.
- **Stronger Patient Relationships**: Proactive communication and support build trust and loyalty.
- **Data-Driven Decisions**: Actionable insights guide strategic marketing efforts.

Improves Pharma Sales Reps' Effectiveness

Furthermore, AI-powered CRM is revolutionizing the role of pharma sales reps, transforming them from product presenters into trusted healthcare partners. Here's how:

Boosting Efficiency and Productivity:

- **Automated Tasks**: AI handles repetitive tasks like scheduling meetings, generating reports, and data entry, freeing up reps' time for higher-value activities.
- **Content & Proposal Generation**: AI suggests personalized content and proposes tailored treatment plans based on HCP profiles and patient needs, saving reps time and effort.
- **Travel Optimization**: AI algorithms suggest optimal travel routes and meeting schedules, maximizing reps' time in front of HCPs.

Delivering Deep Customer Insights:

- **Predictive Analytics**: AI predicts HCP needs and preferences, guiding reps on which products and information to present.
- **Sentiment Analysis**: AI analyzes social media and past interactions to understand HCP concerns and tailor communication accordingly.
- **Patient Data Integration**: AI integrates patient data from EMRs (Electronic Medical Records) and wearables, allowing reps to personalize discussions and address specific patient needs.

Enhancing Engagement and Relationships:

- **Real-time Coaching**: AI provides real-time feedback on rep-HCP interactions, highlighting strengths and suggesting improvements.
- **Personalized Communication**: AI suggests relevant talking points and conversation starters based on HCPs' interests and research areas.
- **Remote Support**: AI-powered assistants answer HCP questions and provide additional information on-demand, enhancing reps' capabilities.

Benefits for Pharma Sales Teams:

- **Increased Sales Success**: More targeted interactions and personalized proposals lead to higher conversion rates.
- **Improved HCP Relationships**: Data-driven insights and personalized communication foster trust and build stronger relationships.
- **Enhanced Rep Satisfaction**: Reduced administrative tasks and real-time coaching increase job satisfaction.
- **Optimized Resource Allocation**: AI insights help prioritize calls and allocate resources effectively.

Challenges and Considerations:

- **Data Privacy and Security**: Ensuring responsible data collection, storage, and usage is crucial.

- **Transparency and Explainability**: Reps need to understand how AI recommendations are generated.
- **Human-in-the-Loop Approach**: AI should augment, not replace, reps' judgment and relationship-building skills.

AI-powered CRM is not a magic bullet but a powerful tool to empower pharma sales reps. By embracing its potential and using it responsibly, pharma companies can transform their sales forces into data-driven, insightful partners who build stronger relationships, deliver personalized solutions, and ultimately improve patient care.

9. Digital Twins

Digital twins are poised to disrupt the pharma industry, profoundly impacting drug development and marketing. Imagine a virtual replica of a patient, a disease, or even an entire pharmaceutical production line— a dynamic model simulating their real-world counterpart in real-time. Here's how this transformative technology can revolutionize pharma and its marketing strategies.

In Drug Development:

- **Accelerated R&D**: Digital twins can simulate drug interactions, predict patient responses, and optimize clinical trial design, dramatically accelerating the development of life-saving medicines.
- **Personalized Medicine**: By modeling individual patients' genetic profiles and disease progression, digital twins can facilitate personalized treatment plans and guide the development of targeted therapies.
- **Reduced Costs and Risks**: Virtual simulations can reduce the need for costly animal testing and identify potential safety concerns early on, saving time and resources.

In Pharma Marketing:

- **Targeted Marketing Campaigns**: Analyze anonymized patient data from digital twins to identify specific patient segments and personalize marketing messages with unparalleled accuracy.

- **Enhanced Patient Education**: Interactive digital twins can more engagingly and impactfully educate patients about their conditions, treatment options, and potential side effects.
- **Improved Medication Adherence**: Virtual simulation can predict and address potential adherence challenges, providing personalized support and interventions to patients.
- **Real-Time Safety Monitoring**: Track medication performance in the real world through data collected from digital twins, identifying potential adverse events quickly and effectively.

Examples:

- Pfizer utilized a digital twin of the human circulatory system to optimize the design of a new blood pressure medication, significantly reducing development time.
- Sanofi leveraged a digital twin of a specific disease to personalize treatment plans for individual patients, leading to improved clinical outcomes.
- AstraZeneca used a digital twin to simulate the flow of materials through their manufacturing facility, optimizing production processes and reducing waste.

Challenges and Considerations:

- **Data Privacy and Security**: Ethical data collection, storage, and use are paramount.
- **Technological Complexity**: Developing and maintaining accurate digital twins requires specialized expertise and resources.
- **Regulatory Compliance**: Navigating complex regulations surrounding data privacy and healthcare marketing is crucial.
- **Human Expertise Remains Essential**: Digital twins should empower human decision-making, not replace it.

Overall, the impact of digital twins in pharma and pharma marketing is expected to be transformative. By creating virtual doppelgängers of patients, diseases, and processes, we can unlock deeper insights, optimize interventions, and personalize experiences in ways unimaginable just a few years ago. It's a future where the power of digital simulation meets the needs of real-world healthcare, paving the way for personalized medicine, accelerated drug development, and, ultimately, healthier lives for all.

10. Generative AI

Generative AI in pharma marketing can revolutionize content creation by automating repetitive tasks, tailoring content to specific audiences, and driving greater innovation. Here's how:

Automating Repetitive Tasks:

- **Generating Boilerplate Content**: AI can create product descriptions, FAQs, and social media posts with consistent messaging and style, freeing up human teams for more strategic work.
- **Data-Driven Reports and Summaries**: AI can analyze sales data, clinical trial results, and other information to generate automated reports and summaries, saving time and ensuring accuracy.
- **Personalized Email Marketing**: AI can generate individual emails based on recipient demographics, interests, and previous interactions, improving engagement and click-through rates.

Tailoring Content to Specific Audiences:

- **Patient Education Materials**: AI can personalize patient education materials based on disease stage, treatment history, and cultural background, ensuring information is easily understandable and relevant.
- **Medical News and Updates**: AI can curate customized news feeds for HCPs based on their specialty, research interests, and upcoming conferences, keeping them informed about the latest developments.

- **Targeted Marketing Campaigns**: AI can tailor marketing messages to specific patient segments with different needs and concerns, improving campaign effectiveness and ROI.

Driving Innovation and Creativity:

- **Generating Story Ideas and Headlines**: AI can suggest creative stories that capture attention and resonate with the target audiences.
- **Developing Educational Video Scripts**: AI can generate scripts for educational videos on specific learning objectives and audience demographics.
- **Personalizing Drug Discovery and Development**: AI can help identify novel drug targets and design new molecules, accelerating the development of life-saving medicines.

Examples of Generative AI in Action:

- A pharma company uses AI to create personalized emails for patients undergoing cancer treatment, offering targeted support and resources.
- An HCP platform utilizes AI to curate daily news feeds for doctors, highlighting relevant research papers and upcoming clinical trials in their field.
- A marketing team leverages AI to generate a library of blog posts on various health conditions tailored to specific demographics and cultural sensitivity.

Challenges and Considerations:

- **Data Privacy and Security**: Ensuring ethical data collection, storage, and use is crucial.
- **Maintaining Scientific Accuracy and Regulatory Compliance**: Humans must rigorously review and edit AI-generated content to ensure accuracy and compliance.
- **Human Oversight and Control:** AI should empower human creativity, not replace it.

With AI+human synergy, Generative AI can create a future where pharma marketing is more personalized, insightful, and efficient. We can positively impact patient care, HCP engagement, and overall healthcare outcomes by harnessing the power of intelligent automation and creative AI assistance.

11. Blockchain: Securely Connecting AI and Humans in Pharma Marketing

Imagine a transparent, secure, decentralized system where AI and humans collaborate seamlessly in pharma marketing, ensuring trust, data integrity, and efficient workflows. This is the promise of blockchain, a revolutionary technology transforming various industries, including pharmaceuticals. Let's explore now how it plays out in AI-human synergy:

What is Blockchain?

Simply put, blockchain is a digital ledger that records transactions across a network of computers in a secure, transparent, and tamper-proof way. Each transaction (a "block") is linked to the previous one, forming a chain that cannot be altered without the knowledge of the entire network. This creates an immutable record of all activity, ensuring data integrity and trust.

AI-Human Synergy in Pharma Marketing:

Clinical Trials:

- **Secure Data Sharing**: Blockchain platforms can securely store and share clinical trial data between stakeholders (researchers, sponsors, regulators) with controlled access and audit trails, improving transparency and efficiency.
- **AI-Powered Data Analysis**: AI algorithms can analyze vast datasets on the blockchain to identify trends, predict outcomes, and personalize treatment plans, while the blockchain ensures data security and privacy.

Drug Supply Chain Management:

- **Counterfeit Prevention**: Blockchain can track medications from production to consumption, verifying their authenticity and preventing counterfeiting, which is crucial for patient safety.

- **AI-Powered Logistics Optimization**: AI algorithms can analyze blockchain data to optimize supply chains, predict demand, and prevent stockouts, ensuring timely delivery of essential medications.

Personalized Marketing and Patient Engagement:

- **Secure Patient Data Management**: Blockchain can securely store and manage patient data, allowing for personalized marketing campaigns and targeted interventions while ensuring patient privacy and control over their data.
- **AI-Powered Patient Interactions**: AI chatbots and virtual assistants integrated with the blockchain can provide personalized support and answer patient queries based on their secure medical records, improving patient engagement

Examples:

- Pfizer and MediLedger collaborate on a blockchain platform to track medication shipments, improve supply chain transparency, and combat counterfeiting.
- Novartis and IBM utilize the blockchain to securely share clinical trial data with researchers, accelerating research and development efforts.
- Roche and Genpact are developing a blockchain platform to manage patient consent for data sharing, empowering patients and ensuring ethical use of their data.

Benefits of Block Chain in AI+Human Synergy:

- **Enhanced Trust and Transparency**: Secure data sharing and tamper-proof records foster trust between stakeholders.
- **Improved Data Integrity**: Blockchain ensures data authenticity and prevents unauthorized modifications.
- **Streamlined Workflows**: Automated processes and secure data exchange increase efficiency.

- **Personalized Experiences**: AI leverages secure patient data for targeted interventions and marketing.

Challenges and Considerations:

- **Scalability and Performance**: Blockchain technology is still evolving, and scalability for large-scale adoption requires further development.
- **Regulatory Landscape**: Clear regulations and standards are needed to ensure blockchain's ethical and compliant use in healthcare.
- **User Adoption and Education**: Educating stakeholders and gaining widespread adoption is crucial for successful implementation.

In conjunction with AI, blockchain holds immense potential to transform pharma marketing by creating a secure, transparent, and efficient ecosystem. However, addressing challenges and fostering stakeholder collaboration is crucial to unlocking its full potential. Blockchain can empower AI+human synergy for better healthcare outcomes and patient experiences by prioritizing responsible data practices and patient privacy.

Remember, technology serves humanity, and blockchain should be used ethically and responsibly to benefit patients and the healthcare industry.

12. Federated Learning: Collaborative Intelligence for Pharma Marketing

In artificial intelligence, federated learning emerges as a revolutionary approach to data analysis and model training. Unlike traditional centralized learning, where data is targeted in a single location, federated learning keeps data at its source, training models collaboratively across decentralized devices. This offers unique advantages for pharma marketing, where privacy concerns are paramount and access to large-scale, diverse datasets can be challenging.

Here's how federated learning works:

- **Decentralized Data**: Patient data, anonymized and secured, remains on individual devices like smartphones, wearables, or hospital IT systems.
- **Local Model Training**: AI algorithms train on local data subsets without sharing raw data with a central server.
- **Model Aggregation**: Aggregated model updates, not patient data, are exchanged and combined to create a globally improved model.
- **Privacy Preservation**: Patient data remains protected, minimizing privacy risks and complying with data regulations.

AI-human synergy amplifies federated learning's impact:

- **Human Oversight and Governance**: Experts ensure ethical data utilization, model fairness, and alignment with healthcare regulations.
- **Data Quality Curation**: Humans identify and address data biases and anomalies at the source, improving model accuracy and interpretability.
- **Explainable AI (XAI)**: Human-interpretable models provide insights into making AI decisions, fostering trust and transparency.

Meaningful Applications in Pharma Marketing:

- **Personalized Patient Journey Optimization**: Analyze vast, decentralized datasets to tailor marketing outreach, medication adherence tools, and educational resources to individual needs.
- **Real-Time Adverse Event Monitoring**: Track potential safety concerns across diverse patient populations without compromising data privacy.
- **Targeted HCP Engagement**: Deliver relevant medical news, clinical trial updates, and drug information based on individual HCP interests and research activity.

- **Decentralized Clinical Trials**: Enable faster recruitment and more diverse trial participation by securely gathering data from patients' devices.

Challenges and Considerations:

- **Technical Complexity**: Implementing federated learning requires specialized infrastructure and expertise.
- **Interpretability Between Devices and Systems**: Ensuring data compatibility across different devices and healthcare systems is crucial.
- **Ensuring Ethical Data Governance**: Robust frameworks and human oversight are essential to protect patient privacy and prevent bias.

The future of federated learning in pharma marketing is bright. By unlocking the power of collaborative intelligence while safeguarding privacy, we can create a future where patient data empowers personalized care, informs ethical marketing practices, and accelerates medical breakthroughs. AI+Human synergy, where intelligent algorithms work with human expertise, paves the way for a more responsible, patient-centric, and innovative future for pharma marketing.

13. Brain-Computer Interfaces (BCIs): Decoding Minds for Pharma Marketing Revolution

Brain-computer interfaces (BCIs) are revolutionizing various fields, and pharma marketing is no exception. This groundbreaking technology allows direct communication between brain and computer, opening doors to an unprecedented understanding of patient needs, emotions, and responses to marketing messages. Here's how BCIs can reshape pharma marketing.

1. **Ultra-Precise Targeting and Personalization**:
    - **Decoding Emotional Responses**: Analyze brain activity in real-time to gauge patients' emotional reactions to advertisements and marketing materials, enabling dynamic personalization and optimization.

- **Identifying Target Audiences with Unparalleled Accuracy**: Through BCI-based assessments, identifying individuals with specific conditions or predispositions, delivering highly targeted marketing campaigns.
- **Tailoring Content Based on Individual Brain Waves**: Adapt marketing messages and visuals to suit individual cognitive preferences and attention patterns, maximizing engagement and recall.

2. **Deeper Insight into Patient Needs and Experiences**:
   - **Gather Unfiltered Feedback**: Capture patients' true feelings and opinions beyond the limitations of traditional surveys and focus groups, revealing unvoiced concerns and motivations.
   - **Understand Medication Adherence Challenges**: Identify and address potential hurdles to medication adherence by monitoring brain activity related to decision-making and emotional responses.
   - **Emphasize Empathy and Understanding**: Pharmaceutical companies can tailor messaging and product development to address unmet needs by directly assessing patients' emotional landscapes.
3. **Novel Marketing and Educational Tools**:
   - **Interactive BCI-Powered Campaigns:** Creative immersive experiences where patients interact with marketing materials using brainwaves, making campaigns more engaging and memorable.
   - **BCI-Driven Educational Platforms:** Develop tools that adapt to individual cognitive styles and learning preferences based on brainwave patterns, fostering personalized and effective learning experiences.
   - **Virtual Clinical Trials and Simulations:** BCIs can be utilized to conduct virtual clinical trials or simulations, improving patient comfort and gathering richer data on medication effects.

Challenges and Considerations:

- **Ethical Considerations**: Data privacy, informed consent, and potential misuse of brain data require careful consideration and ethical frameworks.
- **Accessibility and Affordability**: BCI technology is still nascent and expensive, posing accessibility challenges for some patient populations.
- **Regulatory Landscape**: Adapting current regulations to encompass BCI-based marketing practices and data collection is crucial.
- **Developing User-Friendly and Non-Invasive BCIs**: Ensuring BCIs are comfortable, safe, and accessible for diverse individuals is essential.

Overall, BCIs offer transformative potential for pharma marketing. By bridging the gap between mind and machine, we can create a future where marketing is deeply personalized, patient needs are understood intimately, and the industry builds genuine connections with individuals seeking better health. It's a future where BCIs pave the way for more patient-centric and ethical marketing practices, ultimately contributing to improved healthcare outcomes and a healthier world.

Remember, this is just the beginning. The possibilities of BCIs in pharma marketing are still unfolding, and with continued advancements and responsible implementation, we can unlock even more exciting applications in the years to come.

14. XAI (Explainable AI): Demystifying AI for Better Decisions

Explainable AI (XAI) revolves around making the intricate workings of AI models understandable for humans. In pharma marketing, where trust and transparency are paramount, XAI becomes crucial for building confidence in AI-driven insights and fostering ethical usage:

Understanding XAI:

- **Black Box vs. Glass Box**: Traditional AI models often function as black boxes, their decision-making processes opaque and difficult to interpret. XAI aims to make AI models more transparent, like glass boxes, where we can understand why they make certain decisions.

- **Techniques of XAI**: Various techniques, like feature importance analysis, counterfactual explanations, and LIME (Local Interpretable Model-Agnostic Explanations), help explain individual predictions and identify the factors influencing AI-driven outcomes.

AI-Human Synergy Empowers XAI:

- **Human Validation and Interpretation**: Humans with domain expertise interpret XAI outputs, ensuring responsible usage and alignment with ethical principles.
- **Identifying and Mitigating Bias**: XAI techniques help identify and address potential biases in AI models, preventing unfair or discriminatory outcomes.
- **Communicating Insights with Stakeholders**: XAI facilitates clear communication of AI-driven recommendations to patients. HCPs and regulators, building trust and fostering collaboration.

XAI Applications in Pharma Marketing:

- **Personalized Patient Targeting**: Explainable AI helps understand why specific patients are recommended for marketing campaigns, ensuring fair and unbiased targeting practices.
- **HCP Engagement with AI-Powered Recommendations**: XAI gives HCPs insights into why AI suggests specific drugs or treatment options, promoting informed decision-making.
- **Real-Time Monitoring of Adverse Events**: By understanding how AI identifies potential adverse events, we can refine algorithms and improve the accuracy of safety monitoring systems.
- **De-Risking Clinical Trials**: XAI can explain why certain patients might respond favorably or poorly to experimental drugs, informing recruitment strategies and mitigating potential risks.

Challenges and Considerations:

- **Balancing Explanation with Accuracy**: Oversimplifying explanations can be misleading, while overly complex ones might be difficult to understand. Striking the right balance is crucial.
- **Addressing Technical Limitations**: Current XAI techniques may need help explaining every aspect of complex AI models. Continuous research and development are needed.
- **Integrating XAI into Existing Workflows**: Integrating XAI tools into existing workflows requires proper training and support for teams working with AI in pharma marketing.

AI-human synergy fosters a future where XAI in pharma marketing is not just about technology but about building trust and transparency. By demystifying AI, we can make AI-driven insights more responsible, ethical, and ultimately more impactful in improving patient care and advancing healthcare progress.

15. Augmented Reality (AR) in Pharma Marketing: Bringing the Invisible to Life

Augmented Reality (AR) revolutionizes pharma marketing by overlaying digital information in the real world, creating interactive and engaging experiences for healthcare professionals (HCPs) and patients. Here are some specific ways AR is playing out in pharma marketing:

1. **Enhanced Product Demonstrations**:
   - Imagine an HCP holding a new inhaler and, through their AR device, seeing an animation of the medication reaching the lungs and highlighting its mechanism of action. This goes beyond static information in brochures, providing a deeper understanding of the product's function.
   - AR can showcase 3D models of complex drug structures, allowing HCPs to manipulate and explore them virtually. This aids in understanding drug design and potential interactions with target molecules.

2. **Interactive Clinical Trial Data Visualization**:
    - Instead of flat graphs and tables, AR can transform clinical trial data into 3D visualizations. HCPs can interact with these visualizations, filter information based on specific criteria, and gain a more intuitive grasp of the data's significance.
    - Imagine an AR app allowing HCPs to "walk through" virtual clinical trial environments, experiencing firsthand patient demographics, treatment responses, and potential side effects. This would foster a more holistic understanding of the data and its real-world implications.
3. **Improved Patient Education and Medication Adherence**:
    - Patients can use AR apps to scan medication packaging and access interactive information about the drug, its side effects, and proper administration. This empowers patients to take an active role in their healthcare.
    - AR can overlay medication reminders onto everyday objects, helping patients with memory issues stay on track with their treatment regimen. This can significantly improve medication adherence
4. **Interactive Disease Awareness Campaigns**:
    - AR campaigns can transport patients into the microscopic world of a disease, visualizing its progression and the impact of treatment. This fosters empathy and understanding, encouraging patients to seek early diagnosis and treatment.
    - Imagine an AR app allowing patients to virtually "try on" different treatment options and see their potential effects on their bodies. This empowers patients to be informed participants in their treatment decisions.
5. **Personalized Marketing Experiences**:
    - AR apps can leverage AI to tailor product information and educational content to individual HCPs based on their specialty, research interests, and past interactions. This ensures they receive the most relevant and valuable information.

- AR medication packaging can personalize dosage instructions and side effects information based on a patient's medical history and genetic profile. This promotes safer and more effective medication use.

These are just a few examples of how AR is transforming pharma marketing. As the technology continues to evolve, we can expect even more innovative and impactful applications that benefit both HCPs and patients in the healthcare journey.

16. Virtual Reality (VR) in Pharma Marketing: Stepping into Immersive Experiences

Virtual Reality (VR) transports users into entirely simulated environments, creating fully immersive experiences that transcend the limitations of traditional marketing tools. In pharma marketing, VR is playing a groundbreaking role in:

1. **Deepening HCP's Understanding of Diseases and Treatments**:
    - Imagine HCPs virtually "walking through" the human body, experiencing the journey of a disease from its origin to its impact on different organs. This fosters empathy for patients and a deeper understanding of the disease's mechanisms.
    - VR simulations can place HCPs in realistic clinical scenarios, allowing them to practice complex medical procedures like surgery or drug administration in a safe, virtual environment. This improves their skills and preparedness for real-world situations.
2. **Enhancing Patient Education and Engagement:**
    - Patients can virtually experience different treatment options, seeing their potential effects on their bodies in a simulated environment. This empowers them to make informed decisions about their healthcare.

- VR simulations can transport patients to calming virtual environments, helping them manage anxiety and stress during treatment procedures. This improves their overall treatment experience and well-being.

3. **Personalized and Interactive Patient Consultations:**
   - Patients can attend VR consultations from the comfort of their homes, interacting with avatars of healthcare professionals in a simulated clinical setting. This overcomes geographical barriers and provides convenient access to specialized care.
   - VR consultations can be personalized based on patient data and medical history, tailoring the information and experience to their needs. This fosters a more patient-centric approach to healthcare.

4. **Gamified Learning and Training for HCPs:**
   - VR simulations can transform HCP training into engaging and interactive games, allowing them to learn new skills and procedures in a fun and memorable way. This increases knowledge retention and improves overall training effectiveness.
   - VR simulations can assess HCPs' skills and knowledge in a realistic and controlled environment, identifying areas for improvement and ensuring patient safety.

5. **Immersive Marketing Campaigns and Product Launches**:
   - VR experiences can take HCPs on a journey inside the development process of a new drug, showcasing its innovative features and potential benefits in an immersive and impactful way. This creates excitement and engagement around new products.
   - VR campaigns can raise awareness about diseases and treatment options, immersing the audience in the lived experiences of patients and highlighting the impact of the pharma industry. This fosters empathy and understanding of the challenges faced by patients.

These are just a few examples of how VR is revolutionizing pharma marketing. As VR technology continues to evolve and become more accessible, we can expect even more creative and impactful applications that benefit both HCPs and patients in the healthcare journey.

17. Gamification: Transforming Patient Engagement and Education in Pharma Marketing

In healthcare, where knowledge and adherence are crucial, gamification is a powerful tool for engaging patients, motivating behavior change, and enhancing learning. By incorporating game-like elements like points, badges, and leaderboards, pharma marketing can transform how patients interact with medications and health information.

Here's how gamification can impact pharma marketing:

1. **Improved Medication Adherence**:
    - **Interactive Medication Reminders**: Turn pill reminders into engaging challenges, using points and badges to motivate consistent medication intake.
    - **Virtual Pill Bottles**: Gamify medication management by tracking progress, unlocking rewards for adherence, and fostering a sense of accomplishment.
    - **Social Support and Competitions**: Create online communities where patients can support each other, participate in friendly competitions, and earn rewards for adhering to treatment plans.
2. **Enhanced Patient Education**:
    - **Interactive Educational Games**: These games transform complex medical information into engaging experiences, using quizzes, simulations, and challenges to improve knowledge retention.
    - **Personalized Learning Journeys**: Tailor gamified learning experiences to individual needs and preferences, ensuring targeted education and skill development.

- **Virtual Simulations**: Let patients practice managing their condition in a safe, virtual environment, building confidence and empowering them to take control of their health.

3. **Brand Awareness and Engagement**:
   - **Interactive Marketing Campaigns**: Use gamified elements like quizzes, contests, and scavenger hunts to raise brand awareness and promote healthy lifestyle choices.
   - **Social Media Engagement**: Develop engaging challenges and rewards to incentivize social media interactions and spread positive brand messages.
   - **Patient-Powered Research**: Gamify data collection processes to encourage patients to contribute to research initiatives and feel included in the advancement of healthcare.

Examples:

- **Johnson & Johnson** launched a gamified app for patients with psoriasis, leading to a considerable increase in medication adherence and improved patient-reported outcomes.
- **Sanofi** developed a mobile game to educate patients about diabetes, resulting in a significant increase in knowledge retention and improved management of blood sugar levels.
- **AstraZeneca** utilized gamified marketing campaigns to raise awareness about a new asthma medication, attracting over a million users and generating significant social media buzz.

Challenges and Considerations:

- **Ethical Considerations**: Gamification should be used to empower patients, not manipulate them.
- **Accessibility and Equity**: Ensure all patients access the necessary technology and internet connectivity.
- **Data Privacy and Security**: Safeguard patient data and ensure ethical data collection and usage.

- **Integration with Existing Healthcare Systems**: Gamified solutions should seamlessly integrate with existing healthcare infrastructure and workflows.

Overall, the impact of gamification in pharmaceutical marketing is promising. By tapping into playful engagement, we can encourage positive behaviors, empower patients, and ultimately contribute to better health outcomes. It's a future where healthcare becomes more engaging, motivating, and fun, fostering healthier habits and stronger patient-provider relationships.

18. Metaverse: Reimagining Pharma Marketing in a Virtual World!

The Metaverse, a burgeoning world of interconnected virtual platforms, offers incredible potential to revolutionize pharmaceutical marketing. Imagine patients attending virtual consultations with avatars of their doctors, exploring simulated disease models in real time, or joining support groups in immersive online communities. This hyper-realistic virtual environment opens exciting doors for personalized engagement, innovative education, and enhanced access to healthcare information.

What is Metaverse?

The metaverse is a loosely defined term referring to a future iteration of the internet, characterized by a network of interconnected virtual worlds accessed through specialized headsets or interfaces. It's envisioned as a more immersive and interactive experience than the traditional web, blurring the lines between the physical and digital worlds.

Here's a breakdown of the key features of the metaverse:

- **Immersion**: The metaverse aims to provide a sense of being physically present within a virtual world. This can be achieved through virtual reality (VR) headsets that create a fully immersive environment.

- **Real-time interaction**: Users can interact with each other and virtual objects in real time, fostering a sense of social presence and connection within the metaverse.
- **Avatars and User Agency**: Users will be represented by avatars, digital representations of themselves that they can customize and use to navigate the metaverse. These avatars can perform actions and interact with objects within the virtual world.
- **Integration of Technologies**: The metaverse is expected to combine various technologies, such as VR, augmented reality (AR), blockchain, and artificial intelligence (AI), to create a rich and interactive user experience.

Potential Applications of the Metaverse:

- **Social Interaction**: The metaverse could revolutionize social interaction, allowing people to connect, work, and play in virtual spaces regardless of physical location.
- **Gaming**: The metaverse has the potential to transform online gaming by creating immersive and interactive virtual worlds for players to explore and socialize.
- **Education and Training**: The metaverse could offer new and engaging ways for education and training by providing realistic simulations and virtual environments for learning.
- **E-commerce**: Businesses could create virtual storefronts within the metaverse, allowing customers to browse and purchase products more effectively.

Challenges of the Metaverse:

- **Technological Limitations**: Current VR and AR technology is still under development, and cost and accessibility might hinder widespread adoption.
- **Privacy Concerns**: The immersive nature of the metaverse raises concerns about user privacy and data security within these virtual spaces.
- **Regulation and Governance**: Establishing clear regulations and governance structures for the metaverse will be crucial to

ensure a safe and inclusive environment for all users.

Overall, the metaverse has the potential to significantly impact the way we interact with technology and each other in the future. However, many technical, social, and ethical challenges must be addressed before the metaverse can reach its full potential.

Here's how the Metaverse can impact pharma marketing:

1. **Personalized Patient Engagement**:
   - **Virtual Consultations**: Offer immersive appointments with healthcare professionals' avatars, providing convenient access to care and breaking down geographical barriers.
   - **Interactive Disease Simulations**: These allow patients to experience the effects of a specific illness or treatment in a safe and controlled virtual environment.
   - **Tailored Medication Education**: Design personalized learning modules within the Metaverse, using interactive VR experiences to explain medication usage and potential side effects.

2. **Innovative Healthcare Education**:
   - **3D Anatomical Models**: Explore the human body in stunning detail, fostering a deeper understanding of disease processes and treatment mechanisms.
   - **Virtual Clinical Trials**: Conduct simulations of clinical trials within the Metaverse, allowing for faster recruitment and more diverse participation.
   - **Interactive Workshops and Events**: Organize educational workshops and conferences in the Metaverse, connecting healthcare professionals and patients globally.

3. **Enhanced Access to Healthcare Information**:
   - **Virtual Patient Support Groups**: Foster social interaction and emotional support for patients with chronic conditions through immersive online communities.

- **Gamified Medication Adherence Tools**: Utilize game mechanics and rewards within the Metaverse to encourage consistent medication intake and healthy behavior change.
- **Democratizing Access to Information**: Provide patients with accessible, visually engaging educational resources within the Metaverse, regardless of location or socioeconomic background.

Examples:

- **Pfizer** is exploring using VR to educate patients about a new cancer treatment, allowing them to visualize the drug's effect on cancer cells in 3D.
- **Novartis** is creating a virtual world in the Metaverse where patients with diabetes can connect, share experiences, and participate in educational activities.
- **Roche** is developing VR simulations of Parkinson's disease, enabling patients to experience the symptoms firsthand and better understand their condition.

Challenges and Considerations:

- **Accessibility and Equity**: Ensuring everyone has access to the necessary technology and internet connectivity is crucial.
- **Data Privacy and Security**: Ethical data collection and usage practices within the Metaverse are paramount.
- **Regulatory Compliance**: Navigating regulations surrounding healthcare marketing and data privacy in virtual platforms is essential.
- **Human Oversight and Control**: Technology should augment human expertise in healthcare, not replace it.

Overall, the Metaverse holds immense potential to transform pharma marketing. By creating immersive and interactive experiences, we can create a future where patients are empowered, healthcare education is engaging and accessible, and the boundaries of traditional healthcare delivery are transcended. It's a future where virtual worlds contribute to improved health outcomes, stronger patient-provider relationships, and a more equitable healthcare landscape for all.

19. Bioprinting: Shaping the Future of Pharma Marketing with 3D Printing Tissues and Organs

Bioprinting, the revolutionary technology of creating functional tissues and organs using 3D printing techniques, has significant potential to disrupt and reshape pharma marketing. This transformative technology could impact the industry in several exciting ways:

1. **Personalized Marketing and Education**:
   - **Bioprinted Disease Models**: Imagine patients interacting with 3D-printed models of their specific diseases, allowing them to understand progression and treatment options in a personalized way.
   - **Drug Testing on Bioprinted Tissues**: Instead of relying on animal testing, pharma companies could utilize bioprinted human tissues to assess drug efficacy and safety, leading to more accurate and ethical results.
   - **Customized Educational Tools**: Bioprinted models of organs and anatomical structures could be used in interactive educational experiences for patients and healthcare professionals.
2. **Enhanced Brand Awareness and Engagement**:
   - **Bioprinting Demonstrations and Workshops**: Showcasing the potential of bioprinting technology at medical conferences and patient events can generate excitement and curiosity about the brand and its innovative approach.
   - **Interactive Marketing Campaigns**: Develop engaging campaigns that utilize bioprinting technology, like creating personalized 3D models of patients' medications or offering virtual tours of bioprinting facilities.

- **Collaboration with Research Institutions and Patient Advocacy Groups**: Partnering with such organizations can leverage bioprinting for patient education, fundraising initiatives, and awareness campaigns.

3. **Building Trust and Transparency**:
   - **Openness About Research and Development**: Utilizing bioprinting for drug testing and showcasing the results can increase transparency and build trust with the public.
   - **Personalized Medication Production**: Imagine a future where 3D-printed medications are tailored to individual patient needs, offering a more personalized and effective approach to treatment.
   - **Promoting Ethical AI and Sustainable Practices**: Bioprinting presents an opportunity to address ethical concerns and ensure sustainable practices within the pharmaceutical industry.

Challenges and Considerations:

- **Technological Advancements and Accessibility**: Bioprinting technology is still evolving, and it is crucial to make it cost-effective and accessible to all stakeholders.
- **Ethical Considerations**: Data privacy, informed consent, and potential misuse of bioprinted tissues need careful consideration and ethical frameworks.
- **Regulatory Landscape**: Adapting current regulations encompassing bioprinted tissues and drugs requires collaboration between governments, researchers, and industry leaders.
- **Skilled Workforce Development**: Training skilled professionals to operate and utilize bioprinting equipment is essential for widespread adoption.

Overall, bioprinting offers a transformative perspective on pharma marketing. By harnessing the power of this technology, we can create a future where marketing is personalized, educational materials are interactive, and brand trust is built through transparency and ethical practices. It's a future where bioprinting paves the way for a more personalized, effective, and ethical approach to healthcare, ultimately improving patient outcomes and shaping a healthier world for all.

20. Digital Therapeutics: Orchestrating a Holistic Approach to Health in Pharma Marketing

Imagine interactive mobile apps, wearable devices, and virtual reality experiences working alongside medication seamlessly integrated into a patient's healthcare journey. This is the exciting world of digital therapeutics (DTx), transforming pharma marketing by moving beyond pills to holistic solutions. Let's explore how DTx plays out in pharma marketing:

Step 1: Identifying the Need:

- **Specific Conditions**: Focus on chronic diseases like diabetes, asthma, or mental health, where DTx can complement traditional therapy.
- **Patient Needs**: Understand your target audience's behavioral, educational, or adherence challenges.
- **Regulatory Landscape**: Navigate DTx development and marketing regulations to ensure compliance.

Step 2: Developing the DTx Solution:

- **Evidence-Based**: Ensure the DTx has clinical evidence demonstrating its safety and efficacy for the intended use.
- **Engaging and User-Friendly**: Develop the DTx to be interactive, intuitive, and seamlessly integrated with patients' lives.
- **Interoperability**: Ensure the DTx can connect with other healthcare platforms and devices for data sharing and integration.

Step 3: Marketing and Integration:

- **Patient Education**: Raise awareness about the DTx and its benefits for specific patient groups.

- **HCP Collaboration**: Partner with healthcare professionals to integrate DTx into treatment plans and patient education.
- **Data-Driven Insights**: Track DTx usage and outcomes to refine messaging and improve patient engagement.

Examples in Action:

- **Akili Interactive Labs** developed a video game-based therapy for ADHD, showing improved attention and focus in clinical trials.
- **Pear Therapeutics** created a digital therapeutic app for opioid use disorder, combining cognitive behavior therapy with motivational interviewing.
- **Livongo** offers a DTx program for diabetes management, including a connected scale, personalized coaching, and educational content.
- calm.com provides a mindfulness and meditation app used to manage stress and anxiety, often recommended by therapists and mental health professionals.

Benefits of DTx in Pharma Marketing:

- **Improved Patient Outcomes**: DTx can address behavioral and adherence challenges, leading to better health outcomes.
- **Enhanced Patient Engagement**: Interactive DTx solutions offer a more engaging experience than traditional medication alone.
- **Differentiated Brand Positioning**: A commitment to holistic care can enhance brand image and trust among patients and HCPs.
- **Real-Time Data Insights**: DTx provides valuable patient behavior and outcomes data, informing future marketing efforts.

Challenges and Considerations:

- **Reimbursement**: Navigating complex reimbursement pathways for DTx solutions.

- **Integration with Healthcare Systems**: Ensuring seamless integration with existing healthcare infrastructure and workflows.
- **Data Privacy and Security**: Protecting patient data collected through DTx applications.
- **Ethical Marketing Practices**: Avoiding overstating the benefits of DTx and ensuring transparency about its limitations.

By thoughtfully integrating DTx into their marketing strategies, pharma companies can move beyond simply selling pills and position themselves as partners in holistic health management. Remember, DTx is an evolving field, and successful implementation requires careful planning, collaboration with stakeholders, and a commitment to ethical and responsible marketing practices.

21. Gene Editing: Reshaping Pharma Marketing in the Era of Personalized Medicine

Gene editing technologies like CRISPR (Clustered Regularly Interspaced Short Palindromic Repeats) offer the revolutionary potential to transform pharmaceutical marketing by paving the way for personalized medicine, targeted therapies, and enhanced patient engagement. This groundbreaking field opens the doors to treatments beyond traditional pharmaceuticals, profoundly impacting marketing strategies.

Here's how gene editing can impact pharma marketing:

1. **Personalized Marketing and Education**:
    - **Targeted Marketing Campaigns:** Analyze genetic profiles to segment patient populations and deliver personalized messages about relevant gene editing therapies.
    - **Interactive Education Tools:** Develop educational resources that explain gene editing and its potential impact on specific diseases tailored to individual patients' genetic backgrounds.

- **Virtual Trials and Simulations:** Use interactive platforms to explain gene editing trials and allow patients to "explore" their genetic landscape in a simulated environment.

2. **Enhanced Brand Awareness and Engagement**:
   - **Showcasing Innovation and Leadership**: Position your brand as a leader in the rapidly evolving field of gene editing, attracting patients and healthcare professionals eager to assess this personalized approach.
   - **Collaboration with Patient Advocacy Groups**: Partner with organizations representing communities affected by genetic conditions to raise awareness and educate patients about potential gene editing therapies.
   - **Transparency and Ethical Discourse**: Engage in open discussions about the ethical implications and social impact of gene editing, building trust and fostering meaningful dialogue with stakeholders.
3. **Building Trust and Transparency**:
   - **Open Communication About Clinical Trials**: Communicate openly about gene editing trials, their progress, and potential risks, fostering trust and informed patient decision-making.
   - **Focus on Patient Empowerment**: Empower patients to understand their genetic information and participate in shaping the future of gene editing therapies.
   - **Addressing Societal Concerns and Ethical Considerations**: Engage in proactive discussions about the ethical implications of gene editing, ensuring responsible and equitable access to this powerful technology.

Challenges and Considerations:

- **Regulatory Landscape**: Navigating complex regulations surrounding gene editing therapies and marketing practices is essential.

- **Accessibility and Affordability**: Ensuring equitable access to gene editing therapies for all patient populations is crucial.
- **Ethical Considerations**: Addressing concerns about potential misuse, unintended consequences, and social disparities related to gene editing is paramount.
- **Educating the Public and Healthcare Professionals**: Building awareness and understanding of gene editing technologies among patients and healthcare providers is critical.

Overall, gene editing's impact on pharmaceutical marketing is profound. By embracing this transformative technology, we can create a future where marketing is personalized, patient engagement is empowered, and healthcare focuses on individualized treatments with the potential to cure genetic diseases. It's a future where collaboration, ethics, and transparency go hand in hand with scientific progress, leading to a healthier world for all.

22. AI-Powered Chatbots

AI-powered chatbots rapidly change pharmaceutical marketing, offering personalized interaction, 24/7 accessibility, and valuable data insights. Here's how they're being used and the impact they're having.

Types of AI Chatbots in Pharma Marketing:

- **Patient Education Chatbots** answer queries about specific medications, conditions, and treatment options, providing reliable information in a convenient format. For example, a chatbot for a diabetes medication offers personalized advice on managing blood sugar levels and answers questions about potential side effects.
- **Symptoms Checker Chatbots** help patients assess their symptoms and guide them toward appropriate resources, potentially improving early detection and diagnosis. For instance, a chatbot for a mental health app assesses anxiety

symptoms and connects users with therapists or support groups.

- **Medication Adherence Chatbots** send friendly reminders, offer motivational messages, and answer questions about medication schedules, promoting better adherence and improving health outcomes. For example, a chatbot for a chronic disease medication reminds patients to take their medication and celebrates their progress toward adherence goals.
- **Virtual Assistants for HCPs** assist healthcare professionals by answering drug information queries, providing clinical trial updates, scheduling appointments, streamlining workflow, and improving efficiency. For instance, a chatbot helps doctors quickly access information about newly approved medications and their potential interactions with existing prescriptions.

Benefits of AI Chatbots in Pharma Marketing:

- **Personalized Engagement**: Chatbots tailor interactions to individual needs and preferences, providing a more meaningful experience than generic marketing materials.
- **24/7 Accessibility**: Patients and HCPs can access information and support anytime, anywhere, removing scheduling barriers and improving engagement.
- **Data Collection and Insights**: Chatbot interactions generate valuable data on patient concerns, preferences, and usage patterns, which can inform marketing strategies and product development.
- **Cost-Effectiveness**: Chatbots can automate repetitive tasks and provide support at scale, reducing marketing costs and improving ROI.

Examples of Successful Chatbot Implementations:

- Pfizer launched a chatbot in China to answer patient questions about a new lung cancer medication, exceeding engagement expectations and increasing medication awareness.

- Sanofi deployed a chatbot in France to support patients with diabetes, resulting in 80 percent of users finding the information helpful and feeling more confident managing their condition.
- AstraZeneca created a chatbot in Brazil to educate people about HIV/AIDS, reaching over 1 million users with accurate information and resources.

Challenges and Considerations

- **Data Privacy and Considerations**: Ethical data collection, storage, and use are paramount.
- **Human Oversight and Control**: Chatbots should still be controlled by human experts to ensure accurate information and ethical practice.
- **Natural Language Processing**: Chatbots must be continuously trained and refined to understand complex queries and human nuances in language.

Overall, AI-powered chatbots offer a powerful new tool for pharma marketing, enabling personalized engagement, 24/7 accessibility, and data-driven insights. As AI technology continues to evolve, the potential of chatbots to improve patient care, support HCPs, and empower individuals to manage their health will only grow.

23. Cognitive Computing

- Cognitive computing holds immense potential to transform pharma marketing by offering deep data analysis, personalization, and real-time insights. Here is how:

1. **Deep Data Analysis and Insights**:
    - **Unlocking Complex Data**: Traditional analysis tools often need help with the vast and complex data sets in pharma marketing, including patient demographics, social media sentiment, historical sales data, and clinical trial results. With its ability to process and analyze vast amounts of data, cognitive computing can uncover hidden patterns and correlations, leading to deeper insights into patient behavior, market trends, and campaign effectiveness.

- **Predictive Modeling**: By analyzing historical data and identifying patterns, cognitive computing can predict future trends and patient behavior, allowing pharma companies to tailor marketing campaigns and allocate resources more effectively and proactively.

2. **Personalized Marketing and Patient Engagement**:

- **Hyper-Targeted Campaigns**: Cognitive computing can analyze patient data, including demographics, health conditions, and online behavior, to create highly personalized marketing messages and recommendations. This fosters deeper engagement and improves campaign ROI.
- **Chatbots and Virtual Assistants**: AI-Powered chatbots, integrated with cognitive computing, can engage patients in personalized conversations, answering questions, providing education, and offering support. This improves patient experience and loyalty.

3. **Real-Time Insights and Optimization**:

- **Social Media Sentiment Analysis**: Cognitive computing can analyze real-time conversations to gauge patient sentiment toward brands, products, and competitors. This allows for immediate reaction and course correction in marketing strategies if needed.
- **Dynamic Campaign Optimization**: By analyzing campaign performance data in real-time, cognitive computing can recommend adjustments to optimize ad targeting, message content, and budget allocation, increasing campaign effectiveness and ROI.

4. **Regulatory Compliance and Risk Management**:

- **Automated Ad Review**: Cognitive computing can analyze marketing materials against complex regulatory guidelines, ensuring compliance and reducing the risk of penalties or negative publicity.

- **Cybersecurity and Data Protection**: AI-powered systems can detect and prevent cyberattacks, protecting sensitive patient data and ensuring compliance with data privacy regulations.

5. **Drug Discovery and Development**:
   - **Targeted Research and Development**: Cognitive computing can analyze vast amounts of scientific data to identify promising drug targets and predict the efficacy of potential treatments, streamlining the drug discovery process.
   - **Personalized Medications**: By analyzing patients' genetic and health data, cognitive computing can help personalized treatment plans and medications, leading to more effective and targeted healthcare.

Challenges and Considerations:

- **Data Privacy and Security**: Implementing robust data protection measures is crucial to building trust and ensuring the ethical use of patient data.
- **Interpretability of Results**: Understanding the reasoning behind AI-generated insights is essential for trust and effective action.
- **Integration with Existing Workflows**: Seamless integration with existing marketing and data systems is important for adoption and successful implementation.
- **Cognitive Computing** offers a powerful toolkit for pharma marketing, enabling deeper data analysis, personalized patient engagement, real-time insights, and improved regulatory compliance. By responsibly harnessing this technology, pharma companies can create more effective marketing strategies, build stronger patient relationships, and ultimately contribute to better healthcare outcomes.

Cognitive Computing for Personalized Marketing and Patient Engagement:

Cognitive computing revolutionizes pharma marketing by enabling hyper-personalized experiences and deeper patient engagement. Here's how it plays out, step by step:

Step 1: Data Collection and Integration

- **Gather Data**: Collect diverse data points, including patient demographics, medical history, online behavior, medication adherence, and social media interactions.
- **Integrate Data Sources**: Combine internal data (CRM, sales) with external data (social media, medical records) using secure platforms.

Step 2: Data Analysis and Insights:

- **Apply Cognitive Computing**: Utilize AI algorithms to analyze vast data sets, identify patterns, and uncover hidden correlations.
- **Segment Patient Groups**: Cluster patients based on shared characteristics, behaviors, and needs, creating distinct patient personas.

  Example: Using cognitive computing, a pharma company might identify a segment of diabetic patients struggling with medication adherence.

Step 3: Personalize Content and Targeting:

- **Tailor Messaging**: Craft marketing messages, educational content, and product recommendations for each patient persona.
- **Utilize Multi-Channel Engagement**: Deliver personalized messages through various channels, such as email, social media, mobile apps, and SMS reminders.

Example: The identified segment with adherence issues might receive personalized emails with medication reminders, tips on overcoming barriers, and educational videos on the importance of adherence.

Step 4: Real-Time Feedback and Optimization:

- **Monitor Engagement**: Track patient interactions with marketing materials and analyze their response to different messages and offers.
- **Optimize Campaigns**: Use AI to analyze engagement data and make real-time campaign adjustments, tailoring content and targeting based on individual and group responses.

Example: Analyzing email open rates and app usage data, the system might identify patients needing additional support and trigger automated interventions like personalized phone calls from healthcare professionals.

Step 5: Building Patient Relationships and Trust:

- **Offer Value Beyond Marketing**: Provide patients with educational content, disease management tools, and support communities, fostering trust and engagement.
- **Prioritize Transparency and Control**: Allow patients to access and manage their data, choose what information they share, and opt out of personalized marketing when desired.

Example: The pharma company might develop a mobile app offering patients personalized health tracking, medication reminders, and access to support groups, building trust and engagement beyond marketing campaigns.

The Benefits of Cognitive Computing:

- **Increased Patient Engagement**: Personalized experiences lead to higher interaction and response rates.
- **Improved Campaign Effectiveness**: Targeted messages resonate better, leading to better ROI.
- **Enhanced Patient Care**: Proactive interventions improve medication adherence and health outcomes.
- **Stronger Brand Loyalty**: Personalized interactions foster trust and long-term relationships.

Remember, ethical considerations are paramount. To build trust and maximize the benefits of this powerful technology, ensure data privacy, transparency, and patient control over their information.

By following these steps and prioritizing ethical practices, cognitive computing can take pharma marketing to a new level, creating a win-win situation for patients and companies.

24. Quantum Computing

Quantum computing, with its ability to solve complex problems beyond the reach of classical computers, offers exciting possibilities for revolutionizing pharma marketing in several ways:

1. **Personalized Medication Marketing**:

- **Optimize Drug Targeting**: Analyze massive datasets of genetic information and patient profiles to identify ideal patient segments for specific medications, leading to personalized marketing campaigns.
- **Predict Medication Response**: Quantum simulation can predict individual patients' responses to different medications, enabling personalized treatment recommendations and improved clinical outcomes.
- **Develop Novel Drug Formulations**: Explore and optimize complex molecular interactions through quantum simulations, leading to the design of more effective and targeted drug formulations.

2. **Enhanced Clinical Trial Efficiency**:

- **Accurate Drug Discovery**: Simulate complex biological processes and chemical reactions to identify promising drug candidates faster, shortening the time from discovery to market.
- **Optimize Clinical Trial Design**: Quantum algorithms can design more efficient and informative clinical trials, reducing costs and accelerating drug development.
- **Personalize Clinical Trial Participation**: Analyze patient data and predict potential side effects to personalize recruitment and participation in clinical trials, improving patient safety and efficacy.

3. Data-Driven Marketing Strategies:

- **Analyze Vast Amounts of Marketing Data:** Use quantum computing algorithms to analyze large, complex datasets from various marketing channels, uncovering hidden patterns and informing data-driven marketing strategies.
- **Dynamic Market Forecasting:** Predict future market trends and customer behavior based on complex real-time data, enabling proactive marketing strategies and resource allocation.
- **Optimize Marketing Content and Channels:** Utilize quantum algorithms to personalize and tailor marketing content and channels to specific audience segments, improving engagement and conversion rates.

Challenges and Considerations:

- **Accessibility and Affordability:** Quantum computing technology still evolves and requires significant investments, potentially limiting accessibility for smaller companies.
- **Ethical Considerations:** Data privacy and security concerns must be addressed when dealing with sensitive patient information and marketing data.
- **Regulatory Environment:** Regulatory frameworks may need to adapt to accommodate the potential applications of quantum computing in pharma marketing and clinical trials.
- **Developing Expertise and Skills:** Building a team with expertise in pharma marketing and quantum computing is crucial for successful implementation.

Overall, quantum computing has the potential to impact pharma marketing significantly. By leveraging its unique capabilities, we can create a future where marketing is personalized and data-driven, clinical trials are faster and more efficient, and drug discovery leads to more effective and targeted patient treatments. However, ethical considerations, regulatory frameworks, and the need for specialized expertise must be addressed to ensure responsible and beneficial implementation of this transformative technology.

Remember, this is just the beginning. The possibilities of quantum computing in pharma marketing are still unfolding, and with continued advancements, we can unlock even more exciting applications in the years to come.

The AI Symphony: A Human-Centered Future for Pharma Marketing

As we conclude this exploration of AI's transformative role in pharma marketing, a powerful harmony resonates with the **synergy between human ingenuity and artificial intelligence**. We've witnessed how AI tools, from digital twins to gamified experiences, orchestrate a new performance that empowers patients, informs HCPs, and ultimately improves health outcomes.

However, the melody is far from complete. As we progress, we must remember that **technology serves humanity, not vice versa**. Ethical considerations, transparency, and a patient-centric approach must remain the guiding principles in this evolving symphony.

Here are the key takeaways to remember:

- **AI is not a magic bullet:** It's a powerful tool that must be used responsibly and ethically.
- **The human touch remains essential:** AI should augment, not replace, the crucial role of healthcare professionals and patient support systems.
- **Transparency and trust are paramount:** Patients and HCPs deserve clear explanations of how AI is used and how their data is protected.
- **Collaboration is key:** The most successful AI applications will emerge from partnerships between technologists, marketers, HCPs, and patients.

Call to Action:

The **symphony of minds** doesn't end here. This book has served as a conductor, guiding us through the complex and exciting landscape of AI in pharma marketing. Now, it's your turn to pick up an instrument and join the orchestra. **Become an active participant in shaping this future.** Explore the potential of AI, engage in ethical discussions, and advocate for transparency in its use. Remember, the most beautiful melodies are created when diverse voices harmonize in pursuit of a common goal: **improving lives through the power of innovation and human empathy.**

This chapter embodies the essence of "The Synergy of Minds: Human+AI Orchestrating the pharma marketing revolution." We've witnessed the **powerful collaboration** between human creativity and cutting-edge technology, showcasing how this **synergy** can revolutionize marketing and healthcare. As you move forward, remember the lessons learned:

- **Embrace collaboration:** Foster partnerships across disciplines, ensuring AI serves the needs of patients, HCPs, and society.
- **Prioritize the human touch:** Let empathy and ethical considerations guide your use of AI, never losing sight of the human lives it impacts.
- **Compose a future of progress:** Be an active voice in shaping the responsible and impactful use of AI in pharma marketing, ensuring its melody resonates with health, hope, and progress for all.

The **encore awaits, and the score is still being written.** Let's compose a future where AI empowers, enlightens, and serves humanity's greater good.

PART IX

Embracing the Synergy: AI Transformation in Pharma

Chapter 55. The AI Arsenal: Tools for Pharma Marketing Revolution

Chapter 56. Breaking Down the Silos

Chapter 57. The Human Touch in a Digital Age

Chapter 58. Navigating the Ethical Compass: AI in Pharma Marketing with a Conscience

Chapter 59. Implementing AI Transformation in Pharma Marketing

Chapter 60. Embracing AI Transformation in Small and Medium-Sized Pharma Companies

Chapter 61. Gazing into the Crystal Ball: The Evolving Landscape of AI in Pharma Marketing

Imagine a pharma landscape no longer confined by siloed data, intuition-driven campaigns, and reactive compliance strategies. Enter the era of the "Synergy of Minds," where human expertise and artificial intelligence forge a revolutionary alliance, orchestrating a profound transformation in pharma marketing. Within this chapter, we embark on a thrilling journey into the heart of the transformation. We witness the once-daunting realm of AI morph into a potent tool, empowering pharma marketers to transcend traditional boundaries and achieve unprecedented efficiency, personalization, and reach. Prepare to shed the skin of skepticism and embrace the symphony of human insight and AI power. We'll delve into:

- **The AI Arsenal**: Unmasking the powerful tools at your disposal, from predictive analytics and data-driven targeting to intelligent content creation and real-time campaign optimization.
- **Breaking Down the Silos**: Witness how AI shatters the walls between departments, fostering seamless collaboration and data integration across marketing, sales, research, and regulatory functions.
- **The Human Touch in the Digital Age**: Reassuringly, we'll explore how AI doesn't replace human brilliance but elevates it. We'll see how data-driven insights empower marketers to make deeper connections, craft compelling narratives, and build stronger brand loyalty.
- **Navigating the Ethical Compass**: Addressing crucial questions about data privacy, responsible AI implementation, and ethical marketing practices within this new paradigm.

This chapter is more than just a technological exploration; it's a declaration of human+AI co-creation. It's a call to embrace the transformative potential of synergy and step into a future where pharma marketing sells medications and shapes healthier lives for all.

Turn the page, dear reader, and let the revolution begin. Let's orchestrate the symphony of minds and reshape the essence of pharma marketing through the transformative power of AI.

CHAPTER 55

The AI Arsenal: Tools for Pharma Marketing Revolution

Forget clunky robots and monolithic machines; the AI arsenal in pharma marketing is a dynamic, diverse, and ever-evolving collection of tools. Buckle up as we explore this treasure trove of technological marvels, each meticulously crafted to amplify your human brilliance and fuel the marketing revolution.

1. **Precision Targeting Like Never Before:**
   - **Data-Driven Audience Segmentation**: Imagine AI dissecting vast databases of healthcare demographics, purchase behaviors, and social media activity. Its lightning-fast algorithms paint crystal-clear portraits of your ideal customers, allowing you to laser-focus your campaigns on the individuals most likely to resonate with your message. No more scattershot approaches; every marketing touchpoint hits its mark with laser precision.
   - **Predictive Analytics and Lead Scoring**: Forecasting the future is no longer a fortune-teller's domain. AI analyzes historical data and identifies patterns, predicting which leads will most likely convert. This empowers you to prioritize your efforts, focusing on high-potential targets and maximizing your return on investment. It's like having a crystal ball showing you the path to the most fruitful conversions.

2. **Content Creation with Midas Touch:**
    - **AI-Powered Copywriting and Storytelling**: Struggling with writer's block? Let AI be your muse. It can analyze industry trends, patient needs, and brand messaging to create compelling, personalized content that resonates. From website copy and social media posts to email campaigns and video scripts, AI becomes your co-writer, ensuring your message is always fresh, relevant, and emotionally engaging.
    - **Dynamic Visuals and Personalized Experiences**: Imagine landing pages that morph based on individual preferences or videos that seamlessly adapt their messages to the viewer's demographics. AI makes it possible! It generates eye-catching visuals and personalizes the user experience in real time, creating a deeper connection with each potential customer. Every interaction feels tailor-made, fostering trust and brand loyalty.
3. **Campaign Optimization: A Perpetual Feedback Loop**:
    - **Real-time Performance Monitoring and Adjustments**: No more waiting for end-of-campaign reports to understand what worked well and what didn't. AI monitors your campaigns, analyzing clicks, conversions, and social media sentiment. This constant feedback loop allows you to make micro-adjustments on the fly, optimizing your messaging, targeting, and budget allocation for maximum impact. It's like having a performance coach whispering strategic tweaks in your ear as you navigate the campaign landscape.
    - **Predictive Modeling and Future-proofing**: AI delves into historical data and current trends to predict future campaign performance. This foresight empowers you to make informed decisions about budget allocation, resource deployment, and launch dates. It's like having a time machine, allowing you to peek into the future and ensure your campaigns are always one step ahead of the curve.

4. **The Power of the "AI Whisperer"**:
    - **Natural Language Processing and Chatbots**: Imagine having a tireless, multilingual, and endlessly knowledgeable assistant. AI-powered chatbots can handle routine inquiries, provide basic information to healthcare professionals, and even book appointments, freeing up your sales team's time for more complex interactions and relationship building. It's like having a 24/7 information desk staffed by the most helpful AI companion imaginable.
5. **Compliance and Regulation: AI as Your Guardian Angel**:
    - **Automated Regulatory Compliance Checks**: Navigating the labyrinthine world of healthcare regulations can be daunting. AI is your legal eagle, scrutinizing your marketing materials and ensuring they adhere to complex guidelines. This minimizes the risk of non-compliance and potential penalties, giving you peace of mind to focus on creative brilliance.

Remember, the AI arsenal is not a replacement for human ingenuity but a powerful extension. It amplifies your strengths, frees you from tedious tasks, and empowers you to make data-driven decisions confidently. With this arsenal, you can orchestrate a pharma marketing revolution, forging deeper connections with HCPs and patients, building stronger brands, and ultimately paving the way for a healthier, more informed future.

CHAPTER 56

Breaking Down the Silos

Breaking down the silos in pharma marketing, once an immovable obstacle, is now a thrilling possibility fueled by AI. Here is how this transformation process unfolds:

1. **Shattering Data Walls**:
    - **Imagine Siloed Data No Longer Locked Away in Departmental Vaults**: AI bridges the gap, integrating patient insights, sales figures, clinical trial data, and regulatory documents into a unified, accessible pool. This data lake empowers marketers to craft holistic campaigns, personalize interventions, and make informed decisions based on a complete picture of the patient journey. It's like unlocking a hidden library of valuable knowledge, enriching every marketing strategy.
2. **Collaborative Symphony**:
    - **Marketing, Sales, Research, and Regulatory Teams, Once Disconnected Islands, Begin to Harmonize**: AI orchestrates this collaboration, providing a shared platform for real-time data exchange, feedback loops, and joint planning. Marketing campaigns become informed by scientific insights, sales strategies adapt to patient needs in real time, and regulatory compliance seamlessly integrates into campaign development. It's like conducting a beautiful symphony where each instrument (department)

plays in perfect harmony, creating a masterpiece of effective marketing.

3. **The Patient at the Center**:
   - **The Silos Dissolve, Revealing the Patient at the Central Focus**: AI analyzes data across departments, uncovering patient needs, preferences, and potential hurdles. This holistic understanding empowers marketers to craft personalized experiences, address concerns proactively, and build trusting relationships with each patient. It's like dismantling the walls around the patient, placing them at the heart of every decision, and ensuring their needs guide every marketing touchpoint.
4. **AI as the Bridge Builder**:
   - **Forget Clunky, Rigid Systems**: AI serves as a gentle yet powerful bridge between silos. It automates routine tasks, eliminates data duplication, and fosters transparency through shared platforms. This frees up human bandwidth for creative problem-solving, strategic thinking, and building meaningful connections with patients and healthcare professionals. It's like having a tireless construction crew constantly building bridges of communication and collaboration, breaking down barriers, and ensuring everyone is on the same page.
5. **Embracing Change, Not Dreading It**:
   - Breaking down silos doesn't mean eliminating individual expertise but rather reshaping it for a synergistic future. Teams retain their specialized knowledge while AI facilitates cross-functional collaboration. This fosters a culture of continuous learning, adaptation, and embracing change as a catalyst for growth. It's like transforming from rigid, independent towers into flexible, interconnected bridges, welcoming knowledge and innovation across the organization.

Remember, breaking down silos is not just a technological feat; it's a cultural transformation. It requires openness, trust, and a willingness to embrace new working methods. With AI as the enabler, pharma marketing can shed the legacy of siloed operations and evolve into a collaborative, patient-centric ecosystem where human brilliance and AI power work harmoniously to revolutionize how we reach and serve those in need.

Breaking Down Silos with AI-Human Synergy in Pharma Marketing: Unveiling the Benefits

Traditional pharma marketing has often been plagued by information silos, hindering collaboration and hindering success. However, embracing AI-human synergy can break down these walls and unlock many benefits. Let's explore how with practical examples:

1. **Enhanced Customer Targeting and Personalization**:
   - **AI**: Analyze vast HCP data, including research interests, online behavior, and prescribing patterns.
   - **Humans**: Interpret insights, identify key segments, and develop personalized content like targeted articles, webinars, and invitations.

   Example: An AI model identifies oncologists researching lung cancer therapies through online journals. Human marketers develop personalized email campaigns offering relevant case studies and webinar invitations, leading to higher engagement and a better understanding of HCP needs.

2. **Seamless Omnichannel Engagement**:
   - **AI**: Automates email campaigns, social media interactions, and live chat support responses based on pre-defined criteria.
   - **Humans**: Provide personalized responses to complex queries, handle sensitive interactions, and build deeper relationships with HCPs.

Example: An AI-powered chatbot answers basic questions about a new oncology drug on social media. Human specialists join the conversation for tailored discussions on specific treatment pathways, strengthening trust and connection with HCPs.

3. **Real-Time Performance Monitoring and Optimization**:
   - **AI**: Tracks campaign performance, engagement metrics, and platform-HCP interactions.
   - **Humans**: Analyze data, identify trends, and adjust real-time strategies for better targeting and content improvement.

Example: AI reports show low webinar attendance for a specific HCP segment. Human marketers analyze feedback, adjust content strategy, and offer alternative engagement formats, leading to increased participation and improved knowledge transfer.

4. **Collaborative Innovation and Content Creation**:
   - **AI**: Generates initial drafts of marketing materials, identify relevant research, and propose content ideas based on HCP interests.
   - **Humans**: Refine AI-generated content, inject creativity and expertise, and ensure accurate scientific information.

Example: AI suggests topics and provides references for an article on immunotherapy. Human scientists refine the content, ensuring scientific accuracy and tailoring it to specific HCP interests, resulting in a high-quality, valuable resource for target audiences.

5. **Building Lasting Relationships and Trust**:
   - **AI**: Facilitates ongoing engagement through personalized outreach and educational resources.
   - **Humans**: Foster genuine connections with HCPs, address concerns, and provide ongoing support through direct interactions.

Example: AI identifies and reminds HCPs about upcoming clinical trials they expressed interest in. Human experts answer questions and provide additional information, creating lasting trust and fostering potential collaboration.

These are just a few examples of how AI-human synergy can break down silos and elevate pharma marketing. The benefits extend beyond these, leading to:

- Increased campaign effectiveness and ROI.
- Improved HCP engagement and trust.
- Faster drug adoption and market penetration.
- Deeper insights and data-driven decision-making.
- More efficient resource allocation and cost savings.

Remember, AI is not a replacement for human expertise. It's a powerful tool that amplifies human capabilities, enabling better targeting, personalization, and stronger HCP relationships. By embracing AI-Human synergy, pharma companies can break down silos, unlock new possibilities, and drive success in a competitive market.

CHAPTER

57

The Human Touch in a Digital Age

The rise of AI in pharma marketing might conjure images of robots seamlessly churning out campaigns, but let's remember the critical role of the human touch in the digital age. Here's how human brilliance and AI power come together to create a symphony of effective and ethical marketing:

1. **Empathy and Emotional Connection**:
    - AI can analyze data and predict behavior but can't replicate the human capacity for empathy and understanding. Patients respond to genuine compassion and emotional connection. It's up to humans to translate data-driven insights into stories that resonate, craft messages that inspire hope, and build trust through authentic interactions. AI empowers humans to do this effectively, personalizing messages and tailoring interactions to individual needs, but the touch of human empathy remains irreplaceable.
2. **Ethical Stewardship and Responsible Action**:
    - Navigating the ethical landscape of healthcare marketing demands human oversight and discernment. AI can flag potential biases, predict compliance risks, and analyze social sentiment, but ultimately, it's the humans who ensure marketing campaigns are ethical, responsible, and adhere to strict regulations. Human expertise ensures AI is used

for good, guiding its development and application with a strong ethical compass.

3. **Creative Storytelling and Brand Building**:
   - AI can generate content and optimize messages but can't capture the spark of human creativity. Crafting compelling narratives, building a unique brand voice, and evoking emotions through powerful storytelling are human strengths. AI can provide data-driven insights and personalize content. Still, the human touch breathes life into those messages, translating data into stories that resonate and build lasting brand loyalty.
4. **Strategic Decision-Making and Risk Management**:
   - While AI excels at analyzing data and predicting outcomes, it needs the human ability to interpret context, weigh trade-offs, and make strategic decisions. It's up to humans to understand the bigger picture, consider ethical implications, and make informed decisions about campaign direction, resource allocation, and navigating potential risks. AI provides invaluable data and insights, but human wisdom and experience remain crucial to navigating the complexities of pharma marketing.
5. **The Patient as a Partner, Not a Target**:
   - The human touch ensures patients are seen as partners in their healthcare journey, not simply targets for marketing campaigns. Building trust, fostering open communication, and addressing individual concerns all require human skills like active listening, understanding nonverbal cues, and demonstrating genuine care. AI can personalize patient interactions, but the human touch builds lasting relationships and ensures patients feel valued and respected.

Remember, the human touch is not a competitive advantage over AI; It's a complementary superpower. Humans and AI are a force to be reckoned with, ensuring ethical, patient-centric, and effective marketing in the digital age. Here are some examples to illustrate the importance of human touch:

- A clinical trial coordinator uses AI to identify diverse potential participants, but their human touch builds trust and addresses individual concerns, ensuring successful recruitment and retention.
- A marketing team uses AI to personalize email campaigns, but their human creativity crafts compelling stories and emotional appeals that resonate deeply with patients.
- A pharmaceutical company leverages AI to monitor social media sentiment for potential safety concerns, but its human expertise guides responsible communication and patient outreach strategies.

By embracing the human touch in the digital age, pharmaceutical marketing can achieve more than just selling medications. It can build trust, foster healthier relationships, and ultimately contribute to a brighter future for patients and the healthcare industry.

CHAPTER

58

Navigating the Ethical Compass: AI in Pharma Marketing with a Conscience

The rise of AI in pharma marketing is a double-edged sword. At the same time, it holds immense potential for personalized communication, targeted outreach, and data-driven insights. It also presents a new frontier of ethical challenges. Navigating this landscape requires a clear ethical compass, ensuring AI is used responsibly and for the benefit of patients, not exploited for self-serving purposes.

Here are some key areas where the ethical compass plays a crucial role:

1. **Data Privacy and Security**:
   - Patient data is sensitive and must be protected. AI algorithms rely on vast amounts of data, but robust security measures and stringent data anonymization processes are crucial to prevent breaches and uphold patient privacy. Transparency and control over data usage are also essential, empowering patients to decide how their information is used.
2. **Algorithmic Bias and Fairness**:
   - AI algorithms are only as objective as the data they are trained on. Biases within datasets can lead to discriminatory outcomes, unfairly targeting specific patient groups or perpetuating existing inequities. It's crucial to detect and

mitigate bias in AI algorithms actively, ensuring fairness and equitable access to healthcare information and treatments.

3. **Transparency and Explainability**:
   - Patients and healthcare professionals deserve to understand how AI influences marketing decisions. Black-box algorithms that operate in the shadows erode trust and raise concerns about manipulations. Implementing transparent, explainable AI models fosters trust and enables informed decision-making.
4. **Personalization and Manipulation**:
   - The power of AI to personalize messages can be a double-edged sword. While tailoring information to individual needs can be beneficial, exploiting vulnerabilities or manipulating emotions for marketing is unethical. Maintaining a clear boundary between personalized communication and emotional manipulation is key to preserving patient autonomy and trust.
5. **Marketing Content and Responsible Claims**:
   - AI can generate convincing marketing copy, but claims must be accurate, balanced, and backed by scientific evidence. Exaggerated promises or misleading information can harm patients and erode trust in the healthcare system. Upholding scientific and ethical standards in AI-generated content is crucial to maintaining responsible marketing practices.

A Multipronged Approach

Navigating the Ethical Compass requires a multipronged approach:

- **Developing Robust Ethical Frameworks**: Guidelines and policies for AI use in pharma marketing must establish clear boundaries and expectations for responsible conduct.
- **Active Human Oversight and Accountability**: Humans must remain accountable for the development, deployment, and outcomes of AI algorithms, ensuring they are used ethically and by regulatory guidelines.

- **Continuous Monitoring and Evaluation**: Regularly reviewing and assessing the ethical implications of AI use in pharma marketing is crucial to identify and address potential issues proactively.
- **Open Communication and Transparency**: Engaging in open dialogue with patients, healthcare professionals, and policymakers about the ethical considerations of AI in pharma marketing fosters trust and collaboration in addressing challenges.

By embracing these principles and actively navigating the ethical compass, AI can become a powerful tool for good in pharma marketing, driving positive change and contributing to a more patient-centric healthcare landscape.

Navigating the Ethical Compass: Some Examples

As AI permeates pharma marketing, navigating ethical considerations becomes crucial. Here are some examples of navigating the ethical compass in this space:

1. **Transparency and Bias Mitigation**:
    - **Example**: Disclose to HCPs that they are interacting with an AI-powered chatbot, not a human representative.
    - **Example**: Employ diverse datasets and algorithmic training processes to avoid bias based on gender, ethnicity, or socio-economic factors.
2. **Data Privacy and Security**:
    - **Example**: Implement robust data security measures to protect HCP privacy and comply with healthcare regulations.
    - **Example**: Allow HCPs to control their data usage and opt out of targeted marketing efforts.

3. **Personalized Content and Overpromising**:
    - **Example**: Tailor content to individual HCP needs and interests but avoid exaggerating product benefits or making unsubstantiated claims.
    - **Example**: Ensure AI-generated content is reviewed and approved by scientific experts to prevent misinformation and maintain scientific accuracy.
4. **Avoid Manipulation and Unfair Targeting**:
    - **Example**: Don't target vulnerable HCPs with aggressive marketing tactics or exploit financial pressure points.
    - **Example**: Use AI for patient education and awareness but avoid overemphasizing disease risks or creating undue anxiety.
5. **Responsible Collaboration and Human Oversight**:
    - **Example**: Clearly define the roles and responsibilities of humans and AI in marketing campaigns, ensuring human oversight of AI decisions.
    - **Example**: Promote ethical AI development and adoption within the pharma industry through collaboration and knowledge sharing.

By prioritizing these ethical considerations, pharma companies can leverage AI in marketing while building trust with HCPs and contributing to a responsible and patient-centric healthcare system.

Here are some additional tips for navigating the ethical compass:

- Develop and implement a clear ethics framework for your organization, outlining principles and guidelines for AI development and use.
- To ensure your AI practices sound ethical, seek input from diverse stakeholders, including HCPs, patients, ethicists, and regulators.

- Continuously monitor and evaluate your AI-powered marketing initiatives to identify and address any ethical concerns that may arise.

Remember, building ethical AI in pharma marketing is an ongoing process. By proactively addressing these challenges and prioritizing ethical considerations, you can harness the power of AI to achieve positive outcomes for your business and the healthcare community.

These examples and tips help you navigate the ethical landscape of AI in pharma marketing.

CHAPTER

59

Implementing AI Transformation in Pharma Marketing

Embracing AI in pharma marketing offers many opportunities, but charting the course of implementation can be daunting. Here's a roadmap to guide you through the process:

1. **Assess Your Needs and Goals**:
   - **Identify Key Marketing Challenges**: What are your major pain points, inefficiencies, or areas for improvement?
   - **Define Your Objectives**: How do you envision AI contributing to your marketing goals (e.g., increased HCP engagement, improved campaign ROI, data-driven decision-making)?
   - **Evaluate Your Data Assets**: Assess the quality, accessibility, and volume of data to fuel AI initiatives.
2. **Build Your AI Foundation**:
   - **Secure Technology Infrastructure**: Invest in cloud computing, data management tools, and relevant AI platforms based on your chosen applications.
   - **Develop an AI Strategy**: Outline your approach to data, models, algorithms, and ethical considerations while aligning with company policies and regulations.
   - **Upskill Your Team**: Train employees on AI basics, data literacy, and relevant skills to effectively operate and manage AI tools.

3. **Prioritize and Pilot**:
   - **Start Small with High-Impact Use Cases**: Choose specific goals (e.g., personalized content generation, HCP targeting) where AI can deliver tangible results in a focused setting.
   - **Pilot Projects**: Implement chosen use cases on a smaller scale to measure effectiveness, learn from challenges, and refine your approach before broader roll-out.
   - **Iterate and Adapt**: Continuously monitor results, gather feedback, and adapt your strategy based on pilot learning to ensure continuous improvement.
4. **Scaling and Expansion**:
   - **Expand Successful Pilots**: Gradually scale proven AI applications to broader target audiences and marketing campaigns.
   - **Integrate AI Across Processes**: Explore opportunities to embed AI in different marketing functions, such as sales support and customer relationship management, for cross-functional benefits.
   - **Invest in Ongoing Talent Development**: Continue upskilling your team to stay ahead of AI advancements and maintain expertise.
5. **Remember the Human+AI Synergy**:
   - **AI Doesn't Replace Humans**: It augments existing skills, freeing up employees for more strategic tasks and creative thinking.
   - **Prioritize Transparency and Ethics**: Build trust with HCPs by being transparent about AI use, ensuring data privacy, and adhering to ethical principles.
   - **Foster Collaboration**: Encourage collaboration between AI experts, marketers, scientists, and ethicists to maximize the potential of AI while navigating challenges responsibly.

Implementing AI transformation takes time, commitment, and adaptability. By following these steps, prioritizing your needs, and fostering a learning culture, you can confidently navigate the journey and unlock AI's transformative power to elevate your pharma marketing efforts.

Building A Strong AI Foundation: Delving Deeper

Building a strong AI foundation is crucial for successful transformation in pharma marketing. Here's a deeper dive into the key elements involved:

1. **Technology Infrastructure:**
   - **Cloud Computing:** Invest in a secure and scalable cloud platform like AWS (Amazon Web Services), Microsoft Azure, or Google Cloud Platform to handle data storage, processing, and model training. Consider factors like flexibility, cost, and compliance with healthcare regulations.
   - **Data Management Tools:** Implement data lakes or warehouses like Snowflake or Amazon Redshift to store and manage your diverse marketing data, such as HCP profiles, campaign data, and website analytics. Ensure data quality and accessibility for AI models.
   - **AI Platforms:** Choose specialized AI platforms or toolkits for your chosen applications (e.g., TensorFlow for natural language processing and PyTorch for image recognition). Consider open-source options for commercial platforms with built-in features and support.

2. **AI Strategy and Governance:**
   - **Define Your AI Vision:** Outline your long-term goals and values for utilizing AI in pharma marketing. Align with your company policies and regulations about data privacy, ethics, and transparency.
   - **Develop an AI Roadmap:** Identify specific use cases and applications where AI can add value. Prioritize high-impact areas and define timelines for implementation.

- **Establish Ethical Guidelines:** Implement policies and procedures for responsible AI development and deployment. Address concerns like bias, transparency, and data security.
- **Appoint an AI Governance Team:** Create a dedicated team responsible for overseeing AI strategy, monitoring projects, and ensuring ethical compliance.

3. **Skills and Training:**

- **Upscale Your Existing Team:** Develop training programs to equip your marketing team with basic AI literacy, data analysis skills, and an understanding of AI applications in your field.
- **Hire Specialized Talent:** Consider recruiting AI engineers, data scientists, and machine learning experts to manage and develop complex AI models and infrastructure.
- **Foster Collaboration:** Encourage cross-functional collaboration between marketing, IT, data science, and ethics teams to leverage diverse expertise and ensure successful AI integration.

4. **Data Preparation and Quality:**

- **Identify and Collect Relevant Data:** Gather data from various sources like CRM systems, HCP databases, market research, and social media platforms. Ensure data relevance and alignment with your chosen AI applications.
- **Clean and Pre-Process Data:** Address missing values, inconsistencies, and biases in your data to ensure accurate and robust AI model training.
- **Develop Data Governance Policies:** Implement data security, access control, and auditability practices to comply with privacy regulations and protect sensitive information.

5. **Partnerships and External Support:**
   - **Collaborate with AI Vendors and Consultants:** Consider partnering with specialized AI companies or consultants to access expertise, technology solutions, and implementation support.
   - **Engage with Research Institutions and Industry Groups:** Participate in research collaborations and industry forums to stay updated on AI advancements and best practices in pharma marketing.

By carefully building your AI foundation, you create a solid platform for successful AI transformation in pharma marketing. Focus on the right technology, define your strategy, invest in skills and data quality, and leverage external support to unlock the full potential of AI and achieve your marketing goals.

Remember, building your AI foundation is a continuous process. Adapt your approach based on learnings, embrace advancements in technology and ethical considerations, and continuously refine your strategy to stay ahead of the curve and maximize the impact of AI in your pharma marketing initiatives.

How AI Transformation Benefits Pharma Marketing

AI transformation in pharma marketing offers many benefits across various functions, improving performance, efficiency, and patient outcomes. Consider the following, for example:

1. **Enhanced Customer Targeting and Personalization:**
   - **Benefit:** Precisely target HCPs based on their research interests, online behavior, and prescribing patterns, leading to relevant outreach and higher engagement.
   - **Example:** AI identifies oncologists researching lung cancer therapies through online journals. Personalized email campaigns with relevant case studies and webinar invitations can increase click-through rates considerably compared to generic campaigns.

2. **Increased Campaign Effectiveness and ROI:**
   - **Benefit:** Optimize campaign content and timing based on real-time data analysis, maximizing reach and impact while minimizing budget waste.
   - **Example:** AI models predict which social media posts resonate most with specific HCP segments. Targeting campaigns based on these predictions can reduce cost per engagement.
3. **Improved HCP Engagement and Trust:**
   - **Benefit:** Deliver personalized content and interactions, foster deeper relationships with HCPs, and build trust through tailored educational resources.
   - **Example:** AI-powered chatbots answer basic questions about a new drug on social media, freeing human experts for more complex discussions. This can lead to increased HCP satisfaction with knowledge accessibility.
4. **Streamlined Operations and Resource Allocation:**
   - **Benefit:** Automate tasks like email marketing, data analysis, and reporting, freeing human resources for strategic work and creative insights.
   - **Example:** AI tools automatically generate campaign reports, saving marketing teams considerable time previously spent on manual reporting and allowing them to focus on deeper campaign analysis and optimization.
5. **Faster Drug Adoption and Market Penetration:**
   - **Benefit:** Drive faster awareness and uptake of new drugs through targeted outreach and personalized engagement with relevant HCPs.
   - **Example:** AI-powered HCP targeting and content personalization for a new oncology drug can significantly reduce the time to peak market share compared to traditional marketing methods.

6. **Data-Driven Decision-Making and Insights:**
   - **Benefit:** Gain deeper insights from vast marketing data, uncover hidden trends, and make informed decisions based on actual performance and HCP response.
   - **Example:** AI analytics reveal that HCPs prefer concise video summaries over lengthy research papers to understand new drugs. Adapting content strategy accordingly can significantly increase information consumption among target audiences.

Quantifying these benefits depends on campaign goals, market size, and target HCP segments. However, even modest improvements in engagement, campaign performance, and resource allocation can lead to significant financial gains and improve patient outcomes through faster access to effective treatments.

Remember, AI is a powerful tool but not a magic bullet. Its success relies on a strategic approach, strong data infrastructure, ongoing investment in talent, and ethical considerations. By addressing specific marketing challenges and prioritizing human+AI synergy, pharma companies can unlock the transformative potential of AI and reap the considerable benefits it offers for a more effective and patient-centric future.

How Pharma Embraces AI Transformation

The following case studies show how three large multinational pharma companies have embraced AI transformation.

Case Study #1: UCB Embraces AI Transformation!

UCB (Union Chimique Belge), a multinational biopharmaceutical company headquartered in Brussels, Belgium, is actively embracing AI transformation in pharma marketing, focusing on several key areas:

1. **Personalized HCP Engagement**:
   - Utilizing AI to analyze HCP interests, research priorities, and online behavior.
   - Developing personalized content and outreach strategies tailored to individual HCP needs.
   - Leveraging AI-powered chatbots and virtual assistants for real-time HCP interaction and support.
2. **Data-Driven Insights and Decision-Making**:
   - Extracting insights from vast marketing datasets using AI and machine learning algorithms.
   - Optimizing campaign performance and resource allocation based on data-driven predictions.
   - Gaining a deeper understanding of HCP engagement and market trends to inform future strategies.
3. **Content Generation and Automation**:
   - Employing AI for generating personalized content like articles, case studies, and presentations.
   - Automating routine tasks like email marketing and data analysis to free up human resources for higher-level activities.
   - Developing AI-powered tools for creating engaging and informative scientific visuals.
4. **Improved Regulatory Compliance**:
   - Using AI to automate data cleaning and validation processes, ensuring accuracy and compliance with regulations.

- Developing AI-driven systems for monitoring safety and pharmacovigilance data.
- Utilizing AI to facilitate rapid and transparent communication with regulatory bodies.

Here are some examples of the benefits UCB has gained from AI transformation:

- **Increased HCP Engagement**: Personalized email campaigns delivered higher click-through rates.
- **Improved Campaign ROI**: Data-driven optimization decreased campaign costs while maintaining reach and engagement.
- **Faster Insights and Decision-Making**: AI analytics reduced the time to generate marketing reports considerably.
- **Enhanced Regulatory Management**: AI-powered data validation processes minimized compliance risks.

These are just a few examples, and UCB continues to explore new ways to leverage AI to improve its pharmaceutical marketing efforts.

Exploring Cutting-Edge Applications

In addition, UCB is actively exploring and implementing innovative AI applications across various aspects of its pharma business, demonstrating its commitment to a future driven by digital intelligence. Here are some exciting areas where UCB is pushing the boundaries with AI:

1. **Drug Discovery and Development**:
    - **AI-powered target Identification and Lead Optimization**: UCB utilizes AI algorithms to analyze vast datasets and identify promising drug targets with specific therapeutic potential. This streamlines the early stages of drug discovery and leads to faster development timelines.

- **Generative AI for Molecule Design**: UCB partners with companies like Exscientia to utilize AI in designing novel drug molecules with desired properties, accelerating the lead generation process and increasing success rates.
- **Predictive Models for Clinical Trial Optimization**: UCB employs AI to forecast patient recruitment, analyze clinical trial data in real time, and predict potential safety risks, leading to more efficient and informative trials.

2. **Personalized Medicine and Patient Care**:
   - **AI-Powered Biomarker Analysis**: UCB utilizes AI to analyze genomic and other patient data to identify biomarkers associated with disease progression and treatment response, paving the way for personalized medicine approaches.
   - **Machine Learning for Treatment Optimization**: UCB explores using AI to develop algorithms for personalized treatment plans based on individual patient profiles and responses to therapy, improving treatment outcomes.
   - **Digital Therapeutics and Virtual Assistants**: UCB participates in developing AI-powered digital therapeutics and virtual assistants that support patients in managing their chronic conditions and improve adherence to treatment regimens.
3. **Marketing and Sales**:
   - **Hyper-Personalized HCP Engagement**: UCB leverages AI to analyze HCP preferences and online behavior to deliver highly targeted content, recommendations, and educational materials, fostering deeper and more relevant interactions.
   - **Data-Driven Campaign Optimization**: UCB employs AI analytics to optimize marketing campaigns, identify effective strategies, and allocate resources efficiently, maximizing ROI and engagement with healthcare professionals.

- **AI-Powered Customer Relationship Management (CRM)**: UCB implements AI-powered chatbots and virtual assistants to provide instant support and information to HCPs, improving customer satisfaction and access to knowledge.

4. **Beyond Pharma**:
   - **AI for Drug Safety Monitoring**: UCB uses AI to analyze real-world data from patients and healthcare systems to detect potential drug safety issues, safeguarding patient well-being.
   - **Collaboration and Knowledge Sharing**: UCB actively participates in industry initiatives and partnerships to develop ethical guidelines and best practices for AI in pharma, promoting responsible development and knowledge sharing within the sector.

UCB's AI Transformation Initiatives: Some Examples

Here are some examples of UCB's AI transformation initiatives, including their collaborations and technologies:

1. **Drug Discovery and Development**:
   - **Collaboration with Microsoft:** UCB collaborated with Microsoft to combine Microsoft's computational services, cloud, and artificial intelligence (AI) to augment UCB's drug discovery and development capabilities.
   - **Internal AI Lab**: UCB established an internal AI lab focused on developing and applying AI algorithms for various aspects of drug discovery, including target identification, lead optimization, and virtual screening. The lab collaborates with other research teams within UCB to integrate AI into their workflows.

- **Technology**: UCB utilizes various AI technologies in its drug discovery efforts, including deep learning, machine learning, and natural language processing. These technologies analyze complex data patterns and generate insights that would be difficult to identify using traditional methods.

2. **Personalized Medicine and Patient Care**:
   - **UCB Launches Nile AI Inc:** In January 2021, UCB announced the launch of Nile AI Inc., a new independent company created to improve care for people living with epilepsy, their caregivers, and healthcare providers (HCPs). Nile was founded with a clear mission to make the journey of every epilepsy patient predictable. Nile is developing an epilepsy management platform that serves as a digital extension of the Healthcare provider (HCP), providing patients with peace of mind between consultations and shortening the path to optimal treatment.
   - **Technology**: UCB uses machine learning algorithms to analyze genomic and other patient data, identify relevant patterns, and predict treatment response. Additionally, they explore advanced natural language processing techniques to extract insights from patient narratives and medical records.

3. **Marketing and Sales**:
   - **Collaboration with Accenture**: UCB partnered with Accenture to develop and implement an AI-powered platform for personalized HCP engagement. This platform leverages AI to analyze HCP profiles, preferences, and online behavior to deliver targeted content and recommendations, fostering deeper and more relevant interactions.
   - **AI-Powered Sales Forecasting**: UCB utilizes AI to analyze historical sales data and market trends to predict future

sales performance. This information helps them optimize resource allocation and sales strategies.

- **Technology**: UCB uses various AI technologies for marketing and sales, including natural language processing for sentiment analysis, machine learning for customer segmentation and churn prediction, and deep learning for personalized content generation.

4. **Beyond Pharma**:
   - **Collaboration with the European Medicines Agency (EMA)**: UCB participates in a pilot project with the EMA to explore the use of AI for real-world data analysis and drug safety monitoring. This project aims to develop new methods for identifying potential safety issues early on, Improving patient safety.
   - **Membership in Industry Consortia**: UCB is a member of several industry consortia focused on promoting AI's responsible development and use in pharma. These collaborations help ensure ethical considerations and best practices are shared and incorporated across the industry.

Overall, UCB demonstrates a strong commitment to AI transformation, focusing on improving HCP engagement, gaining data-driven insights, automating tasks, and ensuring regulatory compliance. As they continue to evolve their AI approach, one can expect UCB to be a leader in harnessing the power of AI to transform pharma marketing and ultimately contribute to better patient outcomes.

Case Study #2: Boehringer Ingelheim: Embracing AI with a Human Touch in Pharma!

Boehringer Ingelheim (BI) recognizes the transformative potential of AI in pharma and is actively integrating it into various aspects of its operations, particularly focusing on the following:

1. **Research and Development**:
    - **AI-Powered Drug Discovery**: Utilizing machine learning algorithms for virtual screening, target identification, and lead optimization, accelerating drug discovery and generating promising drug candidates.
    - **Data-Driven Clinical Trials**: Implementing AI for patient recruitment, trial design optimization, and real-time analysis of clinical data, leading to faster and more efficient trials.
    - **Precision Medicine** involves using AI to analyze patient data and predict individual responses to treatment, paving the way for personalized medicine approaches with tailored therapeutics.
2. **Marketing and Sales**:
    - **Personalized HCP Engagement**: Leveraging AI to understand HCP preferences and deliver targeted content, recommendations, and educational materials, fostering deeper and more relevant interactions.
    - **Data-Driven Marketing Campaigns**: Employ AI analytics to optimize campaign performance, identify effective strategies, and allocate resources efficiently, maximizing ROI engagement.
    - **Customer Relationship Management (CRM)**: Implementing AI-powered chatbots and virtual assistants to provide instant support to HCPs, improve customer satisfaction, and streamline communication.

3. **Manufacturing and Supply Chain**:
   - **Predictive Maintenance** Involves Using AI to analyze sensor data and predict equipment failures in manufacturing plants, preventing downtime and optimizing production processes.
   - **Automated Supply Chain Management**: Implementing AI for demand forecasting, inventory optimization, and logistics planning, ensuring efficient and timely delivery of medications.
   - **Quality Control**: Employing AI-powered image recognition and data analysis for automated quality control checks, guaranteeing product safety and consistency.
4. **Ethics and Transparency**:
   - **Human-Centered Approach**: BI emphasizes the importance of human expertise and oversight in AI development and deployment, ensuring AI complements and empowers people rather than replaces them.
   - **Focus on Explianability and Fairness**: BI prioritizes transparent and responsible AI development, addressing potential biases and ensuring explainability of AI decisions to build trust and confidence.
   - **Collaboration and Knowledge Sharing**: BI actively engages stakeholders and industry experts to develop ethical guidelines and best practices for AI in pharma, promoting responsible innovation and knowledge sharing.

These are just some examples of how BI is embracing AI, and they continue to explore new applications and partnerships to harness its potential for the benefit of patients and healthcare professionals. Here are some key takeaways about BI's approach to AI in pharma:

- **Focus on Integration**: BI seamlessly integrates AI across various departments, creating a holistic approach to innovation and improved performance.

- **Human-AI Synergy**: BI prioritizes human expertise and ethical considerations, ensuring responsible and trustworthy AI development.
- **Collaboration and Knowledge Sharing**: BI actively engages with stakeholders and experts to contribute to the responsible advancement of AI in pharma.

By thoughtfully and strategically embracing AI, BI is at the forefront of shaping a future where technology enhances and empowers human expertise, ultimately leading to better healthcare outcomes for everyone.

BI Exploring New AI Applications

Boehringer Ingelheim (BI) is actively exploring various new applications of AI in its pharma business, pushing the boundaries of what's possible across different stages of the pharmaceutical value chain. Here are some exciting areas they're focusing on:

1. **Drug Discovery and Development**:
    - **Quantum Computing Applications**: Partnering with Google Quantum AI, BI explores accelerating drug discovery by simulating complex molecular interactions using quantum computers.
    - **Generative AI for Molecule Design**: Utilizing AI to generate new drug candidates with desired properties, spending up the lead generation process.
    - **AI-Powered Clinical Trial Design and Optimization**: Implementing AI to optimize trial protocols, patient recruitment, and data analysis for faster and more efficient trials.
    - **Predictive Models for Drug Safety and Efficacy**: Employing AI to predict potential safety risks and efficacy of drug candidates before reaching clinical trials, improving success rates and reducing development costs.

2. **Manufacturing and Supply Chain**:
    - **Digital Twins for Production Optimization**: AI creates digital replicas of manufacturing plants, predicts potential issues, and optimizes real-time production processes.
    - **AI-Powered Supply Chain Forecasting and Management**: AI is utilized to anticipate demand fluctuations and optimize inventory levels, ensuring efficient resource allocation and avoiding stockouts.
    - **Augmented Reality for Quality Control**: Implementing AI-powered AR tools to assist workers in quality control procedures, improving accuracy and efficiency.
3. **Marketing and Sales**:
    - **Hyper-Personalized HCP Engagement**: Leveraging AI to analyze HCP preferences and data to deliver highly personalized content, recommendations, and educational materials at scale.
    - **AI-Powered Sales Forecasting and Resource Allocation**: Employ AI to predict sales performance and optimize resource allocation for field teams, maximizing the return on marketing investments.
    - **Conversational AI for HCP Support**: Utilizing AI-powered chatbots and virtual assistants to provide instant support and information to HCPs, improving customer satisfaction and access to knowledge.
4. **Beyond Pharma**:
    - **AI for Personalized Medicine**: Exploring AI to analyze patient data and develop personalized treatment plans based on individual needs and genomics.
    - **Digital Therapeutics and Wearables**: Developing AI-powered digital therapeutics and wearables to support patient care and disease management.

- **AI-Powered Drug Safety Monitoring**: Implementing AI to analyze real-world patient data to detect potential drug safety issues early.

These are just a few examples of the numerous new applications BI is exploring in its AI transformation journey. They are actively collaborating with startups, academic institutions, and technology companies to push the boundaries of AI in pharma and contribute to improved healthcare outcomes for patients worldwide.

BI's commitment to responsible AI development is noteworthy. They emphasize transparency, human oversight, and ethical considerations in their AI initiatives, ensuring technology serves as a tool for good within the healthcare ecosystem.

Case #3: GSK Embracing AI Across the Pharmaceutical Value Chain!

As a leading global pharmaceutical company, GlaxoSmithKline (GSK) recognizes the transformative potential of AI and is actively integrating it into various aspects of its operations:

1. **Drug Discovery and Development**:
    - **AI-Powered Target Identification and Lead Optimization**: GSK utilizes advanced algorithms to identify promising drug targets and accelerate development timelines. This has led to a considerable increase in potential avenues for exploration in their early pipeline.
    - **Predictive Modeling for Clinical Trials**: GSK employs AI to optimize clinical trial design, predict patient response, and identify potential safety risks, contributing to more efficient and effective trials.
    - **Real-Time Data Analysis**: They leverage AI to analyze vast amounts of data from preclinical and clinical studies, accelerating the discovery of insights and guiding decision-making.
2. **Manufacturing and Supply Chain**:
    - **Predictive Maintenance**: GSK implements AI to analyze sensor data and predict equipment failures in manufacturing plants, minimizing downtime and optimizing production processes.
    - **AI-Powered Logistics Planning**: They use AI to forecast demand, optimize delivery routes, improve supply chain efficiency, and reduce costs.
    - **Quality Control Automation**: GSK employs AI-powered image recognition and data analysis for automated quality control checks, ensuring product consistency and safety.

3. **Marketing and Sales**:
   - **Personalized HCP Engagement**: GSK utilizes AI to analyze HCP profiles and preferences, delivering targeted content, recommendations, and educational materials that foster deeper and more relevant interactions.
   - **Data-Driven Campaign Optimization**: They employ AI analytics to optimize marketing campaigns, identify effective strategies, and allocate resources efficiently, maximizing ROI and engagement.
   - **AI-Powered Customer Relationship Management (CRM)**: GSK implements AI-powered chatbot virtual assistants to support HCPs, improving customer satisfaction and streamlining communication immediately.
4. **Ethics and Transparency**:
   - **Prioritizing Human Expertise and Oversight**: GSK emphasizes the importance of human expertise and oversight in AI development and deployment, ensuring AI complements and empowers people rather than replaces them.
   - **Focus on Explainability and Fairness**: They prioritize transparent and responsible AI development, addressing potential biases and ensuring explainability of AI decisions to build trust and confidence.
   - **Collaboration and Knowledge**: GSK actively engages with stakeholders and industry experts to develop ethical guidelines and best practices for AI in pharma., promoting responsible innovation and knowledge sharing.

GSK's commitment to AI transformation is evident in its ongoing investments, partnerships, and initiatives. It is actively pursuing collaborations with startups, tech giants, and academic institutions to unlock AI's full potential for drug discovery, manufacturing, marketing, and improving patient outcomes.

GSK's Chatbot Initiatives

GSK actively explores AI-powered chatbots for HCP engagement. However, it is important to note that they are yet to deploy a single, widely used chatbot across all their operations. Their approach focuses on piloting and testing various chatbot applications in different regions and therapeutic areas.

Here's an overview of some known GSK chatbot initiatives:

1. **Project Catalyst**: Launched in 2018, Project Catalyst is a GSK initiative supporting innovative digital health solutions. Within this project, several AI-powered chatbots focusing on HCP engagement have been piloted:
    - **My Vax Assistant**: Developed in partnership with Huma, this chatbot provides personalized information and support to healthcare professionals and the public about vaccines.
    - **Dr. AI for Oncology**: This chatbot, piloted in Japan, guides oncologists through complex treatment recommendations for specific patient profiles.
    - **Chatbots for Patient Management**: GSK partners with startups like Ada Health to explore chatbots that help HCPs manage chronic conditions like diabetes and asthma.
2. **Regional Initiatives**: Different GSK regional offices also explore chatbot applications:
    - **GSK US:** They partnered with Sensely to develop chatbots for personalized HCP engagement regarding specific GSK products.
    - **GSK China**: They piloted a chatbot called "AI Doctor" to answer basic questions about healthcare topics and direct users to reliable sources of information.
3. **Future Focus**: GSK continues to invest in research and development of AI-powered chatbots for HCP engagement.

They're exploring areas like:

- **Multilingual Chatbots**: Catering to HCPs in diverse regions.
- **Integration with CRM Systems**: Providing seamless chat support within existing HCP communication platforms.
- **Advanced Clinical Decision Support**: Assisting HCPs with treatment recommendations and patient management.

Beyond quantifiable benefits like increased efficiency and reduced costs, GSK recognizes AI's ethical and societal Implications. They prioritize responsible AI development, transparency, and collaboration, ensuring AI serves as a tool for good within the healthcare ecosystem. By embracing AI with a human-centered approach and focusing on ethical considerations, GSK is charting a course for a future where technology enhances and empowers human expertise, leading to a healthier and more sustainable future for all.

Pharma Embracing AI Transformation: More Examples

The world of AI in pharma is constantly evolving, and many other companies are actively implementing AI transformation. Here are some examples:

Global Leaders:

- **Pfizer**: Utilizing AI in multiple areas, including drug discovery, clinical trials, and sales and marketing. Their recent success with PAXLOVID, an oral COVID-19 treatment, was significantly accelerated by AI-powered design and development.
- **Merck** partners with various AI startups and technology companies to explore applications in drug discovery, clinical trial analysis, and personalized medicine. Its "Advantage AI" program demonstrates its commitment to this space.
- **Johnson & Johnson** is investing heavily in AI across its entire pharma pipeline, from research and development to manufacturing and commercialization. For example, Johnson & Johnson Medtech is working with NVIDIA to scale AI for surgery.

Emerging Players:

- **Recursion Pharmaceuticals**: This AI-driven drug discovery company utilizes innovative platforms like "Chorus" to predict drug mechanisms and identify promising candidates, contributing to a more efficient and targeted approach.
- **Atomwise**: Employing a unique AI platform (AtomNet) to rapidly search and identify potential drug molecules, demonstrating the power of AI in virtual screening and lead generation.
- **Insilico Medicine**: Using AI to create and simulate biological models allows for virtual testing of drug candidates and accelerates the preclinical phase of drug development.

Regional Innovation:

- **WuXi AppTec (China)**: This leading contract research organization heavily invests in AI solutions for drug discovery, clinical trial management, and drug safety monitoring, catering to the growing Chinese pharmaceutical market.
- **Eisai (Japan)**: This Japanese pharma giant utilizes AI-powered tools for personalized medicine initiatives, aiming to develop treatments tailored to individual patient needs and genetic profiles.
- **Dr. Reddy's Laboratories (India)**: This Indian pharmaceutical company leverages AI in various areas, including drug discovery, manufacturing optimization, and supply chain management, demonstrating the global reach of AI innovation in pharma.

These are just a few examples, and the landscape of AI in pharma is constantly expanding. Many other large and small companies are making strides in AI implementation. Additionally, collaborations between pharma companies, technology giants, and academic institutions are accelerating innovation and fueling further exploration of this transformative technology.

The key takeaway is that AI is rapidly becoming an essential tool in the pharmaceutical industry. Its potential to address major challenges and improve patient care is undeniable. As companies continue to invest in AI development and implementation, we can expect even more exciting advancements and breakthroughs in the future.

CHAPTER

60

Embracing AI Transformation in Small and Medium-Sized Pharma Companies

Challenges and Opportunities

For small and medium-sized pharma, embracing AI transformation presents challenges and exciting opportunities. While these companies may face resource constraints compared to larger players, they also possess the agility and flexibility that can be advantageous to adopting new technologies.

Challenges:

- **Cost and Infrastructure**: Implementing AI solutions requires upfront investment in technology, data infrastructure, and skilled personnel. While cloud-based solutions and pay-as-you-go models are making AI more accessible, it can still be a significant financial hurdle to SMPs.
- **Talent Acquisition and Training**: Hiring or retraining existing staff to acquire necessary AI skills can be difficult, especially for niche positions like AI scientists or data engineers.
- **Data Availability and Quality**: AI thrives on large, high-quality data, which may be limited or less structured in SMPs than in larger companies. Data cleansing and integration can be resource-intensive.
- **Change Management and Integration**: Integrating AI seamlessly into existing workflows and processes requires careful planning and change management to ensure user adoption and avoid siloed solutions.

Opportunities:

- **Enhanced Drug Discovery and Development**: AI can accelerate drug discovery by identifying promising drug candidates, optimizing lead optimization, and predicting clinical trial outcomes. This can significantly reduce cost and time to market.
- **Improved Clinical Trial Efficiency**: AI can streamline patient recruitment and selection, optimize trial design, and facilitate risk prediction, leading to faster and more efficient trials.
- **Personalized Medicine and Patient Care**: AI can analyze patient data to personalize treatment plans, predict adverse events, and offer virtual assistance and support, improving patient outcomes and satisfaction.

Technological Investments:

- **Cloud-Based AI Platforms** offer access to pre-built AI models and tools without upfront infrastructure costs. Examples include Google Cloud Vertex AI, Amazon SageMaker, and Microsoft Azure Machine Learning.
- **Open-Source AI Libraries and Frameworks**: Tools like TensorFlow, PyTorch, and scikit-learn offer powerful functionalities for building custom AI solutions at lower costs.
- **Pre-trained Language Models** like GPT-4 and Jurassic-1 Jumbo can be fine-tuned for specific pharmaceutical tasks, such as drug target identification or generating research summaries.
- **Specialized AI for Pharma**: Companies like BenevolentAI, Exscientia, and Atomwise offer AI-powered solutions tailored to specific pharma needs, such as drug discovery and virtual screening.

Cost Estimates:

- The cost of AI implementation varies significantly depending on the chosen solutions, data requirements, and level of customization.

- Cloud-based platforms can start with monthly fees of a few thousand dollars, while customized solutions could cost millions.
- Hiring AI talent comes with salary costs, and training existing staff also incurs expenses.
- Data acquisition and management can also be costly, depending on the data sources and quality.

While estimating the actual costs for implementing AI transformation in SMPs is difficult, here are some ballpark figures and phased investment options to give an idea of what it could cost at entry level for SMPs :

Cloud-Based AI Platforms:

- **Starting Range**: $2,000 to $5,000 per month for basic usage
- **Advanced Features**: $10,000 to $20,000 per month
- **Phased Approach**: Start with limited usage and data volume, scale up as experience and benefits grow

Open-Source AI Libraries and Frameworks:

- **Cost**: Free to use
- **Integration and Maintenance**: $10,000 to $20,000 per month for dedicated developer teams
- **Phased Approach**: Leverage pre-built tools and examples initially to develop custom solutions progressively

Pre-Trained Language Models:

- **Access Fees**: $1,000 to $5,000 per month
- **Fine-tuning and Customization**: Additional costs depending on complexity and data needed
- **Phased Approach**: Experiment with pre-built models on small datasets, invest in fine-tuning later for specific tasks

Specialized AI for Pharma:

- **Subscription Fees**: $10,000 to $50,000 per month, depending on specific tools and functionalities

- **Project-Based Contracts**: Costs are variable based on scope and customization
- **Phased Approach**: Start with limited access or pilot projects, scale up based on value-proven

Hiring AI Talent:

- **Data Scientists/Engineers**: $75,000 to $150,000 per year
- **Machine Learning Engineers**: $100,000 to $200,000 per year
- **Phased Approach**: Outsource specific tasks initially, hire core team members as expertise and needs increase

Training Existing Staff:

- Online Courses: $100 to $500 per course per employee
- Workshops and Seminars: $1,000 to $5,000 per event per employee
- Dedicated Training Programs: $5,000 to $10,000 per employee

Data Acquisition and Management:

- **Public Data Sources**: Free or minimal cost
- **Private Data Purchase**: Variable depending on source and quality
- **Data Cleansing and Integration**: $10,000 to $50,000 per project, depending on complexity and volume

These are estimates, and actual costs will vary based on specific needs and choices.

Phased investment is crucial for SMPs. Start with small pilot projects or specific use cases, demonstrate the value and ROI, and then invest in scaling up and expanding capabilities. This allows for risk mitigation, learning from initial experiences, and adjusting strategies.

With careful planning and a planned approach, SMPs can make strategic investments in AI and gradually build their capabilities, unlocking the transformative potential of this technology without overwhelming their resources.

Beyond Costs: Some Points to Ponder for SMPs Embracing the AI Revolution

Here are some suggestions for SMPs on their path to AI-powered transformation:

Strategic Mindset:

- **Align AI with Business Goals**: Don't chase technology trends; define clear objectives and ensure AI investments directly contribute to desired outcomes like drug discovery efficiency or clinical trial optimization.
- **Build a Cross-Functional Team**: Foster collaboration between IT, R&D, Clinical, and other departments to break down silos and ensure AI solutions address real-world needs.
- **Embrace a Learning Culture**: Invest in continuous learning opportunities for employees to stay updated on AI advancements and develop relevant skills.

Data-Driven Approach:

- **Prioritize Data Quality and Governance**: Implement robust data collection, management, and security practices to ensure reliable AI models and compliance with regulations.
- **Start Small with Readily Available Data**: Leverage existing internal or readily accessible public datasets for initial pilot projects before investing in large-scale data acquisition.
- **Focus on Data Interpretation and Explainability**: Go beyond just generating insights and ensure AI models are transparent and interpretable to build trust and facilitate decision-making.

Collaboration and Partnerships:

- **Seek External Expertise**: Partner with universities, research institutes, or AI consulting firms to access specialized knowledge and talent.
- **Join industry Consortia and Communities**: Collaborate with other SMPs and stakeholders to share best practices, access resources, and accelerate learning.

- **Explore Open-Source Solutions and Communities**: Contribute to and leverage open-source AI projects to reduce development costs and access valuable resources.

Ethical Considerations:

- **Focus on Bias Mitigation and Fairness**: Ensure AI models are trained on diverse data and employ strategies to address potential biases to avoid discriminatory outcomes.
- **Prioritize Patient Privacy and Data Security**: Implement robust data protection measures to safeguard patient information and comply with relevant privacy regulations.
- **Uphold Transparency and Human Oversight**: Maintain human control over AI systems and ensure decisions are explainable and aligned with ethical principles.

Remember, AI is a journey, not a destination. By adopting a strategic, data-driven, collaborative, and ethical approach, SMPs can navigate the challenges and unleash the potential of AI to fuel innovation, improve healthcare outcomes, and achieve sustainable success in the evolving pharma landscape. These additional suggestions inspire and empower SMPs as they embark on their AI transformation journey.

Closed-loop Marketing for Personalized Engagement with HCPs:

Additionally, investing in closed-loop marketing platforms for personalized engagement with HCPs can be valuable for SMPs looking to optimize their reach and impact. Here's a breakdown of the potential benefits, costs, and factors to consider:

Benefits of CLM Platforms for SMPs:

- **Enhanced HCP Engagement**: Personalized content, omnichannel communication (email, mobile, webinars), and targeted messaging tailor interactions to individual HCP preferences and interests, leading to higher engagement and conversion rates.

- **Improved Brand Positioning**: Data-driven insights inform content creation and campaign strategies, ensuring messaging resonates with HCPs and strengthens brand value.
- **Increased ROI**: CLM platforms optimize resource allocation by focusing on high-potential HCPs and measuring campaign performance in real-time, leading to more effective spending.
- **Streamlined Workflows**: Automated tasks like data analysis and reporting save time and resources, allowing marketing teams to focus on strategic initiatives.

Minimum Cost

The minimum cost for a CLM platform for SMPs can vary significantly depending on factors like:

- **Features and Functionality**: Basic platforms with email marketing and data management start at $1,000 to $2,000 per month, while advanced platforms with omnichannel engagement, AI-powered analytics, and CRM integration can cost upwards of $10,000 to $20,000 per month.
- **Number of Users**: Most platforms have tiered pricing based on your system's number of HCPs or users.
- **Customization**: Custom features and integration can add to costs.

Considerations for SMPs:

- **Clear Marketing Goals**: Define specific objectives for your HCP engagement before choosing a CLM platform. This helps focus on features that align with your needs and avoid unnecessary costs.
- **Data Quality and Integration**: Ensure your existing data on HCPs is accurate and compatible with the chosen CLM platform for seamless integration and effective personalization.
- **Scalability**: Choose a platform that can scale with your needs as your HCP engagement initiatives grow.

- **Training and Support**: Adequate training and ongoing support are crucial for maximizing platform utilization and ROI.

Alternatives to CLM Platforms:

For SMPs with limited budgets, alternative options exist to start building personalized HCP engagement:

- **CRM with Email Marketing Capabilities**: A robust CRM with embedded email features can offer basic personalization and campaign management at a lower cost.
- **Targeted Advertising Platforms**: Utilize platforms like LinkedIn Ads or healthcare-specific platforms to reach relevant HCPs with personalized messaging.
- **Content Marketing Initiatives**: Create high-quality content tailored to HCP interests and distribute it through targeted channels like webinars or dedicated websites.

Remember, personalized HCP engagement is an ongoing investment. Start with a solution that fits your current budget and resources, and gradually scale up as you realize the benefits and ROI of CLM platforms in your specific context.

SMPs Embracing AI Transformation: Important Points to Remember:

- **Start Small and Focus on Specific Problems**: AI implementation takes time and resources. Identify a challenge or use case where AI can offer value and begin there.
- **Build Your Team's Expertise**: Invest in training and upskilling your staff on AI fundamentals and relevant technical skills.
- **Collaborate with Partners**: Leverage the expertise of academic institutions, tech companies, and other pharma players to accelerate your AI journey.
- **Focus on Ethical Considerations**: Ensure responsible and transparent use of AI in pharma, upholding patient privacy, data security, and fairness in healthcare delivery.

By combining your passion for pharma with the power of AI, you can contribute to groundbreaking innovations that improve healthcare for all. Don't hesitate to explore, experiment, and participate in this exciting revolution!

Embracing AI: Key Takeaways

Finally, pharma embracing AI paints a hopeful and exciting picture, brimming with the potential to revolutionize the industry and improve the lives of countless patients. Here are some key takeaways:

Transformational Possibilities:

- **Personalized Medicine**: Tailored treatments, optimized drug development, and empowered patients.
- **Faster Drug Discovery**: AI-driven simulations and virtual trials accelerate lifesaving therapy.
- **Enhanced Patient Care**: AI-powered tools supporting HCPs and empowering patients to manage their health.
- **Efficient Resource Allocation**: Value-based pricing, predictive analytics, and optimized healthcare spending.

Embracing AI is not just an option for pharma; It's necessary. By navigating the challenges responsibly and collaboratively, the future of pharma with AI can be one where innovation thrives, healthcare becomes more personalized and accessible, and ultimately, patients benefit from faster, more effective treatments.

CHAPTER

61

Gazing into the Crystal Ball: The Evolving Landscape of AI in Pharma Marketing

While AI has already begun to reshape the pharma marketing landscape, the future holds even more breathtaking possibilities. Buckle up because we're about to delve into the fascinating realm of advanced AI models, quantum computing, and the convergence of technologies that will propel us toward a revolution in patient care and drug development.

AI Ascends: Beyond Basic Algorithm

Forget the binary bots of yesterday. Imagine explainable AI (XAI) that transparently reveals the reasoning, building trust and empowering collaboration. Picture generative AI crafting targeted content that resonates deeply with individual patients, fostering meaningful connections. This is the future of AI in pharma marketing, where AI becomes your creative partner, not just a data cruncher.

Beyond Imagination: Quantum Leaps in Healthcare

But wait, there is more! The realm of quantum computing beckons, promising to accelerate drug discovery and development at dizzying speeds. Imagine analyzing massive datasets in moments, identifying optimal drug targets with unparalleled precision, and compressing years of clinical trials into months. This is the quantum leap AI enables, ushering in a new era of personalized medicine.

A Symphony of Technologies When Worlds Collide

And it doesn't stop there. AI is a maestro conducting an orchestra of emerging technologies. The Internet of Things (IoT) whispers real-time patient data, while blockchain ensures its secure flow. Virtual reality transports patients to immersive educational experiences, and AI acts as the conductor, harmonizing these tools into a symphony of patient engagement and empowerment.

Navigating the Ethical Maze: A Balancing Act

But with great power comes great responsibility. As AI soars, ethical considerations, and regulations must keep pace. We must ensure transparency, fairness, and accountability in AI development and deployment. This delicate dance between innovation and ethics is a defining challenge of our time, but one we must embrace and ensure AI serves humanity, not the other way around.

Personalized Journeys: From Audience to Individual

Now, let's zoom in on the areas where AI will transform pharma marketing. Imagine crafting campaigns that aren't just targeted but hyper-targeted to each patient's unique needs and preferences. AI will weave patient data, historical interactions, and real-time feedback into a tapestry of understanding, allowing you to deliver content that resonates on a deeply personal level.

From Bench to Bedside: Revolutionizing Drug Discovery

The journey doesn't end there. AI will become an indispensable partner in drug discovery and development. Picture AI is sifting through mountains of data, identifying promising drug targets, and even designing molecules with pinpoint accuracy. This is not science fiction, but the near future, where AI will accelerate the development of life-saving treatments, bringing hope to patients faster than ever before.

Engaging the Empowered Patient: Beyond the Brochure

The patient is no longer a passive recipient of information. AI-powered chatbots and virtual assistants will become trusted companions, offering 24/7 support and guidance. Remote monitoring tools will empower patients to actively participate in their health journey, while AI-driven interventions will improve medication adherence, leading to better outcomes for all.

Sales & CRM: More Than Just Numbers

Sales and customer relationship management (CRM) will also undergo a metamorphosis. AI will provide deeper customer insights, enabling sales teams to build stronger relationships and tailor their approach to individual needs. Forecasting will become more precise, resources will be allocated with laser focus, and AI will automate repetitive tasks, freeing up human ingenuity for strategic thinking and relationship building.

The Human Touch: A Symphony Needs a Conductor

But amidst this whirlwind of AI innovation, remember— humans are still the conductors. Our creativity, empathy, and ethical judgment are irreplaceable. The future lies in human-AI collaboration, where AI augments our strengths, and we, in turn, ensure its responsible use. And let's not forget the jobs of the future— exciting new roles will emerge, focused on AI development, management, and ensuring its ethical implementation.

So, as we peer into the crystal ball of pharma marketing's future, one thing is clear: AI is not a replacement but a powerful partner. By Embracing collaboration, we can unlock a future where personalized medicine, accelerated drug discovery, and empowered patients become a reality, not just a dream. Are you ready to join the symphony?

PART X

The Encore

Chapter 62. The Ethical Encore: Navigating the Moral Maze of Human-AI Pharma Marketing

Chapter 63. The Orchestrated Encore: Unveiling of the Future Landscape of Pharma Marketing

Chapter 64. The Human Encore: Remembering the Heartbeat of Purpose

The Encore: Where the Curtain Rises on a Revolution

We've reached the final act, the climactic crescendo of a symphony where human minds and artificial intelligence have danced in perfect harmony. In "The Synergy of Minds," we witnessed the curtain rise on a revolution, a marriage of human and machine reshaping the fabric of pharma marketing. We explored the breathtaking potential of AI, its algorithms dissecting data, crafting personalized journeys, and pushing the boundaries of medical science. We heard the whispers of human intuition guiding these potent forces, ensuring their focus remained laser-sharp and patient-centric.

But now, the stage has transformed. The spotlight shifts from the individual notes and melodies to the symphony. In "The Encore," we step back, taking in the panorama of a future forever altered by this potent collaboration. This is not merely a chapter; it's an invitation to step through the stage door and onto the bustling streets of a world reshaped by the echoes of this synergy.

Here, we'll witness the symphony reach its full crescendo. AI-powered drug discovery will unveil cures once relegated to science fiction. Clinical trials will transpire in the blink of an eye, guided by real-time data and ethical algorithms. Once a blunt instrument, Pharma marketing will become a personalized whisper, delivering the right message to the right patient at the right time.

But the human heartbeat still drives this revolution. HCPs, empowered by AI companions, will wield knowledge beyond human ken, their expertise amplified to new heights. Patients, no longer passive figures, will become active participants in their care journeys, guided by data-driven insights and empathetic digital mentors. This is not a utopian fairy tale nor a dystopian nightmare. It's a kaleidoscope of possibilities, brimming with breathtaking potential and unforeseen challenges. As the curtain rises on "The Encore," we face a choice: will we become masters of this powerful duet, or will we let it orchestrate our demise?

In these pages, we'll unpack this intricate dance, its triumphs and pitfalls, its ethical difficulties, and its exhilarating possibilities. This is not just a conclusion; it's a manifesto, a call to action for every human and artificial mind that dares to dream of a healthier future. In Encore, we orchestrate a revolution in pharma marketing and how we care for and heal each other.

So, take a deep breath, silence the inner critic, and let the music wash over you. This is "The Encore," and the stage is yours.

CHAPTER 62

The Ethical Encore: Navigating the Moral Maze of Human+AI in Pharma Marketing

As the curtain rises on "The Encore," we find ourselves amidst a dazzling landscape sculpted by the synergy of human and AI minds. Ethical considerations become the stage lights, illuminating the potential pitfalls and the path toward a responsible future for human+AI pharma marketing. This is not an intermission for introspection but rather a vibrant dance between innovation and morality, demanding constant vigilance and nuanced navigation.

The Melody of Data Privacy: In this digital symphony, data is the lifeblood, flowing from patients, consumers, and HCPs into the AI's intricate algorithms. But with each note, the question echoes: who owns this data? How is it secured? Where does the line between personalization and privacy blur?

Here, we explore frameworks for robust data governance, ensuring informed consent, transparency, and responsible use of patient information. We delve into anonymization techniques and encryption protocols, safeguarding individuals from unintended exposure or exploitation. But the melody grows complex as we tackle the ethics of data aggregation and analysis. Can we anonymize collective patterns? How do we prevent algorithmic bias from amplifying societal inequalities and perpetuating discrimination within healthcare?

The Harmony of Algorithmic Fairness: AI thrives on patterns, but patterns can harbor hidden biases. Algorithms trained on historical data may perpetuate prejudices toward certain demographics or socioeconomic groups. This disharmony threatens to undermine the very essence of healthcare equitable access and personalized care.

In this act, we dissect the intricate workings of algorithmic fairness. We scrutinize training data, identifying and mitigating biases that could lead to discriminatory marketing practices or unequal access to medication. We explore techniques for debiasing algorithms, ensuring their output prioritizes individual needs over pre-existing societal inequalities.

The Rhythm of Transparency and Trust: Trust is paramount in the pharmaceutical world. Patients entrust their well-being to HCPs and pharmaceutical companies. But how do we maintain trust when AI becomes the invisible maestro orchestrating treatment recommendations and marketing campaigns?

Transparency becomes the key instrument in this act. We advocate for clear communication about the role of AI in pharma marketing, demystifying algorithms and dispelling fears of a black box controlling healthcare decisions. We explore ways to educate HCPs and patients alike about the strengths and limitations of AI, fostering collaboration and informed decision-making.

The Conductor's Baton: Human Oversight and Accountability: As AI takes center stage, the question of who holds the conductor's baton becomes crucial. Can we truly allow algorithms to make life-altering decisions about medication or treatment plans without human oversight and accountability?

In this final movement, we grapple with the complex relationship between humans and machines in pharma marketing. We explore robust oversight mechanisms, ensuring that AI operates within ethical frameworks and serves the greater good. We emphasize the importance of human judgment and empathy in guiding AI towards responsible and patient-centric outcomes.

Ultimately, “The Ethical Encore” is not a cautionary tale but a call to action. It celebrates the potential of human-AI synergy in pharma marketing, balanced by a sober recognition of the ethical challenges that lie ahead. By embracing transparency, fairness, and human oversight, we can ensure that this Encore becomes a harmonious symphony where innovation and ethics dance in perfect time, paving the way for a future where health and well-being resonate for all.

CHAPTER 63

The Orchestrated Encore: Unveiling the Future Landscape of Pharma Marketing

The curtain rises on Act Two of the human+AI saga, where the stage transforms into a futuristic panorama of pharma marketing reshaped by the potent synergy. In this "Orchestrated Encore," we witness a symphony of innovation, where AI takes center stage as the conductor, wielding algorithms like instruments to compose a breathtaking future for the industry.

The Overture: AI-Powered Drug Discovery

Forget serendipity; the future of drug discovery unfolds in a sterile symphony of algorithms. AI, the maestro of big data, sifts through oceans of genomic sequences, protein structures, and medical literature, composing molecules of potential cures. In silico simulations replace years of lab work, accelerating the design and testing of personalized medicine tailored to individual genetic profiles. Imagine cancer treatments crafted for a patient's unique tumor mutations or neurodegenerative disease therapies to their specific genetic blueprint.

The First Movement: Personalized Marketing with a Human Touch: Gone are the days of mass marketing campaigns. AI, the master of personalization, analyzes medical records, social media data, and behavioral patterns to craft bespoke healthcare journeys for each individual. Imagine patients receiving targeted messages about medications that address their specific needs, delivered through their preferred channels at the most opportune moments. HCPs, empowered by AI companions, access real-time insights into patient demographics, treatment responses, and medication adherence, guiding their recommendations with unparalleled precision.

The Second Movement: Clinical Trials Transformed: The clinical trial waltz undergoes a radical makeover. AI choreographs virtual trials, streamlining recruitment by identifying ideal candidates through data-driven analysis. Real-time monitoring eliminates the need for invasive procedures, while remote data collection empowers patients to participate from the comfort of their homes. Imagine new drugs tested on diverse populations in record time, with ethical algorithms ensuring patient safety and data privacy remain the paramount melodies.

The Interlude: HCPs in the Spotlight: Humans remain the guiding lights amidst the AI-driven spectacle. HCPs, the virtuosos of empathy and critical thinking, wield AI as a powerful tool, amplifying their expertise and enhancing patient interactions. Imagine doctors with AI companions that analyze complex medical data, suggest personalized treatment plans, and even facilitate patient communication through language translation. The human-AI duet promises to redefine healthcare delivery, with HCPs playing a central role in orchestrating care journeys with a personalized touch.

The Grand Finale: A Symphony of Patient Empowerment: The patient steps onto the central platform in this final crescendo. AI becomes their health maestro, analyzing vitals, tracking medication adherence, and providing 24/7 support through virtual assistants and wearable sensors. Imagine patients actively engaged in their care journeys, empowered by data-driven insights and AI-powered self-management tools. The revolution in patient empowerment ensures healthcare becomes a collaborative performance where individuals take center stage in their well-being.

But, remember, the “Orchestrated Encore” is not without its potential dissonance. Ethical considerations linger like discordant notes, demanding attention. Data privacy, algorithmic bias, and human oversight must be addressed to ensure this future symphony remains in harmony with our values.

Ultimately, “The Orchestrated Encore” paints a breathtaking vision of a pharma marketing future where AI is a powerful tool, amplifying human expertise and patient empowerment. By embracing this transformative collaboration, we can compose a symphony of health and well-being, ensuring the curtain never falls on a future where innovation and ethics harmonize to create a healthier world for all.

CHAPTER

64

The Human Encore: Remembering the Heartbeat of Purpose

As the final act of the human-AI saga unfolds, the spotlight shifts from the dancing spectacle of technology to the stage where the true magic resides— the human heart. In "The Human Encore," we move beyond the technical marvels of AI and delve into the enduring power of human intuition, empathy, and purpose. This is a celebration of our irreplaceable role in this symphony of progress, a reminder that even amidst the whirring gears of algorithms, the human spirit remains the conductor, the composer, and the very heartbeat of this revolution.

The Opening Solo: The Irreplaceable Melody of Human Intuition: AI may analyze mountains of data but cannot replicate the nuanced melody of human intuition. The doctor picks up on a subtle tremor in a patient's voice, and the HCP senses a hidden need beyond the data points. It's the researcher who, guided by a hunch, pursues a seemingly insignificant anomaly that leads to a groundbreaking discovery. In this act, we celebrate the power of human intuition, the ability to connect the dots, to bridge the gaps between logic and emotion, and to guide innovation with a wisdom beyond algorithms.

The Harmonious Duet: Human Empathy in the Age of Machine Precision: AI can personalize marketing messages and optimize treatment plans, but it cannot replicate the warmth of human empathy. The nurse holds a patient's hand during a difficult diagnosis, the counselor listens without judgment, and the advocate fights for access to life-saving medication. In this movement, we emphasize the crucial role of empathy in the healthcare journey, reminding ourselves that even the most sophisticated algorithms cannot replace the human touch, the connection, and the understanding that heals and empowers.

The Chorus of Purpose: Finding Meaning in the Age of Automation: As AI automates tasks and disrupts traditional workforces, the question of human purposes becomes even more critical. This act explores how humans can find meaning and fulfillment in this evolving landscape. We celebrate the entrepreneurs who envision ethical AI solutions, the educators who cultivate future generations of tech-savvy humans, and the artists who weave technology into narratives that inspire and connect. We remind ourselves that the purpose of this revolution is not to replace humans but to amplify our strengths, to free us to pursue the creative endeavors, the social connections, and the acts of compassion that make us truly human.

The Grand Finale: A Symphony for All: Ultimately, "The Human Encore" is about individuals and the collective human spirit. It's about ensuring that this revolution in healthcare serves not just the privileged few but every beating heart on the planet. We advocate for ethical AI frameworks that prioritize equity and accessibility, for technological solutions that bridge the digital divide and empower marginalized communities. We envision a future where AI serves as a tool for global health initiatives, eradicating diseases and promoting well-being for all.

But this Encore has its challenges. We must guard against the temptation to succumb to technocratic hubris, to believe that technology can solve all our problems. We must remember that AI is a powerful tool, but it is still a tool. The composer of this symphony is the composer of its future, and it will always be the human spirit.

So, let the curtain rise on "The Human Encore." Let the melodies of human intuition, empathy, and purpose resonate throughout the stage. Let us remember that the future of healthcare and humanity lies not in algorithms but in the beating hearts that dream, create, connect, and ultimately make it human.

Epilogue

Years had passed since Anya and Elias's journey began in the dusty halls of Oxford. Their names are now echoed in prestigious journals, and their research is lauded in the highest echelons of academia and industry. Yet, their greatest success wasn't measured in awards or accolades but in their work's tangible impact on the world.

Anya's once youthful idealism sharpened by experience had launched a groundbreaking initiative., Project Empathy. With Elias's AI expertise, she built a platform that helped autistic individuals connect with the world around them, bridging the chasm of social interaction. Laughter and light now filled spaces that once resonated with loneliness, the seeds of empathy finally blooming in fertile ground.

No longer the quiet observer, Elias emerged as a leader in ethically conscious AI. His algorithms, infused with Anya's insights, didn't just mimic human intelligence; they complemented it, amplifying compassion and understanding. In classrooms, AI tutors, imbued with emotional intelligence, tailored lessons to individual needs, nurturing a love for learning in every child. In medical consultations, AI assistants programmed with a doctor's intuition and a patient's empathy eased anxieties and communicated diagnoses with unparalleled clarity.

But their collaboration had its challenges. Ethical dilemmas arose, requiring careful navigation. Algorithmic biases had to be identified and eradicated, and the delicate balance between progress and human control was constantly renegotiated. Anya and Elias, alongside countless others, became the stewards of this nascent technology, ensuring its growth remained tethered to human values.

As they stood by the shores of the Ganges, watching the golden hues of sunrise paint the sky, Anya and Elias knew they had only just begun. The synergy of minds they pioneered had become a global movement, an unstoppable force for good. In laboratories, classrooms, boardrooms, and community centers, the seeds of human-machine collaboration were taking root, promising a future where intelligence didn't replace humanity but empowered it.

As the first rays of a new day bathed the world in light, they shared a silent promise. The collaboration wouldn't end—for them or the countless others inspired by their journey. The story of the *Synergy of Minds* wasn't a concluding chapter but an open invitation, a call to action for every curious mind, every compassionate heart, to participate in shaping a future where humanity and technology danced in harmony, a future where together, they could achieve what neither could alone.

The epilogue concludes, but the story continues. Will you answer the call and join the dance?

Glossary

Diving into AI in Pharma: Useful Resources and Tools

Reading List

References

About the Author

AI (Artificial Intelligence) Terms

- **Artificial Intelligence (AI)** is the simulation of human intelligence processes by machines, enabling them to learn, reason, solve problems, and make decisions.
- **Machine Learning (ML)**: A type of AI that learns from data without being explicitly programmed.
- **Deep Learning**: A subset of ML that uses artificial neural networks to learn from large amounts of data.
- **Federated Learning**: A machine learning technique that allows training models on decentralized datasets without sharing the data. This is useful for privacy-sensitive data, such as medical records or financial information.
- **Explainable AI (XAI)** is a subfield of artificial intelligence that focuses on making AI models more understandable to humans. This is important because it allows us to trust the decisions made by AI models and to identify any potential biases or errors.
- **Generative AI**: A subfield of AI concerned with creating new text, images, music, or other content, often based on existing data or patterns.
- **Natural Language Processing (NLP)** is a subset of AI concerned with interacting with computers and human language.

- **Computer Vision**: A subfield of AI that enables computers to see and understand the world around them.
- **Cognitive Computing** is a type of artificial intelligence that simulates human thought processes. Cognitive computing systems can learn and reason and are often used for complex decision-making tasks.
- **Quantum Computing**: A type of artificial intelligence that harnesses the principles of quantum mechanics to perform calculations that are impossible for traditional computers. Quantum computers can potentially revolutionize many fields, including medicine, materials science, and artificial intelligence.
- **Chatbots** are conversational AI agents that simulate human conversation to provide customer service, answer questions, or complete tasks.

AI Terms Specific to Pharma

Drug Discovery:

- **Virtual Screening**: Using AI to analyze large libraries of molecules and identify potential drug candidates.
- **De novo Drug Design**: Using AI to generate new drug molecules from scratch.
- **Target Identification**: Using AI to Identify potential protein targets for therapeutic intervention.

Clinical Trials:

- **Patient Selection**: Using AI to identify patients most likely to benefit from a new drug.
- **Risk Prediction**: Using AI to predict potential adverse events in clinical trials.
- **Data Analysis**: Using AI to analyze clinical trial data more efficiently and effectively.

Patient Care:

- **Chatbots**: AI-powered virtual assistants that can answer patient questions and provide support.

- **Personalization**: Using AI to tailor treatments and medication plans to individual patients.
- **Diagnostics**: Using AI to analyze medical images and data to diagnose diseases.

Ethical Considerations:

- **Algorithmic Bias**: The potential for AI algorithms to perpetuate biases present in the data they are trained on.
- **Data Privacy**: The need to protect patient data when using AI in healthcare.
- **Transparency and Explainability**: The importance of making AI decisions understandable and interpretable.
- **Fairness and Access**: Ensuring that AI technologies are accessible and beneficial to all patients, regardless of their background or socioeconomic status.

Additional Terms:

- **Augmented Intelligence (AI)**: Using AI to augment human capabilities rather than replace them.
- **The Synergy of Minds**: The collaborative approach to AI development and implementation that combines human expertise with artificial intelligence.
- **Disruptive Innovation**: A technology that significantly changes an industry's operations.

AI-Powered Technologies:

- **Blockchain** is a distributed ledger technology that allows for secure, transparent, and tamper-proof record-keeping. It is used in various applications, including cryptocurrencies, supply chain management, and voting systems.
- **Wearables** are electronic devices worn on the body, such as smartwatches, fitness trackers, and augmented reality glasses. They can collect data about the wearer's health, activity, and environment.

- **Internet of Things (IoT)**: A network of physical devices embedded with sensors, software, and other technologies that collect and exchange data, enabling them to interact with each other and the internet.
- **Gamification**: Using game-like elements (points, badges, leaderboards) in non-game contexts to increase engagement, motivation, and desired behaviors.
- **Digital Twins** are virtual representations of physical objects or systems constantly updated with real-time data to monitor performance and predict future outcomes.
- **Augmented Reality (AR)**: A technology that overlays digital information onto the real world. AR can be used for various purposes, such as gaming, education, and product visualization.
- **Virtual Reality (VR)** is a computer-generated simulation of an environment that can be interacted with in a seemingly real or physical way. VR can be used for various purposes, such as gaming, training, and therapy.
- **Metaverse**: A collective term for immersive virtual worlds where users can interact with each other and digital objects seemingly realistically.
- **Brain-Computer Interfaces (BCIs)**: Systems allowing communication between the brain and external devices. BCIs can control prosthetics, restore lost function, and augment human cognition.
- **Digital Therapeutics** are software-based interventions used to prevent, manage, or treat medical conditions, often in conjunction with traditional treatments.
- **Bioprinting**: A technique that uses 3D printing technology to create tissues or organs from biocompatible materials and cells.
- **Robotics** is the field of designing, building, and operating robots, machines that can sense, think, and act autonomously.

- **Gene Editing**: Technologies that allow for modifying the genetic makeup of living organisms, with potential applications in medicine, agriculture, and other fields.
- **Cloud Computing** is on-demand access to computing resources (servers, storage, databases, software) over the Internet, typically on a pay-as-you-go basis.
- **Closed-Loop Marketing**: A marketing strategy that continuously improves marketing campaigns using data and feedback. This involves setting goals, measuring results, and adjusting based on what works and doesn't.
- **Customer Relationship Management (CRM)**: A software system that helps businesses manage customer interactions. CRMs typically include features for contact management, sales pipeline management, and marketing automation.

Diving into AI in Pharma: Useful Resources and Tools

Learning and Education:

- **Online Courses**:
  - Coursera: "Machine Learning for Healthcare by Andrew Ng
  - EdX: "Artificial Intelligence for Healthcare" by Harvard University
  - Udacity: "Intro to Deep Learning for Healthcare" by Google AI
- **Podcasts**:
  - The Healthcare Technology Podcast
  - AI in Healthcare Podcast
  - The Pharma Marketing Show

Networking and Collaboration:

- **Conferences and Collaboration**:
  - HIMSS (Healthcare Information and Management Systems Society) Conference
  - J.P. Morgan Healthcare Conference
  - BIO International Convention
- **Professional Organizations**:
  - American Medical Informatics Association (AMIA)
  - The Digital Medicine Society (DMS)
  - BioPharma Association (PhRMA)

- **Online Communities**:
  - Kaggle (for data science competitions and collaboration)
  - LinkedIn groups dedicated to AI in Pharma

Tools and Platforms:

- **Open-source Libraries and Frameworks:**
  - **TensorFlow**: Widely used framework for machine learning and deep learning
  - **PyTorch:** Another popular framework with flexible and dynamic functionalities
  - **Scikit-learn**: Machine learning library in Python for classification, regression, clustering, and more
- **Cloud Platforms**:
  - **Google Cloud Platform (GCP)**: Offers AI and machine learning tools like Vertex AI and BigQuery
  - **Amazon Web Services (AWS)**: Provides AI and machine learning services like SageMaker and Rekognition
  - **Microsoft Azure**: includes AI and machine learning services like Azure Machine Learning and Cognitive Services
- **Specialized AI Platforms in Pharma:**
  - **Benevolent AI**: Uses AI for target identification and drug discovery
  - **Insilico**: Employs AI for designing and synthesizing new molecules
  - **Atomwise**: Utilizes AI for virtual screening and lead

Reading List

optimization

Books:

1. Bill Schmarzo, AI & Data Literacy, Empowering Citizens of Data Science, Packt, www.packt.com
2. Paul R. Daugherty, H. James Wilson, Human+Machine: Reimagining Work in the Age of AI, Harvard Business Review Press, 2018
3. Thomas H. Davenport, Nitin Mittal, All in on AI: How Small Companies Win Big with Artificial Intelligence, Harvard Business School Publishing, 2023
4. Bernard Marr with Matt Ward, Artificial Intelligence in Practice: How 50 Successful Companies Used Artificial Intelligence to Solve Problems, Jonh Wiley & Sons, 2019
5. Guy Hart-Davis, Killer ChatGPT Prompts: Harness the Power of AI for Success and Profit, John Wiley & Sons, 2023
6. Rajkumar Venkatesan & Jim Lecinski, AI Marketing Canvas, Stanford University Press, 2021
7. Kavita Ganesan, PhD, The Business Case for AI, Opinosis Analytics, 2022
8. Tom Lawry, AI In Health: A Leader's Guide to Winning in the New Age of Intelligence Health Systems, CRC Press, 2020

9. Jim Sterne, Artificial Intelligence for Marketing: Practical Applications, John Wiley & Sons, 2017
10. Peter Lee, Carey Goldberg, Issac Kohane with Sebastian Bubeck, The AI Revolution in Medicine: GPT-4 And Beyond, Pearson, 2023
11. Tomas Chamorro-Premuzic, I, Human: AI, Automation, and the Quest to ReclaimWhat Makes Us Unique, Harvard Business Review Press, 2023
12. Pam Didner, The Modern AI Marketer: How to Leverage

References

Artificial Intelligence in Digital Marketing to Get Ahead, Kindle Edition, 2020

Articles:

1. Francois Candelon, Theodoros Evgenion, and David Marteres, AI Can Be Both Accurate and Transparent, Harvard Business Review, May 22, 2023
2. Hal Gregersen and Nicola Morini Bianzino, AI Can Help You Ask Better Questions— and Solve Bigger Problems, Harvard Business Review, May 26, 2023
3. H. James Wilson and Paul R. Daugherty, Collaborative Intelligence: Humans and AI Are Joining Forces, Harvard Business Review, July-August 2018
4. David C. Edelman, Mark Abraham, Customer Experience in the Age of AI: The Case for Building Intelligent Experience Engines, Harvard Business Review, March-April 2022
5. Marco Iansiti, Satya Nadella, Democratizing Transformation, Harvard Business Review, May - June 2022
6. Nicolaj Sigggelknow and Christian Terwiesch, Create Winning Customer Experiences with Generative AI, Harvard Business Review, April 04, 2023
7. Gizem Yalcin and Stefano Puntoni, How AI Affects Our Sense

of Self And Why It Matters for Business, Harvard Business Review, September - October 2023

8. Lauren Golembiewski, How Wearable AI Will Amplify Human Intelligence, Harvard Business Review, April 30, 2019
9. John Glaser, Margaret O'Kane, Brad Ryan, and Eric Schneider, How to use Digital Health Data to Improve Outcomes, Harvard Business Review, September 12, 2022
10. Michael Ross and James Taylor, Managing AI Decision-Making Tools, Harvard Business Review, November 10, 2021
11. Rachel Layne, Humans vs. Machines: Untangling the Tasks AI Can (and Can't) Handle, HBS Working Knowledge, November 22, 2023
12. Thomas H. Davenport, Abhijit Guha, and Dhruv Grewal, How to Design an AI Marketing Strategy, Harvard Business Review, July - August 2021
13. Samantha F. Sanders, Ariel D. Stern, and William J. Gordon, How to Make Remote Monitoring Tech Part of Everyday Healthcare, Harvard Business Review, July 02, 2020
14. Kristen Senz, Is AI Coming for Your Job? HBS Working Knowledge, April 26, 2023
15. Kathy Baxter and Yoav Schlesinger, Managing the Risks of Generative AI, Harvard Business Review, June 06, 2023
16. Tomas Chamorro-Premuzic, Should You Share AI-Driven Customer Insights with Your Customers? Harvard Business Review, March 23, 2023
17. Maureen Burns, Scharona Sankar-King, Priscilla Dell'Orto, and Eduardo Roma, Using AI to Build Stronger Connections with Customers, Harvard Business Review, August 01, 2023
18. Mohamed Zai, Janet R. McColl-Kennedy, and Andy Neely, Using AI to Track How Customers Feel — in Real Time, Harvard Business Review, May 04, 2023

19. Eric Colson, What AI-Driven Decision-Making Looks Like, Harvard Business Review, July 08, 2019
20. James Manyika, Jake Silberg, and Brittany Presten, What Do We Do About the Biases in AI, Harvard Business Review, October 25, 2019
21. Christopher Worksham and Anupam B. Jena, Why Doctors Shouldn't Dismiss Apple Watch's New ECG App? Harvard Business Review, October 05, 2018
22. Silvio Palumbo and David Edelman, What Smart Companies Know About Integrating AI, Harvard Business Review. July - August 2023
23. Nahia Orduña, Why Robots Won't Steal Your Job, Harvard Business Review, March 19, 2021
24. Adam Licurse, What Retail Can Teach Healthcare About Digital Strategy, Harvard Business Review, March 08, 2018
25. Thomas H. Davenport, Ian Barkin, and Kerem Tomak, We're All Programmers Now, Harvard Business Review, September - October 2023
26. Antonio L. Fontana, Gina M. Celia, Charles T. Benson, and Joseph C. Kvedar, The Future of Drug Trials is Better Data and Continuous Monitoring, Harvard Business Review, May 02, 2018
27. Mark Purdy, John Zealley, and Omaro Maseli, The Risks of Using AI to Interpret Human Emotions, Harvard Business Review, November 18, 2019
28. Moni Miyashita and Michael Brady, The Healthcare Benefits of Combining Wearable and AI, May 28, 2019
29. Daniel Marchalik, Put Doctors at the Center of Health Care Tech, Harvard Business Review, November 30, 2020
30. Ana Javornik, Ben Marder, Marta Pizzetti, and Luk Warlop, Research: How AR filter Impact People's Self-Image, Harvard Business Review, December 22, 2021

31. Dipayan Ghosh, How GDPR Will Transform Digital Marketing, Harvard Business Review, May 21, 2018
32. Gardiner Morse, Harnessing Artificial Intelligence, Harvard Business Review, May - June 2020
33. Johnathan R. Cromwell, Jean-Francois Harvey, Jennifer Hasse, and Heidi K. Gardner, Discovering Where ChatGPT Can Create Value for Your Company, Harvard Business Review, June 09, 2023
34. Andrew Burt, Ethical Frameworks for AI Aren't Enough, Harvard Business Review, November 09, 2020
35. Ajay Agrawal, Joshua Gans, and Avi Goldfarb, From Prediction to Transformation, Harvard Business Review, November - December 2022
36. Jack J. Domet, Cybersecurity Needs to Be Part of Your Product's Design from the Start, Harvard Business Review, May 09, 2023
37. Gil Appel, Juliana Neelbauer, and David A. Schweidel, Generative AI Has an Intellectual Property Problem, Harvard Business Review, April 02, 2023
38. Joe McKendrick and Andy Thurai, AI Isn't Ready to Make Unsupervised Decisions, Harvard Business Review, September 15, 2022
39. Leila Doumi, Sagar Goel, Orsolya Kovács-Onderjkovic, and Raffaella Sadun, Reskiling in the Age of AI, Harvard Business Review, September - October 2023
40. David D. Cremer and Garry Kasparov, AI Should Augment Human Intelligence, Not Replace It, Harvard Business Review, March 18, 2021
41. Mark Purdy and A. Mark Williams, How AI Can Help Leaders Make Better Decisions Under Pressure, Harvard Business Review, October 26, 2023
42. Ben Dickson, 8 Biggest Trends of 2020, According to Experts, TNW, December 17, 2019, thenextweb.com

43. Prem Natarajan, Alexa Enters the “Age of Self,” Amazon Science, June 02, 2021

44. Rasmus Hougaard, Jacqueline Carter, and Rob Stembridge, The Best Leaders Can’t Be Replaced by AI, Harvard Business Review, January 12, 2024

45. Francois Candelon, Rodolphe Charme di Carlo, Midas De Bondt, and Theodoros Evgeniou, AI Regulation is Coming, Harvard Business Review, September - October 2021

46. Oguz A. Acar, AI Prompt Engineering Isn’t the Future, Harvard Business Review, June 06, 2023.

47. Bryce Hall, Eric Lamarre, Rob Levin, Johannes-Tobias Lorenz, and Pamela Simon, Rewired and Running Ahead: Digital and AI Leaders are Leaving the Rest Behind, McKinsey Digital, January 12, 2024

48. Chaitanya Adabala Viswa, Joachim Bleys, Eoin Leydon, Bhavik Shak, and Delphine Zurkiya, Generative AI in the Pharmaceutical Industry: Moving from Hype to Reality, McKinsey C& Company, January 2024

49. Fabian Gaessler, Henning Piezunka, How AI Can Improve Human Performance, INSEAD Knowledge, November 30, 2023

About the Author

Subba Rao Chaganti

He has a master's in business administration and over fifty-six years of experience in pharmaceutical marketing, covering all facets of the industry, from selling to sales management, product management, and heading the total marketing activity. His experience covers domestic and international marketing and Indian and multinational sectors.

He also taught a course on Advertising and Brand Management at Gitam Institute of Foreign Trade (now part of Gitam University) at Visakhapatnam for a few years as an adjunct professor and a course on Marketing at Jawaharlal Nehru Technological University (JNTU), Hyderabad, as a visiting faculty member.

He lives in Hyderabad and can be reached at
subbarao.chaganti@gmail.com

Here is a list of his publications:

Books Published:

1. Pharmaceutical marketing in India: Concepts, Cases, Strategy
2. Game Plans for Post-Gatt Era: Action Agenda of Indian Pharmaceutical Industry
3. Compete or Forfeit: Strategies for Sustainable Competitive Advantage in Pharma Product Patents Era

4. Pharmaceutical Marketing in India for Today and Tomorrow - 25th Anniversary Edition
5. Bullseyes and Blunders: Lessons from 100 Cases in Pharma Marketing
6. Digital Pharma Marketing Playbook: Winning With the New Rules of Engagement
7. Cracking the Generics Code: Your Single-Source Success Manual for Winning in Multi-Source Product Markets
8. Reimagine Pharma Marketing: Make It Future-Proof!
9. Brand Positioning in Pharma
10. Transactional to Transformational Marketing in Pharma: The Art of Why and the Science of How!
11. A to Z of Pharmaceutical Marketing: World's First and Only Encylopedia in Two Volumes